OKANAGAN COLLEGE LIBRARY

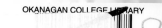

MW01101914

WITHDRAWN

"NO FIVE FINGERS ARE ALIKE"

WITHDRAWN

OKANAGAN COLLEGE
LIBRARY
BRITISH COLUMBIA

"NO FIVE FINGERS ARE ALIKE"

What Exiled Kurdish Women in Therapy told me

Nora Ahlberg

The International Series of Psychosocial Perspectives
on Trauma, Displaced People, and Political Violence
SERIES EDITOR: Renos K. Papadopoulos

KARNAC

First published in 2007 by
Karnac Books Ltd
118 Finchley Road
London NW3 5HT

© 2008 Nora Ahlberg
Foreword copyright © 2008 by Renos K. Papadopoulos
Copyright © Solum Forlag a.s, Oslo 2000.

The rights of Nora Ahlberg to be identified as the sole author of this work have been asserted in accordance with §§ 77 and 78 of the Copyright Design and Patents Act 1988.

All rights reserved. No part of this publication may be reproduced, stored in a retrieval system, or transmitted, in any form or by any means, electronic, mechanical, photocopying, recording, or otherwise, without the prior written permission of the publisher.

British Library Cataloguing in Publication Data
A C.I.P. for this book is available from the British Library

ISBN: 978-1-85575-512-3

Printed in Great Britain
www.karnacbooks.com

To my husband and our children Mildrid and Ernst Hugo

CONTENTS

7

Part two:
THERAPY IN A CROSS-CULTURAL SETTING

POSTSCRIPT

ACKNOWLEDGEMENTS
People and Subjects

This work is based on the analysis of refugee narratives related to me – the therapist – by traumatised kurdish clients in exile who have given their permission for these accounts to be published. To my knowledge, no similar material has been gathered before. What little research there has been on Kurdistan has either been philological or based on ethnographic fieldwork in the area, while Amnesty reports restrict themselves to describing human rights violations. In addition, clinical works in which kurds might be involved, if ethnically differentiated at all, give cultural and religious identity secondary importance.

I am grateful for the professional support of professor in psychiatry Nils Johan Lavik, former head of the Psychosocial Centre for Refugees (PSCR), University of Oslo, professor Fredrik Barth, the founder of the study of social anthropology as well as the study of Kurdistan in Norway, and my teacher in comparative religion professor Juha Pentikäinen, University of Helsinki, whose work on the world view of a karelian refugee woman (1978) was my first introduction to the subject. Dr Barbara Harrell-Bond, anthropologist and at the time Director of The Refugee Studies Programme at the University of Oxford, has a share in the fact that this book has come about. I have repeatedly been able to draw on the courtesy and expertise of this unit, where I was a Visiting Fellow in the autumn of 1994.

I also want to acknowledge my gratitude to professor of kurdology Joyce Blau at the Sorbonne, professor of medical anthropology Benedicte Ingstad, professor of clinical psychology and member of the Board of Directors (PSCR) Anni von der Lippe, professor of developmental psychology Karsten Hundeide, professor of cultural studies Saphinaz Naguib, and professor of south asian history Pamela Price, all at the University of Oslo. My indebtedness extends to an interdisciplinary inspiring milieu at The Norwegian University of Science and Technology and, especially, previous dean of the Faculty of Arts Håkon With Andersen and his successor Petter Aaslestad. The appreciation shown by practitioners and students of many diverse subjects have been an additional inspiration for me while paving the way for an interest in the area of cultural psychology and comparative religio-cultural analysis.

Moreover, I want to mention professor of social psychology Karmela Liebkind, University of Helsinki, whose keen intellect and refined quantitative analysis constitutes a continuing challenge for my own work, and the host of finnish colleagues, particularly folklorists, who have put various themes of tragic or violent culture such as siberian shamanistic healing practices, female wailing, blood feuding and extraordinary death on the international research agenda. In Norway, not least as a result of the seminal work on migration and mental health carried out by Ørnulf Ødegaard and Leo Eitinger, disaster psychiatry under the leadership of professor Lars Weisæth, University of Oslo, has attained an international reputation. The obviously important links between these fields, however, has not yet been fully explored, and much work remains to be done.

The present work has been financed mainly by the Norwegian Research Council, especially through the programmes of International Migration and Ethnic Relations, and Mental Health. The Norwegian Academy of Science has contributed by funding a preliminary study, as has the Finnish Academy of Science by funding an inter-nordic follow-up study within the framework of its programme on Cultural Traditions and Internalisation Development. Dr. Mette Rudvin, University of Bologna, has greatly improved my language, while Ernst Hugo Bjerke has proof read the manuscript. Besides the administrative support from which I profited at the Psychosocial Centre for Refugees, University of Oslo, I have, since its foundation in 1986 on the initiative of Dr.med. Edvard Hauff among others, here also profited from a milieu of warm collegiality. I would especially like to mention psychoanalyst Dr. Carl Ivar Dahl for his supervision regarding the therapeutic aspects of my work whenever I needed him, as well as Dr. Sverre Varvin, director of the Psychoanalytic Institute in Oslo, Dr. med. Sol Dahl, Dr. psychol. Ellinor Major and Dr. Øivind Solberg, head of the outpatients' unit, because of our common academic interests. Fellow Nora Sveaass, Department of Psychology, has repeatedly joined me in teaching psychology students on issues discussed in this book. There are, of course, many more who remain unmentioned to whom I extend my gratitude.

Apart from time spent with the clients, most of my time collecting material was spent with one particular interpreter, Zarin Pettersen, who loyally supported me all the way. Together we have pondered the many relational difficulties encountered during the course of our work together, and their possible personal, professional, ethical and even political ramifications, and have in the process created a mutually satisfying working relationship. However, I alone bear responsibility for the views put forward in this publication, as Zarin does for any opinions pertaining to the matter that she will hopefully come to pursue in her own professional work.

Last, but not least, I would like to thank the clients themselves for their willingness to share with me and the readers such painful experiences and memories. Since those of them who appear in this study are marked by an oral tradition, it is difficult to render justice to the richness of their communication, especially while working with an interpreter at a distance of two or even three languages. But their narratives, told from a subjective point of view, are nevertheless all-important in expanding our understanding of what it is like, mentally, to cross borders and, perhaps, prepare us to respond more adequately to the challenges involved.

This study will hopefully add to our professional knowledge of traumatisation generally, and its relationship to the adjacent cross-cultural problems developing in the wake of exile in particular.

While my themes covers widely and 'holistically' both from within the fields of psychology and psychiatry (i.e. as related to its clinical aspects) as well as from comparative and, especially, anthropology of religion when it comes to cultural understanding; however, the empirical material is based on a few indepth cases of clients whose therapeutic contacts with me, the resercher, extends over years of weekly or, at times, other-weekly, sessions. It has taken some time to prepare the text for publication because – in addition to the ordinary difficulties of balancing between family life and a university career – the personal nature of its content reckoned such a delay advantageous from the point of view of ethical considerations. However, I am rather confident that its subject matter remains relevant for an inter-disciplinary interested readership, though it is of course ultimately for the informed reader to judge.

This remarkable book is the second in the International Series of Psychosocial Perspectives on Trauma, Displaced People and Political Violence and it continues with what the first one offered – a unique opportunity to the English speaking readers to familiarise themselves with important European contributions in this field that usually are not accessible to them.

Nora Ahlberg allows us to get a privileged close look at her practice and to listen to the voices of her refugee clients. But her book is much more than a reproduction of their tumultuous experiences. It manages to achieve a most sensitive balance between providing authentic testimonies of suffering and endurance, and articulating an authoritative and scholarly methodology for treating this delicate material. I am not aware of any other book that addresses so ably both of these facets of the refugee experience.

Moreover, this is (to my knowledge) the only book of its kind that focuses exclusively on refugee women, and one of the few that limit their scope only to one group of refugees – the Kurds, in this case. Although the book is about Kurdish women in Norway, nevertheless, its appeal and contents are of universal value and applicability. Also, although it was first published in Norway in 2000, by no means is it dated.

The general reader will get an unparalleled insight into a therapeutic way of working with refugees and the specialist reader will have a vast range of themes to feast on. These include theoretical considerations of ideas about collective trauma, narrative life stories, working cross-culturally, mental health perspectives on refugees, the formation of meaning, to mention but a few.

Professor Nora Ahlberg is an eminent academic and clinician, immensely experienced in working with refugees. She is head of the Norwegian Centre for Minority Health Research and professor of psychology at the Medical

Faculty at the University of Oslo as well as associate professor at the University of Helsinki. Before taking up her present position she was professor and head of the Psychosocial Centre for Refugees at the University of Oslo and the Department of Religious Studies at the University of Trondheim. By combining the academic disciplines of psychology, religious and psychosocial studies with clinical sensitivity, Professor Ahlberg succeeds in producing an outstanding book that can become an invaluable resource for everybody working in this field.

Renos K. Papadopoulos
Series Editor

ABOUT THE AUTHOR

Dr Nora Ahlberg (b. 1952) has a background as full professor – alternately of psychology and comparative religion – at three out of four Norwegian universities, in addition to the Oslo University College, and as associate professor at the University of Helsinki. She is presently head of the Norwegian Centre for Minority Health Research and professor of transcultural psychology at the Medical Faculty at the University of Oslo. Before taking up this position she was professor and head of both the Psychosocial Centre for Refugees at the University of Oslo and the Department of Religious Studies at the University of Trondheim.

Her interdisciplinary background covers clinical psychology and comparative religion, in particular anthropology. Her main fields of research are minorities, issues of world view and migration, especially refugees and the Muslim diaspora. Through her attachments to the faculties of arts, social Sciences and medicine, she has gained genuine interdisciplinary experience from counselling, teaching and evaluation within the fields of psychology, the history of religion, anthropology and psychiatry. She has lectured at several foreign universities; and outside of the university her competence has been utilised by various clinical or political bodies and NGOs as well as by the media. Her doctoral thesis was made use of for making a television documentary.

Many things have changed since the therapies described in this book were conducted. Wars, terror and polarised debates about negative sides of cultural traditions complicate attempts to speak cross-culturally. Although issues of health are not 'hot' in the same sense, there is more to them than meets the eye. So what lessons have we learnt?

Personally I would still stress a need for acknowledging the cumulative aspects of trauma within "the extended refugee scenery". Forced migration and a subsequent resettlement as a member of a minority group in a new sociocultural setting, increase the risk for somatic and mental health problems. Different illness profiles in the countries of origin and exile, painful events before and during relocation, as well as problems of integration, all influence the situation. But while cumulative traumas go together, our more specific therapeutic tools may fall short of acknowledging this reality. An example could be a circumcised girl, who is also a distressed refugee, and suffers from retraumatisation while giving birth, involving several of these aspects.

We must to a much larger extent consider an extra-therapeutic framework or the existence of many-sided problems, which are not easily resolved within the consultational space alone.

Also, the fact that the therapeutic alliance is under such extraordinary challenge, actualizes issues of professional closeness and distance. Due to mutual avoidance behaviour, migrants tend to be in a poorer condition when they arrive for treatment, a fact that might lead to more drastic measures, such as enforced committal or heavy medication. Working in a cross-cultural context increases the risk of inappropriate reactions of over- and under involvement. We may avoid treating Third World migrants altogether, or give them different services, frequently of lesser quality, such as medication in the absence of a more demanding and time-consuming "talking cure". Also, the use of an interpreter increases the time for consultation at least two-fold; while introducing a triadic constellation that may activate competition about who is in charge, or, alternatively, who is to take the blame when things go wrong.

Cross-cultural migrants are particularly vulnerable in relation to health care because it frequently involves the most personal, intimate or private sphere meeting interventions located in a public space. The problems may not be exclusive to migrants, but there are few instances in which they are as obvious as in a cross-cultural setting. Such is the case, for example, with regard to existing tensions between the protection of citizens in times of ill health or misfortune versus forced intervention in their lives, even when these are seen as part of preventive measures. Between public and private or even transnational micro-space important ethical challenges, which affect our professional work, are thus rendered visible. It may therefore be wise to try to unpack our interpretational frames in order to reflect on the conceptions of clinical reality that we have created.

Nora Ahlberg
October 2007

INTRODUCTION

Towards Interdisciplinary Theory and Understanding

NOTES ON A WARTIME PICTURE

One of the clients brought me a six hour long video tape filled with human tragedy, raids and killings of adults and children alike. Though it was simply overwhelming to view, her point was a different one; that these were the only remaining pictures of her dear *Home*. It seemed like a compulsive backward glance at a happy childhood through the spectacles of organised social violence; while being, moreover, cast away on foreign soil.

While many minority studies have been written by, and implicitly concerned with men, this one focuses on woman brought up in a traditional setting dominated by gender segregation[1]. At the same time, however, it is a work about displaced persons whose stories remind us not only of the atrocities of wars fought in their homelands, but of the extent to which wars continue to be waged on the psychocultural level even after its victims have reached what they believe to be a safe haven in a cross-cultural exile.

As for the subject matter, I have tried to present the clients' truths as I have understood them as a therapist/researcher invited to hear and feel their tragedies and separation from their loved ones. The narratives on which I base my analysis are thus in themselves the products of a cross-cultural encounter involving three people including the interpreter. I feel fairly safe in alleging that it has been an experience of mutual challenge and confidence building. Writing on the life history approach in general, Catani (1981, 212) aptly describes it as "a two way seduction, a love story that recounts the development of an intense affective relationship whose exchange exists on a purely oral basis". To ignore this fact in favour of an exclusively documentary approach would be to renounce the fundamental importance of interpersonal communication generally, and therapeutic relationships in particular.

It goes without saying that the mental hospitality of these women, reflecting a more general kurdish attitude of sharing with your guests, has made a deep impression on me. The same applies for their pride despite feelings of desperation and 'shame' that have been brought about by traumatic experiences in their old as well as in their new lives. I also want to point out that the pure duration of these treatments, extending over many years, allows for a unique material as compared to what therapeutic experience we have hitherto had from cross-cultural settings involving tradition-oriented third world clients and their western-educated therapists.

An extended focus, comprising also the field of cultural study, makes this study somewhat different from those of my psychologist/ psychiatrist colleagues working within the field of traumatology, despite the fact that it is based on the same empirical foundation. While I hope I have avoided oversimplification, I am afraid, however, that my emphasis on issues, which I find worthy of criticism from a human rights perspective within the fundamentalist islamic tradition, may be held against me. I therefore wish to point out that transgressions of this kind are in no way restricted to one particular – religious or secular – ideology. Moreover, recent developments in Iran have lessened the negative focus on that country in order that my findings may be judged more unrestrained by high-level political connotations.

There is no shortage of bad prognoses concerning the coping of tradition-oriented refugee clients in exile, or of the threats to their familiar way of life. The present work is, symptomatically, in many ways, a reflection of an integration or a mourning process, and, therefore, has some affinities with the assimilation analysis used by Varvin (1998; 1999). Because of the additional factor of severe trauma, many have reached a breaking point, generally diagnosed as post traumatic stress disorder (PTSD), when entering treatment. New conditions, such as the fact of receiving therapy, bring about new ways of viewing problems where the old ways brought no relief. I have tried to avoid overemphasising the clients' cultural past by simultaneously relating it, with due respect, to their present exile conditions. Because this past is less known or present in other clinical works, it might, therefore, seem accentuated here.

Though third world refugees are generally associated with the drama of international politics, their presence among us presents a range of profound, although less obvious, issues. For example, as migrants from muslim tribal areas they meet opposition in areas of family law and custom, where their religious custom involves diverse forms of marriage practices, as well as those related to the custody of children and the elderly, practices which are rooted in deeply felt humanitarian considerations. Seen from this perspective, their exiled predicament is a far cry from the ideals of unambiguous acceptance of the rights of individual citizens in the West without regard to gender or culture, who may freely choose with whom or how they prefer to pursue their lives. My material shows that traumatised refugees who harbour tradition-oriented norms and values that are perceived as alien by the majority, are especially vulnerable, sometimes resulting from pure misunderstanding, but also due to the more or less conscious use of institutionalised violence.

Working within a therapeutic setting, one is, from time to time, privileged in being able to venture beyond the boundaries of one's own professional realm when faced with wider ethical or cultural perspectives in the clients' accounts. What is likely to begin as a case of post traumatic stress might end in a tale from inside a life story marked by culturally alien and psychosocially extreme circumstances. And, in the midst of all the despair and failure, also one of basic human trust and coping. It is at this point in a therapeutic relationship that the diagnostic estimates and their carefully assessed causes will start to appear as being meaningful. This, of course, happens in any fieldwork setting, but here with the added obligation required by medical ethics to do what is in your power in order to ease the victims' burden. From this point of view – and the fact that the treatment has been free of charge for the clients – the setting is more characterised by 'a give and take' than the case is in ordinary fieldwork.

The ethnography of the clinical context can never be regarded purely as an issue of acquiring the greatest possible amount of correct information. For such a venture, the manner of relating problems is all too sensitive. To be allowed to live together with one's kinsmen, to keep one's secrets in peace or to protect one's dead, such issues all present complications that result from specific belief systems and which add to other psychosocial problems. These are complications that we cannot avoid dealing with if we are to acquire an accurate picture of the situation of traumatised refugees cast in the role of patients on foreign soil, and consequently of our own role as psychotherapists working in a cross-cultural context.

PART ONE:

A Cultural Study of Clinical Context

THE INTERDISCIPLINARY CHALLENGE

The Extended Use of Clinical Data

This work is a study of trauma, not from the narrow perspective of psychiatric pathogenesis, but from a wider, interdisciplinary viewpoint, that is, including a comparative psychocultural analysis. It takes as its theme two rather problematic concepts – namely *trauma* and *culture*. Both of these concepts are highly relevant to the research on forced migration from the developing countries and so called 'traditional settings' to the urban western context. My ultimate aim is to reconsider the impact of trauma and culture on victims of forced migrants in order to further our theoretical insights in this area. However, the themes of this study also carry other implications for the analysis of cross-cultural treatment and the psychological consequences of cultural change and migration more generally.

Because of the fact that illness and suffering always originate within a particular psychosocial environment any investigation of its patterns must also relate to the cross-cultural aspects of this fact. In view of the traditional religious settings from which the migrants at issue here come, it becomes particularly obvious how illness and suffering are intertwined with moral problems, and how recovery and further coping are therefore not only dependent on modern medicine, but ontological validity as well.[1] It is my firm conviction that any successful psychotherapy is dependent on getting things right from the patients' point of view, i.e. the *emic* perspective of the insider, which the medical anthropologist Arthur Kleinman (1980; 1988 a) calls illness. And which he saw as distinct from the external *etic* concept of disease that denotes the theoretical interpretations of pathology as used by professional helpers.

In the anamnestic efforts to understand, a psychotherapist is, however, largely dependent on the patients' retrospective reconstruction, because he or she seldom meets them outside the office in the way the fieldworker does. This fact acquires added importance in therapeutic work with victims of organised social violence because the emerging trauma story, in directing attention to the atrocities committed, may in retrospect also function as a sort of political condemnation of the perpetrators of the violence. It was for this reason that the therapeutic method of *Testimonio* (witness story) was introduced in Chile in the 1970s as a means of re-establishing the personal and political ties severed as a result of extensive political repression[2].

These and similar concerns have led me to engage in the present research, the material of which was collected in a clinical setting, with all the limitations that this entails. A wide range of interdisciplinary variables influence any cross-cultural therapy with traumatised refugees. Besides the psychological factors involved in victimology, there are social factors reflecting the marginalisation of third world migrant patients, and somatic factors following hardships during combat or in prison. Legal and spiritual problems should also be added to the list as they reflect the various sociocultural discourses at hand. Furthermore, all these different variables affecting the individual clients will, in the long run, promote the accumulation of collective memory and traditional lore.

The qualitative approach used in this study is based on an effort at increasing understanding of what psychoculturally meaningful connections occur within such diverse conceptual frames. In this aspect, then, its scholarly aims coincide with psychodynamically oriented forms of therapy. According to Varvin's report on the 1991 Standing Conference on Psychoanalytic Research by the International Psychoanalytic Association, psychoanalysis can be defined as 'a search', while *re*-search is simply a systematic revision of the material by 'seeking again'. In other words, the process through which results is construed into ideas or concepts. Gagnon (1981, 52) similarly defines data collected by the life history approach in the following way: "Each account expresses a critical reading of a situation; a reading determined by a project, and constructed with the help of signification acquired through biographical experience." This statement is likewise relevant for understanding the therapeutic process when it is viewed as a means of fostering the progressive unfolding of a meaningful life project. As a therapist, I see my task as coming to terms with this continuous process without 'premature closure', and as a researcher, as describing it at length from the point of view of certain multidisciplinary conceptual frameworks.

Working with refugee clients' trauma stories, the therapist/researcher can in a clinical setting benefit by borrowing skills from biographers and historians, particularly from the life history or history of mentality approach[3]. As I have not personally collected other documents than the client's verbal reports themselves, *focused life story* is, for my purposes, a more accurate term than life history, and a somewhat broader concept than that of illness or trauma story used by the medical professions. There is, according to Bertaux (1981, 7), a certain terminological confusion within the field owing to the use of overlapping concepts such as autobiography, personal document, life record, case history and so on. My own approach covers only partial life histories. It is topically restricted, on the one hand by what the clients spontaneously brought to the therapy sessions, and on the other by the therapist/researcher's interest in the field of comparative cultural analysis and knowledge of the field of traumatology.

Related life course research being carried out in the social sciences tends to focus on patterns of deviation or divergence. Studies are frequently made of juvenile delinquents, drug addicts or the mentally ill, more recently extended to include third world migrants.[4] What is common to these categories of people is that they have been denied the right to belong to a given community as full social subjects. A recent extension of such scholarly interests deals with victims of social violence, such as women subjected to sexual assault, children exposed to incest or refugees who are victims of torture.[5] Besides the after-effects of interpersonal violence, the larger focus of the study of trauma encompasses the effects of other stressful events, such as those resulting from natural disasters or serious accidents. In clinical studies the ensuing disturbances in 'belonging' are then analysed as they appear in therapeutic sessions through verbal material and behaviour, as well as by generating emotional climates. A micro traumatic situation is often found to have been provoked in the helper as well.

A more recent trend, however, is that of extending the focus from merely researching misery towards protective and rehabilitative factors and the patients' ability to cope with stress and unhealth. This accords with a shift in the World Health Organisation's focus from merely curing disease towards preventing it, and the promotion of health. In a similar way, in the field of psychology, the concept of learned resourcefulness has been launched in contrast to what could be described as learned helplessness[6]. The refugee situation represents a rare opportunity for understanding not only the pathogenic effects of trauma, but also mechanisms that explain the ability to 'not let oneself down' – i.e. resilience – or to cope in the face of massive trauma[7]. Within the field of cultural studies, the ensuing criticism of conceptualising the world view of the individual as a sort of static prison which hinders development has brought a parallel search for approaches in which the subjects are seen as active rather than passive agents in their own lives.

Likewise, ethnographic monographs tend to focus, if not on deviant, then certainly on exceptional people, such as leading shamans or tradition-bearers. The same is largely true of the history of religion, of literature or of philosophy, in that they unfailingly emphasise great and exceptional men and the systematically developed beliefs of such men – and more lately women, assuming that they are generally shared.[8] In my opinion, however, the extent to which beliefs are uniform or elaborated varies depending on a number of factors. Besides, the aforementioned scholarly approaches tend to obscure the beliefs of ordinary people such as the subjects of this publication. Despite the fact that they have been struck by extraordinary circumstances in their region of origin they still represent quite ordinary kurdish women whose knowledge of the world outside of their own restricted female sphere and folk beliefs is fairly limited, i.e. prior to their exile.

While systematised belief systems or 'grand theories' may be a practical necessity, according to the finnish philosopher Kurten (1990), theoretical issues do not necessarily concern most humans. A prevalent life story is therefore primarily a way through which the individual expresses those aspects of the past, which are relevant to the present in terms of his or her future-oriented – and quite practical – intentions. From the perspective of Berger and Luckmann's world view analysis[9] it could, moreover, be said to be part and parcel of the external and objective impact 'out there', but simultaneously internalised by the individual. This is why the subjects at issue here can be considered both products and producers of a history, which can, therefore, be studied from *within* and *below*. Because the refugees are actors in a specific psycho-socio-cultural context, their narratives will contain both collectively and individually, subjectively, construed meaning.

Despite the fact that intrapsychic and interpsychic meanings cannot be equated, one should nevertheless try to find ways to conceptualise and explore their connections without reducing the one to the other. Through a heuristic movement back and forth between individual and collective levels, the analysis of the separately emerging narrative accounts of this study, not only focuses on understanding individual particularities, but becomes, rather, a method by which one can identify elements contained in them that might lead to analytical generalisation (i.e. *not* statistical generalisation). The specific themes that have emerged from my study, during therapy sessions with the participants, have subsequently been analysed on the collective level across cultures, as well as in terms of individual relationships and private solutions. The material ensuing from a micro level analysis might, but does not necessarily, coincide with the collective one, for example, where clients – like mine – are undergoing change as a result of alien majority pressure; or it may include mere fragments of the collective patterns involved[10].

Indeed, the need for a general shift in research focus towards the interface between a number of ideologically divergent and distinct cohort groups becomes evident in this study. Such a shift is particularly important when analysing the multicultural identities of second and subsequent generations of acculturating migrants groups. But the adaptational choices of other groups, such as the more conservative pakistani foreign workers of Norway, are increasingly present also in the views of the first generation kurdish subjects of this study. Their reference in this respect is thus not only to the majority 'Norwegian culture' as understood by them.

With only a few cases at hand, I have followed a 'replication logic' rather than a 'sampling logic' in agreement with the multiple case study design presented by Yin (1991, 52ff). The analysis of the research propositions have been conducted separately for each case by relating its data to the particular individual context, that is without pooling across data. Each individual case consists of a separate study in which convergent evidence is sought regarding the facts interpreted on the single case level. The findings pertaining to each individual case are then considered the information needing replication in the results of other individual cases. In other words, the patterns of explanation given for each single case are cross-checked or compared across cases in order to reach cross-case conclusions, following the replication model of multiple cases. The theoretical propositions are thus tried out in a variety of contextual circumstances, and alternative patterns are pursued in order to reach an interdisciplinary, differentiated understanding.

In our scholarly efforts to build on systematised beliefs that serve the organisational needs of scientific constructions or 'grand theories' some things may go unnoticed. For example, one should bear in mind the extent to which a coherent world view or identity psychologically may constitute an extraordinary achievement, even under unicultural conditions. Compared to what holistic knowledge we may have constructed about particular cultures from a number of mostly written sources, in most people, identity remains a partial, fragmentary and somewhat irrational unit. Man, according to such a view, is no more a purely calculating rational being than an emotionally reacting one, who carries conflicting and irrational elements in his basic assumptions and identity. The impossibility of uncovering such personalised elements under ordinary fieldwork circumstances is apparent, and a clinical setting, such as the one used in this study, therefore seems to be more profitable.

A more particular aim of mine has been to analyse the emerging refugee narratives in the light of the deep-seated normative ruptures encountered by the clients at home as well as in exile, whose sources are often twofold; traumatic events in the countries of origin and cross-cultural migration. Following the humanities approach, my primary objective has not been to produce 'progressive' or applicable results, but to acknowledge what forms of interdependence there exists between our long term goals and certain issues of ultimate importance which require renewed treatment by each successive research cohort. In so doing I also hope to avoid the saturation of knowledge resulting from a mere quantitative analysis; an issue to which I will return in chapter 14 on methodological choice and the study of sensitive issues.

ADVANTAGES OF THE APPROACH:

— Since very little concerning the lives of tradition-oriented kurdish women has been written down, and since many of the subjects at issue here are illiterate, their stories have to be recorded at source. Hence, the advantage of an oral – i.e. face to face – approach;

— In a therapeutic setting, informants themselves choose to come to me (the therapist/researcher), and, presumably, I may provide some relief to their problems;

— The therapeutic setting offers opportunities for the researcher of attaining a certain amount of cross-cultural intimacy or looking

'behind the scenes' while ideally remaining an outsider, in no way a matter of course for a participant observer in the field;
— It may offer the clients the chance to reflect on the norms of their own culture as well as those of the alien culture;
— Transference relations and emotional climates are made explicit as a variable of the research;
— During the course of the therapy the knowledge gained by both therapist and clients may become all the more profound and thus objective, as it is increasingly subjectively felt during the course of year-long treatment processes;

DISADVANTAGES OF THE APPROACH:

— Loss of context-specific observational and source-critical data. This is all the more important when considering the desire migrants might have to break with their former patterns. Their point of view as expressed in the therapeutic setting might not necessarily coincide with those that are dominant in their own milieu, but, might, rather be considered marginal in the eyes of their own people;
— Although the client is free to stop coming at any time, the explicit/greater power in the relationship still lies in the hands of the therapist. One related problem is the ability to draw a neutral line between the assumptions of caregiver and care-receiver as further discussed in Part two of this publications.

Inside-Outside the Therapeutic Room
and Migrant *Problem Families*

By emphasising the relationship between treatment variables and belief systems, it is likely that elements which are relevant to the analysis of the expanding health care system in general and the mental health care sector in particular, elements that may otherwise go unnoticed, will emerge. Mental health workers must, from time to time, unpack their well interpretative schemes and rethink the versions of clinical reality that they themselves have created. Such pursuits are, perhaps, nowhere more promising and potentially profitable than in the cross-cultural setting. Indeed, the interdisciplinary lesson is derived from this incorporation of certain intervening socioculturally determined variables into our psychological models and vice versa.

The methodological disparities of researching a unicultural psychotherapeutic setting and a cross-cultural one cluster around various points on the axis of particularism/universalism. Moreover, while subjects are actively sought by the fieldworker, participants in a therapeutic context generally – and ideally – seek treatment themselves; and differences of this nature will clearly affect the asymmetrical balance of the subject-object relationship. However, this distinction seems to diminish in importance for cross-cultural migrant-clients in that they are frequently referred to specialists – like psychotherapists – for treatment by various authorities. Besides, they tend to arrive in therapy expecting treatment that is different from what is on offer, and consequently must learn how to make use of the help received. For example, the therapist frequently encounters a request for treatment of a somatic complaint or advice on problems concerning the social welfare system.

Referring to the concept of *parsities* ('persian syndrome'), a term used by frustrated health care professionals in describing their ethnic minority patients, Pliskin analyses an encounter between jewish-iranian patients and their israeli doctors. She concludes, somewhat bombastically, that

> Failure to comprehend the sociocultural factors involved in illness expression, exacerbated when patients and practitioners come from two different cultural backgrounds, contributes to faulty labelling, unsuccessful treatment, frustrated practitioners, unhappy patients, and the failure of therapy (1987, 238).

Recognising the need to pay special attention to the way in which health services are provided for minorities is not a matter of course, but ignorance of the customary practices and beliefs of such patients on the part of health care professionals is only one aspect of this issue. Problems presented by ethnic minority clients often have causes, which lie outside the control of the help providing system. This may, furthermore have an adverse affect on the helpers themselves as they often eventually become 'burnt out' by continuously having to share in their patients' misfortune over sustained periods of time (cp. the concept of secondary traumatisation[11]).

While many customary practices have no bearing upon health, a few are nonetheless crucial to the provision of culturally appropriate and sensitive health care. In the field of psychotherapy, we have no choice but to take these issues seriously. The high level of anxiety found in the refugee population has alerted their minority representatives, and especially their clinically educated compatriots, to the danger of misdiagnosis that results from overlooking the psychosocial and cultural context. And the growing awareness of the ethnocentrism inherent in our scientific concepts has brought an increasing concern for overcoming such tendencies also within the field of psychology[12]. One reaction that has resulted from such efforts has been that of emphasising the primary importance of cross-cultural studies and therapy carried out by insiders as a priority, thereby counterbalancing the tendency by western scholars to monopolise the presentation, also the history of the others. This has particularly been commonplace where outsiders have not taken into account the 'colonial stranglehold' or accompanying racism, so acutely felt by many minorities.

There are, however, good reasons to scrutinise this position from the point of view of the desirability of creating scientific or therapeutic 'ghettos'. It might lead to the exclusion of researchers belonging in a minority group from free choice of the subject of their study in a neoimperialistic manner. Such endeavours are, in my view, better served by a model in which the minority is free to scrutinise the majority, and vice versa. The ensuing debate has led to further disagreement as to whether or not refugees are in need of psychological help at a more general level (e.g. "Forced migration is not mental illness"). From this point of view, the rehabilitation centres for refugees which have largely been established in the West are even accused of creating de facto psychological quarantines where dangerous migrants (read terrorists) accustomed to resorting to violent opposition and fighting are 'disempowered' so that they no longer constitute a threat[13].

Culture, of course, is just another term for the psychosocial heritage or prism through which, and the prison from which, we view the world. Therefore, it must not be forgotten that this concept is equally applicable to the therapists as well as their clients, even though cultural understanding has never been central to psychiatric nosologies. It is also true, however, that the conflict between sensibility to cultural context and various human rights issues can at times become difficult to handle. However, post traumatic stress in combination with the additional stress of a cross-cultural migration often creates difficulties in the exile situation without the parties being aware of its causes. Furthermore, families belonging in ethnic minorities' that are perceived as 'problematic' by their helpers share certain characteristics which render them particularly vulnerable from the point of view of popular western notions about psychological well being. Among such characteristics we find a background in a traditional, often muslim, community, as well as severe traumatisation.

A typical case is the following:

> The parents are more often than not illiterate[14], the husband worn down by prolonged torture or warfare as the wife seeks help for social or somatic problems while carrying secret traumas of her own. Frequently, there is also an excessive recourse to medical examinations without this having, to any appreciable degree, lessened the high level of anxiety. There are four or more children who will in time be exposed to the scrutiny of a professional system of helpers. The apparent unity of the family and problems of interpretation has, however, left outsiders without much knowledge about real problems. Nevertheless, many a suspicion has been raised about family violence, mismanagement of the children, incest and the like.

After a couple of years as *a problem family* 'in orbit', a cumulative crisis may occur, and desperate professional caregivers often feel that the ensuing despair is directed against themselves. This is the point at which the expertise of a centre such as the Psychosocial Centre for Refugees is frequently called on. The child welfare authorities or the police might already have become involved in the case, or the parties may have been separated, but, from the point of view of the largely medical staff, we find that:

— the reasons for referral seem vague;
— the opportunity to work undisturbed for the therapist is limited by distracting external conditions related to problems of housing, language or even residence permits;
— the only thing that is fairly certain is the accumulation of psychosocial and cultural stress factors; albeit often not explicitly manifested.

From an outsider's point of view, the subjects of this study are refugees recognised as such by the United Nations High Commissioner for

Refugees, and, moreover, here in the role of patients. They are all adult muslim females; married, and members of what has been perceived by their helpers as such multiproblem families mentioned above. Three of them are disability pensioned for psychological reasons, just as their husbands were before them, and the others are sustained by other types of refugee or unemployment aid. In all but one case, several family members have also received treatment. All of them, without exception, have a history of problems with professional helpers such as the child welfare authorities, social workers, the police, or the primary health care system.

Despite the lack of any active research done outside of the therapeutic space on my part – to be further discussed below – some background material throwing light on that sort of strained relationships and the general pressures/expectations from various authorities directed at the therapeutic staff of the centre, has reached me.

*All ex. 1: TIME AND MANNER OF REFERRAL

1. *Aisha*; referred to the centre about a year after her arrival in the country via an interpreter, for failure to perform her housekeeping duties. She arrived at the centre, accompanied by her husband, complaining of somatic pain and continuing problems with the Social Services. She was to remain with us for six years, including a one year intermittent break.

2. *Nasreen*; referred about two years after her arrival in the country following an 'unsuccessful' treatment period at another psychiatric outpatients' department. Her husband was already receiving treatment. Complaints about 'nerves', somatic pain as well as disobedient children. She stayed in therapy for four years.

3. *Fatima*; referred about one and a half year after her arrival in the country via her solicitor because of an acute conflict with the immigration authorities who refused to allow her husband to be reunited with her. There turned out to be some confusion regarding her legal status due to contradictory evidence allegedly produced in police interrogations. She was to stay in my therapy for four and a half years.

4. *Layla;* referred about a year after her arrival via an interpreter who had worked with the family in an outpatients' setting. She arrived at the centre accompanied by her husband, determined to move away from the area against the will of the local authorities. Complained

about 'nerves' [15] following failure by the said authorities in investigating a serious attack on her family that was thought to have been motivated by racism. She got two years of therapy with me.

5. *Shirin;* referred a year after her arrival by a frustrated primary health care system following a stormy family crisis, including much violence, which had taken her both to hospital and to the local Centre for Battered Women. There were further problems with the authorities concerning reunion with her family. Her therapy was short-lived as compared to the others: a duration of less than a year.

In order to attempt to understand such cases and the confusion, which they create in their host surrounding, we can turn to many different conceptual models. Roughly speaking, however, they divide into two types of explanations across professional demarcation lines: one is based on the social criticism inherent in theories of racism or discrimination and a parallel philosophy of liberation, the other on cultural explanation and relativism. In addition to this, of course, we find those professionals who shirk their responsibilities by altogether refusing to deal with this group of clients or types of problems.

The general problems inherent in prolonged idleness, xenophobia and loss of status is a recurrent story repeatedly and continuously unfolding in the lives of third world migrants and in their stormy relationships with the social services. Adequate housing and meaningful employment on equal terms with their host would give better opportunities for a happy life despite cultural differences. However, psychocultural alienation and the lack of language skills, combined with difficulties in understanding a complex social security system, add to the difficulties of those who are already afflicted by torture and other trauma.

The number of third world migrants receiving disability pensions has been growing steadily. Among immigrants from Pakistan, Turkey and Morocco, resident in the country for 15-20 years and aged between 40 and 54, the frequency of disability pensions are three to five times higher than among norwegian born citizens[16]. This means that 10 per cent of men in the age group 40-44, and 40% of those aged 50-54, receive such benefits. Among moroccan men in the 50-54 age group, for example, two in three are in this category. The reasons given for requesting benefits are mainly muscular and mental afflictions. Many are illiterate and live in ghetto-like conditions where the sociocultural integration process has failed, at least as perceived by the majority. In addition, because the labour market no longer needed migrant workers, the arriving refugees (at issue here) were encountering increasing difficulties in getting jobs. Some 20 per cent of those in receipt of social security benefit in Oslo in 1969 were born in the Third World, as against 6 per cent who were born in Norway[17]. A fact that the more recent shortage of work force has, however, not relieved to any great extent; not even in the case of well educated migrants from the Third World.

* Husband of Aisha upon referral[18]:

FROM PRIDE AND HONOUR
TO SOCIAL SECURITY AND INFERIORITY

In our country of origin you could say that we had everything, our garden gave plenty of fruit. We owned the very village and needed neither money nor education. But what on earth could I contribute here? Do you need a good reindeer hunter?

* Aisha ex. 1 (initial):

"THERE IS NOTHING BEAUTIFUL ABOUT US"

On the whole I think that life is very beautiful. It is good to be able to live and be content. If it only could always be that way, but I do not think it is like that for anybody. You know, it is like this – if you are in a foreign country, life is all worries and such unfortunate things. It has no other meaning then; just worries and problems. At least, for most of the refugees I have talked to, it is like their life is not very beautiful. It isn't like that. That's because no matter where you are, you cannot think about the beauty of life: one just has to think about the awful things.

Half mankind, those who have grown up with injustice cannot find any meaning in life. (That is what you think?) Yes, because those who have experienced repression, endured misery, have had no opportunity or time to think about anything else. (Those who have been deprived of possibilities?) Yes. (It makes one angry). Yes, it's like this: If someone has no power or strength left, if I am weak, for example, and unable to fight or make war with you, I will not dare to express my opinion, not even to breathe freely. I'm unable to use what rights

31

everybody else has and can make use of. Because I have to hide all, I hide it in my heart. This makes me angry, and when I'm angry, there is no point to it all, no meaning to life.

Therapists working with refugees often have a sense of being obliged to pick up the threads at the point where the social services have failed, and they themselves frequently lack qualifications for functioning as advisors on legal matters or on the welfare system. But who betrayed the social security system? As in many other areas, in addition to reflecting the status quo of a particular society, such questions emphasise the importance of an interdisciplinary approach to these issues. The (inner/outer) vulnerability which marks many traumatised refugees, and may be expressed either as withdrawal or acting out behaviour directed at their surroundings, can be explained psychodynamically by reference to an injured basic trust and the use of maladaptive defence mechanisms. This is because the effects of organised social violence can in retrospect be psychologically understood as a forced regression to a dependant condition with malignant consequences. Moreover a protective detachment or estrangement from others is associated with post traumatic stress disorder as further elaborated in the next chapter.

On the other hand, exiled refugees often inhabit a borderline existence marked by a high level of de facto present loneliness in socioculturally alien surroundings. Like the many others who carry some form of unresolved/painful social experience in their psychological luggage, third world refugees are marginalised as peripheral outsiders with the resulting vague effects on the mind (learned helplessness; post traumatic stress) which may but, of course, do not necessarily follow from this. A similar type of affliction seems to occur in a range of different situations such as unemployment, admission into various totalitarian institutions like prison or mental hospitals[19], or forced migration, all of which have in common a lack of power and control over decisive issues in the lives of those afflicted. Under such conditions a crisis may be sparked by a mere trifle in their relationship to professional helpers.

* Aisha ex. (1 continued) 2 (initial):

"WHEN THEY TRAMPLED UPON OUR HONOUR"

Aisha's husband went on the rampage at the social security office, attacked equipment and threatened to kill himself. She was so ashamed of this behaviour that she claimed never to set foot in the place again. Like her husband, she spoke of taking her own life because 'Fate had turned out to be so awkward'. The children could not accept this treatment of their parents on the part of the authorities involved, and sought help. After this several people, headed by a chief psychiatrist and the head of the social security staff, arranged an impromptu meeting in the home of this family, without giving them prior notice.

The dispute went on about the family's request, now supported by the children's therapists, to have steady housing in the area in order to avoid, once again, moving when their current housing arrangement came to an end. Aisha strongly disliked the way her children were used as interpreters and "had to speak in a sharp voice to their Father" in order that they – according to her – broke down in hysterical fits of crying. She threatened to set the house on fire, after which the police were called. She described the episode in the following words:

> That quarrelling lady tried to overrule me in my own home, accuse me in front of the Police, so I refused them entry. Now they state that it would be best for us if we were under the control of a doctor – what does it mean?

From my own experience of working within the field, *authority incidents* such as this are, unfortunately, not seldom occurrences. It is typical of the escalation in these types of 'incidents' that the clients – the weaker party of the relationship[20] – justify their expressions of anger by proclaiming to defend their honour. They might invoke oaths and threaten physical violence while, however, expecting to be prevented by others from carrying out these threats. While occurring in certain interpersonal contexts, such displays of having 'lost control of oneself', which would otherwise be considered outrageous, are, however, socioculturally sanctioned. In situations where one's honour is perceived to be unjustly defamed, one is expected to react rather vividly in many parts of the world and social strata, as may happen in the case of these clients, subject to various types of interpersonal violations and subjugation as they are, even in exile. This picture is

33

complicated by the fact that irritability and temper are, moreover, a most troublesome symptom of post traumatic stress disorders across cultural divides. Clients often claim to be terribly upset or angry over small things (L ex. 3: Layla's Secrets). And such outbursts of anger are, according to Lipton (1994, 45), apt to be quick and explosive and may cause marital problems.

Problems such as those described here can – in addition to the reference to power relations involved in deprivation per se – be analysed; either on an exterior level of cultural diversity reflected as it is in a range of symbolic items connected to dress, food, religious ritual and so forth, which depict a multitude of customary practices undergoing change; or on a deeper level of psychocultural understanding of what mental effects are involved in the process. The positioning and movement of an individual client between various 'systems', however, depends on the sociocultural variation within the group itself as well as on its reciprocal relationship to the outside world, in this case represented by the norwegian ethnicity. It is just as important to learn about cultural variation as it is to avoid pressing clients into anticipated readymade categories. After all, they may want to make use of the chance offered by the host country for testing or breaking with traditional practice.

It would be ironic if professional helpers turn out to be too busy to protect the 'honour' of their clients out of sensitivity for values, which are alien to themselves. In the 1980s a lower court in Norway thus gave a divorced husband custody of the children in a trial brought to the court due to his violent behaviour towards the family, by reference to the prevailing muslim practice. Before venturing further into the impact of differing value systems on the cross-cultural treatment situation, I will, however, review the concept and available knowledge of trauma from the point of view of the psychological tragedy involved.

PSYCHOLOGICAL TRAUMA RECONSIDERED

The Weakness-Exhaustion-Demoralisation Constellation and Post Traumatic Stress

One of Freud's major early discoveries was the fact that certain childhood experiences had had a crucial influence on the subsequent adult lives of his patients. This discovery impressed him because of the specific role they played in the development of illness and the formation of symptoms. Although practically all children have such experiences, events which result in pathological formations in some, are experienced by others without ill effects. Judging by the results obtained from research in the emerging field of traumatology, there is little doubt that intrapsychic factors play a decisive role here.

In medicine, the concept of trauma denotes physical injury, but when transferred to the psyche, it refers to emotional shock. In the process of defining psychological trauma in more detail, Freud himself was to view it from many interrelated angles:

— In *Studies on Hysteria* (1893/See 1964) trauma is described as any experience which calls up distressing affect such as fright, anxiety, shame or physical pain.
— In *Introductory Lectures* (1917/See 1964) he used the term to describe excessive stimuli too powerful to be worked off in a normal psychological way.
— In *Beyond the Pleasure Principle* (1920/See 1964) he launched the idea of breaking through the psychic stimulus barrier or protective shield.
— In *Inhibitions, Symptoms and Anxiety* (1926/See 1964) he distinguished between a state of psychic helplessness resulting from actual experience of danger and that of the mere expectation of danger.

Thus, from initially conceiving of trauma as an essentially environmental factor, the paradigmatic case being sexual seduction, Freud moved towards viewing trauma in terms of inner psychic reality and unconscious imagination, that is, fiction. This development unfortunately brought about a temporary decline in scholarly interest in the matter. However, a host of related concepts were soon worked out by the emerging psychoanalytic movement concerning various forms of defence mechanisms, anxiety and infantile or intersystemic developments. According to Khan (1963, 288) this process culminated in an integrated point of view, which took into consideration both the intrapsychic and the environmental factors as envisaged by relational concepts such as the 'good enough mother' or 'containing other'.

The explanation of trauma thus moved from an outer exterior scenario towards an inner, fiction based one, from where it was again later to move back, among other things, as a result of the emphasis placed by the feminist movement on the frequency of external de facto occurring incidents of sexual assault and incest. In fact the difficulties involved in upholding any clear-cut division between inner and outer realities from the point of view of clinical material should by now have been demonstrated. It is no accident that Freud's interest in trauma arose after the 1914-18 war when Europe was filled with shell-shocked soldiers. Similarly, the study of trauma from the point of view of psychiatry as well as other related disciplines, is on the rise again when world opinion perceives a growing refugee problem and widespread ethnic tension.

The outcome of trauma in any given case depends on a number of interrelated interdisciplinary variables. Apart from personality factors and pretraumatisation determining the strength of the so called psychic stimulus barrier, they include the content of the malign stimuli comprehended as subjective meaning, as well as the sociocultural context surrounding and defining the event. The degree of preparation as well as subsequent life experience could be added to this. In the case of the kurds, the subjects of this book, the environmental and psychosocial setting in which trauma occurs can be said to include the iranian revolutionary process and the Iran-Iraq wars, prolonged and extreme living conditions of mountain-escapees, prisoners or refugee camp dwellers, and the severe long term repression and massive loss of human lives affecting the whole population. These events are, in the case of my clients, followed by forced cross-cultural exile that takes place while the subjects are still in a highly vulnerable state of mind.

'THE FROG IN THE WELL' (Aysha)

This image is meant to illustrate Aisha's fate in exile and the trauma related to her own (increased) expectations of honourable conduct accompanying her position as the *strictly segregated* eldest daughter of a family of *Agha* landlords, and, the age long intergenerational harmony which has suddenly been threatened by the unexpected cultural circumstances of her exile. However, hers is also the generation old tragic history, going back to her *Zardushti* (zoroastrian) roots[1]. Her father died from *sekhte* (shock, presumably, heart trouble) following her brother's death by torture under the shah's regime. These events were succeeded by uninterrupted repression throughout the Khomeini period, imprisonment and detention for a decade in a refugee camp.

THE WOMAN OF BAD DESTINY (Nasreen)

Nasreen's tragedy began at a time when her contemporaries were actively involved in militant opposition during the period of revolutionary fervour. This was followed by her father's subsequent death from shock (again, *sekhte*), general harassment, imprisonment, torture and spending a prolonged period under emergency conditions while hiding in the mountains. There followed a decade of detention in a prison-like refugee camp. Despite an ambivalent attitude to religion resulting from socialist leanings among the younger members of her middle class family, Nasreen takes refuge in the supernatural concept of 'destiny' (*adjal*) in dealing with trauma and the subsequent dissolution of her extended family in exile.

THE 'BAD' WOMAN (Fatima)

Fatima's family background remains something of a mystery, her parents having died in a most tragic accident. Her somewhat tolerable life in exile and her dissociation from religion will be shown to be linked to a pronounced premigrational deviation resulting from, among other things, the shi'ite faith of her father in a predominantly, self-conscious sunnite kurdish (though not persian) environment, and her status as an orphan, with no family support; i.e. a relative 'benefit' in exile when considering her problems back home?

THE DAUGHTER OF THE IMAM (Layla)

Layla's flight was initially described by herself as a mistake (and shameful to her family) following her husband's sudden and unexpected imprisonment, although it turned out that some close relatives had been involved in the opposition movement (and had paid for it with their lives, L ex.1). As the eldest daughter of a local imam and sufi sheikh, her suffering is closely related to the religious idea of a century old succession of a beneficial godly light in her family line, and its subsequent abrupt interruption by the unexpected and forced migration which was followed by harassment of her kin at home, some of whom, to her despair, have died since she went into exile.

THE DIVORCED WOMAN (Shirin)

The semi-nomadic lower middle class Shirin likewise came from a ten year long detention in a refugee camp, but her family had been only marginally involved in opposition activities. Despite being depressed as a result of her separation from her kin and continuing severe maltreatment by her husband, she was free from PTSD symptomatology, which is why she was included in this study as a control case of primarily adaptational problems. As a way of coping, when left to manage by herself on foreign soil without male protection, she took refuge in 'compulsive' prayer, nurtured by a 'compensatory' comforting view of herself as being of special importance to Allah.

The traumatic events in the lives of refugee clients can be infinitely varied, but the ensuing traumatic mental state is a rather uniform reflection of a specific type of mental breakdown which occurs when the mind is presented with a quantity of stimulus too great to be dealt with in the usual way by any healthy normal person. Trauma causes the mental apparatus to be flooded to the extent that it cannot master the situation. Its psychic content involves a feeling of helplessness in the face of overwhelming danger. Phenomenologically, it appears sudden and totally disruptive. The world as previously known to the survivor somehow ceases to exist through external events.

* Nasreen ex. 1 (pre-medial):

A TOPSY-TURVY WORLD

(Did you cry when you left Iran?) No, not at all (Now she re-experiences it all in tears). You cannot know what it is like inside me. Now, I just have to smile as if nothing had happened, but it is all black; terrifyingly painful. How could anyone suffer like me – have to leave everything. Our home became mere soil, and the family was killed. How much can a heart endure? I cannot go home anymore, but must go to a strange place. The trees, walls, birds – everything is strange to me; I have no home. The house is strange, like a sculpture. When the revolution came, we had to flee to the mountains while they were bombing people, we saw children and women being killed in front of our eyes.

Once, in Iraq, during a large wedding celebration, bombs started falling. We could not identify the bridal couple – they were just mud. 200 were killed and 150 injured that day. Another time a small village was hit in early spring. The children were out picking fruit, the sheep grazing. 50 sheep were blown up in the air, and a neighbouring family of four. I have seen so many killed. I've seen too much, many families who have lost their breadwinner. I see it all the time, tormenting me terribly. When I left I had no white hairs, now my hair is grey. Only God can know how painful my memories are. I have heard so many aeroplanes arrive. Even after three months in Oslo, the children tried to run away when they heard an aeroplane. I will never be able to fly. When we were to leave for Norway the children wanted to travel by donkey. For three whole years they could arrive night and day, there was no difference. (Do you think there is some meaning to all of this?) Yes, I have thought of that. Life is not to be reckoned with at all. In a matter of seconds, it is all over, one is finished even if one is healthy. This is the way I am even now. God only knows how frightened I am. If the children do not answer me in the morning, I think they are dead. *You know one gets so immensely confused. It is not only me, everybody is like this.*

For trauma survivors, according to clinical experience, a feeling of unreality penetrates many aspects of their lives[2]. Irrespective of its context, traumatic damage seems to undermine the basic psychocultural assumptions by which people live, including their sense of control over their body and mind as well as their hopes for the future that seem to have become somehow foreshortened: i.e. their normally expected *myth of invulnerability*. Frequently experienced symptoms are a feeling of unreality, "of watching a movie", of having changed completely as a person subsequent to the traumatic events [3] (especially in the cases of Aisha and Nasreen who, unlike Fatima, were free of primary traumatisation), of numbing and somatic pain. Diffuse bodily pain[4], decreasing in time, was marked during the initial phase of all therapies excepting that of Layla in whose case the pain remained throughout our contact.[5]

* Nasreen ex. 2 (1 continued/medial):

"LIKE PARTING WITH MY SISTER"

Once when Nasreen (that was after having parted with her niece at the end of a reunion abroad shortly before) hadn't shown up for her session, she later motivated her absence by unspecified bodily pain. And then she was, once again, to re-experience *'it all'* as she herself put it, this time with even greater affect. As it turned out, years before, this niece had been the only one among her kin to suspect that Nasreen's family was about to escape (such plans had to be kept strictly secret under the circumstances) when she had shown up unannounced just prior to their departure.

> We said that we weren't going anywhere, but she suspected it anyway. (Did you bring anything with you?) Nothing apart from a bag of some children's clothing we later left with a friend of my husband in Iraq. It was heavy, I could not take anything with me. We hid our money on the children and bought what we needed on the way. (So, you never got a chance to bid farewell?) No, we locked the door and left. Now everything is levelled to the ground, destroyed. But we would have been killed if anybody had known we were about to leave.

> (Is there anything special you miss?) I've stopped dreaming; many things I got from Mother, old things: some gold, china, clothes my mother had made – a white wedding gown, with a little blue. (Did you get time to prepare yourself for leaving?) I couldn't imagine that I was going to leave for such a long time. 13 years have passed... (She cries a lot during this session, but manages to smile towards the end). I was sure that we were going to be away only for a while. (How did you travel?) By car, driven by a friend of my husband, on horseback, on foot... (I point out that this time she had similarly left her niece in a car driven by the friend of her husband, upon which she comments). This time it was so difficult

to say goodbye, we sat in the car for hours on end crying, all of us. I wish I had never gone! Neither had my niece brought anything with her (that is, from home, while fleeing herself).

(Cp. F ex. 10: Nothing but a Widow)

Under such extraordinary circumstances the inability of the suffering person to deal with the impact of outside events and related impulses from the inside is followed by clearly discernible changes in appearance and behaviour. The victim may appear immobilised, infantile and submissive, or else trauma may be followed by disorganised, frenzied behaviour bordering on panic. In addition, signs of automatic dysfunction (such as hyperventilation, muscle spasms, sweating, dizziness) contribute to the picture. Intense anxiety can appear suddenly and without apparent reason combined with fear of dying or going crazy. When the defence capacity of the synthetic functions of the ego break down, a defensive or adaptational regression occurs in which modes of functioning considered developmentally earlier, such as denial (here, a delayed or postponed sorrow reaction in N. ex 2), splitting (such as in the next example F. ex 1 below) or fixations dominated by repetition-compulsion, are, according to therapeutic theory and reasoning, resorted to. For this reason, making the correct diagnosis even under unicultural conditions, requires perseverance and ability to detect clues in the face of denials and other averting measures.

The general effects of trauma may thus fluctuate from a general numbing or loss of affective response to the opposite, a *startle response* aptly illustrated by Nasreen's case ex. 1: A Topsy-Turvy World above and an emotional storm in affect and behaviour.[6] Depending on its more or less specific characteristics, psychiatry has included the cluster of psychological reactions to trauma in a significant number of victims in its diagnostic systems, such as the International Classification of Disease (ICD) and The Diagnostic and Statistic Manual of Mental Disorders (DSM). As pointed out by Lavik (1994) among others[7] psychiatric experts were initially summoned to investigate and treat soldiers with psychological reactions from battle trauma beginning with the United States Civil War. But it was not until the World Wars that any systematic investigation was carried out. In addition to soldiers on duty, these have included the study of prisoners of war, political prisoners in general, holocaust victims and wartime children.

The diagnostic categories in use, such as traumatic neurosis, stress

41

response syndrome, concentration camp syndrome or the now widely applied *post traumatic stress disorder* (PTSD) naturally reflect the various psycho-historical settings present at their emergence[8]. Recently this picture has been complemented by a category called *disorder of extreme stress not otherwise specified* (DESNOS), which is the result of the interest in sexual and domestic violence as evidenced, among other things, by the feminist movement. The diagnostic criteria of DESNOS, which presupposes the existence of PTSD for at least three years, include changes in consciousness, belief system, self-image and the perception of the assailant(s), as well as changes in interpersonal relations and the ability to regulate feelings, resulting from *prolonged* situations of totalitarian control.

As such, these mental states could be compared with the concept of altered state of consciousness (ASC) – and viewed as a sort of ASC-*in-the-negative* – while many of the same characteristics that we know of from the study of drug induced or religious ASC such as, for example, the lessening of identity boundaries, high emotional alertness and suggestibility, and a retrospect feeling of having changed completely as a person, are present. However, in this instance depending on the cruel realities surrounding the events, the very same characteristic that we find in creative or other peak experiences are here perceived negatively, as horrific/painful and unreal; a form of enforced and prolonged 'bad trip': i.e. as opposed to, for example, the conviction of the mystics of having experienced the truly real or sacred[9]. Following such a negative/positive experience the subject may feel so different from others that even communicating their experiences becomes difficult, if not impossible; someone who has not been through it simply could not understand.

Long term danger from which a subject cannot escape, such as that facing severely abused children, enables the victim to mobilise a defence mechanism in the form of constant arousal and manipulation of consciousness such as focused attention, amnesia or the creation of a dissociative and highly personal fantasy world.

* Fatima ex. 1 (medial):

THE PRETRAUMATISATION PERIOD

Fatima told me that she had an older sister and brothers (observe that she did not at the time mention her deceased sister, see below) as well as a younger brother. It was only much later that she disclosed that he had been martyred in the war. She said that her father had died from an illness when she was six ("As children, we were always discreet when he was around – afraid of being beaten to death. But we nevertheless considered him to be fair").

She is close to her mother who, when she became a widow, had to provide for her children on her own and never remarried. "Mother", she says, "has lost me." (i.e. through the client's flight, and, despite the very opposite fact that in real life 'she had lost her mother', which was to be revealed only later). Fatima's father had no kin, and according to her they would have been better off without her mother's few relatives (who turned out to be of no help to the family in distress). Currently, she is very concerned that no one is taking care of her mother (she cries while telling me this). Later it turns out that her elder sister had badly maltreated her from an early age on "without anyone acknowledging it".

She was disturbed by intrusive memories when she first disclosed her subsequent maltreatment at the hands of her first husband. Her husband was in the habit of attacking her in a towering rage, leaving scars all over her body except for the face. He sometimes hit her with a belt buckle; once, when a local police station was ransacked during the revolution, he had, according to her, got hold of an electric rod which he later used to torture her. At this point Fatima maintains intense eye contact with me – during our early sessions she consistently kept turning to the interpreter. The reason she was so upset and unable to sleep was that she had met a compatriot whom she could not recognise at first, but who turned out to be a former acquaintance who had always pitied her because of the awful treatment meted out by her spouse.

> But there is nothing you can do about such things in our culture. No one dares to intervene. For many years I endured it because there was no way of getting a divorce. But when the revolution broke out – I really do owe them this – all those snobs who took bribes disappeared. At first they really tried to be good. It was what we called a *komiteh* (police force) group which gave me a divorce (due to her husband's alcohol abuse).

Even so, unwanted by her kin as she was, she had to leave without possessions and with nowhere to go.

(cp. F ex. 10: Nothing but a Widow)

Dissociation is a frequently observed protective mechanism in the victims of social violence which has gained increased attention only recently[10]. The Diagnostic and Statistical Manual of Mental Disorders, DSM-III (1987) by the American Psychiatric Association, defines it as a disturbance of, or an alteration in, the normally integrative functions of identity formation, memory or consciousness. Like the phenomenon of trauma itself, dissociation has not received much attention from the mainstream of mental health studies, despite the fact that both phenomena are, especially through the works of scholars like William James, Pierre Janet and Sigmund Freud, at the very foundations of the discipline. Renewed scholarly efforts have, according to Spiegel (1991) since revealed trauma to be a common thread in the aetiology of dissociation.

Because the essence of trauma is the loss of control in a situation where the subject's will is overridden by the brutality of others, by accident or by nature's indifference, mental control becomes paramount. Psychogenic amnesia or inability to recall trauma related topics are among the most prominent symptoms, while the person's general fund of knowledge remains intact. The portion of the episode not remembered is apt to be the most traumatic one. This phenomenon is also coherent with the theory of state-dependent memory linking affect to content in hypnosis and other forms of altered states of consciousness[11].

* Fatima ex. 2 (1 continued/post-medial):

"PROMISE ME NEVER TO SPEAK OF MY MOTHER AS BEING DEAD"

> For years, during our sessions Fatima had spoken of her mother as though she was alive and referred to their continuing contact. She included her in the previous life story (as depicted above) and worried herself sick about her mother's loneliness, abandoned by all her relatives except for herself. She told me that she had shared her experiences of torture with no one but her mother, she told me of her mother's inability to speak for a year because she was mourning her little brother who was martyred in the war; about her mother's refusal to receive the 'blood money' meted out by the regime and so on.

> After insulting the iranian-born interpreter in order that she should withdraw from the therapy sessions and, thus, from witnessing her further narrative as described below (F ex. 17: "I will never go back to

interpreting for her or I lose all my credibility"), she brought a female friend to help her tell *the real story* as quoted here: A story about her fate as an *saghir* (orphan), which for a kurdish female like her was equivalent to that of being an unprotected and socially stigmatised person.

(Now, do you feel strong enough to use your friend for what you wanted to tell me?) Yes (She starts spontaneously to speak Norwegian). I will try, but I don't know how to start... My mother married when she was nine years old. She had a few children but then lost one. When she (her other sister) was nine, she died at school. I was five. My older sister was born when my mother was ten. There was only ten years difference between them. And then, I don't know how to talk about this...

I was the fourth child of my parents. I was so very much attached to them when I lived with them. But when I was six, I lost my mother and my father. I didn't tell you about that (she is very moved). But, my mother will always be alive for me. *I do not believe that my mother is dead*. No. (You were six when both your parents died?) We had bought a little house because they had always wished to own one, we worked very hard to be able to afford it. This house was destroyed (Her friend now interrupts: It was in such a bad shape). My mother and my father were underneath...

(Buried underneath the house?) Yes. It was spring, so there was a lot of snow. It was very slippery, water mixed with dirt; so difficult to get them out. It took a long time, for ten hours they lied buried underneath the house. Nothing happened to us. We were... (She shows me how they were buried to their waists)... People came, and at once they pulled us out (So your home did actually fall down on you?) Yes. When they were pulled out they died. They dug them out using a pickaxe, but the axe went into my mother's ear and came out on the other side; this killed her. (Her friend: She died because they dug her out with the axe; Fatima shows me how the axe jutted out on the other side of her head). Father died of the dust because he was asthmatic.

They died when they came out. We just cried; me and my little brother just cried. When they came out they buried them (Her friend: There is a special word which means to be orphaned in Iran). (A hard destiny?) And so we were orphaned, which meant that my elder sister had to look after us. (So that was why your sister brought you up?) (Her friend: She was the eldest one, there was nothing else to be done). She was 18, married and very afraid of us (At this point, I see a faint smile on her face). After all, there was no choice.

My other sister died when mother was alive. I told you before. A friend hit her at school. She had heart problems. When she came home from school she complained "I have pain in my heart". Mother said "Okay, you need a doctor, do you?" But she could not speak any longer. (Fatima now pauses, crying quietly.)

Mother takes my sister like this in her lap (She shows me) and I take sister's shoes, and we leave for the doctor. On the way, she said "Ah, ah, ah" three times, and then, she died. The doctor examined her and said "She has been dead for an hour". She died; we were only four children. My little brother and I were orphaned. We were very young, could not choose for ourselves. (What about your older brother?). His fate was different, not like ours. (Her friend explains that he was only half orphaned. He didn't spend much time with them. The court decided that her sister was to take care of them.)

(Are you able to remember the events yourself, or has someone told you? The friend: No, it is herself.) I remember exactly how it was, as if it were happening again, right here. (As if apologising for Fatima's 'madness', her friend corrects her: She forms a picture of it in inside her head.) (It comes back the way it did when you told me about your torture?) Yes... (She is very moved). Yes, I see... have seen it with my own eyes (Her friend again specifies: She was there when they took her parents out).

They had buried them very close to each other, so close that the wall between them collapsed. It was almost like the same grave (I couldn't follow you now?) (Her friend: They were buried in separate graves, but the wall between the graves was so thin that it almost became a single one, her father's leg could touch the other side.) (Do you think this is somehow a good thing?) No, it is just what happened (Do you remember it like that, that they were allowed to stay together or that it was a bad thing to happen?) Perhaps it was a good thing, because they lie so close that they merged. (A good thing somehow?) Hmm (Her friend is restless: She only remembers it all, because she saw it with her own eyes.)

(Were you present at the funeral?) (Her friend: She was not allowed to be there, but she went anyway) (I remember that you told me about witnessing the washing of your father's corpse,

46

but you never managed to say that your mother was there too?) Yes...

(I suppose this is the worst experience you ever had?) Yes. And that is why I had to live with my sister, and she was not kind to us. Her husband kept nagging her because he had married only one person, not three. (He didn't want you? Is that what it is like to be a *saghir*?) Yes. My sister quarrelled with me a lot, kept criticising me. (I remember you told me about your bad relationship, her actually maltreating you, but I had difficulties understanding why your mother didn't hinder it? Now I do.) She treated me badly. After my mother's death it was worse. (I remember you told me about the episode with the fire irons?) Mother was alive at the time, but afterwards she hit me with a brick (she shows me a scar which is still visible) Look. Can you see it? It went like this. (Her friend: She smashed her head.) The doctor said: "How can you hit her like that, one can stick a finger in the hole. It is very dangerous". But one thing, Nora. *You must promise me never to talk about this thing, concerning my mother.* My mother will always be alive for me. I don't want you to say to anyone that yes, my mother is dead. *Perhaps in your opinion my mother is dead. But not for me!*

This piece of information about her mother's death conveys both Fatima's culturally determined evaluations of her lack of social status as an orphan, *and* the impact of trauma, while mutually amplifying its effect. It was consequently to remain a sensitive issue throughout our subsequent contact despite the fact that in time she was able to accept it as a fact, at least between the two of us.

(Cp. F ex. 19: "Dear Nora" & F ex. 20: The Home Destroyed)

The caprice of memory is well known, as depicted by Fatima's concealment of certain personal material attached to the trauma which consistently evaded my anamnestic efforts for years. The story told by Fatima combines PTSD with other factors involved in dissociation such as child and/or sexual abuse (F ex. 8: One who Lost both her Money and her Honour); the loss of significant others in childhood, especially, witnessing their death or deliberate destruction[12]; the torture of prison inmates (F ex. 14: Accused of Lesbianism) and threats to her own survival and bodily integrity (F ex. 5: Memories from Inside the Prison); besides cross-cultural dislocation. These elements may not have been detected if it were not for overt symptoms, in her case including hospitalisations for episodes of brief mental breakdown.

The symptoms associated with DESNOS, whether in the form of psychogenic amnesia, depersonalisation, so called fugue or multiple personality disorders, may appear strange[13]. According to Spiegel (1991, 169) this may be due to the fact that the ability to assemble a coherent and unified self concept is taken for granted within the field of psychology. However, given the complexity of mental functioning, unity of consciousness, continuity of experience, memory or identity, is rather an achievement, not a given fact.

Chronic abuse causes serious psychological harm. Instead of analysing the consequences of the abusive situation, however, a tendency to blame the victim has sometimes influenced the direction of psychological inquiry, as it has the general public of our own society for long. In her book *Trauma and Recovery* (1992), Herman argues that people who suffer from the complex effects of chronic trauma risk being misdiagnosed in an attempt to fit the symptoms into the mould of existing diagnostic constructs. The most frequently used diagnostic categories considered doubtful by Herman and others[14] are, besides depression, anxiety or psychosomatic and personality disorders.[15] These disorders may conceal a multitude of severe traumas.

On the whole, clinicians deal with those formal and dynamic aspects of traumatic events that determine their pathological outcomes, but the study of the mechanisms involved also offers a productive avenue for gaining a fuller understanding of normal psychic functioning. This is because traumatic regression as a psychic event sets in motion 'unusual' attempts to *master* what could not be mastered in the usual way, a process which manifests itself on a continuum of severity from normal to pathological coping[16]. To the extent that such manoeuvres succeed in ensuring a gradual release of the overwhelming memories involved, the trauma is dissipated and, at best, gradually assimilated, as happens in normal pain reduction.

While, at first, the symptoms are helpful in separating the victim from the impact of the malign traumatic event, they later may serve as a defence against the painful/warded-off effects following from it. Thus, the very same mechanisms that in the traumatic situation itself serve as coping mechanisms become, in the long run, maladaptive if the victim remains unable to integrate the experience or provide it with mental content which makes cultural sense[17]. Short term positive effects may thus be converted into poor long term adaptation and persistent chronic forms of PTSD as the cumulative effects of trauma seen in these clients unfold.

The *Unspeakability* of Trauma and Broken Narratives

Psychodynamically oriented psychotherapists working with victims of organised social violence have called attention to what amounts to 'a conspiracy of silence' as an element of transference in both patients and therapists[18]. After a time, PTSD patients learn to avoid specific triggers associated with the trauma, whether thought or activities. The unbearable aspects of torture are perceived of as having a destructive impact on mediation, and this also blocks the therapeutic exploration of its psychological effects. Various averting manoeuvres, such as an exaggerated absorption in somatic, culturally exotic or political aspects, may come to overshadow the affective ones also in a listener. To which list, may be added the premature eagerness to heal or master the trauma whatever the costs (cp. the issues of retraumatisation and countertransference reactions below). Moreover, such 'unspeakable secrets' may become the heritage of the children passed on by their overwhelmed parents, as shown by the studies of children of Holocaust survivors[19].

For all of us, the unspeakable and secret nature of scenes of massive intense aggression links them in our minds to other secrets of intra-psychic life[20]. In the torture situation the victim is invaded from the outside by those mechanisms involved in the process, but simultaneously overwhelmed from the inside by aggressive and libidinal impulses[21]. In the discussion, which follows, I have chosen to compare the experiences of Fatima with those of an opponent of the 'modernist' shah regime, called AD, in order to counteract the impression that it would somehow be a solely islamic matter[22]. Apart from certain ideological modifications, the new regime has continued with the same torture methods as the old regime and even is said to employ some of the same staff.

In comparison with the orphaned Fatima, AD was privileged to be, to some extent, a mentally prepared believer in her cause, as well as member of the opposition movement before her imprisonment and torture. In the *Memoirs of a Woman Guerrilla*, she quotes a prison guard saying to another:

> You have no idea what 'love' is, have you really? It is not something you can prove or disprove with talking. And there is not one kind of love only. Some people love their kids, others love their mothers. Well, these people are also in love and you can't do anything with them (No date, p. 91).

Deghani describes how, in her experience, and in accordance with what the victims of the Khomeini era tell me, the maltreatment often starts with obscenities before one is attacked by punching, kicking or other physical brutalities. In the case of women prisoners their gender is frequently used as a weapon[23]. The victims are often blindfolded, undressed and strapped to a bench in utter helplessness before torture begins. But the ultimate target is the morale rather than the body, as illustrated by the following story, which is so typical of these clients' allegoric way of presenting their problems.

* Fatima ex. 3 (pre-medial):

'THE POWER OF HARSH WORDS'

Such stinging words, I don't know how to explain it. Such hard words they say. Cold ones. The pain from beating disappears faster than the pain from those who somehow strike with their tongue. It is said that the wounds you get from a sword soon heals, but cold words are not forgotten that fast. There was once a lion, and his best friend, an old man, who shared their lives without animosities of any kind, peacefully. One day, when the old man was busy gathering wood for a living, undisturbed by the lion, he told the lion to draw back a bit because he was bothered by the lion's bad breath when they ate together. The lion on his part helped the old man out with his work on that particular day, but afterwards asked him to leave on pain of death. The old man did this, but only after first wounding the lion with his sword. Weeks later, believing the lion to be dead, the old man returned, but found the animal to be in good shape. The lion showed him its healed wounds and said to him that physical scars are for healing, but the cruel, insulting words you utter can never be taken back. And so it all ended tragically after all.

(This seems to be an important story for you?) Yes, when old friends start hurting each other with cold words, that is very important for me[24]. You know, mother was so good at telling stories to us. As long as we remained awake in the evenings she told lots of stories like this one. When she quarrelled with her brother, he used such cold words (Was this after your father had died?) Yes. *It is better to be alone than in bad company.*

(cp. N ex. 3: A Sexually Tortured Woman's Secret; A ex. 8: She who would have Cared for her Old Mother).

Fatima's destiny was to end up alone in prison, victimised by the gender politics of the revolutionary regime: she had chosen to oppose both her husband's domestic violence (depicted above) as well as the paramilitary *pasdaran* force of revolutionary guards patrolling the neighbourhood. Like thousands of political prisoners, she had to endure arbitrary pretrial detention followed by a summary trial before an islamic revolutionary court, deprived of any defence counsel or the right to call witnesses in her defence or to appeal. According to Amnesty International (1993), no political trials before the islamic revolutionary courts have been prompt. Most are held in secret inside prisons without any outsiders present, often lasting only a few minutes.

* Fatima ex. 4 (3 continued/medial):

THE ARREST

(Why did they arrest you?) There was a birthday party. We danced and had a good time, men and women together, and there was some alcohol as well. The music was loud, and a neighbour called the *pasdaran*. Three of them arrived, beating their way through with guns to frighten us. Everyone, 30-35 persons including the children, was imprisoned. Raiding my apartment they found a music cassette (in which she herself sang). I asked, "What now?" "You ask too much", they answered and threw me into solitary confinement. It was terribly difficult. A secret cell it was, far removed from all the others, the size of a cupboard. (She shows me how she had to sleep squatting in order to avoid the ice-cold damp walls.) No light, no window. It was very dark and there were many crawling creatures. It was winter; I had no blanket, only the thin clothes I was wearing at the party. I was never allowed to change. Once a day, I was given food and allowed to go to the toilet. Only once! As for the other times I had to soil my cell, and live in the smell and shit[25]. Nora, no one can understand me, how I feel today, what is inside me. No one explained why. I remained in this cell for forty[26] days, not understanding anything.

(Cp. F ex. 2: "Promise me never to speak of my mother as being dead")

The use of indeterminate imprisonment without the right to visitors or legal procedure; the extreme physical conditions; difficulty in keeping track of time or sleep, or performing sanitary functions; the use of demeaning language and treatment or giving confusing and contradictory information were part and parcel of the overall prison routine. A publication by The People's Mujahedin of Iran[27] lists other forms of systematic torture which can be added to the experiences of the inmates. The most widely used are blindfolding, flogging, electric shock and other bodily or sexual assault forms, as well as solitary confinement in small windowless or cage-like cells under the most deplorable conditions. Other methods of torture reported by the subjects are forcing prisoners to stay half-naked in the open during winter time, starvation, burning with cigarettes and tearing out nails or eyes. In the experience of Fatima, however, the latter were meted out according to 'Islamic reasoning', for offences such as petty theft – major theft being punished by amputation – or looking at the opposite sex illegally. Especially bad conditions are associated with Evin prison in Tehran, where both women spent some terrifying days, despite the change of regime.

Evin is a large prison with overcrowded cells where the prisoners were locked up except for ablutions, when, in a few minutes, all the prisoners had to go at once to the toilet and wash in the few available showers; a moments delay was punished by severe beating. A body search coupled with kicking and punching regularly occurred already on admission to prison, after which the prisoner was taken away for interrogation accompanied by agonising physical or psychological torture.

* Fatima ex. 5 (3-4 continued/medial):

MEMORIES FROM INSIDE PRISON

What I described about psychological torture happened in that prison. The prison I went to is for murderers and those who have committed very serious crimes, who are never freed. Here they find any excuse for killing you. They told us it was the terminus when they arrived one day, just like that, saying "Pack up your things, we are going to leave". They never said anything about where or why. We were blindfolded and had no idea where we had been. (Were you afraid of dying?) For me, life or death was not an issue at all, the way they kept going on. It was exactly the same whether one died or not, better if I had been killed. They killed us a hundred times a day... This is a way of killing very slowly. If only they would have killed us once and for all, but one is tormented like that all day long...

In addition to mock executions with intensely amplified sound echoes, capital punishment was broadly applied. Since the introduction of the Anti-Narcotics Ordinance in January 1989, which prescribed mandatory death sentences for those caught carrying or smuggling drugs, hundreds of people have been executed on charges of being drug traffickers or drug addicts. According to World Watch, the Iranian government itself claimed that of 113 people executed during seven months in 1990, 71 belonged in this category. Amnesty (1993) recorded more than 260 executions in 1992, noting that the true number may have been considerably higher than this.

Reports from all parts of the country reveal anti-drug operations as a cover up for political arrest and summary executions amounting to acts of genocide[28]. Political prisoners thus bear the brunt of executions and atrocities alongside criminals, as do ordinary poor people, especially women who might have broken the law out of desperation, by petty theft or by having extramarital affairs in the absence of money for contracting a marriage (F ex. 13: Secrets of the Prison). In my view these represent *the forgotten victims*, who, for lack of proper 'political' motive, have not attracted the attention of world opinion.[29]

The *Behesti Zahrah* cemetery in Tehran has allocated separate quarters for the rich, the poor and 'the unknown opponents of the regime'. The latter, the *Place-of-Shame* or *Disgust* as the clients call it, is seldom visited by the bereaved for fear that they may be persecuted themselves. Such ostentatious and, it could be added, shameless public demonstrations of the power of the regime are amply referred to in the testimonies of the survivors. According to *Human Rights in Iran Newsletter* (9, 1993), the regime had, for example, killed two highway robbers and paraded and displayed their blood stained bodies in the streets of the southern town of Kajnun. Except for the control case of Shirin, none of the women who form the subject of this book escaped such horrid public spectacles mounted by the regime to make an example of 'the outlaws' to the public too.

* Layla ex. 1 (pre-medial):

PUBLIC DEMONSTRATIONS

While FATIMA's repression never involved her kin (save the fears she expressed for her long-dead mother), in Layla's case the fate of kin seems to have played a decisive role in her later symptoms. Among the most sensitive moments is one where she relates having found, unexpectedly (while browsing the morning paper) the photographs of three young relatives publicly hanged in the street (she had previously known nothing about the incident).

A revolutionary guard had been assassinated so they needed scapegoats. Either they shoot them in the morning at four o'clock or hang them publicly later. This concerns especially 'victims of the first degree' (cp. *second shahids* in Aisha ex. 12), the *peshmerga*. A girl who had recently given birth and was already the mother of another four year old (who had at the time been torn out of his mother's lap), had been hanged (observe that fear of suffocation figured as a prominent psychosomatic complaint in her therapy) together with her two brothers, one of whom was only 14 "and could not have understood a thing". Another cousin bribed himself free with one million *toman*.

> They are buried in a place called 'The Place of Disgust' where no one dares to go. No one has any idea of what they do with them. If something tragic happens to the family, everyone suddenly just disappears, and the rest are left on their own because no one dares to visit them for fear of repercussions.

The photographs now in a very disturbing way; perhaps even reminiscent of survivor's guilt remind her of those later published, in the same paper, of her own children subsequent to their success in school.

Before her own detention (but after her husband's), she also found the body of the wife of a detained neighbour buried in her own courtyard with her legs protruding out of the ground. However, Layla's worst agony while in exile is about the reprisals to which the regime has resorted, first with her parents-in-law and, subsequent to their death, with her elderly father.[30]

Again, AISHA's family had to witness the torturing to death of several inmates while confined to a small three-cornered and windowless cell in prison; among these inmates was also a young friend of her own children. NASREEN and FATIMA had both witnessed sexual violations *en masse* in prison, and the latter had also seen inmates being stoned and molested.

The purpose of the act of torture itself is to create an extremely unpredictable or chaotic and aggressive space where some people may pose as rescuers while others act as murderers in abruptly changing role patterns. The constant threat of injury and even death, combined with extreme helplessness calls for what in psychodynamic theories are called *the internal caring objects* of infantile development while enabling the assailant to act on different aspects of them by abrupt shifts from a *good* to a *bad object*. We owe to Melanie Klein (1940[31]) the clinical description of the internal splitting process of the real caretaker's/mother's good and bad aspects inherent in psychic life, both normal and abnormal. Aspects that are, again, tied to the existing cultural symbolism inherent in the available interpersonal roles.

Like a Therapy-in-Reverse

According to western clinical experience, uninterrupted good 'mothering' saturates a child with libidinal joyful experience that promotes psychological integration and health.[32] The severe deliberate frustration of the basic need for support and trust in others, consciously played upon during torture, may come to reverse an otherwise healthy development by exceeding the subject's capacity for keeping the good and bad objects united as a tolerable whole. An internal structure comprising cruel and deceitful relationships is created, which may reactivate related *part-self* or *all-bad* objects connected with feelings of rage, despair and shame.

In this sense, because of the premigrational difficulties of Fatima going back to her childhood dilemmas, even before the 'politically' motivated harassment or trauma, AD obviously fared better than her. Mentally prepared for the possibility of torture before her internment, AD's reflective account describes the hazards involved in the changing positions of her persecutors as between the 'kind-hearted' and persuasive few doing the soft talk ("Come on girl, don't hurt yourself needlessly, talk"), and others oscillating between indifference and fury. To quote from her initial confrontation with her assailants:

> ... he burst into the room swearing "Where is this...? Look into my eyes, darling, into my eyes". I would look down, or around, I did not want to pay him any attention. He was furious, shouting, jerking me, repeating "Into my eyes...". What did the criminal savage want of me? What did he expect? Perhaps he thought he could hypnotise me.

> Gradually he got bored and told one of the underlings to get the whip. Turning to me, he said: "Do you know me? I am Hossein Zadeh, the famous torturer, executioner". So they even take pride in that! Pulling his ghastly face, he would growl: "This is Evin, and I am the expert torturer". He was truly the embodiment of ugliness... When tormenting a victim, particularly when this involves the private parts, they expect cries of anguish and indignation. I wished my hands were free to strangle them all. Being tied up, helpless, was terribly frustrating. Those filthy mercenaries who would tremble when faced with a revolutionary guerrilla, were now displaying bravery against a powerless fighter in chains. What admirable courage!... I could only retaliate against their shameless, impudent insolence with eyes saturated with hate (28-9).

The change in the guards' treatment of her in her case led to a room with comfortable mattresses and treatment marked by great respect and witty remarks. Though the food was worse than previously, at least it was enough. And she was allowed to go to the toilet at any time.

> The jailer shrews must have been ordered to try to be kind and to calm me down. They were constantly talking of the future and the promises it held... insisting that all the torturers were really very nice and kind people! It is only that they go berserk at times when they have to torture people ... At any rate, now that the torture is over there is no point in being unfriendly! We don't have to bother one another. We are like a family in this room (...) Some family I thought! I saw myself totally apart, not so much apart, as opposite (44).

Such mechanisms of splitting and projective identification explain facets of normal identity development as well as serious personality disturbance, in which case they come to dominate the subjects' relationships also in adulthood. The less reliable or more intrusive the primary love object has been, the greater the extent to which it remains an unassimilated foreign object in the intrapsychic economy, which may later be uncontrollably released. In the torture scenario an externalisation of the harmful internal situation otherwise typical of the borderline patient with a psychotic core, may surface again as it did in Fatima's case. The situation leaves the torture victim in a state of paranoid transference, convinced of the total badness of the surroundings long after the immediate danger is over, and may cause panicky acting-out or even psychotic disturbance in an otherwise non-psychotic patient. Furthermore, torture victims are frequently forced to act out inner conflicts by betraying or assaulting their kin.

* All ex. 3: IMPOSSIBLE CHOISES

Again, due to her marginal position in relation to her kin, Fatima escaped such brutalities, but the other clients' narratives abound with them: for example Layla's feelings of betraying her family who knew nothing about and was to be harassed because of her husband's political involvement before their inevitable escape, and Nasreen's father who was tortured to death "because of us" (see F ex 4) while she herself was released from prison on condition that her husband agreed to be imprisoned and severely tortured. But the methods of divide and rule in use in the prison is all too well known to Fatima as well, even if, again, she is less aware of their rationale than AD.

Every subject has a certain amount of choice in terms of how to belong, but, in violent social situations, one is deprived of this choice. Like a staged psychotic fantasy, the performances of the torturers enhance regression and activate extreme protective mechanisms and persecutory primary objects. It becomes very difficult to preserve the memory of caring and protecting others in the subject's internal world, and thus to integrate what is happening or give it any meaning. Thus Laub and Auerhahn (1993, 287) depict trauma as disrupting the link between self and empathic other, originally built upon the mutual responsiveness in the nurturer-child bond. The point is that the victim's protective shield or psychic skin is somehow punctuated from without (i.e. the outside), here resulting in a profound ego split which cause later relationships to be impaired or invaded by chronically ambivalent behaviour.

In this way, torture acts as a kind of 'therapy-in-reverse', impregnating the inner world of the victim with a distorted human context. According to the clinical experience of Varvin and others (1995, 4;1998, 66), it is as though the traumatic situation implies not only the destruction of the future, but also a re-transcription of earlier object relationships (cp. the concept of *nachträglichkeit*). Massive atrocity thus may leave its imprint on the quality and resolution of infantile conflict, i.e. in retrospect. Torture penetrates the deepest layers of the personality and renders its victims susceptible to further traumatisation.[33]

AD somehow finds scant consolation in her ability for suffering during childbirth, another critical incident in life. After describing the pain from torture growing increasingly difficult to endure, when there is no longer any way out, she declares:

> I was like a mother delivering a baby. The pain is there and goes on. Nothing can be done but to wait for the birth of the child. And in that situation, the birth of the child was the arrival of death. I had to wait for that (29).

But for the unprepared Fatima, as for so many others, the situation turned out to be a more difficult one, one, which was to throw her into repeated episodes of mental breakdown.

In conclusion, defining the concept of trauma raises further problems in the relationship between the inner and outer worlds; of causality and time. Massive trauma renders fiction and fantasy dealing with the darker sides of life or demonic art – as they are envisaged by the collective traditions – both historical and personal. It represents 'danger come true', a nightmare realised. In facing massive acts of interpersonal aggression, the blurring of the boundaries between reality and fantasy conjures up an emotive experience so violent that it exceeds the ego's capacity for regulation. The pervasive destructive impact on the basic assumptions governing our lives (balancing between the good and bad sides of it) may result in a cognitive and affective paralysis.

From this vantage point, we can only relate to the events as though they had not happened. We defend ourselves against intense feelings of rage, cynicism, shame or guilt by not recognising them consciously. At times, such normally limited manoeuvres extend to the denial of historical veracity by its narrators, and might thus become reflected also on the collective level. Knowing the events, making sense of them, and putting them in the normal order of things seems to be an insurmountable task. The victims *cannot* make sense of it, they *cannot* know it cognitively. Indeed, they may not even be able to remember what happened, except for the haunting and fragmented precepts that torment them. At times, such problems may also intervene with the clients' ability to keep their appointment times (cp. p. 199ff).

Regarding trauma, we move into an area where mere knowledge may function as a sort of renewed encroachment or retraumatisation. Even so, the majority of mental health professionals working in the area agree on the necessity of talking it all through as further discussed below. However, the situation is further complicated by the fact that 'knowing' in the sense of articulation requires the preservation of a detached sensibility, which is destroyed in situations of horror. From this point of view, trauma can only be defined from a certain distance, that is, in retrospect as an experience, which has given rise to certain psychological damage. That is precisely why a narrative approach is so suitable for its investigation. Moreover, the traumatic state seems to impose a conspicuous fragmentary structure upon refugees' accounts of their traumatic experiences, such as those of the clients at issue here, which can therefore be conceived of as conveying a quite accurate diagnostic reflection of the ongoing intrapsychic processes. For example, the information obtained from asylum seekers thus often leaves a conflicting and distrustful impression, which is reinforced by the fact that the subject is simultaneously thrown head first into the general confusion accompanying the exile with no prior preparation. This is elaborated further in the next chapter: The *Torture* vs. *Exile Trauma*.

* Fatima ex. 6 (initial);

MARRIED OR NOT?

Against all expectations, the orphaned Fatima managed to obtain an education, got a divorce after many years of struggle, and remarried, despite opposition, to the man of her own choosing. She also refused to accept a morning gift from her husband's family in order that the civil servants who should register this matrimony failed to obtain their share of it, a fact which was later to create unexpected problems (i.e. its authenticity was questioned) while she was in exile, in connection with the reunion with her husband. However, this was only after she managed to flee, through a third country, and after many hardships, to 'freedom' in the West. Once again, she met with renewed and quite unexpected resistance towards the acceptance of both her love marriage and her acquired education reminiscent of that which happened at home.

Having produced contradictory statements during police interrogation, which had again reactivated the events of her previous experiences of torture and had led to a mental relapse, she suddenly stood in danger of losing her political refugee status, and, consequently, her husband's right to repatriation. According to the charges put forward by the authorities, she had, among other things, claimed to be married while simultaneously comparing her marital status to those couples who live without formalities in the West. This was correct, in so far as she had contracted a temporary *mut'a*[34] marriage, the existence – in shi'ite Iran – of which the said authorities were quite unaware at the time.

The culturally conditioned misunderstandings and re-emergence of fragmentary traumatic memories reflected in the conflicting evidence brought against her, was the reason for her being referred for treatment (cp. All ex. 1: Time and Manner of Referral). The authorities followed her case with suspicion while she herself was struggling to reconstruct a life in exile, dashed to pieces by a series of traumatic events haunting her. Events, which were to reveal themselves in time only, from behind the fragmented accounts that accompanied them due to her own prolonged inability to understand, and thus, communicate the facts to me – another likewise perplexed therapist-receiver of such a deeply moving narrative.

(Cp. my own distrust of her story, F ex. 13: Secrets of the Prison)

Despite the client's own overt silence regarding traumatic events, knowledge nevertheless does occur on some level, although in a restricted and defensive form, as manifested by its clinical symptomatology. The various ways in which we attempt to know or to not know the horror of atrocity range from erecting barriers against remembering and reclaiming undigested fragments of memory which break into consciousness, to phenomena wherein the traumatic legacy is somehow lived out as an unavoidable faith or self-fulfilling prophesy, or actively recapitulated in an analogous relationship with someone else, that is, as transference reactions; further treated in Part Two. On a narrative level, trauma is thus reflected in a range from its partial, hesitant expression by way of an overpowering but fragmented story, to its potential subsequent reorganisation into a coherently structured witness story.

The general purpose of these fluctuating and even contradictory symptoms is twofold: to defend the subject against the trauma by means of avoidance, and its opposite compulsive repetitive reactivation[35]. Building barriers against knowing is often the first response. An adult facing severe trauma will re-experience infantile remnants of primary traumatisation, while attempting to ward them off by a sequence of defensive mechanisms resulting in a lack of receptivity to and splitting off from shared reality. In contrast to the disappearance of memory, other forms of defensive measures are marked by the opposite reaction: intrusive reappearance of traumatic, dissociated or split behaviours, cognition or affects. PTSD patients often drift into re-experiencing the trauma in intrusive 'flash-backs' during which episodes they might behave as they did during the original traumatic episode. The trigger can be something experienced through any of the senses such as sound of aeroplane described by N. Ex 1; A Topsy-Turvy World above.

This kind of traumatic re-experience is decontextualied in the sense that the individual is not reflectively present or even able to communicate it in words as a coherent narrative. The moment the trauma comes to mind, it obliterates or obscures current reality and the narrator loses perspective; she is reliving the original experience once again, as reflected, for example, in the use of past versus present tense in the examples included here. In this kind of memory, the story overpowers the subject without emotional perspective, the very narrative text acquiring a somehow timeless quality of frozen images[36].

The intruding memory may also be manifested in post traumatic anxiety dreams in which the trauma is repeated, a process known to all those clients reliving it in waking life[37]. Recurring distressing dreams about the events including the full emotional impact may occur for many years.

* Fatima ex. 7 (3-6 continued/post-medial, conducted without interpreter):

ON MENTAL INTRUSIONS

Many years after the actual torture, three norwegian police officers made a nightly routine visit to the block where Fatima now lives in exile. Unaware as they were of the similarities with her former arrest, their visit triggered a new wave of severe anxiety: Here again were three uniformed men called by a neighbour for a domestic disturbance late at night, beating fiercely, as it appeared to Fatima, on the front door. Initially unable to respond herself, and although she was only an innocent bystander to the events, she fell into a nightmarish re-experience. The police had apparently just wanted to check her out of the case[38].

> (Do the bad thoughts still often haunt you?) Yes, like the other day when I had a dream that someone captured me. "Come on, to prison with you". I say "Please, please, don't do it to me. It is so painful for me". I cry, and my husband immediately intervenes "No, you are here, not in prison". "Am I really here? – ooh". I was so very, very relieved. I was so terribly frightened when I had this dream. I thought I was in Iran and somebody took me (Before you had frequent bad dreams, but nowadays they seem more seldom?) I don't get them so often now.

The ultimate aim of therapy is to enable the individual to hold the painful memories in the form of a true memory in which the event can be recalled by the internal witness, that is mediated by the client herself[39]. When an individual tells her story on this level (i.e. under normal circumstances), a certain distance or psychoculturally meaningful perspective is retained by the observing ego. Although the memory is vivid, it is neither *overwhelmingly immediate* nor motivated by way of distortive and projective mechanisms but is rather an external historical reality.

Traumatic experiences are thus repeatedly reactualised in the survivors' lives and narratives with the purpose of trying to master the helpless situation. This simultaneous acknowledgement of the trauma – and the lack thereof – may continue to exist for years without integration taking place. There is an intrinsically paradoxical on/off element in this, namely that the information, which is unavailable to the consciousness, can still reveal its mental presence. The alternations between memory impairment and intense reliving of events in vivid flashbacks show that the event is not really repressed but rather transformed into subsequent history, as Spiegel (1991, 266) formulates it. The different forms of knowing trauma, whether by verbal or non-verbal behaviour, form a continuum of 'mental distance', reflecting the degree of encapsulation of the trauma as something odd or foreign to the subject as opposed to its integration as a fact of one's life. The outcome – or degree of distance – depends upon the balance of power between the experience itself and the ego's capacity to deal with it[40].

Most clinical literature points to trauma as a necessary primary focus of interest in psychotherapy with refugee patients. The experience of the therapeutic staff at the Psychosocial Centre for Refugees does, however, not quite agree with this position[41]. It might be just as important to pay attention to the client's internal reservoir of earliest 'good', 'containing' or 'holding' relationships, as a buffer for the *de facto* painful traumatic experiences, or the emphasis on them may become too great a burden (i.e. retraumatisation) for them. It follows from this logic that the therapist must become like a *trauma membrane* by which is meant someone who personifies predictability in order that such memories can be endured or housed within a safe relationship[42]. Neither should the possibility of "being trapped in the trauma story" as Mollica (1988) has it, be underestimated as a process parallel to the other forms of somatic, political or cultural avoidance manoeuvres mentioned by Bustos (1990) above.

I do believe that we have learned much since those pioneering days when it seemed that the answer would lie in diagnosing trauma and getting it all out, no matter what the cost, based as it was on an almost automatic belief in undoing trauma by a relatively short abreaction through a talking cure. Today we know better. We know, first of all, that in order to protect ourselves from and intermittently adapt to massive trauma, we must at times also avoid knowledge. The second lesson traumatic experience teaches us, is that there is undesired and undeserved pain that must, however, somehow be dealt with, psychologically as well as socioculturally. Beneath the facade of bland optimism regarding the natural order of things, there is a deeper apprehension of a dark, harmful stream of negative events and difficulties. There are diverse ways of managing this on a personal as well as collective level, which depend on a number of cross-cultural and interdisciplinary variables. Thirdly, we have learnt that the deliberate destruction, or social chaos, resulting from the emergency-like situation at the client's home, in combination with a forced change of abode, challenges the psychocultural order we are led to believe – need to believe – exists.

3.
THE TORTURE VERSUS EXILE TRAUMA

Collective versus Individual Meaning
and Management of Trauma

At this stage the question arises as to what the trauma actually constitutes for these exiled clients. Traumatic experiences do cause PTSD,
but cannot of their own create the type of anxiety which appears
from these clients' stories. A traumatic experience, especially when
inflicted by others during torture, is generally assumed to damage
the victims to the extent that they actually lose touch with common
sense reality. To be 'one of the living dead' is a common description
of the subjective experience of such total helplessness reported in the
clinical literature reviewed in the previous section. Moreover, under
such extreme circumstances, socially authorised shared values prove
to be insufficient for imbuing meaning into what the victims have
experienced. By their very nature such *abnormal* experiences initiate
a sense of discontinuity, which threatens the clients' confidence in the
construction of reality as simultaneously internalised by him or her,
and externally anchoraged in a collective world view, and thus their
ability to cope with life.

However, irrespective of what type of traumatic luggage they might
be carrying, tradition-oriented migrants who suddenly find themselves
in what seems to them to be culturally unpredictable alien western
surroundings, will have to deal with increased expectations in the
host community about the creation of individual meaning of the kind
that is associated with the modern discourse. Despite the fact that
they may experience an increased freedom of personal choice (from
having escaped the repressive situation at home), many third world
exiles are, however, left entirely on their own to substitute for previously close-knit and collectively anchored normative regulations as
best they can.

ABOUT THE MEANING OF LIFE

When I cannot sleep, I think of those thoughts from the old days, and then I think about what it is like now. I wonder what this life is about after all. Why life has turned out like this. I reflect on the good and the bad. What is it about, all this? There is no meaning in everything going 'up and down' all the time. Over there, in those days, there were not the same possibilities which you find here. If there was pain, one just carried it inside, and things just went on like that, life continued. People over there believed that that was all there was to life, until death, and so they never searched for other things, but here things are somehow different.

(Some people say man is not supposed to think because thinking is the task of God?) Yes, they've said that to us. So when anything happens to us, we say, 'Yes it is the will of God'. We've heard this from everybody. Ever since we opened our eyes in this world, we've heard nothing else. When you've got it on your brain, this meaning which one is given in childhood, I do not believe there can ever be any space left for any other way of thinking. Because when I was a child, there was no one who could answer my questions, because when they were children no one had answered their questions. This is how it has been all along.

For example, my brother was executed and there was no one who could tell me why. Because they would say that power was in the hands of the unjust, and that that was God's will. It is God who wanted the Shah to have power. It is his will, and it is the Shah who has the power. So you just have to hold your tongue! That is how it is. (When you say that, you mean that asking questions was not allowed?) Yes, at times it happened that I turned to ask some casual passer-by, woman or man, but how could it be that my brother died if they had not put the rope around his neck on that particular day and hung him in the air? And they would answer me that even if he had been in his own home, his life would have been over, he was to die on that day.

(As a small girl you did think about this issue to the extent of turning to strangers?) Yes. I am like that. If someone falls down from a bridge into the water and dies, they claim that the meaning of that life has come to an end, he had been called. You use a certain word for it, *adjal* to be summoned. When this happens, everything is finished.

But I might think that someone hadn't been there to save his life, or that the bridge was not properly built. That this was the reason for that person's death. But they would say 'No, *adjal* came to summon him, he was meant to die on that day even if everything had been all right.

At that time children were not paid attention to at all (she laughs). If the kids kept asking questions they thought that, oh no, it must be the end of the world when children start asking questions. Well, in those days no one answered children's' questions. But now it is different. My children ask me, is it not you who are our mother? Then why is it that you cannot answer our questions as a mother is expected to? For example, they ask me whether God is male or female. How am I supposed to answer that?

In my opinion, those who call themselves priests over there, *akhund*[1] – forgive me, but if those simpletons had taught people anything, because they should have known something about the meaning of life, about the Koran, about God, and about everything it means, so we could have learnt it. But the women had no access to the mosque – perhaps the Farsi women had, but we didn't. They believed that women are not complete. Since they were wrong in the head there was no use in having them present, to teach them. They were to make food, deliver babies and take care of children, wash clothes and cook, over and over again. Women learnt nothing, they just used us all along.

(You are angry because you were not allowed to attend school?) Yes, you know my wish has always been to be able to write what is in my heart, on paper. But I have never managed to. I don't want to give the impression that the interpreter wouldn't translate correctly, but if I had managed to get my thoughts down on paper myself it would have been different.

Social uprootedness is a recurrent theme – which is closely related to the world of religion – and which has gained renewed scientific interest as a consequence of contemporary sociopolitical upheavals and intercontinental migration. Many refugees come to experience the loss of their *proper* abode or *meaning*, and subsequently find themselves in the middle of a perpetual struggle between tradition and renewal, a struggle between a sense of order and of chaotic adventure. Since, there is no automatic merger between a displaced person's *psychoc-*

ultural birth as a migrant and their sociopolitical one as citizen of a foreign culture.

Between the Devil and the Deep Blue Sea

In what follows I will present a range of psychocultural variables involved in interpersonal cross-cultural encounters, which are marked by conflicting normative claims. These will then be expanded in subsequent sections, as they are relevant for gaining a fuller understanding of the experience of traumatised and tradition-oriented refugees undergoing therapy. Belief systems include certain basic propositions which cannot be separated from the cultural context in which they appear, and the cross-cultural aspects of psychotherapeutic work are often due to variation in such self evident, and often unconscious, elements. Elements, which are, however, rarely questioned and the frames of which are neither merely private nor explicit. Often, we simply assume them to be fundamental without having made any conscious reflection.

Indeed, it often takes an accident to reveal such elements of cultural consciousness that have earlier simply been taken for granted without question, and cross-cultural perspectives are highly conducive in this respect. Mobility across culturally distant areas frequently entails a revival or a reconsideration of such self evident elements of distinctive mentalities or normative styles. This is the case, for example, where diaspora or migrant religion as an approximately total and unfragmented code of life encounters specialised (i.e. secularised) areas of the host society which disregard it as a purely private affair[2]. An allied issue touching upon that of the refugees is that of human rights which, according to its critics in the Third World, depend on their origins in western, secularised environments. Here, man has become, if not the measure of everything, at least the standard by which everything is measured, that is, in terms of human rights and to the exclusion of other concerns.

The present situation calls for a cross-cultural analysis in many sectors of society, including the expanding health care sector, and especially the mental health care sector. The christian belief system, which until the Renaissance constituted the basic assumption for western people, has today lost its predominance and is now frequently regarded critically, especially within psychological discourses. Diluted versions of psychotherapeutic assumptions have subsequently appeared in competition with other ideology producers as heirs to this same market. It has even been asserted that health has become an almost sacred aim of the modern gnosis.

It might be interesting here to turn to Skorupski (1976, 25-29) who makes a distinction between *cosmocentric* and *anthropocentric* religion. He defines the former as that which concerns itself with the relation between god(s) and the world of nature, including man as a part of nature. Here the supernatural is firmly rooted in an understanding of reality that considers it an active agent in everyday life. While the traditional world view – whether christian or other – thus makes repeated reference to the supernatural impact on natural and social phenomena, anthropocentric religion focuses on the world of man. In anthropocentric religion, the supernatural is accorded a marginal position in relation to science, except on the level of the utmost generality as the creator of a self regulating universe.

TRADITIONAL MIGRANT
COMMUNITIES

cosmocentric

contextual ethos
(duty-bound)
past-priented hierachical
(respect for the elderly)

sociocentric embedded self
(scribed roles)
extended joint families

segregating/expulsive
shame-conscious
('external voice')

kin network-care

indirect/metaforical

| direct/ rational communi- cation | institutional/ self-care | assimilating coercive guilt-laden ('internal voice') | expressively individualistic (chosen roles) nuclear families | de-traditionalised ethos (rights-oriented) future-oriented non-hierarchical (revolt of the young) | anhropo- centric |

DE-TRADITIONALISED
WESTERN HEALTH IDEOLOGY

69

Tradition-oriented refugees who have left repressive third world contexts for freedom of conscience in the West may find themselves vacillating between two largely incompatible authoritative stances: one requiring loyalty to the old order of things, and the other demanding change and adaptation as depicted on the continuum below (see figure). Here individual persons could be placed and given a profile according to their relative affiliation with a range of distinct characteristics of the normative styles involved[3]. It is to be observed that the adaptational process is a multidimensional one in order that the individual can be involved in conflicting collective discourses across the divide, thus making up a rather complex web of profiles.

In the de-traditionalised western view, here represented by the prevailing health ideology of the host country, it is taken for granted that freedom of expression is ideal for the individual, whereas a duty-oriented morality characteristic of traditional migrant communities favours submission to authority, god, and existing traditions. Yet other differences between a rights-oriented and a duty-oriented morale accompany this choice.

Culture shapes the course of a life in various ways according to prevalent normative styles, for example, by determining the relative amount and type of stress allocated 'the golden' childhood, youth 'revolt', adult 'responsibilities' and old age 'privileges'. This formative influence of culture as it is reflected in primary loyalties, may be illustrated by considering a south asian sculpture portraying a family threatened by extinction[4]. During a famine, a nursing mother is confronted by the following dilemma: should she give the milk in her breasts to her old, starving mother, or use it to save her last surviving child? The woman is portrayed as turning away from her crying baby and bends towards the kneeling grandmother who is depicted as the one suckling at her breast.

Where modern western man gives priority to an unknown future, here symbolised by the baby, this woman instinctively submits to the rights of elders – for who is to replace a long life full of experience? (cp. as against a nine month pregnancy). Notions of constant change and progress permeate modern western thinking[5]. Life is viewed as evolving towards constantly further developed states through modernisation, reform or revolution[6]. A result of this has been that third world cultures are more often than not viewed as dependent on developmental aid in order to 'catch up'; Islam, and other ideologies too, is thereby stigmatised as being inherently 'backward'[7]. The central tenets of western modernisation, and its criticism, depend on the necessary preconditions of democracy, capitalism, and an individualistic social system. Just as social progress is believed to depend on ideological emancipation from the past, the continuing development of man is seen as being dependent on a capacity of the individual to free himself from the context of the family in order to achieve independent adulthood. The ultimate value of a society is seen to lie in its potential; the value of an individual is seen to lie in what he may become, that is, a process of self actualising, frequently posed in terms of good health and economic/social success rather than moral anchorage.

Decrying such presuppositions of western models of conceptualisation as being permeated by evolutionary optimism and change, the ideal of islam as envisaged by its modern islamist proponents is grounded in a permanent, divinely revealed morality[8]. In Islam, the guidelines of normative consensus, built upon the history and traditions of a past epoch (i.e. the time of Muhammed), have supreme priority even in a revolutionary setting. From this viewpoint, the potential freedoms of western ideologies seem irrelevant, even self righteous, since the future is seen as residing in the past. No one can make themselves god-like by ruling merely according to their own albeit democratic will[9]. In the traditional hierarchy of power, god reigns supreme, followed by the prophets, kings and the like, then men, women and children according to their gender. This is a fact that even the most liberal muslim reformers cannot bypass in their efforts to render islam more up-to-date. There are – of course – a large literature on the matter: i.e. revising the islamic law, *sharia* on issues such as democracy, criminal or family law and gender, which must remain outside my primarily concern here.

Despite the generally coercive nature of orthodox renditions of islam, the shi'ite, and particularly the kurdish minority, exhibit a peculiar blend of submission and nonconformist or indirect resistance, nurtured by a long history of persecution. Notwithstanding its present opposition to the iranian clerical regime, the kurdish nationalist movement is itself intertwined with religious leadership and sentiments hailing from *naqsbandi* and *qadiri* sufi fraternities, and even 'zoroastrianism'[10]. Along with the family, the tribe and the tribal leaders, these fraternities make up the primary loyalties.

According to van Bruinessen (1989, 16-17), attempts to break such

71

loyalties have not met with any great success. While, on the one hand, national unity depends on the support of the traditional leadership for gaining popular legitimacy, on the other hand the ever present rivalries among the same leaders hinder its development[11]. The extent to which the clients at issue in this book are influenced by, or even related to, such a leadership has also been reflected in the present analysis; their loyalties include both *barzani* and *talebhani*, and, more loosely, the *mujahediin* as well as non-political sufis as indicated by All ex. 2: The Kurdish Legacy.

All societies offer time honoured socially sanctioned privilege corresponding to certain performances. While, for example, human rights thinking assumes the western ideal of autonomous individuals, islam – just as christianity in its traditional and popular religious form – gives priority to social arrangements and is generally in favour of a more dependent man, embedded as it were in his collective categories. This fact, that social roles are perceived as permanent compared to the individuals who fill them at any time, accentuates the problem of those, such as potential refugees, who opt out. As illustrated by the tragic destinies of a long line of writers and freethinkers, the most famous case of which is Salman Rushdie, one does not have unlimited freedom to publicly plead deviation, even in exile.

The private domain remains subordinate to role expectations, unless one is expelled for being morally corrupt. To a lesser extent, western society limits personal expression, but not necessarily social opportunities. Since social roles do not come in ascribed clusters predetermining life at birth, one is to a greater extent left to interpret them for oneself. This freedom of choice has largely come to mean, however, that whatever rules chosen by a democratic majority vote should ideally be transformable into universally binding laws[12]. Despite the ideal of multiculturalism which is inherent in official migrant policies in Scandinavia, the principle of equal opportunity is in fact often put into practice as a result of psychocultural similarity, a process (read: integration) which is more in tune with assimilationist politics than with individual liberalism.

In contrast, islamist policy, which explicitly classifies all citizens according to mutually exclusive categories of faith, favours segregation and the formation of ghettos based on variation in beliefs. In many muslim countries, there are separate electorates, educational institutions, jurisdictions and so on, which are allocated to the respective publicly acknowledged religious minorities, the so called "Minorities of the Book". It cannot, therefore, be assumed that the mere separation of state from religion ensures non-discrimination. Despite every assurance to the contrary by official freedom of religion policy, in fact pre-eminence is still accorded beliefs that are in accordance with a particular ideology also in the democratic western setting.

Because the demands of various belief systems differ, the law of the country, though equally applicable to all, will in certain important matters reflect the concepts of the dominant group. For example, due to a strong pressure towards seeing islam as an inherent element of the public sector, it is almost inevitable that muslim practices occasionally end up becoming incompatible with the host society, as shown by Ahlberg (1990, 186-202). Indeed, a number of liberation movements have drawn attention to the conflict between the egalitarian values of a self-advertised democratic society and its parallel exclusion of certain minority groups from sociopolitical participation.

In response to Norway's refusal to accept ahmadi refugees (i.e. without proof of personal persecution), their leader Kamal Yosuf perceptively stated that:

> Western individualists do not understand that person and family are, for us, part and parcel of the same thing, and that asylum seekers might therefore be only indirectly (that is, through their kinship to others who are considered traitors) but all the same real political refugees" (*Aftenposten* 3.10.1984).

When considering, for example, the impact of blood feuding or its less dramatic forms of face saving measures (as described in chapter four and eleven below) on the large number of relatives, regardless of their personal participation in the actual deed, this statement appears even more to the point as an illustration of our case.

Normative Transgression and *System-Oscillation*

The formative influence of culture on the development of personality as well as on the underlying notions behind western psychotherapy cannot be overlooked. Whether individuals choose to conform to these pre-set standards or to break away from them in various ways,

73

their ensuing 'badness' or 'madness' is still influenced by the norms and sanctions contained therein, the culture providing, as it were, the psychosocial patterns of misconduct. Even under conditions of the most extreme stress the individual is still dependent on cultural conventions and traditions of coping, even though under extreme conditions they might not be sufficient to prevent a personal breakdown.

The narratives of refugees frequently confront us with such wider perspectives of cultural psychology and religious theodicy, and with the fact that our own therapeutic standards are governed by certain seemingly *self-evident* propositions that are seldom made explicit. These elements are surfacing in the current criticism of 'the therapeutic culture' from philosophical quarters[13]. According to this criticism the principle of self-actualisation has become the most widespread official meaning of life as envisaged by the welfare state, the central question being: 'To what extent are we left merely to ourselves and to what extent is there any outside authority?' This basic assumption of western modernity, that everything rests with the ego, presents some additional problems that further complicate the analysis of traumatisation. The reason it complicates matters further is that it might undermine the basic trust in something outside of oneself, an essential feature in interpersonal relations, and thus strengthen the already existing mistrust in these clients caused by the traumatic events. Where should one draw the line between healthy scepticism and destructive distrust? Under normal conditions basic trust in others is inextricably bound to ethics in the sense that when confronted with trust, we tend to develop a mutual responsibility for living up to it.

While the psychocultural gap between normative systems might be big, obviously neither the 'sending' nor the 'receiving' country fits perfectly well into such idealised sets of paired comparisons. Depending on the perspective cultural variation includes both inter-group differences such as those related to ethnicity and religion, and intra- or subgroup differences such as gender, age and socioeconomic status. But irrespective of whether a particular case rests on inter- or intra-cultural variation, any invasions of one system by the other inevitably sets various mechanisms of reception and resistance in motion. Reactions, which are then played out in the lives of its actors as well as reflected in the therapeutic relationship as further discussed in Part Two.

Because the macro level drama of migrational upheaval thus always is demonstrated by personal problems being solved and private lives being lived, an analysis of the processes involved, therefore, requires relating variations in collective value systems to the detailed empirical material, which reflects the individual oscillations between these diverging systems; what I have called *system-oscillation*. The focus of this study is on the meaning of such normative dichotomies as they are woven into the daily lives of exiled and traumatised refugees. It is evident from the material at hand that deep-seated problems related to a range of psychocultural and social values are embedded in their narratives.

It is against this background that our patients' traumas must be understood. The most conspicuous of these traumas seem to be:

— the disruption of their meaningful environment without any accompanying change of purpose, as already envisaged above, and

— the vulnerability of women resulting from the absence of their male protectors, a discussion of which follows in the next chapter. With virtually no control over the making of war, women and children nevertheless become the targets of family crimes of honour and violent retribution. Moreover, in the absence of their fighting or imprisoned men, women frequently have to bear the main burden of caring for an impaired life during exceptional times of war or in distant exile.

4.

VIOLATION OF GENDER

The Silence of Women – the Shame of Men

Social violence is widely practised by, and directed at men, just as torturers are as a rule male[1]. However, the sexual violation of women is a widespread war crime, which has not been accorded corresponding status, despite the increased attention given to it recently[2]. Out of a desire to help it is, however, easy to forget that the rape of a tradition-oriented woman is always also a rape of her male protectors. This being the case, focusing on it on the level of a particular case, if public revelations are involved, adds to the dilemma of all those involved in this kind of suffering. Indeed, I would go so far as to say that no rehabilitation which ignores this fact, and thus also the problems confronting men in bringing their women home after such acts of violation, can possibly succeed.

Episodes of this kind will, irrespective of any individual guilt, risk bringing the whole family into disrepute. Sexual violation and the torture of women and children therefore remain underreported, and it takes much courage for clients to reveal them, even in the course of therapy[3]. According to Mollica (1989, 374-5), non-western women generally do not seek help for the medical and psychological effects of sexual violence. Instead, they are referred for treatment of problems related to the trauma, such as pregnancy or suicidal behaviour, while at the same time the women deny sexual abuse or keep the fact that it has taken place a secret.

* All ex. 4:

THE SHAME FACTOR VS. SOCIO-RELIGIOUS STATUS

It took the less religious clients a couple of years of reluctance to disclose sexual trauma. In one case, revelation was followed by subsequent intermittent denial (cp. dissociation in chapter two). Again, a higher social status seems to have hindered a client from more than hinting at 'the very worst' while choosing to postpone the issue altogether until she could manage without an interpreter. But those whose

76

therapy did not reveal sexual trauma were nevertheless tormented by a fear of such incidents, described by one of them as "arrests accompanied by *foul words* and *forced marriages* to oppressors"; i.e. rapes rendered 'lawful' prior to execution in iranian prisons.

The medical complaints related to sexual trauma that these clients have brought to my attention include menstruation disorders, vaginal discharge, and unspecified but persistent abdominal or pelvic pain, as well as symptoms of PTSD.

* Nasreen ex. 3 (medial):

A SEXUALLY ABUSED WOMAN'S SECRET

After four years in Norway and two in therapy, Nasreen offered the following story depicting how 'shameful issues' are brought to light. It turned out to be a sort of testing prelude to her subsequent disclosure of devastating secrets in the next session.

A young girl asks to be allowed to take a walk outside and, when she doesn't return, a search is initiated. Her naked body is found; she has burned herself to death. Her clothes are neatly folded alongside the corpse, and sewn into the waistband of her skirt her mother, sometime later, finds a piece of paper which discloses that she has been raped.

As it turned out during a period in a 'refugee camp' a man posing as a gynaecologist would have a group of women brought in for 'medical examinations' every day. Every day, a group of silent women returned without disclosing the terrible facts, that they had been subject to electric, genital torture. To this day, Nasreen hasn't told her husband about what happened. But the matter didn't end here. When she eventually sought medical help, in Norway, for consistent vaginal discharge and abdominal pain from having been "burnt inside", as she put it, she felt that she was rejected as a mentally unstable person by an unsuspecting norwegian medical practitioner who was not aware that any such 'medical practice' (could not reckon with torture of the kind – the genitals being probed with electrical rods) existed.

At that time not even the client herself had been fully aware of the nature of this form of torture. She had never visited a gynaecologist before. Not knowing whether or not it might after all have been some sort of standard procedure, the tying up of 'patients' and the unbearable pain involved, accompanied by the echoing screams of violated women, and her subsequent confinement to a mattress, unable to stand on her feet for weeks, confused her. Alone in her agony, she had no one to turn to for further explanation during all these years.

Sexual atrocities such as this must be understood within their psychocultural and particularly, their religious or regional, context as an issue regarding the proper place of women or "what it means to be female"[4]. The same client subsequently reported how husbands were condemned as unbelieving *kafirs* (unbelievers) by the local *pasdaran* (revolutionary guardians) who viewed their flight as synonymous to religious defection. Such an act of desertion meant that they had relinquished their faith, and had left their wives unprotected. This is – among other things – borne out by the fact that the number of women who were raped was in direct proportion to the number of male relatives who were perceived as having fled from their responsibilities; that is as defenders of their women's honour. According to the clients' testimonies this is what happened to the women at issue "hundreds of times at the hands of several men".

As far as women prisoners and girls are concerned, sexual abuse has been widely practised in iranian prisons. According to a Khomeini decree, all arrested girls were to be regarded as slave girls – and thus mistresses – of the guards[5]. This information is supported by Fatima's account according to which the female prison ward (referred to as 'the harem') functioned as a brothel for the guards, conveniently equipped as it was with a photo register making the choice easier for males who were not, according to her, allowed to visit their segregated quarters except for during the dark hours.

* Fatima ex. 8 (3-5 continued/medial):

ONE WHO LOST BOTH HER MONEY AND HER HONOUR

There are two pillars in the life of a man. His *namus* (honour) is dependent on his wife and on the soil, both for whom the *shahid* (martyr) gives his life. In the Iraqi war, one had to fight for one's country because if it fell into the hands of the enemy they would rape and plunder the land and women. Even in prison one had to get used to it in spite of being innocent. Many are those who have committed suicide following rape. I have seen them kill pregnant females, and you will not find any argument for that in the Koran. This was to prevent the filth from getting out. It is easy to lose one's faith from less. Every dead person gets a stone on his or her grave but all these women get is a so called unknown grave. A mother whose child is killed doesn't know where to go and cry. Their destiny is to be flung into a big, godforsaken hole.

The malignant social consequences of sexual trauma may include rejection by the woman's kin and community, such as disownment and divorce, or even murder by family members if the rape victim herself is blamed for the loss of family honour. As a consequence, victims are frequently unable to turn to the support of their own and must suffer in silence: in certain circumstances they might risk desolation and even prostitution if what has happened becomes known. Related to this reasoning is a set of notions about the nature of female sexuality, such as women's inability to control their sexual impulses, and the necessity of external constraints.

Such concern with female sexual vulnerability, while predominantly associated with middle eastern islam, is by no means uniquely linked to this area or religion. Reports of gender segregation and arranged marriages are found in many parts of the world; right across Eurasia, from India to the Balkans, in some parts of northern Europe and in the iberian peninsula[6]. It is important to acknowledge how sheltering honourable women from unauthorised sexual advances is felt to be necessary not only for the woman's own sake, but, primarily, for the sake of maintaining the honour of the male members of the group to which they belong.

The segregation of families and communities along gender lines in the domestic field is, however, one of the pillars of islamic hierarchy. Islamic legal discourse neutralises the bodies of young girls by creating social space in various ways, for example by using so called *purdah* ('curtain') seclusion practices to keep them apart from certain designated men.[7] These purdah practices range from the most extreme – confining women by a physical shield in the home (such as defining separate women's and men's quarters) or manipulating clothing (for example by wearing a veil, also while in prison) – to many other kinds of avoidance and modesty behaviour.

* Aisha ex. 4 (medial):

PURDAH OF THE HEART

Aisha, whose childhood setting is depicted as a 'Guest House' (A ex. 17), has moved a long way from the position of an illiterate, closely watched and segregated upper-class lady (All. ex 2; "frog in a well") to the shameful position of a *problem patient* in exile, deprived of the fruits of her honourable struggle for her children, and not able to enjoy the respect traditionally accorded to an ageing mother in her home context. This development, however, had already began at home when, after her father's death, and according to customary practice she was married to the son of an uncle. His part of the family turned out to be more relaxed than hers regarding purdah arrangements, embarrassing the newly wed bride by expecting her to share food with the men of the family, and later to move to a separate house with her husband. Later, in Iraq, she was again confronted with others who showed greater laxity with issues of gender, before such problems become vastly accelerated in Norway.

> You know, this is what it was like. But I remember once when we were in Iraq and there came many strangers, Farsi, Turkish and Kurdish. They were all having dinner but I couldn't sit down with all those people I didn't know. So they asked "Where is Aisha?" and my husband said "Never mind her, she is used to eating on her own. They prefer that, to keep to themselves". I was raised that way, and thought that whether it is good or bad, that is simply how it is. Then there was a man who was older, around 40 I guess, who came to me and said "But, Aisha, you have to join us for dinner. After all you are no Gypsy girl who has to eat all by herself, all alone". That was very difficult for me to hear, because, I mean, it was a matter of respect. It wasn't aversion I felt for those people; it had nothing to do with being Gypsy. They saw this as something disgraceful, as if one was somehow to throw dirt on, that in that way I became a little less important than they were. They didn't consider it from the point of view of respect, but as for me I am actually proud of being what I am... was.

> When I was a child, girls were not allowed to move outside of the house, except perhaps for once a month to go to the market place. Father was of the opinion that girls should keep their honour and stay indoors. For girls it is not worth going about drifting outdoors like that, but that's how it was at my husband's place. Not that they could go as they pleased, either, but it was less strict

than at home. I mean, they had separate rooms and women as a rule dined with women, men with men. But it wasn't as strict, there was no wall or door or such things (cp. A ex. 17: The Guest House). If they wanted to chat with the young ladies, whom they called "the brides", it was allowed. It wasn't like at home.

(What about your mother-in-law?) She was very kind. She had the last word. Actually, my father-in-law had two wives and the stepmother of my husband lived in the same house. But I was the bride of the eldest son. Actually, for the whole of the first year one is labelled newly wed or called a new bride. That means that one is regarded as a guest, whom the others are expected to serve, look after and treat very well. But after one year, his father built a separate house for us in the neighbourhood, because he had 14 sons. (When you moved into a separate house, did things become even more relaxed then?) Yes, I mean, this freedom was difficult in a way because, when left alone with my husband I didn't know how to behave. I could not sit alone and let him eat separately. I simply didn't know what to do. When his siblings visited us and there were guests it was okay because he could eat with them. That made it easier, but mostly I just didn't know how to go about it. For me it was also difficult because after that year had passed, I had become more used to talking to both women and men. And when I returned home to my Mother. She said to me "So you have started to learn disrespectful ways, to behave impolitely", because I thought it was okay to talk to a man. But actually, as a child, I was a little freer than my siblings were because I could go to my Father – because he sent for me – and I could talk to my brother too. But for me it was so strange when I arrived there, that women and men could sit in the same place and eat or have tea, and the girls could sit chewing chewing-gum and things like that. This I learnt little by little, but when I returned home they said "No, you must not behave that way, you must keep control of yourself". So it turned out that it was not a good way of behaving. (You mean that men and women mixed?) Not always, only occasionally. If the father was present, there was no way, but if not, it posed no problem.

(Did you prefer a freer arrangement?) No. Because I felt like having a sort of respect which I had managed to keep, but I lost it little by little. (Did you long for the way it was at home?) Yes, I was only allowed to visit Father's house once a year. When I was with my Mother, however, my husband could come and talk to her. And Mother could tell him: "You must be a good husband for Aisha and take good care of her" and things like that. And this could pass easily. But he wasn't allowed to talk to me, or sit together with me or anything like that. He had to remain on the other side. (Even when you were married?) Yes, and had got children. You know, they were born in Iran but then the whole world went helter-skelter, when my husband was in hiding. Everything changed...

You see, what have been the past remains in the past. Now they will not even listen to me or bother about what I have to say. When I want to tell them something they just answer me quite shamelessly "But what is this then? Are we not allowed to talk to men?" or something like that. Then they open their mouths wide. And I wonder whether they are right. Perhaps we have been old fashioned while the world has changed. But, nevertheless, inside of me I do respect what has been (Is it important that you will somehow find peace which also includes your respect for yourself?) You see, it is such a dilemma: On the one hand, you cannot throw away your own values, but on the other hand, it can never be the way it was ever again. I believe that most grown ups will remain the way they are. But the children are different. I do not know how to explain this, but sometimes it is like we were in the hands of the girls. Because we do not know how to do what is the best thing for them. That is, we do know which way is best, but they don't accept us choosing for them. But we do not want them to get out of control just in order to please them. Since we do not want them to end up in the streets and become unhappy and shame themselves, or even not dare to come back. Well, we do not want it to be like that.

You know, at home, everybody respected their parents. For me it is very difficult that girls should be allowed to behave that way when their Father is present. I have never seen such things, I am not brought up with such things. Having to behave that way didn't hurt us, we somehow became very respectable people from behaving the way we did, everybody. In the end I just had to give it up. But inside of me, in my heart, what I was taught and brought up with in my home by my Father remains. It is in my blood. But the world is just like a merry-go-round. In a sense, I have to go along with it whether I want to or not. Now I can sit together with 20 other people and eat, but each time I put the spoon in my mouth I remember the words of my Mother, the words the grown-ups said to me. For me it appears to be a violation of respect. My wish is to be able to pass at least something of it on to my children, in order that they can learn from it. But unfortunately in this country it isn't like that. They somehow do not appreciate that which in my opinion is really dignified, in the real sense of the word. It isn't like that here.

The deference practices expected by this client from her daughters include certain explicit standards of female behaviour when they find themselves, unavoidably, in the presence of men. These include shyness of demeanour, gestures such as rising in the presence of men or crouching on the floor, bowing the head, and avoiding eye contact, loud speech or laughter. According to this etiquette, the strictest sanctions are put on the expression of anger directed towards their father by children; the kind of pique that western children direct toward parents would be considered outrageous. Sisters may not initiate an argument against their elder brother, even if he has the right to control them, as Aisha's eldest son did in her daughter's case depicted below, nor may wives do so against their husbands even if they are violent as in Shirin's case.

The following extract depicts the behaviour that Aisha expects from her daughters at the graveyard, and her subsequent disappointment resulting from their failure to live up to her expectations.

* Aisha ex. 5 (4 continued/medial);

THE SHAMEFUL PHOTOGRAPHS

(I refer to Aisha's son's death in A ex. 11 & 12). Aisha complains of being obliged to visit her son's grave while at the same time having to stay away from the graveyard lest her children think that their brother did a good thing. She feels abandoned to herself, 'standing right in the middle', as it were.

If I had been in our country, everyone around me would have understood how I felt. But here, the children cannot understand. You have to learn it from someone, and there is no way here to show them how.

This clearly seems to be the sorest point for her: not to be fully understood, even by her own children (cp. A ex. 15: Hospitalised for Heart Trouble).

If the kids quarrel about the smallest thing, even the youngest one may say "It is better not to mention his name because mother will start crying". I am completely stuck. I can't take anymore. I used to go out with the children if, for example, there was a Kurdish celebration or a wedding, or something happened where a mother was expected to be present. But now I cannot go because my son isn't with us anymore. I simply can't manage to go because he isn't among us. Nevertheless, I do go occasionally, but it isn't the way it should be. I decorate myself and sit there smiling, but suddenly it all comes up. I see him underneath kilos of earth. All smashed up (cp. intrusive symptoms in chapter two: Psychological Trauma Reconsidered).

(Because you still see yourself as being in a period of mourning?) I do not manage to mourn like I should, it has become stuck in my heart. If I had been at home in my own country, perhaps I could have found a way. (Could you imagine how it would have turned out?) You know, their way is like this: I was about the same age as my daughter H. when Father died and my brother was put to death. I understood my Mother's sorrow, but my own children do not. I was 15, and stayed around my mother. All of us were there in order to lessen her sorrow – share it with her. (What did you do?) Nothing in particular. We would cry together, tell her that she should not be so sad. If you cry like that, you will destroy your eyes. Try to cheer her up: It is sinful in the eyes of God to cry like that. Help her with housework – somehow accommodate her sorrow. If she was alone in the wilderness, we immediately went along. She wasn't allowed to be alone (cp. sociocentric coping). You are not allowed to remain alone, not for a moment.

(Do you also mean that one was able to cry without concern for the reactions of others, that they understood that it was all part of it?) Such things they cannot understand in this country. The kids keep asking "Why do you cry, Mother?" They don't understand! So I tell them that it is because I dreamt about my Mother (cp. A ex. 14; N ex. 9). You see, my Mother had to carry ten times my sorrow. When my brother was killed, they didn't even give her back his corpse, so she had no grave to visit. She had Father's grave though, but you see Father had been allowed to live his life. But my brother's grave was empty. He was still so young. That's why everybody gave her the right to mourn, no matter where or when. No, here you are not allowed to mourn like that. Here no passer-by has ever sat down to share my sorrow. (So, in fact, it is difficult for you to visit the grave on your own the way you do?) You are not permitted to be alone. Never is a mourning Mother permitted to visit the grave alone. No, to do that she would have to smuggle herself out and if it is discovered, someone immediately turns up for support, comforting her "It is a sin that you should cry like that and complain against God. God punishes such behaviour"; they calm you down.

At this point I suggest taking a photograph of the grave which she could share with her relatives back home. It had already been considered by her family at the hospital staff, but it never materialised. She isn't sure whether it would be the right thing to do ("Everything is so new to me"). Eventually she tells me quite frankly: It would only increase the sorrow to see such shameful pictures.

At home they would become so sad from seeing my loneliness at the grave (i.e. here in Norway). When we were with Mother at home, everybody went with her to the graveyard. But here it was like this: we merely sat there at the grave, myself and two ladies. They couldn't mourn like at home, we were not even related to each other – but we just sat there on the stone. They were outsiders. Not like my sisters. They didn't even realise how they were expected to behave around me at the graveyard. I will show you the photographs (taken at the grave) so you can see for yourself. The children do not understand in that (culturally proper) sense either. It was just like taking a picture of them anywhere. They simply posed for the picture as it were, but were not attentive to the requirements of the (culturally expected) situation. They are unable to display their sorrow (i.e. properly). It is a pity, for them, that they do not catch up with the (culturally given) meaning, manage to get hold of the extent of the sorrow. They are somehow just obliged to be present.

The Complementary Role of Women as Agents of Male Honour

Tied up with norms relating to gender, such features as above described are a constant element in the interaction with these clients. If, for example, a muslim woman behaves in the proper manner required of her by the rules of purdah during a therapy session, a western male therapist may easily confuse the situation with manifestations of a

85

depressed mood. Equally, it must be acknowledged that the rules pertaining to gender are reciprocal, and are restrictive to males as well as females and they cannot therefore be understood from one point of view only. The exclusion of females from the formal spheres of power is paralleled by norms relating to manliness which demand that men spend no more than the minimum necessary time among women, even with those to whom access would be legitimate. It is often the case that tradition-oriented men only go to their home to eat, and, occasionally, at night for sex. This is reflected in the design of houses and sleeping arrangements[8].

* All ex. 5:

IN THE ABSENCE OF MEN

After years in exile Aisha still reports a sense of nakedness and vulnerability when going about alone without a scarf, although she frequently avoids using it for fear of racist remarks. A sense of vulnerability from the lack of protection by their men is a prevalent feature of these female clients in exile, a situation which is increased by the frequent marital discord and their husbands' disappearance acts (cp. divorce rate on p. 94). They may also sleep separately from their husbands, frequently with their children, and on the whole – again with the exception of Fatima – speak little about them except when facing issues of respect or protection.

It is precisely because of the complementary structure of gender segregation and the accompanying division of labour that the other party cannot, will not or may not move into the other's sphere. A feature that is even more marked among males who cannot under any circumstance risk appearing feminine, while the flexibility involved in women's roles make their movement in his sphere somewhat easier, after all[9]. This does not reduce mutual dependency but, on the contrary, increases it, to the extent that women go to great lengths to restore or maintain the disrupted balance of power and protection in exile. Indeed, at the Psychosocial Centre for Refugees, we have seen widows who keep contact with their deceased husbands through dreams in order that they may continue to be protected and have decisions made for them. The fear of the awful consequences resulting from lack of male protection already experienced by these women at home, thus recur in exile.

Female value and identity is closely tied to a woman's affiliation with and contribution towards the men in her life. The idea that an individual embodies important characteristics of other members of his or her family is central in understanding the sanction pattern involved in normative transgressions. A man is known by the qualities of his female relatives. The honour of an unmarried girl's father and brothers, and a married one's husband and male in-laws, is totally dependent on her ability to remain inviolate and avoid the slightest appearance of being accessible to unauthorised advances.

Responsibility for the maintenance of purdah practices thus falls heavily on males, notwithstanding their personal views on the matter. A man of honour should be able to control his women, that is his mother, his sisters and daughters, using physical violence if needed. For example, when stoning an unfaithful woman to death, it is the father or brother of the accused who is expected to throw the first stone because they have failed in their protective roles.

* Aisha ex. 6 (4-5 continued/medial):

DONKEY RIDE INTO DEATH

Aisha relates how, during her childhood, the hair of a bride who had lost her virginity before marriage was shaven before she was sent home, riding on the back of a donkey in order to publicly shame her family. Her own father or eldest brother was then obliged (unwillingly, we may assume) to take her life. Now she is afraid that Father (as she sometimes calls her husband) or someone else (a kurdish male) take the lives of her daughters if there were to be a shameful incident.

(Cp. A ex. 7: Children Drowning as in an Enormous Ocean & 10: The Case of Aisha's Daughter Continued)

As a mother, a woman's main educational responsibility is to protect her daughters from such a tragedy; managing this in exile is perceived as her biggest dilemma. It is to be expected that she will find it difficult to succeed considering her new environment, and the 'impossible' situation has increased her panicky behaviour. Moreover, this situation – when added to other trauma – has brought her husbands suicidal tendencies to the fore, overtaken as he himself is by the possibility of shame from the lack of respect that his daughters exhibit and its terrible consequences.

Separate living arrangements are initiated in order to prevent affairs of the heart, but constantly watching young girls, who must remain chaste until marriage, presupposes the relatively visible conditions of village life and a group support exceeding the ability of a nuclear family.[10] In the eyes of these clients, life in the West seems full of dubious and even dangerous sexual conduct in which their children may become lost for ever, as if "drowned in an ocean" (cp. also the purity of the women *of the underdog* as compensating for their husbands' lack of worldly status in chapter 13: Symbolic Shelter in a Changing World). In a world increasingly constructed in terms of personal choice and responsibility, violations of honour cannot be reciprocated by revenge, but have to be managed through the intricate rules of 'romantic' love. Rules that are quite incomprehensible to educators who have always been led to believe that liaisons of the heart always end in tragedy, as portrayed, for example, in the traditional folk stories.[11]

* Aisha ex. 7 (4-6 continued/pre-medial):

CHILDREN DROWNING AS IF IN AN ENORMOUS OCEAN

First to leave home was the eldest son, aged 17, who had formerly behaved exemplary, but then had an extra-marital child across ethnic boundaries, and started a separate household, a form of behaviour that brought fear of bloodshed among his kurdish kin in Oslo, and sent his father to hospital from shock (cp. the fear of *sekthe*, f.ex. in N ex. 8: When you are Prevented from Disclosing your Pain).

He's become very big and quarrels so much with Father that soon it won't pass anymore. The children are frightened. I cannot take any more. He won't listen to us anymore, he is completely changed. Since his brother died, we need him so much. Life has become a hell. We try to stop him from leaving us, don't want him to lack anything if he stays with us. But there is so much alcohol and drugs in this country that we have to walk around with our heads bowed down (an expression of lost honour). He just disappears. Once, five youngsters arrived in our house and behaved exactly the way which is improper. In front of women and children they carried cases of beer (she is very upset). When he ventures out of the house, it is just as if he disappears into an ocean, and we have no way of knowing what's going on.

Next out of the house, about a year later, was their eldest daughter of 16:

You see it has become very bad, because something has gone wrong. Because you can make a mistake. Perhaps you face some disagreeable thing but lack any power to refuse. Because we aren't in our own country, we asked for help and advice. But instead they keep coming in such a wrong way. It is just as if they had smuggled my daughter away somewhere. We asked for help but instead of helping us they made her run away from us. It seems like they decide over her themselves. You know, something has gone wrong, but I must know what it is. What does she want? To get her side of the story. But they (the professionals) decide for themselves, as if we were mere weed, nothing. They keep moving her here and there.

It is like I said, no one knows what the Kurds are like. For Kurds, when it comes to honour, there is a limit. If she is ever seen walking alone in the streets, it could be misinterpreted, if something happens to her or she is known to be fast – that type of unpleasant conduct... If this happens, nothing can help her, not even if there were 70.000 people from the child welfare authorities to assist her. Because, in that case, the Kurds will not let her live one more day, that's for sure. They simply do not understand what the difference is between Kurdish culture and the culture here. They don't understand how this case should be handled. They simply try to remove the girl from her mother and father and make her move away from us. If I go there to explain, they won't listen to me, they aren't able to understand the background I refer to. But they will regret it, I'm sure...

A Kurdish lady had seen my daughter. She came to tell me that she had coloured her hair and shaved her eyebrows. She's got a ring in her nose. I told her that my husband doesn't know, that "Yes, she is young, perhaps she is merely trying it out". But the lady said that if she has started behaving like that, she must have gone astray. As long as she stayed with the other lady (i.e. of a christian foster home) she behaved properly, politely. But now she talks rudely to her siblings and scolds her father and mother in every way. She has changed and has adopted a different line of conduct. They said it was too expensive in the former place. But I told them

"I will not need any money to take care of her. Move her back and she will get her own room and you can visit her every day. But don't flirt with her future". They said "No, (your daughter) thinks like a Norwegian and has pain inside of her and all this.

I do not know what to do because Father threatens that he will not have anything to do with her at all. He says he has cut her off, but this will change if he sees her in the streets accompanied by boys. In that case, he says, he will not worry about any child care authorities, but handle this issue the way he himself sees fit. Because, in his view, he has lived his life in honour until reaching Norway, but if it turns out to be a matter of honour... And it would have disastrous consequences. So I urge him not to think about it in that way, I tell him that "It isn't sure that you will be ruined and all that". But I really am afraid that this thing will end like that ...

Where the extended family has hitherto been protected by seclusion practices and collective interests in marriage arrangements, children, and especially young girls have been taught to defer to their elders. However, cross-cultural migration causes an abrupt break in the traditional gender patterns of these multitraumatised refugees who are unprepared for the challenges involved. Compared to other culturally alien immigrant groups, such as the pakistani community, whose networks are kept intact through the processes of ghettoisation, the development is indeed dramatic, a fact which they themselves are well aware of.

The ideals of mutual love and trust implanted in youngsters by the norwegian school system are not enough to ensure psychosocial change where there is no community support from within their own ethnic milieu or where power still rests with the elders. This also explains why the grand parental generation in the countries of origin are largely kept unaware of the problems confronting the refugees in exile, such as the 'shameful' behaviour of a child, divorce and so on. However, because of this lack of ethnic network support and the additional shame (and subsequent silence) resulting from the damage caused by trauma-related problems (i.e. that, again, may already have been present *prior* to migration), the inevitable changes resulting from life in exile may become very traumatic for all those involved including, not infrequently, the helpers themselves who may be pushed

to their professional limits without adequate support from their surroundings (cp. secondary traumatisation).

The link between male honour and social status explains why
public transgressions of the norms are so severely punished, and why
the punishments have to be publicly visible (L ex 1: Public Demonstrations; F ex. 14: Accused of Lesbianism). Where marriage is based
on kin interests to the exclusion of love matches, impulse control is
externalised in complementary ideas about male honour and female
shame, but punitive reactions are similarly externalised. They are public and directed against the body in an almost ritualistic way rather
than being private or directed towards the consciousness (*the internal
voice*), as further discussed in chapter eight: The Millenarian Heritage
of the Modern Age. The fact that the ultimate fulfilment of one's duty
plays such a central role in their interpersonal discourse has been put
forward, by Beeman (1986), as explanation of the iranian propensity
to attempt suicide in situations where honour or duty to another is
at stake.

Gender segregation thus represents a specific but complex form
of conduct prevalent in societies where kinship plays a decisive role
in leadership formation and where in Boserup's (1970) words "the
plough is used", i.e. agriculturally based communities[12]. The vulnerability of women and the concomitant demands put on men depends on
the interaction between the tense field of the private, sheltered sphere
and the public sphere, as further described in Part Two. The survival
of the institution of gender segregation and, in the last example, that
of the whole group when perceived as a culturally distinct and static
entity, depends on the role of women as agents of the public honour
of their men as further elaborated in chapter 13: Symbolic Shelter in a
Changing World. The dual notions of male honour and female shame
thus serve to foster and protect the kinship group.

5.
VIOLATIONS OF
INTERGENERATIONAL OBLIGATIONS

The Dutifulness of the Young
– the Right of their Elders

The techniques used for establishing a distance between the genders, however, are not purely addressed to sexual issues. Protecting women from undesirable sexual contact is not the sole purpose of *purdah* practices, even though this is offered as a rationale by the subjects themselves, but must rather be viewed as part of a larger pattern of *avoidance behaviour* influencing group cohesion[1]. While honour is considered of utmost importance for one's status, the extent to which it is attainable is dependent on one's kin group as an entity. Besides concern for collective disgrace through the interaction of female relatives with outsiders – particularly men – the structural integrity of, and the need to preserve at least formal harmony within the confines of the kin group is a very important by-product[2].

Gender segregation thus becomes a useful means of maintaining internal cohesion in the extended family, while the patterns of deference involved prevent conflicting interests from undermining its social fabric. Kurds live in families, for their families, and, often, from their families. As long as the prosperity of the kin group is bound up with a means of production that renders everyone economically dependent on everyone else, this makes it necessary to prevent overt discord between its members. The nuclear family group is, therefore, not considered to be extraneous to the rest of the joint family; husbands have no means of contradicting their elders, even on issues concerning their own household, nor do parents have any right to display overt preference for their own children who are brought up to regard half-siblings and cousins as brothers and sisters without partiality.[3]

The extended family has come to comprise of an ambivalent and potentially conflict laden arena, which demands much sacrifice from the individuals within it in terms of self-sacrifice for it to function at all. A large family group cannot afford to have several masters and mistresses. The purpose of the elders is to keep harmony between generations. A quarrel within the family is considered a serious business, as reflected in the endemic threats, though not necessarily implementations, and strong sanctions attached to it: for example in Aisha's case, concerning her children's antagonistic behaviour (A ex. 7: Children Drowning as in an Enormous Ocean).

Divorce is generally considered to be the fault of the wife, whose primary responsibility it is to create harmony at home. The social status of a divorced woman is very low, in some cases, a divorced (read: unprotected) woman frequently has no other choice but to resort to the streets (cp. orphaned and later divorced Fatima's vulnerable situation). The divorce rate in Iran, for example, is thus six times lower than in the USA, whereas – when the number of couples living together without formalities are included in the statistics – the nordic countries have the highest divorce rate in the world. Similarly, ten per cent of family units in Iran are dissolved, compared with 50 per cent in Sweden[4]. For the parent generation of exiled migrants enculturated with the values of honourable behaviour, the mere thought of divorce (though not of polygamous marriage) seems horrific, despite the frequently occurring factual separations and separate living arrangements made in exile where the option of taking an additional wife is ruled out. In most instances, however, solutions are found that do not overtly split the family.

* All ex. 6:

INCONCEIVABLE DIVORCES

According to Aisha, a divorce would never be accepted among her own (A ex. 13: *Havvu*). She does not even like using the word for it. Others conceal their separations from their families back home, finding all sorts of cover up tactics to get round it, such as pretending that their husband was only out for the moment if they receive a call from home, subsequent to which he is hastily fetched home in order to phone back.

* Shirin ex. 1 (initial):

THE FATE OF A DIVORCEE

Following violent abuse which sent Shirin to hospital for two weeks and which subsequently led to a public court hearing, her husband left to live elsewhere. This illiterate mother of eight still kept pretending on the telephone to her family (trapped in Iraq without possibility of escape or return), that he was only out on business, because "the shame was so immense": a pattern which recurs in all but the Fatima's case, who was already divorced and remarried under extraordinary circumstances back home (F ex 10: "Nothing but a Widow")

Dervishpour (per. comm. 1994) has in fact found the frequency of divorce statistics among iranian immigrants in Sweden to have risen dramatically.[5] Among those migrants who have spent a few years in Sweden, it is twice that of the swedes. He points to certain traits in the iranian migrant group – such as their middle class background, opposition to the clerical regime, high level of education, uneven gender distribution (two men for a woman in the age group of 17-35 years), and age profile – which make them statistically likely candidates for a divorce; increases the lack of trust which is, according to his view, typical of iranian interrelationships in exile; a fact that also counteracts any tendencies towards ghettoisation among iranians as compared to, for example, the pakistani group.[6]

In agreement with my view, Dervishpour sees the changed power balance in favour of women, which follow from the exile experience as the main reason for this state of affairs, relating it to modern versus traditional modes of social organisation. In addition, most returnees are also male. And – like many male migrants – exiled iranian men prefer to bring a new wife from home rather than marry a divorced iranian female of the host country. But again PTSD may be involved. Family members who live with an affected person, according to Lipton (1994, 80), tend to develop similar symptoms that accelerate marital discord, which is why he sees family therapy as essential for these patients if break-ups are to be avoided.

Traditionally oriented migrants often confront their host community with what is perceived in the West as a repressive family system and the suppression of self-expression. This issue especially concerns the socialisation of girls and other issues to do with gender, which are becoming a point of increasing concern to representatives of the majority culture, accelerating mutual lack of comprehension and criticism. Social workers and other involved professionals are prone, more or less consciously, to undermine prevalent patterns among the tradition-oriented migrant groups because psychological growth, in a western sense, demands clarifying or cultivating the specifically individual in relation to the collectivity of the family.

The freudian paradigm – as popularly understood – in particular has come to constitute an ideological justification for individual liberalism that regards 'traditional man' as a psychological victim trapped in corporate units. While traditional collective units are seen as inhibiting free enterprise and political freedom, their weakening becomes a sort of tacit assumption behind notions of happiness. The oedipal struggle can thus be viewed as an individual counterpart to collective societal liberation. From puberty onwards, the individual's foremost challenge is to disengage himself from the parent generation, and those who fail in their effort at achieving autonomy are seen to be in need of professional help. On the face of it, this could be the fate of any respectable muslim (irrespective of gender) in a twofold sense, both as a religious person and as a member of an extended family, which promotes the values of interdependence, respect for authority and conformity to parental standards. From an ideal muslim point of view, there can be no islamic brotherhood (*umma*) without the extended family because there can be no *ummatic* fraternal feeling bred in its members. For a man, however, his family is only one of many arenas where he may express himself, while a woman will be viewed against, and to a much larger extent restricted to her familial background.

Despite their involvement in the iranian resistance, the family structure of these clients remains tight and extended, at least as a psychic reality requiring loyalty even in exile. This is well illustrated by the case of Nasreen's sore memories and belated wisdom following from her particular relationship to the revolutionary events in Iran (All ex. 2: The Kurdish Legacy).

* Nasreen ex. 4 (pre-medial):

"IF IT HAD NOT BEEN BECAUSE OF US..."

(Are females allowed to be angry?) No – Those who are around me are of that opinion; my brother, my husband and my children. No, it is not allowed to show anger. Girls are not to feel sorry, nor angry. (Have you ever seen your mother angry?) Yes, but then she had every right to. If children do something wrong and the husband blames his wife even if it isn't her fault, then she may. It was during the early days of the revolution when the kids were out demonstrating. Father said it was Mother's fault because she had brought them up like that. He said that this is why they are going to die. The older people wanted

95

peace, but we did not. It was wrong of us. They had life experience; they had, after all, lived through it. Today, I am of the opinion that they were right. Our people used to say that Kurdistan will have to give much blood, but parents were afraid that it would end nowhere. They knew how life was from experience.

Why are we homeless? Is this – being a stranger – never going to stop? We had no problems before the revolution, then Mother died and they arrested Father. *He was tortured to death because of what we had done.* There were many more.

(Had you ever any doubts?) We say they were right now. Today I will have none of it. If it starts all over again here, that I will be homeless again, then everything will start again. If something happens here, and someone does something – if they open their mouth. You can never know, perhaps tomorrow – no one knows. The Iraqi Kurds began to talk a little and 20 000 people died. No authorities have done anything to stop it. If we had not talked, then the Shah wouldn't have left, if we hadn't made the revolution it wouldn't have turned out like this. No, I put it simply, it didn't help a thing. All the homes, large families were eliminated. It was like that, no one knew how it would turn out.

'She who would have Cared for her Old Mother'

The development of traditional muslim identity seems to be less a question of breaking loose than of growing increasingly submissive to the extended family and to a system of authority where elders – including women – gain more rather than less relative influence. However, as compared to their male compatriots aging women seem to have less to win and more to lose from a change of the circumstances, because they are about to enjoy – at last – a well-earned elevated status within their family group (cp. what is said about Aisha having lost this possibility in A ex. 4: Purdah of the Heart).

* Aisha ex. 8 (pre-medial):

SHE WHO WOULD HAVE CARED FOR HER OLD MOTHER

I rang my Father's second wife who could not tell me anything about my Mother's illness. (Is it usual to keep such things secret?) As far as they are able to, they do that. Actually they shouldn't, but even if I try to find out, they conceal it. This especially concerns girls in need of protection. It is considered wrong to tell them if they are in a foreign country, alone, pregnant, ill or have small children to care for. Men are stronger, they forget more easily. It is concealed especially if it is some close person such as a Mother, Father or brother. I am so very attached to my Mother, she's the nearest one to me. If she were to die I will have no hope left. That road, which leads to death, we all have to follow, it is so. God gives and He takes, but the wishes I carry inside are very painful.

Mothers and children want more than anything else to be together until the last minute. This is especially the wish of a daughter, to be able to stay with and care for her Mother in her last days. It is difficult to be so far away and carry such wishes. I cannot see any way out. You know, it is like this: If there was to be the slightest of chances (i.e. to go home), since Mother is the one I am most fond of ... When I left for my husband's house she said something I will never forget. She said, you must remember that when I become sick, you will be the one to stay by my bedside; when I die you shall be there. These are wishes we both carry inside of us.

(If you were at home, would you have gone to her by now?) You know, a Mother is much more important than a spouse. Even if the husband disagrees it is taken for granted that one leaves in order to stay with your Mother during her last days. Even if the husband opposes, it is allowed. Your Mother should never be left lying alone, even if the marriage should break down. (But it seems to me that you are a bit worried anyway?) I don't know, I always think about my Mother, about this road which is closed, the country far away. Conscience leads us, if not, you shame your neighbours. You know, as a young girl I've seen old people who have had daughters-in-law who haven't cared for them. They just had to sit by a wall all day long while the sand and dust covered them. They were not properly cared for, they were not served. Not in my family. But it isn't that either, it's that I should be the one to serve her, to talk about everything that's in my heart. It is said that those who respect their Mother respect others; they come home because of her. If God can give one the opportunity to do so, it is the best thing for oneself.

(cp. A ex. 14; the complications following upon her mother's death)

If a woman is to acquire status in the system, she must be seen as little as possible but still be of maximum utility. This invisibility should, however, not be taken to mean that women are wholly without influence, but rather that the required modesty of demeanour keeps them from assuming authority before it is given to them at a later point in the developmental cycle. This benefit seems to be lost to these exiled women. It is thus not only a woman's ability to threaten the honour of the whole group, nor is it merely her role in the socialisation of children, especially girls, that gives her power. Mothers in general, and the older women in particular, acquire importance primarily through their knowledge of what goes on within the inside spheres of the kinship group *from which men are kept at a distance*, because men need that information for decision making, especially as pertaining to marriage brokering.

The role and importance of women in the upkeep of the extended family cannot be underestimated because their sphere of activity is of such decisive importance when considering the respect of the kin group and the importance of the marriage arrangements linked to the survival of the extended family. Islamists emphasise "the sacredness of the family" so much so that it has been presented as a counterclaim to be added to the Universal Declaration of Human Rights as well as further claims, such as "the right to avoid sin"[7].

In chapters seven through eight I will examine the legal status of women in such a familial setting, and, by extension, the ways in which their status has been put onto the international agenda connected as it is with the issue of human rights. So far, it is enough to conclude, that in addition to the violation of *internal* boundaries resulting from *organised social violence* (i.e. the 'torture trauma') and especially the sexual assaults directed at women *under emergency-like cultural circumstances* as depicted above, there are other ways in which women come to play an important part when considering the overall context of *refugeeism*. In particular, that is the case where their positions as guardians of the sociocentric family structure is called into question by their host communities, thus further aggravating their predicament.

Because the extended family is perceived as the main building block of the traditional, muslim or other, society, its continuation becomes such an important obligation for many migrant parents from the Third World. And a factor, which is, again, dependent upon the honourable behaviour of its young women. Virginity is considered to be of the highest priority; indeed, it is considered to be the single most important reason for a woman's happiness and well being. The loss of virginity before marriage is regarded as an irredeemable situation, threatening the future of the whole kinship group. Only in a context where participants have a non-individual understanding of themselves, can someone so low down in the social hierarchy as an unmarried young girl here represents be attributed such power over superiors that her deviant behaviour is considered a threat to the whole group.

6.
CLIENTIFICATION AS A RE-ACTUALISED TRAUMA

'Guilt' and 'Shame' in Culture and Treatment Ideology

According to Varvin's (1998, 67) clinical experience many refugees manage fairly well while they are living under a repressive regime or are in flight; i.e. as long as they have the possibility of projecting their painful experiences – as I would add, rightfully – on to the enemy. However, as soon as they reach the country of exile, they are, it seems, often left on their own to cope with their painful inner objects and anxieties as these have been presented in previous chapters. Confronting an understanding or, possibly, rejecting authority can precipitate a feeling of misery, but it may also, according to him, allow for the projection of 'bad' parts of the self onto the former. My own focus has been more on the fact that by the time they arrive in the West many third world refugees harbour phase specific unrealistic expectations of what their new life in a western welfare state holds for them. Such expectations may be of decisive importance for further developments, especially their relationship to the host authorities; here evidenced by Shirin, who was in danger of losing her children[1].

* Shirin ex. 2 (1 continued/initial):

FROM DOMESTIC VIOLENCE TO VIOLENCE PERPETRATED
BY THE CHILD WLFARE AUTHORITIES

For years Shirin had patiently suffered harsh treatment from her politically active husband in the hope of one day being able to escape to the West, where she had heard that men are not allowed to hit and where females, as opposed to what happens in islamic culture, obtain custody of the children in the event of a divorce. However, she did not reckon with the eventuality of a 'emergency' resolution by the Child Welfare Authorities that was to remove her six children to an unknown place, out of reach of both their parents. This was to follow from her seeking refuge in a centre for battered women and after she had also contacted a range of local authorities, all of whom had been, according to her experience, however, unable to respond to her needs and had therefore responded with frustration (cp. All ex. 1: Time and Manner of Arrival).

As a result of this experience, she was in constant fear of her now separated husband, who also opposed her treatment. The latter had eventually obtained custody of their sons, even, to Shirin's despair and contrary to the practice at home, the youngest son, a two year old. This was the same man who had, Shirin claimed, married her for the sole purpose of bearing him sons while all along planning to take an additional wife, physically untouched by deliveries. This plan of his, to take an additional wife was, however, thwarted by their flight into exile, just as it was in the case of Aisha's husband (A ex 13: *Havvu*)[2].

The extent to which the initial contact between refugees and their scandinavian hosts has become regulated by the influence of professional help is noteworthy. For many refugees, these professionals have somehow come to constitute a kind of alternative social network, compensating for the lack of support from lost relatives.[3] However, in time, and because of their different ways of tackling problems and interpreting social etiquette, both sides run the risk of becoming frustrated. The clients may come to view the contact with so many different professional helpers as a violation of their personal integrity or privacy, despite the well-intentioned efforts of the helpers.

* Aisha ex. 9 (1-2 & 4-6 continued/initial):

"WE CAME AS GUESTS BUT ARE TREATED LIKE BEGGARS"

The social services tell us to write applications. But, I mean, well, it is very hard, very difficult to reach for the hand that holds the money. I mean, in this country we live like beggars. We beg! When money comes to us from another place, in our view, it seems like begging. Perhaps God will help me, but I don't know for how long I can endure this. At times I feel that somehow I am absolutely powerless in this life; I haven't raised my children as I would have been able to do at home (she is very upset).

But, you know, this thing of taking the children away from their parents, the children will not be happy. There was once a duck which laid some eggs, and we had a hen too. My sister-in-law had taken an egg from the duck and laid it under the hen. The hen believed it to be her own. And when it came out of the egg, the baby duck went straight into the water because it was able to swim. As you know, though, hens never go into the water, but, because it was the mother, though actually the eggs were from the duck... It was a big river with much water, but the mother, the one who was a hen, threw herself in the water after her child, in order to come to its rescue. But she couldn't swim, so she died.

This is what it is like. *Somehow they (the professionals) haven't understood that these are the wrong eggs, you know.* My Mother said, now you can see for yourself what you have done – the small ones were left without any Mother in the water, and the Mother died. In this country, this is the way they do it: they decide very hastily, and then they take the child from its Mother and Father. They have this idea that it would be best if you parted since you are clearly fed up with one another as a couple. It is very frightening, just like a sickness that splits us from the inside. It is so dreadful to think of what to do about this matter. *Well it's terrible shameful to us and then the children will also be ruined forever.*

Although the problems encountered in the meeting with the host culture and the professional helpers are great and add to the refugees' already heavy burdens, this does not necessarily mean that these kind of problems could have been dealt with easily within their traditional setting either. This is because the differences in experience between those who left and those who stayed behind – for example, as a result of the long periods of separation and severe trauma suffered by the exiled – are similarly so great that the former tend to keep 'such terrible secrets' from their own, again, adding to their silence behaviour. The ensuing conflicts reflected in the narratives of these clients point towards colliding expectations in interpersonal communication: on the one hand there are the professionals who are under double pressure from demands of control and help giving (chapter one: The Interdisciplinary Challenge), on the other we might find their clients in a state of confusion.[4] Particularly in Scandinavia, perhaps, a quasi-therapeutic rhetoric has saturated the lower level education and health care systems, reflecting a view of man which legitimise public intervention in private life more easily than the case is in the rest of Europe and the USA.[5] The statistics show an increased incidence among cross-cultural migrants, not only of people in receipt of disability pensions and in the process of obtaining a divorce, but also of child welfare cases, as demonstrated by a report from The Academy of Child Welfare Care in Oslo[6].

If experiences of commonality are scarce in the case of many refu-gee-clients following the combined effects of their migrational margin-ality and unemployment, vague psychological symptoms resembling and reinforcing those of PTSD may appear. However, the social sphere of the clients may also become overloaded, especially if too many helpers who have been taken into their confidence populate it to the exclusion of other types of non-professional 'ordinary' relationships. Distance is a social need akin to closeness, and the lack of it may result in similar adverse effects on the subject's peace of mind[7]. This is compounded by the fact that the issues involved in a cross-cultural exile are frequently considered to be of such a 'shameful' nature that it is compelling to keep them concealed. In such circumstances the very act of receiving help may be perceived as yet another situation in which a painful story is to be ripped up once again, evaluated and substantiated once more[8].

* Fatima ex. 7 (5 continued/medial):

KEEPING RECORDS IN AND OUT OF PRISON

Problems regarding intervening, note-taking and record-keeping as experienced by refugees were brought to my attention by Fatima's description of the keeping of inmates' records in the iranian prisons. She made me aware of their overt resemblance with the procedures which accompany the rehabilitative efforts of western professional helpers, both in terms of the terminology used and their agendas. Both include *screening the problems* of particular cases during *team sessions* held by employees while discussing possible *measures of rehabilitation*, and *following up* their 'progress' (cp. the notion of *therapy in reverse* above).

According to Eriksen's (1991[9]) strong criticism of popular western therapeutic rhetoric, Freud's liberating truth has come to conquer this world as a mere adaptational technique for eliminating traditional wisdom. Many a professional psychoanalyst would, perhaps, agree with him in that the popularised use of freudian psychology have replaced metaphysics with an ideology which, although it may look like an anarchic assault on the establishment, has in actual fact turned into an instrument of standardisation. In this sense, like Marx, Freud has triumphed and lost. While western reality has changed in relation to Freud's theories, what was once progressive freudian thought has now become mere rhetoric phraseology in everyday usage.

Freud was, however, right in his views shared by social scientists like Durkheim and his followers, that concepts like *god* or *the evil* are redundant if the individual is considered apart from the rest of society because these concepts are justified by collectively anchoraged realities. In contrast to the sociocentric third world contexts under scrutiny here, de-traditionalised western health ideology is marked by manifestly decreasing co-operative obligations towards a group in favour of the right of individual self-realisation as an ideal principle. According to Eriksen's assessment, the latter ideology may sanction, narcissistically, mistaken attempts at liberating *others*. I have already in chapter one pointed out how *the victims become the problem itself*, not the victims *of* the problem.[10] All too often, we have seen survivors of genocide and organised persecution, as well as causalities of war become economic migrants, displaced persons and illegal aliens, if not *problem patients*.

Frequently though, as the refugees are relabelled with these terms, we begin to forget their preceding traumas and how these people's negative experiences may interact with the further problems of life in exile. While prescribing the best rehabilitative strategies, 'problematic' case presentations like the ones at issue here, simultaneously also depict a different way of living, which may be at odds with certain norms and values that the clients themselves hold.[11] I have, for example, throughout this publication tried to show how an increased confidence in the idea of self-realisation as a basic human need in the West governs our general attitudes towards alien features of the cross-cultural encounter and, thus, also quite easily therapeutic efforts.

For better or worse the life history approach and therapeutic assistance are in themselves the products of western self-reflection and the development of bourgeois individualism. While emphasising the need to plan for a new future, perpetual change, and more or less complete autonomy in respect to kin, these values may collide with the veneration of the past and the relatively conservative attitude towards change among these clients, imbued with a strict, indeed often harsh, code of traditional morality (cp. the distinctive normative styles on p 69). Culture is a potent modifier of basic human needs, whether children are considered basically independent beings in whom dependence needs to be fostered (the case with these families) or as dependent beings in whom independence needs to be developed (the case in the modern western family setting). This means that phenomena which would be viewed as detrimental to the development of a child in the one context, may be considered highly progressive in the other. Parental behaviour which is defined as a failure in the West may thus be a part of a consensually held parental regime in other places.[12] In this sense, besides its possible pancultural ingredients, a diagnosis always also is a cultural construct.

* Nasreen ex. 5 (medial):

THE BOY WHO SHOULD NOT HAVE SURVIVED

I feel so down that I want to hit the children or throw myself from the balcony. Why should I not have a right to be angry? *Naturally, I have never talked about things like this. No, I cannot talk about them.* Those things which attach me to my son I cannot tell others. As his mother I am the only one who understands him. You cannot imagine what I have been through. I watched a girl on TV who was raped by her father, who talked about it and recovered. I could never say anything like that.

It is so completely terrible that I cannot even manage to talk about it, even to talk to myself. We were in the refugee camp when my son said that a man has done that to me. At first I could not believe him, but then I took his trousers off and saw for myself that he was fouled with that which comes out of the man. His sisters and brothers were very sad. They said to Father (referring to her husband), that if we were you we would have gone to kill that man. Then they didn't talk about it anymore.

He himself was so young that he kept talking about it to everyone. Young and old, they all laughed with him about it. He just thought that it was a very strange thing that had happened. He was too small to understand. I wish that it could have remained that way. You know, we just wanted to forget, leave it behind us. But now the problem is that they (mental health professionals) talk to him about it all the time, so that it is driving him crazy. "A lady said it to me," he told me. "I will go and kill her with a knife." I get so angry when they talk about it. I have told them many times over, that they must not talk about it with him, and then they do it anyway. He was only a child and would have forgotten it all if they hadn't talked about it anymore. But they say that they have to talk to him in order to get it out, because otherwise he will blame himself.

(If you were among your own, would you never have talked about it again?) If it happened to a child – never! No Mother could say a thing like that about her own son. It isn't right while your child is growing up that people talk about what happened to him. I believe that he doesn't want to show that he has been crushed. He doesn't want to lose face. It's nothing to go boasting about. Because it isn't only a matter of getting a wife (i.e. which would be very difficult), but if he gets into trouble with someone they may open their mouths. If others get to know about it they could always use it against him, make fun of him, raise the issue time and time again. So they must not talk about it. (Are you afraid that he will some day disclose himself?) No, because now he is so big that he can understand for himself that he shouldn't talk about it. He doesn't want anybody to know now that he has grown up. After all, he is almost grown-up.

She seems anxious nevertheless and expresses a feeling of going completely mad by the turn of events. She even claims that he would have been better off dead rather than to have understood what actually happened later.

Everyone dies at some point, but this is something you think about every day, you're somehow never through with it. (Should he have fought till the end?) Yes, because it will always follow you if others understand what has happened. I wish that neither I nor my husband had got to know about it (She regrets having told the professionals) (Is it considered (i.e. among your own people) your own fault that it has happened?) That is what everyone says, for sure. You are considered a bad person, of inferior quality. Yes, that is what they say, they cannot understand that he was only three years old and unable to defend himself. He gets the blame (Even if he is innocent?) The boy is to blame, they will most certainly say! If he had not allowed it, it would never had happened, but the man was so big and he was so small. Certainly, that is how the others think. (Are you afraid that he will give himself away at some point?) The fear is there constantly, at all times.

(cp. the *unspeakability* of trauma in chapter two: Psychological Trauma Reconsidered)

The Child Welfare Authorities later took custody of this young boy, so very dear to his mother. She was left with the agony of having lost him, not only in such a shameful way, but also after first having managed to rescue him from all the horrors that they and he had faced at home during the war (cp. N ex. 1: A Topsy-Turvy World). This interference was, in my opinion, brought about by an unfounded suspicion of incest directed against his father, (my opinion was shared by the boy's father's therapist). Among other things, he was referred for a rectal examination without his parents being notified.

This unauthorised intervention was, however, postponed by the medical personnel who were to carry it out, upon discovering the error. That is, until the mother had agreed to what according to her testimony was, after all, presented as a general medical check-up by an interpreter, who probably felt unable to mediate the shameful facts/ accusations *in toto*.[13] Had the facts of this case come to the knowledge of the father at the time, this would, according to the mother, undoubtedly had resulted in violent retribution as he would have been forced to act out a defence of his/their lost honour.

This case is full of curious facts, breaches of confidence and of professional ethics. Indeed, it is symptomatic that representatives of the Child Welfare Authorities appeared quite prejudiced as to the need for removing the prepubertal child from his family no matter what the actual circumstances were. Illiterate and initially co-operative as these parents were, they were persuaded to sign the papers of custody *voluntarily* in the belief that this was beneficial for their son. Only in hindsight did they sorely regret this act, when they felt rejected by the same Child Welfare Authorities. After a long period of separation and change of executive personnel, the boy was allowed back home to the satisfaction of everyone. This, however, was only possible – again according to the client – *on condition* that other members of the family split up: in this case his elder brother wasn't allowed to return home (which in fact he did, in the words of Nasreen "hidden away in a cupboard during visits by the authorities") and the father moved nearby (i.e. was divorced from the boy's mother; cp. what is said on the divorce rate above).

In a life marked by deficiency, warring and repeated sudden deaths, parents frequently cannot protect their children from the malignant consequences of these events. Moreover, the recurrent breaches of honourable behaviour involved in the lives of many refugees lead to a sense of shame which, if the breaches become public, could only be dealt with by strong, possibly violent, measures. In addition to this, the very high expectations the parents have for their children (for good or bad) are evidence of the extent to which they become important carriers of hope. It is also important to acknowledge how certain problems within the area of child custody increase in cases involving cross-cultural migrants. For example, refugee children who, like their parents, may have been exposed to sexual trauma or have witnessed such unspeakable atrocities may exhibit symptoms, which are recognised by professionals trained and attuned to detecting cases of incest. When problems regarding communication and mutual taboos inherent in cross-cultural encounters – often involving an unprofessional interpreter – are added to the uncertainty of diagnostic methods, the aspects of legal protection and personal prestige involved in such cases of suspected incest become worrying[14].

A duty-oriented normative system emphasises the quality of a particular act rather than the moral intentions or contractual rights between voluntary actors. Where a rights-oriented normative system avoids involuntary choices (compulsion/fraud, and so on) by way of exceptions, which disqualify the contract or exclude certain categories of actors (such as mentally ill/minors), a duty-oriented one assumes that *all* actors are more or less vulnerable. Because they frequently exhibit weakness of will, lack of knowledge or dependence, the freedom to enter into a contract is not considered a general benefit in such an understanding[15].

* Aisha ex. 10 (4-7 continued/post-medial):

THE CASE OF AISHA'S DAUGHTER CONTINUED

You know we asked for help ourselves. If we had thought of hurting her we would have hit her. But she is our child, we won't hurt her. Naturally, if it turns out to be something like a question of honour. You have got your own eyes which created the shameless one in order that one just take one's own eyes and throws them away, because there is no more to it (what the client here is referring to in such an unclear way is the biblical idea of removing those eyes involved in shameless viewing).

They were supposed to help that girl, they were supposed to take her back home in order to talk about what she wants. They call them the "Child Welfare" (authorities), but they don't know their business; I don't know how to explain this thing without being able to use my own language. I could have told them that the way they work they will ruin people, one after the another. In this way, they actually work against their own intentions. She is only a female child who cannot decide for herself. When it comes to what is right and wrong, they should not teach children from when they're little that they are allowed to decide for themselves. We are to look after them, wait until they grow up, show them the way and help them on that way. In a year's time she'll be spending time, alone, outside in the streets, and then they will have ruined her. If she refuses to go to school, then the social services will give her 'a salary' (she refers to national insurance contributions) and that kind of thing. Then everyone will see, how they have wronged her.

(I don't believe that they will allow her to come and go as she pleases. But as for how she dresses or does her hair, I presume they will let her choose for herself. But then you have to remember that Norwegian youth may look rather odd to you. If you saw one of them at home, you might mistake it for bad behaviour. Is that why you're afraid?) No, I really do believe them to be ruined. If they weren't they wouldn't go about behaving like that, colouring their hair purple, using ragged trousers and the like? If they are not ruined, why do they look like that? (What I want to say is that it doesn't imply that they let her stay away for the night. Many norwegian youngsters are allowed to try out different looks, but it is outward appearance.) It is true that it is on the outside, but it is a sign that she may end up on the wrong path, that she might make a mess of her life. The fact that you dye you hair doesn't mean that a person is ruined, but if you first land on the wrong path – one day she will end in disaster. It's like I said, only three weeks ago she was respectable, and now she has changed, just like that. And so I think that it will only change for the worse.

You know, the Child Welfare Authorities want her to decide for herself from when she is 15 years old. If that happens, all I can see is a very black future. As her mother, I feel sorry for her, no one in the whole world can be more worried about her than I am. After a while, perhaps, Norwegian children calm down and return. But it turns out that foreign children don't. They carry something inside themselves in order that they have to take revenge, a feeling of having been treated unfairly all along. Most of those who behave like that are foreign youngsters, not Norwegian youngsters, in order that one might wish that they (the foreign youngsters) disappear, not go on living the way they behave when they are allowed to choose for themselves.

(But your son came back?) He has become better, yes, but then he was a boy. Gender makes a big difference. He got a child with a Moroccan girl and started his own household[16]. For a girl it would

109

be quite impossible. Girls are completely ruined, they drag themselves down like filth. Norwegians think it's okay to experience life before calming down, because they believe that it's merely a matter of staying alive. They tell me "She has a good time, she attends school, and she's alive". I know that she is alive, but would have wished her to be dead rather than alive in this way. Because now she doesn't just go to school and then come straight home. I know that she does a hundred other things which are completely disastrous.

I wanted to know what kept her down, why she was angry; they haven't told us. When we went to ask for help, they accused us of all sorts of things. I want to know what it is that she is dissatisfied with, what her pain is, what is wrong with her. But they keep hiding her from us as though we were somehow crazy people; they do things like that. Once I had got an appointment with her doctor. While I sat there in the doctor's office the phone rang and it was to inform her (i.e. the doctor) that my daughter had arrived (i.e. for an appointment the doctor had forgotten all about). "Oh no, is she here? In that case, it's all gone wrong" (the doctor cried out). My daughter was to visit her that day, you see. She (the doctor) told them that her mother was at the place "Quick, hide her in another room (she laughs while telling me) so that her mother won't see her" (i.e. the doctor was heard saying). This doctor was so stupid that she didn't know that I understood Norwegian. They are so stupid that they go about hiding my own daughter like that (we all laugh and it becomes difficult for the interpreter to translate because the situation seems so immensely comical; at this point Aisha herself continues in norwegian.). I told her "Just calm down, don't be afraid, I won't hurt my daughter. Then the doctor said "Oh no, her mother is here – oh, oh. Now we have to end this talk. No – Aisha I'll send you a new appointment time by letter, goodbye.'

Feelings of guilt and shame are clearly psychoculturally conditioned and dependent upon variations in child rearing practices. Like the issue of psychosomatisation, they too should be an important focus in the treatment of victims of organised violence due to the wily humiliations involved, all the more so because of the cross-cultural differences which are frequently involved. For example, western mental health professionals tend to focus merely on survivors' guilt, which is a concept that again presupposes the individual subject's attribution of cause to personalised acts of commission or omission in a way that is less common in the tight kinship groups of many third world contexts. Thus...

* Nasreen ex. 6 (medial):

A MEMORATE OF 'ADJAL'

... Nasreen recounts how she herself experienced the death of a neighbour on her own door-step after she had tried to warn him of the approaching bombs by motioning him away. Her version is that he waved back believing that she was calling him, not waving him away. However, because Nasreen firmly believes that this (i.e. misunderstanding) was the work of adjal (destiny) which had arrived to summon him, and that her own actions had no effect on the outcome, she did not to my initial surprise seem to have experienced the event as particularly traumatic from the point of view of her own action.

(cp. A ex. 3/14)

A canadian study by Allodi & Cowgill (1982) of 41 latin american victims of torture, reported only two cases of guilt feelings. Similarly, Eitinger's (1964; 1969) highly reliable epidemiological study on the psychiatric morbidity of Holocaust survivors in Norway and Israel did not find such feelings to be prominent. Anthropologists such as Mead (1949) and Benedict (1946) are famous for their studies on the distinctive cultural contexts of guilt and shame. According to their reasoning emphasising the integrity, rights and privileges of the individual marks the economical, political and psychological thinking of the guilt-prone environment. The individuals have a right to privacy and spare time to develop their own interests, and the surroundings identify them on the basis of their personal characteristics. However, in a group-oriented (sociocentric) context (conductible of feelings of shame), interpersonal obligations and obedience are more valued. A woman is thus known as someone's daughter, cousin, or wife, depending on her *relation to other members* of the joint family or tribal group. People stick together for the sake of the group, towards whom the individual has responsibilities rather than personal rights or freedoms. He or she is expected to fulfil collectively ascribed responsibilities, economically, practically or emotionally (L ex. 3: Layla's Secrets), and exhibit strict social control while acting as a sort of external police force in respect of each others behaviour. If rules are broken, the group as a whole is liable to *lose face*, as described above.

As a psychological concept, shame just as guilt can be linked to the dynamics of the ego in relationship to both intrapsychic processes and their external sociocultural contexts.[17] It entails a conscious experience of painful affect, that may cast its shadow on both body and soul. From the point of view of the intrapsychic factors at work, however, the immediate reaction to shame seems to be a passive desire to erase the external observer by means of hiding oneself or severing all contacts with the eyewitness[18], that is, in contrast to the element of repression of the psychic conflict itself which is present in guilt. In this sense, shame can be said to have a more pronounced interpersonal profile, the norms being, so to say, externalised onto a *punitive Other* seen as embodying the collective which sets the rule and accompanying *group pressure* (cp. the discussion on the *public penalties* propagated by islamists in chapter 8, and further arguments in Part II). In the case of shame, one learns to adapt more out of a fear for reprisal by real other people rather than by *an introjected ('imagined') parent/other.*

Moreover, shame seems to differ somewhat from guilt in the behavioural options which accompany transgression. While guilt may to a larger extent inhibit/repress outward expressions of aggression which are directed inwards, shame is characterised by more diffuse aggression which may be aimed both at the self and others; cp. the destructiveness following from loss of respect that becomes *publicly known*, for example in 'authority incidents' or 'incidents' related to the honour of young girls, which may be directed at self/others/the offender and/or the physical environment.

The indices of both the behaviour and dynamics involved in shame thus imply a link with sociocentric patterns which, in western mainstream (i.e. traditional) psychological thinking, have been assumed to be characteristic of earlier undifferentiated phases of development. According to this line of reasoning, shame does not preclude the same degree of division between self and other as the case is in guilt. Among the kurds as an example of a more traditional muslim context, quite to the contrary, a readiness for experiencing shame is in fact *a highly valued feature* for men, but even more for women. The ideal of psychological maturity for a woman is quite compatible with an ego which is relatively passive and less 'differentiated' or more considerate in respect of others. In kurdish society a woman's honour (ideally guarded by an appreciation of shame) is, thus, constantly and actively maintained and protected not only by herself but by designated men in her surroundings, for fear of retaliation from the larger kin group. Those whose shame has become public in such a setting – *no matter what personal feelings are involved* – are clearly pressured to act out in public in order to recover the lost equilibrium. That is, if the frequent and primary resort to avoidance behaviour as further presented in chapter 11 on courtesy and withdrawal behaviour, has failed, there are, according to this logic, few remaining options if violent confrontation is to be avoided (cp. how Aisha depicts the 'absolute kurdish limits', the transgression of which will *force* a father to react, in A ex. 10: The Case of Aisha's Daughter Continued, above).

While largely context-bound, such external sanctions operating in the sociocentric surroundings of these cross-cultural migrants' native environment, however, may lose their effect in exile, an issue to which I will return in Part Two. Let it suffice, here, to say that the importance of the context of the extended family as an organising principle is a central demarcation line, not just between tradition-oriented clients and their western-oriented doctors, but also between the mental health ideology of the latter and deviations in their own recent history. This is one reason why the role of the muslim woman is so difficult to come to terms with by many westerners, because it touches upon a sore point in the changing gender relationships in the western context itself pointing a finger at the many still unsolved problems of readjustment accompanying womens' liberation. It is, however, not a simple issue to do with mere male power, but more fundamentally of the continuing presence of the children in the lives and efforts of their parents. The kin group as a hierarchical unit takes priority over the unfolding of its individual members. But at the same time, the future of the community groups' elders is dependent upon loyal and faithful children: children who are strongly and genuinely attached to them as Nasreen's children have remained through all the problems they have experienced in exile, in contrast to the more confrontational choices made by Aisha's children.

The sanctity and priority of this kind of reciprocal attachment tends to be overlooked by western commentators when the restricted freedom of young migrant women is unilaterally criticised. It is important to acknowledge not only the weaknesses but, moreover, the strengths of the bonds of solidarity inherent in collective networks, as these networks operate also in the exile situation. A situation in which a lonely migrant as compared to someone with a socially supportive network will easily become prey to the malignant forces of 'the market'; that is, the debilitating effects of unemployment and extended reliance on social and health care benefits referred to above. It was precisely because of their lack of interest in the central issues of family law based on the collective ideal of 'traditional man' that the colonial powers only managed to gain partial sovereignty in the conquered parts of the muslim world.

Facing western power and culture muslim women seem to have become – at least in the eyes of their men – elevated to a historical role as *guardians of the indigenous tradition*, an issue to which I will return and further develop in chapter 13: Symbolic Shelter in a Changing World. From such a point of view, gender segregation as a facet of kin solidarity, has in fact historically turned out to be an effective strategy against foreign intruders and defence against the loss of cultural identity. Today there is a subtler but nevertheless real threat to muslim migrants that will, however, come from the *inside*. In sum, the individualistic nuclear family, pursuing self-realisation and differentiation through negotiation and achievement as well as fostering stimulation-seeking behaviour, novelty and change, can be contrasted with a more communal structure of extended primary groups. A group that is again coupled with an implicit metaphorical mode of expression as depicted in these narratives, and a mode of relating to others which is in conformity with pro-social values promoting smooth intra-group relations.

7.
THE COLLECTIVE DIMENSIONS OF TRAUMA

Violation of Ritual and Ritual Emotion

I will now again shift focus to include the issue of whether the changes in living conditions, which have provoked such traumatic experiences in the clients, are in any way related to collective ritual requirements of the ingroups at issue. The psychological foundations of *rites de passage* have long been debated within the history of religion and related subjects.[1] The significance of such rites for facilitating emotional readjustment to a new life situation has been particularly stressed. However, the available material has been able to verify this only indirectly as it has mainly consisted of merely observing the rituals or collecting traditional lore.

The interpretation of emotions raises particular problems in cultural research because of its primary preoccupation with collective analyses. The emotional reactions of the individual therefore remain largely outside the scope of ethnographers' focus. Although researchers such as Clifford Geertz (1973) and Victor Turner (1969; 1974; 1979: 1991) have suggested that ritual symbols affect the way individuals experience their world, they have not looked in detail at the individual subject in order to substantiate their ideas. Since the functions of rites are frequently depicted as dependent on personal meaning, the perspective of participatory observation is not sufficient ground on which to base an analysis.

Irrespective of ideological affiliation, the forced migratory process, like the ordinary transitions of life, involves psychosocial 'wandering' that activates feelings and fantasies preserved through time in age-old mythical motifs: of painful longing for and the pain of what is lost, but also of new possibilities and triumphs over the old, inhibiting, world. In many third world migrants' tradition-oriented past, such shifts have been accompanied and made possible by collective binding rituals which ascertain a smooth transition, such as the elaborate mourning customs accompanying loss under ordinary cultural circumstances.[2]

FEMALE GRAVE-DIGGERS

(Who took care of the burials?) Everyone could join in – often parents didn't even know whether they actually got their own children's bodies. Perhaps they were buried with a wrong foot or arm. You just had to do it fast in order to prevent the smell because we had no cooling room there. Whoever felt like it was free to join. According to our customs, the corpse should be washed and such thing, but this didn't happen. We merely had to pick up the parts separately in sacks. Men picked men and women picked women and girls. (In order to show a last respect?) Yes. Each one in a separate grave, according to custom; they have to.

If someone dies in my home country it is a big ceremony, you take your time, for example for washing, and you make large quantities of food, and many other things which happen on different days. Here, it was as if you were dead in a matter of seconds and one just had to get it over with. The grave had to be dug deep in order to hinder the smell. You put stones on each side, building a sort of wall around the hole in which the corpse lies, at the bottom of the grave (Is this to enable the angels visit?) That is what they say. You know, Esrael, the angel of death, will visit and question the dead person (about matters of faith). This is why he must be able to sit up. But you put the stones because when you leave the place, the dead one will wish to follow you back home and will rise up while pronouncing the name of Allah. At that point he will hit his nose against the stones, realise that he is dead, and lie down again.

However, it depended on how much time there was. At times there was such a hurry that they had to use a bulldozer for turning the earth. Put the corpses in a row and just drive earth on top of them. Finished with the business. After all, it was war. (Did you mark the graves?) Yes, of course, one always does. With a stone in order that no one should touch the spot. One stone for each person.

(Did you take part in the digging of graves yourself?). Yes, I did help along with families. It was a very painful task (Whose grave did you dig?) No – I buried too many, I don't know whom. (Did you pick corpses?) Yes, a little girl of four. Her stomach had split open and the insides were pouring out but her head and limbs were in place. I put her in a sack, there was lots and lots of blood everywhere.

At home it was like this; for example when Mother died only the men-folk were allowed to accompany the dead person to the grave, no matter what the gender was. But there it was different. Everyone just went along. It had to be that way.

(Did it feel right?) Yes, it was a good thing. Close relatives cry a lot, they throw earth on their heads and scratch themselves in the face, quite irrespective of gender. – Yes, because otherwise, you would have gone completely mad, if you hadn't been allowed to take part in the burials and the like...

Where expressions of grief remain unrecognised, this will, according to the mainstream psychological discourse, result in the misconstruction of this grief as pathology. In the case of forced migration, the sudden change of social, material and cultural conditions without the benefit of ritual or network support may foster a chronically painful marginality. Kashani's (1988, 2) survey supports the presence of such a grief response in recent iranian migrants to the USA marked by intrusive thoughts and a preoccupation with the past. However, in the cases discussed here disengagement from the old order of things had already begun prior to migration itself because of the quite exceptional circumstances in the country of origin or because of lengthy stays in the primitive and harsh conditions of many refugee camps.

Psychiatric material from Iran shows many links between psychological stress and forcibly altered ritual circumstances.[3] Ritual pollution from corpses during combat, or the general absence of washing facilities, might for example result in obsessive behaviour. In the shi'ite and, by extension, iranian tradition, the ability to express sadness is highly valued. Because historical events are interpreted as evidence of the cruel suppression of the righteous by unjust rulers, grieving becomes the proof of commitment to righteousness: "We have been crying for a thousand years, so what does it matter if we cry for another ten million in order to bring justice against tyranny. I cannot laugh as long as tyranny is ruling. I cry in order to resist"[4].

However, the political annexation and glorification of martyrdom as the paramount ethos for revolutionary iranian society poses unexpected emotional complications for opponents of the present regime. The iranian revolution grew out of the kerbela[5] paradigm, its rotes anchored in the idea of mourning and martyrdom. The so called ta'zieh passion plays include dramatised scenes of separation from important episodes in the shi'ite mythical past, such as when the young son of Hussein takes leave of his father and then implores his mother to let him proceed into the death of martyrdom, or caresses his little sister in a tearful farewell. Paralysed with sorrow, his mother wraps him in a shroud and clings to him. He tears himself away, only to be returned later, dead, into the arms of his mother by the imam. Similar emotionally compelling events supersede one another as many more relatives of the prophet are martyred.

The ritual re-enactment of tragic events is intended to evoke anger at injustice as well as an accompanying dedication to the establishment of a righteous society among the participants. In the present situation, according to Good and Good (1988) emotions such as this have become charged with powerful contemporary political symbolism. While mourning rituals have become mandatory symbols of political commitment to the regime, their ability to comfort the opponents has simultaneously decreased. It has been said that in the past villagers used to go to the cemetery in order to cry, but nowadays they go there to celebrate. This change has taken place during a period when life affirming rituals are – simultaneously – being repressed.

Under the heading "Where Mullahs rule though shall not enjoy life" Human Rights in Iran Newsletter (9, 1993) quotes a poll carried out by the *Hamshahri'a* , published by the mayor of Teheran, according to which an overwhelming majority of Teherani residents cannot recollect a joyous occasion during the past ten years of their lives. In addition to the economic hardships endured, this curious piece of news may reflect the interference of the present regime in the private lives of iranian people. Episodes narrated by the clients suggest that public and private emotional discourse have become subjugated to the scrutiny and control of revolutionary gangs of vigilantes posing as guardians of morality. According to clients' accounts, which are supported by Amnesty reports, these 'Islamic sisters and brothers' feel free to harass offenders for example by removing make-up with a handkerchief filled with broken razor blades or cutting away any visible strands of hair with scissors, and attacking or arresting people while meting out 'Islamic punishments' as further described below.

* Layla ex. 2 (pre-medial):

KILLJOY

Now you are not even allowed to celebrate a wedding in the cellar anymore, because of our many martyrs. It isn't like in the old days. Suddenly the *pasdaran* arrive and you almost get a heart attack. The ladies have to hide, put a scarf on their head and such things. But, after all, we were lucky because at worst, they could take both bride and bridegroom. You are not allowed to use any wedding garment or make up. You have to use thick clothing, and merely sit there until it's over.

Once, the kids of our neighbour celebrated their birthday. Luckily, my son wasn't there. The parents were present. Suddenly four cars full of, perhaps a hundred *pasdaran*, arrived at their house taking everyone away, both boys and girls. They had been flogged so that their bodies were very swollen. They had to have medical attention for a week. But they insisted that even if they were flogged, they somehow had to laugh – do the opposite of what was expected. At least one should not cry. I actually got this suffocating feeling in my throat[6], I felt like killing them. I may lose my temper and become irritated, but I must not cry. It is very bad the way they go about.

It was a week before *Id*[7]. My eldest son had just come home from school. They took him and shaved his head. He came back home afterwards quite beside himself. On that particular *Id* he did not accompany us to the family gathering because he said "It is such a shameful thing to have happened, so I cannot go". But he did get a present for Christmas – I mean for the New Year ...

(What about here then?) No, here it's different, because Nora doesn't force me to cry. But that's how it was in Iran. In a different way, they wanted to force me to be sad. You see, there are many painful memories which emerge, but I've forgotten many of them. Because, you know, it is like this; if you as much as catch a glimpse of their face, a most horrible fear overcomes you. They can be the very *killers*, they can do anything to you. There's only one thing I actually do remember. One of the 'sisters' said that if first you do one thing then you have to reckon with the rest if you do something bad, you must be ready to take what comes. I will never forget that. I keep thinking about her disgusting appearance, I have such an aversion for her. An old unmarried woman, with a moustache and so dreadfully ugly.

I said "My Father is *ruhani*"[8] (All ex. 2: The Kurdish Legacy), and they said "If that was true you would not have done punishable acts". We used the *chador* (the Muslim female dress) but did not cover the whole face and hair. They had a different opinion. It was somehow as though neither a man nor a woman should see anything beautiful in themselves. They wanted you to be frightened by your own face. (You were not allowed to be happy or beautiful?) Yes, that is exactly how it was. If a person was beautiful, they gave her a warning not to make herself look more beautiful. But, after all, it happens that people are beautiful by nature. You should be happy that you didn't have to grow up under that regime.

When I was at home in my Father's house, I used such beautiful fabrics, with flowers and such things, and some colour in it. We were not allowed to walk around in black clothing; my Father disliked them. He said "One should use animated colours because they influence your mood". (So that you get happier yourself?). Yes, that's right. With some glitter or thin material as a final touch. Regrettably, I have not that heritage with me because in all those years from the beginning of the revolution until this very day, I own only one red sweater. And when I have worn it a couple of times at home, it feels just like someone is about to tell me that it is very improper. You become dead inside yourself. You even get a sort of aversion to bright colours somehow...

Thus, in a bid to maintain islamic standards, the police in the ancient iranian city of Shiraz, according to Human Rights Newsletter (1993, 6), had imposed wedding regulations forbidding a range of traditional ceremonies. As part of these measures, all printing houses had to submit a copy of wedding invitations and keep the police informed about the events; restaurants must notify the police within 24 hours prior to a wedding, and bar music and dancing on the premises. Music and dancing during traditional wedding parades in the streets is also forbidden, and permits have to be issued separately for every such ceremony.

Open manifestations of happiness are officially discouraged as being somehow associated with permissiveness since they are thought to facilitate infiltration by decadent western culture. Instead, the iranian media encourage people to seek pleasure by participating in official religious ceremonies of mourning accompanied by frantic beating of one's chest and other forms of self-flagellation, or visiting cemeteries and graves of martyrs. In addition, all sorts of rules circumvent individual freedom in most areas of life from writing to clothing.

One of the more problematic aspects of this situation is linked to the reliance of kurds on the preislamic zoroastrian traditions that are viewed with great suspicion by the regime. For example, the iranian islamic leaders have strongly criticised the persian new year *(no ruz)* celebration, while intensifying, during that particular period, public funeral marches for troops killed at the front in order to produce a general atmosphere of mourning. In parts of Kurdistan, new year's celebrations are likewise viewed sceptically or banned altogether by the authorities, and the same hold true for preislamic customs generally in all areas of intensified islamisation efforts[9].

Culture-in-the-Negative and
the Innocent without Status

Lavik (1977) defines life cycle rituals from a psychiatric point of view as collectively institutionalised solutions to problems of separation and belonging. In traditional societies, social (as against physical) facets of birth, puberty, or an approaching death may overshadow biological development, the result of which may be broken or forced developmental leaps, for example, resulting in unwanted infants left to die, immature brides or prematurely dead persons. Various expelling mechanisms on the collective level may also pose problems for individual participants in ritual events. From this perspective, rituals are useful as much for securing scapegoats as they are for easing individual adaptation. Where rules are broken, a range of sanctions and symbolic measures associated with that particular deviation, or with the person who has abandoned or betrayed her own kind, are jointly activated.

I will take Fatima's wedding under 'normal', premigrational conditions in lower middle class Teheran as an example of a *rite de passage* celebration which left her with deep psychological scars, despite the fact that it may have functioned, normatively, as intended on the collective level. As a consequence of the ritual, the client-protagonist was left stigmatised by the community and vulnerable to her husband's subsequent maltreatment.

* Fatima ex. 10 (medial, before disclosing maltreatment and sexual trauma):

'NOTHING BUT A WIDOW'

One day, after several years of treatment, Fatima arrived for an appointment complaining of diffuse pains in her left side. She remembered very well the first time she had had a similar kind of pain: With no foreboding of what was happening to her, she one day returned home from school with blood-stained trousers. Her older sister, who carried the responsibility for her upbringing, became furious. Battered, and confused by accusations of having lost her virginity, she was taken for a gynaecological examination where the onset of menstruation was confirmed.

The real catastrophe, however, happened during the celebration of her wedding, in the presence of a considerable number of guests who had come a long distance to attend the celebrations. When the celebration was reaching its climax by dinner time, the bride and bridegroom were left alone to consummate the marriage in the ritually prepared bedroom of her parents-in- law. To the linen were according to tradition fastened four pieces of cloth with safety pins, which were later to be distributed among those present as evidence of the consummation of the marriage and of the virginity of the bride. The client was unaware of her husband-to-be as well as totally unprepared for what was about to happen.

> Everybody eats quickly in order to be the first one to peep through any available keyhole or window. There you do it for the first time in your life in front of everybody.

Earlier, on other occasions, she herself had taken part in this race for the fun of being the first to get the blood-stained trophies; by triumphantly waving about 'the evidence', the lucky possessor receives a reward in money.

> Sometimes they come into the room even before the bride and bridegroom has had the chance to get their trousers on.

But this time things did not turn out the way they expected; instead, after the act, her husband-to-be yelled out – in order to save his own honour before it was to be too late:

> "You are no virgin! I have been deceived; I believed I was getting a proper wife, and what have I got here, nothing but a widow".

To her desperation, there was no trace of blood to be seen. She had only recently turned sixteen, and the unfolding scene scared her stiff; meanwhile, a horde of furious onlookers poured into the room in order to defame her. She was not able to repeat to me what they said or did at that point except for that:

> My mother had to walk with her head bowed, the celebration was brought to an end, and everybody went home. Often violence, hospitalisation and visits by the police follow from these kinds of things.

And so it turned out that she was to become a person regarded with contempt by other compatriots, in a lonely and nightmarish marriage.

> But it was even worse for my mother who at nine years old was married to a man twelve years older than her. When he used to come home from work she would be playing with her dolls, the demands of house work were beyond her abilities. For this, she was severely punished. At only ten years of age, she gave birth to my elder sister.

This episode clearly illustrates that ritual marking of the transitions of life gives no assurance of psychological well being. While assuming emotional subordination in relation to collective demands, they limit individual freedom of choice. Regardless of whether or not one has personally experienced real sorrow, for example, participants in shi'ite celebrations are expected to cry aloud, just as traditional wedding rituals gently but firmly gives the marriageable girl a new status, irrespectively of her own wishes. Burkert (1979, 37) defines ritual as stereotyped action redirected for demonstration, displays of solidarity and separateness. I share his view according to which it is important to acknowledge how ritual is learned in a negative way: to know the ritual is to know what is forbidden.

In this sense, ritual is regressive, the message transmitted being primarily concerned with the solidarity of the group to the exclusion of personal interests. It is easy to see how ritual in this sense works for the group's advantage in a durkheimian (1947) sense. Traditionally fixed rituals may thus achieve the opposite effect of the generally assumed instrumental moderation, where the emotional aspects work against the involved parties' interests. During the ritual act of circumcision many young people, like the young mother in the above example, do

123

not really understand what is happening to them, thus, ending up as passive and emotionally perplexed onlookers at their own celebration. One cannot assume that ritual expression harmonises with inner feelings. Rather, the participants, who are obliged to attend, will adapt their behaviour in accordance with ritual expectations.

* Fatima ex. 11 (10 continued/medial):

TAKING PART IN MUHARRAM CELEBRATIONS[10] AS A LITTLE GIRL

"Why do people flog themselves to death in the streets?" Fatima asked her shi'ite father as a young girl. Contrary to the existing gender rules, she was once carried on his shoulders during a Muharram procession in which she was to witness the 'incomprehensible' and unexpected death of another participant as a result of the ritual flagellation involved. The answer she got at that time that it was God's will was to haunt her for years, and well into adulthood she remained deeply perplexed as to why God allowed such things to happen.

(cp. A ex. 3; All ex. 2)

A movement in psychocultural time or social space always involves the risk of imbalance *in* the individual and *between* individuals and the society. The tragic fate that greets many third world refugees reaching the borders of our welfare societies reveal that intercultural migration does not automatically solve distorted development, but might, on the contrary, reinforce it. For example, when the refugees' expectations concerning how to manage the fundamental transitions of life do not correspond with current practice in the host society, this might result in increased fear of these unknown circumstances where 'anything could happen'. For example, unforeseen problems in connection with the washing and tending of the dead body, or other mortuary practice which is related to the management of the corpse, frequently arise. There are many things that can go wrong, and a simple mistake in the burial ritual could, in the eyes of the tradition-oriented migrant, lead to the dead person becoming and 'outlawed ghost' and thus leave their kinsmen in a state of almost unsolvable mourning and grief.

* Aisha ex. 11 (medial):

FROM GHOST TO SECOND 'SHAHID'

When Aisha's prepubertal son suddenly died after they had gone into exile, she expressed herself in the following way:

> Sometimes I wonder whether the people in this country are cruel, unacquainted with law and justice, since they allow so many dead bodies to be put into the same grave and risk desecrating a pure soul with a sinful one? Do they really turn up the graves after some time and sacrilege their dead?

The family, Aisha says, was asked to control their sorrow "as was expected in this country where people mourn with dignity". To me, this seemed to have been a paradoxical reaction by the professional staff in a hospital corridor at such a tragic moment marked by strong traditional expressions of sorrow on the part of the grieving family. This family had certain expectations concerning the handling of a relative's death which were not in accordance with prevailing practice in the norwegian health care system. The result of this lack of mutual comprehension was a mother who remained 'stuck' in the grief, bewildered because of her son's 'disappearance', and feeling shameful for not having been able to fulfil her last obligations towards him: "Our child was simply taken away from us and we were instructed to meet up for the funeral".

Such statements reveal an uncertainty gnawing at her heart, a constant fear, as to whether the correct funeral practice had been followed. Clearly, she was deprived of her traditional right to take care of the corpse herself – to wash, dress and perfume her son properly for the grave. But what is more: "Now he will never have peace, but will forever lie restless in his own blood". An autopsy had been performed without consulting the parents, an act which was perceived as desecrating his corpse. "Why, why did they tear up his stomach and destroy him? The wounds will never heal," she lamented.

However, the fact that the traditionally required (ritual) leave-taking, intended to release a child from the obligations to which he is considered bound from the infantile tie to his mother's milk, was verbally mediated according to custom before the moment of death by herself has been a consolation to her (cp. A ex. 14: One Year Past her Mother's Death). But there was more to it, for, as she pointed out, this child, who should have been buried in the mountains of Kurdistan, was now left, abandoned and blood-stained in a far corner of a christian/non-muslim cemetery.

> Why did they choose a gravesite at the bottom of the graveyard? I
> would not have wanted it that way. My child is so pure. He should
> have lots of space in order that no dirt will touch him. Those who
> have lived a bad life get a narrow grave, but pure people should
> have lots of space.

Aisha further tells about how her own father, on his death-bed, expressed the wish that his family should be buried beside him, which is what he thought was best for them.

> I wish to be buried there too. Father's grave is on top of a small
> hillside with many trees, behind mountains and valleys. My
> Mother also wishes to be buried there, at my Father's grave, and
> so do I. As far as possible, one has to comply with the wish of a
> dying person. (Do you ask the dying person?) No, you do not have
> the heart to do that if he doesn't raise the issue himself. Otherwise,
> the dying person may be upset by the question – it may incur a
> heart attack (cp. the notion of *sekhte* A ex. 7, N ex. 9). However
> weak the patient, no one will utter a word about death, but rather
> comfort them and pray for recovery.

For a long time, following the tragic death of her son, Aisha would offer his favourite dish to the children of the neighbourhood, whom she would gather at a local playground every Friday. She dared not approach grown-ups for fear of being considered mad, "but children do not understand what this is all about". Thus, she managed to fulfil one 'last obligation' as ritually prescribed by tradition (i.e. giving alms or *kheiret*). For some time she also searched for her son near the place of his death, fearing that he might not have found peace among the dead. She described his state as that of a person being locked up in a room equipped with many doors, but unable to find his way out. In this example, we find an actual, rather than perceived or feared, norm transgression further complicating the matter: the young boy, her son, had taken his own life.

A couple of years and many sessions later the picture is, however, changing. The client alleges to have visited her son's dwelling in the beyond, describing it in an animated way. In this dwelling, to his mother's despair, he is found walking back and forth. According to Aisha, because his life was prematurely cut short he has even become capable of mediating between God and man. This is because he now represents what is generally referred to as a 'second' *shahid* (martyr).

Aisha now claims that he reveals himself to her in order to comfort her when his siblings are quarrelling, putting his arm around her while they sit on the sofa together.

(Do you do know of others who experience similar things?) It is quite a common occurrence if a person close and dear to you dies. God will release from their graves those who have lived a good life in order that they may visit home, for *namaz* (prayer), for example. My Mother did not exactly tell anybody either, though my brother, who died from torture, appeared to her for years in exactly the same way. If I asked her, she just answered that it was no business of children. But naturally my sisters and I understood because we always had to bake a certain type of bread when the deceased had visited. We were not allowed to throw away any leftovers, but distributed them among the poor on those particular days.

Her feelings still overwhelm her from time to time, as they did on that particular day when my routine question (What is most difficult for you right now?) had unexpectedly renewed her pain. She looked at me for a little longer than usual, and I understood what she was thinking about. She broke down in tears and told me about talking to her son, all the while crying in an agitated way.

(What do you talk to him about?) I don't know, it's difficult to express in words. (Do you communicate without words?; She nods, adding that she hopes that no one will ever have to experience her pain.) It is something very special. I have to follow him all the time while he is growing up. He would have attended the ninth grade by now.

She asks for a glass of water, and dashes off to the toilet, from where a lonely weeping can be heard. Whereupon the interpreter fetches a cup of tea for her and we wait for her to return. I reassure her that it is quite all right for her to cry here if she wishes to, but she stops crying.

(Has it been worse lately?) Yes, if the children even mention anything to do with my son, I start crying heavily, and that is not a good thing because it is setting a bad example for them because they might think that "Look, mother is crying for P. He must have done a very good thing. Let's do the same". I'm permitted to cry, but not in front of the children.

(Where were you permitted to cry at home?) In front of anybody, and anywhere. Everyone would have understood my situation. But here, if I cry, people from the outside immediately assume that there must be some disagreement at home. (If you cry, you are misunderstood?) Yes, in this country, no matter how much you suffer, they think it is strange to cry. They do not know you, but at home (i.e. in Kurdistan) I can go outside and cry. Everybody would take their time, sit down and comfort me.

I point to the reaction of the hospital staff in connection with her son's death mentioned above, and ask whether there have been other incidents of this kind. She denies it, but nonetheless relates that people stare at her, as if she were somehow odd, when she lets her feelings loose at the graveyard.

I just go there to cry. I don't care what the others think – I cry and cry until I am completely exhausted . (How long would the mourning period last at home?) It differs according to whom you are mourning. If it is a young person, it lasts for a very long time. Father was 40-50 years old and had lots of small children. If you are old, that is old and full of days, it takes 40 days. You do some *kheiret* (give away some alms, for example, food as referred to above), sing and things like that. But if it is a young person, then the sorrow will never end. For a Mother, it never stops, as for siblings. (She seems anxious about the inevitable changes following from the exile.) I imagine that my mourning period will end the day I am allowed to visit my family and be able to tell them myself about what happened to my son.

Hodne (1980) has analysed the changing attitudes to death in the norwegian countryside prior to the First World War. While people today confront death privately in a hospital setting surrounded by professionals, at that time it was an occasion of concern to the larger community also in the case of the host society; and one in which attendance was likewise obligatory in order to ascertain the status of the dead and protect the living from unwelcome apparitions. Taking concrete, ritual leave of the deceased, was imposed even on small children for edifying reasons. This practice, according to Hodne (ibid), resulted in traumatic experiences and the subsequent western denial of death, a practice which is in strong contrast to the practice of certain migrant groups today.

Among the many unforeseen – and cumulative – problems of exile, is the impact of forced migration on traditional ritualisations and vice versa. Through the use of clinical examples, I have been able to elucidate the relationship between the subjectively felt refugee trauma and collective ritualisations: all the examples show a psychosocial imbalance thought to be characteristic of exceptional ritual situations, in which something has gone wrong from the perspective of the individual, but not necessarily from that of the collective. Imbalances which are related, on the one hand, to physical, psychological or ethical transgressions such as autopsy, suicide or other kinds of norm breaches in chastity and/or purity, which are made public by the demands of that particular ritual (cp. ways of circumventing them on pp. 266ff); and, on the other hand, to their social consequences in the form of 'fallen' or uncircumcised women, mutilated apparitions (such as the above mentioned ghost), young martyrs or otherwise socially somehow 'improper' or problematic categories of persons.

There is a concept for covering the various ways of conceptualising or explaining away the extraordinary disturbing fact of innocent suffering, namely *theodicy* – the vindication of divine providence in view of the existence of evil – leading one to ask: "Why, if God is almighty, is evil allowed to happen?" In the face of the immensity of human suffering involved in organised social violence and torture, no religion has come up with a wholly satisfactory answer. In other words, a misfortune that lies *outside the normal range of experience* remains confusing both to the individual personally and to his or her community. Such a traumatic event may appear existentially isolating or unbearable in the face of its large scale collective dimensions, as depicted in more detail below. It is worth pondering in this respect that DSM-III-R included the experience of an event that is "outside the range of usual human experience" as a diagnostic criterion for PTSD.

Another concept denotes those persons who, by way of their highly extraordinary experiences, come to challenge our theodicies, which therefore fail to offer meaning (appear meaningless). The *innocent without status* are those who, independently of their own actions, are expelled into such a vulnerable position. The category may include extra-marital children or children who have died prematurely, 'self-murderers' and others who, in various ways, have suffered an extraordinary fate, including victims of violence and especially rape. Less often, such people may alternatively be elevated to a supernatural status. (cp. the ambivalent fate of Aisha's son in the example above, which embodies both solutions: his becoming both a restless ghost and, upon resolution of the worst grief, moreover, a secondary martyr).

Not fitting into the classificatory scheme, the innocent without status are generally expelled to a marginal condition, apart from others. Perhaps, then, it should come as no surprise when the clients describe their situation as wholly different from others, and their extraordinary experiences as something which defies description, i.e. in common words[11]. But this solution, which may offer some people meaning at the cost of self-condemnation (e.g. rape victims who blame themselves), gives the victim of torture only two options: either to accept stigmatisation, or otherwise somehow transcend the sociocultural setting (cp. 'the limits of honour' as described by A in ex. 7: Children Drowning as in an Enormous Ocean).

* Aisha ex. 12 (11 continued/post-medial):

ABOUT THE 'SECONDARY SHAHID'

(Aisha tells me about the kind of trees that grow by her father's grave). It is the responsibility of the children to cultivate the trees on the grave. On Thursdays the graves are lit up in order that they be kept watch over for the night. It is very beautiful (Are the trees holy?) If the grave belongs to a Sheikh, no one can touch them or break a twig, or throw a stone there. They grow small fruits, which only children under 13-15 years are allowed to pick – if you've started to menstruate, you are impure, you see. When they visit the graves they have to prepare themselves like for prayer (namaz), doing wuzu (ritual cleaning) and the like. This is how they learn respect for the dead. (Do they have healing powers?) The successor of the Tenth Imam does heal, for example, if you cut a piece of white or yellow material and stick it to the trees and afterwards put it around your children's wrists. Such graves are marked by a green flag. But it isn't the same all over Kurdistan. A Sheikh or young person's grave, somebody who has died quite suddenly, for example, or was put to death without having committed no fault, is a victim and gets a white flag. Those who died in the war while young may have a pistol, or its imprint, or their gun belt around the grave stone. For example, if someone is killed in an accident while hunting in the mountains, hunters will visit his gravesite and fire a salute.

There was this meeting place for women and children by a river, where they prayed. Once we were there in order to do *wuzu* (ritual ablution) and there was a girl of F.'s age (her own daughter of 8) who was busy washing her hands, together with her Mother. A boy threw a stone from above the hillside, which hit her on the head so hard that her brains split open. I saw it with my own eyes. If you get convulsion with fever you can be healed at that grave spot (Because this innocent girl was buried there?) If you die young, innocent, or in an incomprehensible way, like she did just before *namaz* (prayer), white cloths are attached to that place; they call them *tabbor*, which, in this case works against fever, as an antidote.

At another gravesite, a young man who was martyred is buried. As young girls approach, they take a stone and put it underneath their clothes to function as a curtain between themselves and the boy. It is said in the Koran that a stone will become a thick curtain between them. But only if they are unmarried; it would be improper otherwise. Actually, it is out of respect that this curtain is created between the young people, out of a sense of respect.

This is why young people should refrain from visiting the cemetery, because they laugh and chat and so on. But, in order that they may recover (i.e. if sick) one can take children there and read *Fatiheh* (the opening Chapter of the Koran frequently thought to have magical powers). No, a child is only permitted to go if in need of healing or the deceased is close kin, and, in that case, together with grown-ups such as with the other women of the family or their Mother. Otherwise, *akhund* (the village priest) will forbid it.

(Is it permitted if you want to get married – to visit the grave?) Perhaps you confide in a female friend but not to anyone else. On the tomb-stone there are 40 small stones called *morad*, good wishes, which you divide in four parts three times. If it doesn't come out even, then your wish won't be fulfilled. If it does, you kiss the stones, and give some *kheiret* (alms), for example dates, to the children in the hope that your wish will come true. But it isn't sure, God only knows. You can also do it if you have lost your children, for example, or they are in prison and you want them to come back (Have you experienced that such a wish has come true?) Yes, I have met people whose wishes have come true from 'taking 40 stones' (as this ritual is called). If someone dies too young, they say that he didn't get all his wishes fulfilled in this life, which is why he can pray to God for the benefit of others – because God owes him, because of his premature death.

131

In terms of object relations' theory, as discussed in Part Two, Fairbarn (1943; 1952) stresses the partial identification of a trauma victim with the bad (internal) object. According to this kind of reasoning, the survivor manages to retain a normal and sane part of their personality by the creation of other split-off parts. The price to be paid for this is the deformation of these latter, split-off parts, which remain outside conscious control as depicted in Fatima ex. 2: "Promise me never to speak of my mother as being dead". My point here is in the need to acknowledge the existence of similar mechanisms of splitting and projection into *all-good* and *all-bad objects* as embodied in traditional collective motifs, for example the christian notions of the angelic versus devilish. Coupled with the mistrust and insecurity frequently first experienced by and, then shown by multitraumatised persons (as depicted earlier), again, one could add a reference to a more general belief that one's life is outside of one's own control (cp. the concept of *external locus of control* within psychology and the dependence on fate or *adjal* as described by N ex. 6, A ex. 3).

The problem of unjust suffering (theodicy) is given due attention in all religions, and some even take them as a starting point for the main tenet of their message. Whereas, for example, suffering from a buddhist point of view is due to a lack of proper knowledge or insight, and therefore illusory, and from a christian point of view is about justification (human free will and god's mercy), the problem is almost non-existent in islam. If, in islam, emphasis is placed on god's omnipotence, humans are mainly obliged to accept this fact. There are a number of implicit consequences that follow on from this, such as that it might be commendable to expose oneself to voluntary suffering in the cause of god (cp. the idea of shi'ite martyrdom). At the same time, though, the preoccupation with suffering can, in islam, be taken as a mark of insufficient faith, in others words, that despair can be labelled blasphemous[12]. On the other hand, the christian emphasis on the innocent suffering of Christ as something beyond the imaginable raises the further problem of innocent refugees and others who have endured even worse destinies. If priests or imams – and their respective ideologies – have nothing to add, the task is left to 'new priests' or to the mental health- or other relief workers.

I will conclude this section by quoting a letter addressed to the immigrant authorities of Norway concerning the anguish of a male client, whose traumatic background in war torn Iran had caused extensive obsessional practices of the kind that was not found among the other clients, such as ablutive showering – for hours – in ice-cold water. The letter, of which he himself gave me a copy during a consultation and the permission to publish, illustrate a similar kind of problematic situation in which extraordinary/rare circumstances are not attended to by his, in this case, religious (collective) ideology.

*WHERE EVEN DAY AND NIGHT SEEM ABNORMAL

To the responsible authorities in Norway.

The undersigned wishes to offer his thanks to the responsible authorities for the efforts and endeavours sustained by the personnel working with refugees. We are quite content with the opportunities offered and for the good relationships with locals in this town. But due to certain problems related to our religion, which have led to a number of psychological problems, we have applied for change of abode to a southern town, where day and night are normal.

There follows an explanation concerning prayer times in relationship to the movement of the sun, supplemented by references to relevant texts and the varying practices of different islamic sects. The letter is concluded in the following way:

Because of certain obligations, we are required to live in places where day and night follow a normal pattern. We never expected to be sent to a place (i.e. of the midnight sun) where such problems would arise. (My italics.)

Violation of Human Rights and the Legacy of Despair

Research into cross-cultural encounters and migration, on the one hand, and traumatology as a field of mental health studies on the other, are rapidly advancing areas of study, and are, furthermore, somewhat overlapping. Some of the findings of these areas of research are compared in the course of the present work. One especially interesting phenomenon which both touch upon, is that of the religio-political revolutionary movements found among the oppressed, who might themselves again turn into oppressors[13]. The key credo here is an emotionally charged investment in and remodelling of the past as a paradise lost (labelled nativism), or of an imagined future, *a mil-*

lennium. The ghost dance of the sioux indians, the cargo cults of the melanesians and, more recently, the rastafarianism of the Caribbean, all are well known examples of tribal communities facing an overwhelming sociocultural onslaught by western colonialism, long before human rights had become an issue on the international agenda.

However, the concept of a total, imminent and mundane transformation which will abruptly, and by way of external impact, place man in an ideal society is not the sole preserve of religious thinkers. It is also closely related to a secular tradition of utopian speculation, which has been at the heart of every revolution arising out of disordered societies. The far-reaching totalitarian movements of the twentieth century, be they nazism, soviet or chinese communism, were all built on 'millenarian' foundations. Their common utopian aim was a drastic this-worldly transformation for the benefit of groups of people who had come to perceive themselves as threatened by prolonged periods of misfortune and social discontent. With a somewhat paradoxical logic the socially organised encroachments to exterminate the jews in the name of the Third Reich preceded the founding of *the promised land* of Palestine, which literally rose from the ashes of Buchenwald and Auschwitz. Moreover, the religious fundamentalist currents could, when articulated in revolutionary or nationalistic terms, as in shi'ite Iran or sikh *Khalidistan*[14], be added as a modern extension of this phenomenon.

Both christianity and islam began as opposition movements propagating supernaturally induced dramatic change, only later to become part of the establishment. In this way, they have both figured as ideologies of both opposition and oppression. As presented by its mythology, islam originates in the pitiful situation of an illiterate and orphaned *refugee*[15] whose followers literally was to conquer, 'by the grace of God', first their enemies, and then large parts of the world as known at the time. During subsequent events, the expectations of the muslim believers has, from time to time, been turned into guidelines for building a theocratic model state, in imitation of the Medina of muhammadan times. Again, today we witness such endeavours in the form of the fundamentalist islamist resurgence which is spreading across the muslim world, especially in the Third World where islam has come to represent a powerful ally against the colonialism of the West.

When, during the reign of the iranian western-oriented modernist shah, all opposition was suppressed, this opposition moved into the mosques where it was nurtured by confrontational shi'ite doctrines[16].

However, as a result of the successful iranian revolution, the emphasis has now again moved towards the preservation of the new power structure. The emancipating and all-embracing sharia (islamic law) of the post-colonialist era has become just as useful as an instrument of repression and division as it earlier was of nationalist liberation. Moreover, the supremacy of a dominant group associated with the arab world, whether urdu-speakers in Pakistan, arabs in Algiers or persians in Iran, have been backed up by elitist cries for islamisation. Minorities that constitute a threat, like the largely sunni kurds, bahai, ahmadies or zoroastrians, are subordinated or persecuted on the basis of religious reasoning. Islam has come to be exploited by its adherents in the same way as other rationales; protection of national security, the justification for or continuation of the revolution, combating communism or the prevention of threats to public order. The rulers seem more comfortable defending themselves against human rights charges from abroad when claiming an islamic rationale for their acts. There is a significant, though naturally not exclusive, correspondence between sharia and human rights violations as elaborated in chapter eight below.

In a somewhat similar way christianity was at the outset a religion of the downtrodden, with its emphasis that "the last shall be first" through the second coming of Christ. The unintentional exportation of such ideas around the world through proselytisation and its secular counterpart, the concept of progress, has incited counter-cultural activity in its oppressed recipients. It has been said about the missionaries, who worked with black slaves in America, that they "went into a gun-powder store carrying a flaming torch". The consequence was that *the official theology concerning the slaves* came to be paralleled by an *invisible church run by the slaves* themselves, and that both sides used biblical arguments to justify their opposite concerns for the relationship between slaves and their masters[17].

The oppressive theologians gave special consideration to the story of the curse of Ham, the unfortunate son of Noah in Genesis 9, who was considered to be the progenitor of the black race. Moreover, the pauline letters were interpreted as assuming that, since human beings, irrespective of their social status as slaves, were free in the eyes of god, there was no need to abolish slavery[18]. Indeed, evidence of Paul sending a converted and escaped slave back to his master was found in Philemon 10-18.[19] And today the christian fundamentalists, for example, in Latin-America are still engaged in a one-sided defence of

135

'the (white) American way of life' as superior to the native way of life, while liberation theology operates more to the spiritual and material empowerment and benefit of poor converts[20].

Where oppressors emphasise submission to the will of an almighty god or principle, the oppressed will find other options, such as the departure of the chosen people, the israelites, from slavery in Egypt to the land of milk and honey. The israelites' flight from Egypt as told in the Old Testament has been linked to the end of the world and to the millenarian marvels of the New Jerusalem by passages in the Revelation. The reality of the believers in any faith is shaped by the topography of its mythology; Here then, the Southern States of the US was likened to 'the Egypt of the black slaves', and the North States was seen as the site of 'their Saviour' Abraham Lincoln. Moreover, these two worlds were perceived as separated by 'the river of Jordan' (in this case Ohio) from the Freedom sung about in the negro spirituals.

In islam this kind of 'exit option' or *motive of Abraham* (i.e. by way of his claim on 'the promised land of Canaan'), was to become the starting point for its very chronology. But here it lacks any association with a *particular* promised land such as we find it in the biblical tradition; it represents only an incentive to start anew somewhere else without specification. Muhammed left his home in Mekka because 'the infidels' refused to accept the veracity of his revelations, and Muhammed's subsequent emigration (*hijra*; see ch. 7, fn. 15) could in actual fact have ended anywhere it was possible to practice the word of god. Since that time, it has been obligatory for practising muslims to leave any place where they feel that their faith is endangered and they cannot resist or fight back as implied in the concept of *jihad*, holy war.

While the *hijra* of Muhammad took the form of a withdrawal to a place of safety where islam could flourish and expand (i.e. Medina, the city of the prophet), the motivating forces behind the present muslim migration to the West are more secular than religious. Like adherents to other religions, the muslims too have come to the West for the material advancement of their families, or to seek protection from political repression. However, where fundamentalist muslim regimes such as those in Iran or Sudan have expelled their own citizens, religious persecution is clearly involved[21]. Moreover, the migrants of today generally join communities whose values are not only alien to islam, but have a history of hostility, confrontation and even bitter occupation of muslim land[22].

136

These various utopian endeavours, covering diverse historical times and places, demonstrate what religion can offer in situations of oppression, but they are also evidence of the ways in which man reacts in situations where his culture (more generally) is threatened. Though slogans vary among oppressors and oppressed of different denominations, the structure of apocalyptic social behaviour, as well as the basic utopian fantasies differ far less.

The colonial hypothesis regards millenarian movements as a result of the clash of technologically unequal and otherwise dissimilar cultures. While impinging more and more upon the world beyond Europe, western imperialism has confronted and overwhelmed many different indigenous communities, a confrontation which has proved traumatic because, for many members of non-western societies, meaning and self-esteem as traditional modes of action and belief have been discredited. In a bergerian (1967) sense, just as expectations are a product of society and culture, changes in society and culture may reciprocally alter expectations. Since these movements are the syncretistic products of traumatic culture contact, attempts have followed to distinguish the old pre-colonialist world view from that of the colonial and post-colonial oppressive ideology impinging on it. The motivating force behind the 'return' to islam among black americans as representing the religion of the pre-colonial Africa was similar. This phenomenon turned the racist tide once more, while giving rise to further counter-developments in which a "blue-eyed, devilish and shameless" white race (i.e. the conquerors) is portrayed as a product of the black man's opposition against Allah. Such myths of the *Nation of Islam*, as one example of these movements, strike deep into the black psyche and may help explain the suffering inflicted upon it[23].

When the gap between what are perceived to be legitimate expectations and the means for satisfying them widens, the result is *relative deprivation*. If the gap continues to widen, and affects a sufficient number of people, social violence may erupt. Extremist movements are thus associated with marginal status groups, just as millenarian activity frequently originates in areas of intense colonial pressure. The millenarian groups in western societies are themselves made up of surplus groups[24]. At varying times and to varying degrees, religious, social or ethnic minorities have found their expectations rising in the face of decreasing resources for their fulfilment.

Large-Scale Loss and Multiple Disaster:
The Kurdish Case

So why have millenarian movements formed in these particular circumstances? Besides the general assumption of an overwhelming cultural impact, there is a more specific idea linking their emergence to disaster situations and catastrophe. While any disaster victim will experience a temporary sense of incapacity, vulnerability and confusion, some continue to manifest a stunned, withdrawn and suggestible condition for a prolonged period of time. Such people tend to operate with diminished mental efficiency, and may not be able to perceive reality correctly due to anxiety and/or the recurrent catastrophic intrusions described in chapter two. These individually based clinical observations are, however, largely restricted to *short-term, small-scale disasters* in well-defined populations that have received a rapid response from the outside. Moreover, the diagnostic categories in use, according to Summerfield (1995, 18), rests on a faulty assumption that the essence of the impact of war and atrocity is in its individual psychological effects, as we understand them in the West[25].

When disaster strikes on the level of the individual, the infrastructure remains more or less intact, but when a whole community, or even a native culture, is under threat, the institutions for coping with stress may themselves become unable to function. In this sense, then, one may compare the traumatic effects on the level of the individual-refugee with that of the communal-millenarian movement. If the problems are perceived to be beyond common experience either by the afflicted individual or on the level of the community (insufficient 'solutions' as given by collective traditions), they become more difficult to deal with and to explain. The torn fabric of interpersonal relationships renders traditional authority less effective and less meaningful. Because of this radical break between collective culture and here, the extraordinary traumatic content of the events, victims are often not able to formulate, mentally or verbally, their experiences. People who embody shared values of the community, such as religious and other leaders, or health workers and teachers, are moreover frequently themselves the very targets of attack.

By removing the familiar environment and transcending the normal range of experience, traumatic disasters remove those frames of reference by which we normally evaluate beliefs. In the absence of reliable guides from the past, suggestibility is heightened. Massive trauma does not only cause problems, but makes potential converts since the victims' experiences will have left them receptive to suggestion and in need of a substitute environment. The process involved resembles that of forced migrants, who, on top of their previous traumas, come to experience the unpredictability, disorientation and cultural bereavement resulting from exile. Compared to other empirically studied acculturating groups, they are thus found to experience greater psychological distress and dysfunction[26].

Much of the impact of a disaster comes from the suddenness with which it overpowers *unprepared* societies, institutions and individual psyches. On the other hand, preventive measures aimed at maintaining familiarity and structure in order to neutralise the effects of trauma may be taken. That is why rehabilitative efforts should ideally offer afflicted persons firm and consistent therapeutic boundaries as presented on p. 224; and even 'time-out' from what migrational pressures might be involved (p. 278). The more specific the trauma, the easier it is to deal with. The greatest damage seems to arise as a result of the inability of people to take such counteracting measures on their own behalf. Under such conditions, millenarian movements seem to be a means of explaining what has happened, as well as functioning as a promise that a seemingly insoluble problem can be dealt with, totally and favourably, in the twinkling of an eye.

As disasters multiply, it becomes increasingly difficult realistically to explain losses and to replace what has been lost. The military defeat of the kurds and the subsequent forced migration and destruction of their traditional way of life is a vivid example of such cumulative damage resulting from a series of traumas, as described below (cp. chapter 9). But disaster alone, even when multiplied manifolds, is not sufficient as an explanation of the phenomenon of millenarian movements. When analysing the disaster-prone environment surrounding millenarian phenomena, Barkun (1974, 62-5) extends his analysis to include disasters that do *not* result in millenarianism. Where, for example, mass emigration serves to empty the affected village, or the situation proves so disabling that the effort involved in simply staying alive prevents 'the dreaming of dreams', as the relative apathy of slaves and prison-camp inmates demonstrates. Moreover, where essentially the same forms of deprivation affect the expectations of successive generations, these expectations and their potential fulfilment may eventually coincide, when, in time, individuals come to expect less from life. The situation is then no longer perceived as disastrous, since it is neither sudden nor unanticipated, but eventually may become an established fact of life to which one must adapt.

The kurdish case, which has caught world-wide attention as part of the present agony of third world refugees, would be an example of this. Squeezed between the persian and ottoman empires, this area has remained a more or less neglected enclave since mediaval times[27].

Since the 1914-18 war, Kurdistan has been divided between five different states, and in all of these five states, the kurdish parts remain socially and economically peripheral and underdeveloped. "How could a small and divided people such as the Kurds rise up against several governments at once? Have not various uprisings been crushed by the joint efforts of these very governments?" asks the head of the iranian branch of the Kurdish Democratic Party (KDPI) A. Ghassemlou (1980, 133), assassinated in Vienna in 1989. Defeat following upon defeat has given rise to a legend that kurds have no friends. Their tragedy seems to be an endless list of historical misfortune, starting with the arab invasion of the seventh century and proceeding right up to the Gulf war of 1991 which, once again, solved no problems for the kurds.

During the 1914-18 war iranian Kurdistan, which is my primary area of interest, became a battlefield for the turkish and russian armies. After 1945 it saw its most notable victory in the proclamation of the Kurdish Republic of Mahabad by Ghazi Muhammad in 1946. A year later, he was publicly hanged in the very same square where he had earlier proclaimed independence. Between the wars, the iranian government used force to sedentarise the kurds with disastrous consequences, virtually exterminating whole tribes. The overall economic infrastructure was later again altered by the agrarian reforms implemented by the shah, without, however, any significant change in the traditions or mentality of the kurdish people.[28] But the efforts to modernise the country marginalised the iranian masses, who were later to use religion as an ideology of resistance during the iranian revolution.

Zarathustra, that celebrated prophet of ancient Persia, is said to have been born in the heart of Kurdistan (cp. All ex. 2). Today however, the majority of the kurds belong to the sunni muslim *shafi'i* school of law[29] which distinguishes them from their turkish *hanafi* brothers as well as from their persian shi'ite oppressors. In addition to some shi'ite kurds in the south, various syncretistic and esoteric sects sometimes referred to as ultra-shi'ites, are found among them, such as the alawis in the north-west (primarily Turkey), *ahl-i-haqq* in the south (iranian and iraqi Kurdistan), or the secretive yezidis, most of whom live in northern Iraq and the former soviet republics of Armenia, Georgia or Azerbaijan and Syria, but some also in exile in Germany to where they have fled mainly from Turkey, and even in Norway[30]. There are also, some christian and jewish kurds; most of the latter have migrated to Israel (cp. the notion of *parsitis* on p. 26).

On the whole it can be said about religion in Kurdistan that ancient non-islamic beliefs seem to flourish despite the gradual introduction of islam up until this day. The isolation of many kurdish communities and their strongly group-oriented and oral character, together with the traditionally low level of formal education, has caused the influence from outside mainstream islam. In other words, there is a conservatism in religious matters or persistence of preislamic elements, which has favoured sufi-like mysticism above legalistic islam, and even that sufism is known for a range of unorthodox ecstatic practices, such as eating glass, walking on fire or piercing the body with knives in its qadiri forms[31].

So what about millenarism in this area? Van Bruinessen's (1989) theoretical interest in peasant revolt, nationalism and messianism has led him to analyse the kurdish case. Millenaristic connotations in the islamic context are found in its various concepts of prophetic leadership, such as mahdi[32], imam (leader), *bab* (gate), *gawth* (helper), *qutb* (pole, axis), etc. Despite the fact that even today kurdish leaders such as Mela Mistefa Barzani, and to a lesser extent his rival Celal Talebani[33], draw their authority from their religious as well as tribal legitimacy, to Bruinessen's surprise, there was little evidence of millenarism among the kurds in that area. Where it did occur, it was mainly due to the sufi sheikhs whose influence has, at times, been very great indeed among the kurds. In the mid-1920s Sheykh Ahmad Barzani, a brother of the nationalist leader to whose followers Aisha's family belong, was thus declared divine (his followers directed their prayers towards him instead of towards Mekka and broke the muslim ban on eating pork) but his movement was crushed in 1931 by the british.

The overthrowing of the shah's regime in 1979 put the kurds' hopes for independence on the agenda again, only to be crushed once more. Soon after the revolution, Khomeini was making use of islamic tribunals to impugn his earlier allies, giving the *pasdaran* revolutionary guards free reign in the country. In the 1980s, Saddam Hussein's use of chemical gas against civilians and the Iran-Iraq and Gulf wars were added to these hardships, which eventually aroused world opinion. By targeting the whole population, these events left millions of kurds as trauma victims, disrupting the social, economic and cultural fabric of kurdish society[34].

On the basis of a more recent study tour to iraqi Kurdistan, Lionel Bailly & al (1992) of A.V.R.E. in Paris[35] estimated that nearly 100 per cent of the general population in this region had symptoms of PTSD, and that there were "optimistically about one million patients in a population of three". The kurdish people's history of long-suffering endurance has contributed to their collective ability to survive under conditions of severe deprivation, embodied in the traditional kurdish notion "We bend but we do not break". Given the scale and duration of such conflicts, whole generations of children might bear witness to the unravelling of society and its norms. Whereas only five per cent of the casualties in the First World War were civilians, the figure in modern times has in many instances, according to Summerfield (1993, 1-4), risen to over 90%. And this is in traditional settings where its inhabitants may not be able to imagine personal survival without the survival of their traditional way of life.

Since neither the culture nor previous experience under extreme conditions thus provides structures for formulating acts of such massive aggression, neither does it, by its very nature, allow for mediation. This is what is meant when traumatic experiences are described as being 'unspeakable' (p. 49ff.). As a result, the subject is left with experiences that are not given their proper place in the common objective realities created and recreated in the community and in its ritual traditions. The survivors are thus easily alienated by their experiences, both in respect of themselves individually and their collective culture. Man-made trauma should always be understood in terms of the relationship between the individual and society[36].

By exceeding the capabilities of a society to deal with stress, multiple catastrophes, according to Barkun (1974, 77-8), create a situation which provides fertile terrain for either of three patterns of response: millenarism, apathy/decay or defensive structuring. In the case of the apathy/decay reaction, the stress is so severe that it precludes any affirmative action, and may perhaps be paralleled by withdrawal and severe depression in individuals[37]. Due to the absence of future-oriented beliefs or charismatic leadership, it serves only to numb (cp. the PTSD symptomatology), a response which bears a resemblance to that of rejecting one's own culture as well as that of the majority, as illustrated by the concept of alienation in acculturation theory.

Studying similar types of phenomena Hirshman (1972) has analysed ideological reaction patterns in times of decline. According to him, such difficult situations can be solved either by what he calls a *voice option* – that is raising one's voice in opposition and getting into trouble – or by removing oneself from any given environment i.e. according to the *exit option*. A third alternative, namely that of loyalty to their aggressors, is the opposite of the exit option which it, so to speak, holds at bay, while at the same time activating the voice option. This latter *loyalty option* somewhat resembles Barkun's (1974, 77) defensive structuring through the establishment of mechanisms which neutralise the effects of stress. It represents a coming to terms with a threatening outside world by keeping it deliberately at arm's length, the paradigmatic case being the self-created ghetto. A group that lacks the means to confront the stress-creating factor turns inwards and carefully regulates its transactions with outsiders. Rather than cutting themselves off from society in the expectation that the stress will shortly disappear, the ghetto seeks a long term, though restricted, relationship with its surroundings. As such, it is associated more with threats to collective culture or ideology, than mere physical survival, and typical of the less educated immigrant pattern as perceived in many western urban contexts.

Analysing the individual psyche in confrontation with a totalitarian regime, the czech psychoanalyst Sebek (1992) further clarifies the defensive option. Where the option of physical flight is ruled out, the individual trapped by a powerful *enemy from within* the community either identifies with the persecuting system or protests against it to the extent of self-destruction, if not by becoming a hero of a new revolution (cp. millenarism). He further envisages the possibility of survival in a form of internal exile through the creation of a false self-structuring, a process which resembles the notion of dissociation referred to in connection with DESNOS above (p. 42).

Referring to Winnicott (1953; 1958), Sebek describes the suppression of individuality and the ensuing internal conflict between 'truth'

143

and 'falsehood' as one of the principal features of totalitarian psychology. Sustained by a high level of conformity, a false self manages to protect the survival of the real one but simultaneously provokes shame and what he describes as 'loosely defined threats in the air'. He views the post-totalitarian eastern european societies as afflicted by a crisis in which remnants of a previously shared intolerance of the freedom of truth persists alongside increased competition and fragmentation, seen for example in emergent nationalistic ideologies. And he takes this even further, pointing out that collectively experienced traumas become epitomised as *mythologised injuries to the ancestors* and passed down through the generations as part of a national identity. Unspeakable events can thus be managed through the religio-political matrix of self-objects. The mechanisms involved are, of course, not obsolete phenomena. Religiously charged symbols are still widely used to divide the world into 'good guys' and 'bad guys', such as viewing the USA – from an islamic – perspective as 'the great Satan', or communists by christian fundamentalists as representatives of the Anti-Christ.

8.
THE MILLENARIAN HERITAGE
OF THE MODERN AGE

Urban discontent and Islamic Fundamentalism

According to Barkun (1974, 166-167) millenarian activity tends to flourish in backward areas and agrarian segments of the population and almost disappears with urbanisation. If disaster strikes an agrarian population it is likely to assume collective proportions, since the imagined society and actual place of residence coincide. For those of fixed abode, the loci of personal identity and actual life coincide. Where there is a feeling that such a whole life is in the process of being lost, this is likely to be perceived as disastrous to the subject's way of life. Disturbing events are thus more clearly shared by highly homogenous communities.

On the other hand, urbanisation draws discontented people from a rural setting into a pluralistic setting, but without an accompanying identification with place of residence. Many migrants continue to internalise as their 'true' society the place they left, and thus possess it internally in an idealised, stable form[1]. It remains their area of primary identification even after they have been forced to leave, thus creating a disjunction between their locus of personal identity and the physical existence of their present life; so aptly portrayed by Nasreen when describing the sculpture-like quality of her exiled home (N ex.1: A Topsy-Turvy World), or as reflected in Aisha's dynastic coping strategy described in chapter twelve: On the Narrative Approach and Meaning-Formation.

There are, however, two categories of migrants to address here: the large majority of those who are internally displaced by socio-economic devastation and war in the Third World and remain there[2], and those relatively few who settle in the inner city areas of western towns at issue here. In the case of the kurds, the constant instability and fighting in kurdish areas has brought about a regionally external as well as internal migratory exodus[3]. The arrival in Europe of kurdish immigrants from eastern Anatolia via the urban centres in Turkey was soon followed by kurdish refugees from Iraq and in this case Iran.

Many more, however, never made it across our borders, and it seems probable that an increasing number will find their lot as *refugees in orbit* without hope of valid exile abroad or protection at home such as in the case of Shirin's family[4].

Barkun (1974) summarises by arguing that societies differ in their likelihood to disaster and their vulnerability to these events, its impact falling more heavily on rural than urban areas, and when moving from single to multiple disasters. Millenarism is an anachronistic fringe phenomenon, politically, sociologically and intellectually on the margins of modern society. Flourishing in relatively isolated, compact and yet vulnerable agrarian environments, it is, according to him, unlikely to occur in a cosmopolitan city life. There are, however, other possible manifestations to these classical, predominantly rural movements and one of these, which could perhaps be described as a manner of 'thwarting' the inexorable process of urbanisation, is ghettosation as already referred to above. Whether by force or voluntary association, individuals from similar backgrounds tend to form strictly delineated enclaves in otherwise heterogeneous cities throughout the world. It is within these ghettos that the phenomenon of urban millenarism often originates, partly because incomplete urbanisation leaves some groups more vulnerable than others; cut off in impoverished social enclaves, their misfortunes are personal as well as communal: unemployment, drugs, crime and familial dissolution[5].

The culturally distinct enclave may breed messianic dreams of its own, but, according to Barkun (1974, 176-179) only in so far as the city shelters quasi-villages within itself. It is not, therefore, surprising that the most sustained tradition of urban millenarism in the twentieth century has taken place in the black ghettoes of the USA. This phenomenon connects american black separatist movements with the millenarism of the West Indies through such leaders as Marcus Garvey (d. 1940) and Elijah Muhammad (d. 1975). Their message, which prescribes a radical surgery through the formation of a separate black nation, was rooted in the social transitions brought on by migrations from rural areas, a world wide depression and two world wars. Anger and bitterness from defeated hopes exploded in large scale urban rebellion after the assassination of the legendary leader Malcolm X in 1964.

The resurgence of inner city violence that is currently being witnessed in many parts of the world leaves a growing number of its deprived inhabitants living in a war-like atmosphere under constant pressure. Today, cities seem to be the primary places where human conflicts are expressed. Since PTSD as a disorder is connected to problems in the environment, especially social violence, it is also worth considering in relationship to the mass of people living in overcrowded and tumultuous urban surroundings. According to Costa e Silva and Lemgruber (1992, 33), it could well be that the chronic problems related to urban violence today in fact incapacitate many more people than war or natural catastrophes do.

Particularly suited for a modern mobile urban setting islamic fundamentalism starts from here. By encouraging a restricted set of common obligations such as *hajj* (pilgrimage), joint prayer or fasting, islamist muslims obtain an increased uniformity which breaks with traditional tribal loyalties because they regard islam as superior to ethnic/national attachments, and as being marketable anywhere. Thus normative islam offers a *boundary-transcending identity* especially suited to rootless migrants in that it emphasises increased individual responsibility and a universal belonging while minimising involvement in matters of local patriotic interest[6].

Despite its lack of any emphasis on sudden change, or of a *particular* promised land (see page 136) fundamentalist islamic discourse nevertheless stresses purity in teaching and practice within the confines of an ideal state. According to this way of thinking, Allah is the sole legitimate legislator, the function of parliament being to execute, not instigate laws. Khomeini fought the persian monarchy because he believed that human sovereignty, western democracy included, is opposed to the belief in the sovereignty of god in islam. Hjärpe (1980, 44) thus demonstrates how the islamists' intent to fight oppression actually meant, much to the confusion of the western viewer, opposing secular legislation[7].

When democratic decisions are at odds with the islamic law, they too represent a kind of tyranny for islamic communities because their law, the sharia, is comprehended as a normative law which, like the laws of nature, it is in the eyes of islamist believers perverse to oppose. Because the true revolution, like the new millennium, is distinguished by the total commitment of its members, competing non-islamic tendencies are banned and there is a collective, conscious, distancing from the old way of life. It is for this reason that the iranian clerics have been waging their ideological war against dissenters. According to Human Rights Watch World Report 1990, those who have suffered most in post-revolutionary Iran from such persecution have been secularly minded women, left wing militants, the predominantly sunni kurds and adherents of the bahai faith.

The recent debate on human rights has tried to find a solution to the cross-cultural difficulties involved; i.e. when they are accused of selective favouring of a western liberal tradition of freedom of speech at the expense of economic, social or cultural rights. Much of the problem is due to the fact that most african and asian countries never took part in the UN's initial formulations. This is done by pragmatically separating a minimum of universally binding common denominators in the human rights from their particularistic ideological justifications (i.e. that may vary across cultural boundaries). In order to secure real pragmatic progress, it is thought that cultural antagonism across boundaries for example by adherents of different religions, might very well exist on the latter level, i.e. of justifications[8]. One would thus overlook whether, for example, a person's right to his/her life depends on considerations rooted in a humanitarian ethos and deliberations, or, whether it is simply perceived as a commandment of a god to be collectively implemented.

The problems inherent in debates on universal human rights resemble those arising in cross-cultural psychology, which are often dependent on assumptions favouring individual choice over collective solidarity. For example, should the right to choose one's spouse freely be considered an unconditional human right in a world where the majority still prefer arranged marriages? Where should the line be drawn between individual choice and common considerations? Human rights violations as formulated under the existing international standards are thus occasionally justified by muslim oppressors by reference to the imperialistic or anti-islamic character of the latter referred to above.

Among the various distinctively islamic factors that depend on the interpretation of sharia which are of relevance here, are the treatment of apostates and what is considered 'fallen' women. In a document issued by the London based Islamic Council (1982), entitled *Universal Islamic Declaration of Human Rights* and published in accordance with the views of one of the chief ideological architects of contemporary islamic resurgence, Abul A'la Maududi's (1980), the right to life is brought to the fore as the first and foremost of human rights. Just like the other controversial rights on this list, it is, however, made *conditional upon the limits imposed by sharia (i.e. the law of god)*. For example, the saudis have objected to Article 18 of the UN Declaration of Human Rights because it is in conflict with the prohibition on a muslim to change his religion. A memorandum, *On Moslem Doctrine and Human Rights in Islam*, issued by the Ministry of Justice in Riyad (1972) justifies this refusal with:

> ... the need to curb the intrigues of the plotters who are addicted to the spread of evil in the world. Every one has his own interpretation of things, and we have our own interpretation which is supported by historical facts, and our concern of not letting any one join Islam excepting those who believe in it in a positive and decisive manner. This shows the extent of sacredness attached to the faith which Islam does not allow to be superficial and subject to the misleading actions of evil persons. (55-56).

The Islamic Ideology Council in Pakistan has taken a similar approach when underlining creed as an irrevocable stance and overlooking the fact that for most of its adherents it is a matter of descent and not choice: thus they have repeatedly proposed the death penalty for conversion. Somewhat paradoxically, this standpoint have been extended to include the imposition of prison sentences on those who, on the basis of sectarian schisms, are thought to make illegal *claims of being a muslim*. 'The Anti-Islamic Activities of Quadiani, the Lahori Group and Ahmadies Prohibition and Punishment Ordinance No 20 of 1984' applies to anyone, who:

> directly or indirectly, poses himself as a Muslim, or calls, or refers to his faith as Islam, or preaches his faith, or invites others to accept his faith, by words, either spoken or written, or by visible representations, or in any manner whatsoever which outrages the religious feelings of Muslims.

Ahmadi muslims can thus be punished by up to three years' imprisonment for a number of activities which identify them with islam. For example, they are not allowed to call their places of worship mosques, they are expected to change their ritual practices and they must forsake many elements of central importance to their faith. Certain offences, such as affronting religious feelings, are so broadly formulated that considerable discretion is left to the courts[9].

Many criminal cases have been tried on this basis, for (mis)using quotations from the Koran, the call to prayer, or using muslim forms of greeting. The number of violent attacks on sect members has also increased due to the fact that the law and order authorities have remained more or less passive to such attacks. There have even been cases of dead bodies being exhumed in order to be buried again, according to islamic custom, on new, segregated burial grounds[10]. In 1986 the Pakistani Parliament further implemented the Criminal Law Amendment Act of 1986 according to which any imputation, innuendo, or insinuation which directly or indirectly, defiles the name of the holy prophet, was punishable with death or imprisonment for life, in addition to being liable to a fine. Nevertheless norwegian authorities have not considered it necessary to give ahmadies refugee status.

Similarly, in Iran individuals are imprisoned and executed on grounds of their deviating religious beliefs according to recurring Amnesty reports. Moreover, several leading members of iranian opposition groups based abroad have been assassinated in circumstances suggesting that they may have been extra-judicially executed. The reports of my clients also reflect a widespread, and apparently well founded, fear of retaliatory harassment directed at their relatives back home (for example N ex 4: The Arrest), in addition to what takes place in the exiled milieu itself.

Fundamentalism repudiates the idea that religion should not mean what its scripture declare literally, that it should be more tolerant and less demanding[11]. Such resistance against the dilution of religious claims is naturally found in most religions, but is currently most conspicuous – apart from the muslim – in some parts of the christian (the USA), hindu (India) and jewish (Israel) world. Gellner (1992) tries to give an explanation as to why islam has shown such a resistance to secularisation. He takes as his starting point the difference between the high and low traditions of islamic learned *ulama* scholars and the common muslim people. Although the divergence between orthodox and popular islam is expressed in de facto ritual variation[12], it has not gained any official status in islam as a sectarian demarcation line such as that of sunnism and shi'ism. On the contrary, this difference has largely been ignored, the adherents of the folk variant acknowledging the authority of the scholars while continuing to indulge in their own popular practices. Especially the realities of religion among the kurds cannot be understood apart from such a demarcation line because so much of the orthodox practice have shaped it to a limited degree only as pointed out above.

At times, this latent tension has, however, caused high islam to launch an internal purification in order to reassert its influence on the whole of society, for example through the iranian revolution. This 'purified teaching' has seldom turned out to be useful in the long run for the common people, however, who tend to relapse almost as fast as they have been reformed. According to Gellner, the political developments in the Third World made possible by modern communication have changed this picture. In the process brought about as a result of modern communication, local bonds are disintegrating, and shrines are being abandoned. However, in my view (1988), migration gives precedence to normative interpretation; The islamist answer to the colonial dilemma is neither an imitation of the West nor an idealisation of indigenous popular tradition, but a return to strict observation of the successful early policy of islam as interpreted by its own ideologists. The power of sharia often derives, moreover, from its spiritual authority and its role in the socialisation process, relatively independently of the degree of official enforcement of its juridical norms. This particularly concerns muslim family law, which the western colonialists left relatively intact despite extensive judicial reforms in other areas.

For many minority groups, the recent process of islamisation in the muslim world has entailed that human rights violations, which were earlier directed against themselves on political grounds, are nowadays often motivated by the dissidents' religious or alleged criminal status. There are obvious conflicts here between the sharia and certain human rights involving gender and religion, which are therefore difficult for some muslim countries to deal with. For example, the fact that *ahl al-Kitab*, the non-muslim 'People of the Book', cannot occupy positions of official authority which give them power over muslims, or publicly promote their faith in a strictly islamic context. The iranian constitution supports the human rights only of the officially accepted minorities (christians, jews and here zoroastrians), unless they become involved in *anti-islamic conspiracies* and activities directed against the state[13]. It can be deduced from this that the same rights are not, however, extended to other minorities such as the bahai, even though this is not made explicit. Moreover, the iranian constitution does not even include any category of non-believers, be they atheists or other ideological groups than those mentioned herein, since there is an obligation to belong to one of the officially recognised religions.

From such a perspective the Universal Declaration of Human Rights is seen as representing a secular understanding of the judeo-christian tradition which, according to this argumentation, cannot accord with the system of values recognised, for example, by the Islamic Republic of Iran. This is since they are ultimately perceived as deriving from the mere relationship between men, rather than the anchorage of islamic rights in the all-inclusive tie between man and god. According to this logic, the rights of an individual are thus primary dependent on a person's relationship with god. If one refuses to submit oneself to the obligations required by god, such behaviour will entail a loss of rights put into effect by other organs, such as the *pasdaran* in Iran, the duty of whom it is to make sure that individual muslims submit to the will of god, even if by way of external sanctions. Only through submission can people share in the rights which are inherent in the *ummatic* community (muslim brotherhood).

Islam as here interpreted, guarantees equality only inwards, while outsiders, by way of their so called *dhimmi* status, may be left in a state of permanent submission and discrimination, a situation which is at odds with western thinking about the universality of human rights. In islamic thought, if human rights are not to be found within the law of god, they must be merely the work of man, and therefore redundant if not actually a sign of revolt against god's will. From this point of view, sharia has often been convenient and useful as an instrument of repressive and undemocratic third world regimes such at that of Iran, Sudan or Pakistan. As such it has, according to a muslim critic Khalid (1992, 6), a function not unlike that of nazism. In the iranian case under scrutiny here, however, it is directed against the *kafir* (unbelieving) kurdish defectors or other political opponents, the bahai, ahmadies and so on. It is important to recognise the difficulties inherent in islamic teachings which finally 'seals' the possibilities of any further prophetic developments since Muhammed was considered to have brought the final authority. This means that there is a theoretically more tolerant attitude towards 'mistaken' older religions of the preislamic era such as christianity or judaism, than what is possible to accept when it comes to successive 'prophesies' like that of the bahai or ahmadiyya.

Sharia (the Islamic Law) and Morally Corrupt Women

Subsequent to the imposition of an islamic state in Iran in 1979 a plan for enforcing islamic regulations regarding proper modes of attire was implemented. Especially women who infringed the official islamic dress code or were accused of the provocative use of cosmetics or of exposing their hair, were subjected to indecent language, fines, imprisonment, or even flogging. According to Amnesty reports, in a national crackdown on 'vice and social corruption' undertaken in June 1993, hundreds of women were thus reportedly arrested in Teheran, a number of whom were then sentenced to flogging.

I will now consider some aspects of this situation in order to illustrate the above discussion through Fatima's traumatic experiences and destiny as a 'fallen' woman. Fatima's first experience of the revolution was as a young energetic woman in one of the less prosperous quarters of Teheran. After having stressed to me that, as a rule, in the past her countrymen were known for encouraging talented people who, such as herself, could dance and sing (skills that are clearly frowned upon in an islamist context), she told me the following story:

* Fatima ex. 12 (3-4 continued/medial):

'THE ISLAMIC SISTERS'

When the new regime was introduced, my friends and I were harassed for years. I remember standing on a street corner with a friend who wore a somewhat revealing dress and nylon-socks under her *chador* (female islamic dress). The 'Islamic sisters' appeared and asked why we had bought so much fruit (i.e. they had been grocery shopping). We answered that it was no business of theirs!, after which they took us to the local *komiteh* (police station) in order to be brain washed. Later on, I protested by using make-up. These sisters carried broken razor blades in their handkerchiefs to remove the lipstick. I was taken to the station many times (she continued to rebel against the restricting gender rules) until my mother became very distressed. It was only for her sake I did not take all the consequences of my actions...

Paramilitary so called *pasdaran* forces of young men and women, 330 000 of whom, according to the Human Rights Newletter (1993, 5) were undergoing training in July 1993, patrolled the neighbourhoods in order to counter social corruption and secularisation, and to impose islamic norms. These people were responsible for such crackdowns on women, which president Rafsanjani himself has called a duty equal in importance to praying or fasting[14]. According to prevailing law in Iran, 34-74 lashes are prescribed for women appearing in public without the veil[15].

The demand for proper dress or the veil, *al-hijab*, however, implies much more than that women should cover their bodies except for the face, hands and feet when moving outside home[16]. On the history of the veil *as a protection against assault*, the saudi ulama (learned men) writes:

> Due to this innovation, they (i.e. muslim women) could be identified, and could not be assaulted by pretended mistakes by those who try to offend the dignity of women and even of men. And you see, it was a measure intended to prevent public disturbance. (*On Moslem Doctrine and Human Rights in Islam* 1972, 182).

Due to later efforts to islamise it, the veil has had a renaissance in Iran as it has elsewhere in the muslim world, especially among unmarried female students who want to use it both as a progressive political symbol, and in order challenge a tradition which prohibits their moving outside the home unaccompanied, or prohibits them from seeking education [17].

The veil, however, is not the most important sharia rule influencing the position of women, but rather the concept of *qawama* (protection, authority), which has its source in the koranic verses 4:36-38:

> Men are the managers of the affairs of women
> for that God has proffered in bounty
> one of them over another, and for that
> they have expended of their property.
> Righteous women are therefore obedient,
> guarding the secret for God's guarding.
> And those you fear may be rebellious
> admonish; banish them to their couches,
> and beat them. If they then obey you,

look not for any way against them; God is
All-high, All-great.

(Arberry 1964)

In exchange for provision and protection, men are entitled to obedience from their women, and have the right to punish them for violating this principle as described above in chapter four (Violation of Gender) in relationship to the clients of this publication. This obedience includes the supremacy of a husband's sexual wishes over his wife, with regard to frequency, timing, and to a certain extent even forms.

Apart from this general paternalistic attitude, women endure a multitude of legal and social restrictions regarding work, education, the custody of children, inheritance, and marriage practices[18]. For example, muslim women may risk further disempowerment by being forbidden – in analogy with the *people of the book* – to occupy official positions of power over men. The identity and prominence of women in an islamic context, from the wives of the Prophet to Benazir Bhutto of present day Pakistan (i.e. daughter of a late prime minister), rest on their relationship to the men in their lives (cp. chapter 14: Symbolic Shelter in a Changing World). Mainstream interpretations of koranic injunctions[19] maintain that women are not allowed to leave their home without good reason or without permission from their husbands (A ex. 4: Purdah of the Heart).

According to the views of learned men like Maulana Ashraf Ali Thanawi – who characteristically addressed his *Bahisti Zewar* (1979) as a warning to women – "the best mosque for a woman is the inner part of her house". Even if kurdish women do not, as a rule, wear a *chador,* the female dress which literally means a tent, their world still remains a 'tent' and when they are confined to this 'tent', they are not expected to associate with strangers without a protector. Probably, for these reasons it took such a long time before Fatima managed to tell me about her lower class background and drastic fall in status after the tragic death of her parents, an incident through which she was deprived of proper protection (F ex. 2: "Promise me never to speak of my mother as being dead").

The fact that when sharia was originally introduced it did in fact improve the position of women by trusting them with independent legal status is overlooked as a motive for improving their lot, especially in rural areas where such progressive rights of the sharia might

155

conflict with age-old tribal customs. In defending their cause against western accusations, however, orthodox islamic scholars emphasise this fact, that womanhood in islam can be understood only by reference to the 'barbaric' conditions prior to its advent[20]. But by any modern western standards, certain regulations of the sharia clearly propagate the inferior position of women in respect of family, inheritance and criminal law, just as a certain fundamentalist interpretation of the christian Bible still discriminates against both women and homosexuals world wide.

From a human rights point of view, the right of men to marry four wives, for example, remains problematic, despite the fact that polygamy is generally presented as a remedy for preislamic spousal abuse and degrading concubinage by its islamist proponents. Let it be further noted that although most polygamous marriages are contracted against the will of the first wife, she is, according to the sharia, permitted, at the time her marriage is contracted, to stipulate monogamy. Should her husband contract an additional marriage, the wife is according to the sharia in such a case entitled to a divorce. Despite attempts to abolish or modify the practice of polygamy, it has, however, survived even in relatively liberal countries[21]. Polygamy affected all my clients whose marital problems was complicated by the additional marriage plans that their husbands harboured.

* Aisha ex. 13 (3 continued/post-medial):

'HAVVU' ('SECOND WIFE' OR 'ENEMY')

You see, it was like this with us Kurds, that they are of the opinion that you had better not marry out of your kinship group or into another. (But there were many uncles with many sons to choose from?) Yes, but I was never interested in boys in that sense. I was only fifteen when my uncle asked my Father for my hand in marriage with his son. But then both my Father and brother were killed, so it was five years before I moved in with his family, because we were in mourning.

(Did you suspect that it was to be him?) It was unexpected that it was to be him, but I never thought much about it. So I was happy to wait – actually I didn't want to move away from my family at all, never wished to be given away in marriage. But Mother said that I had to because Father had decided. In Iran, he would have taken another wife by now, for sure. (Would it have created problems for you?) Yes,

156

it would have, for sure. You call it *havvu*, an enemy. A husband who isn't content with his wife brings a new one. It isn't so easy for the old one to cater to a new wife. And she is unable to get a divorce. If there comes a *havvu* in the house, the husband will not be as kind to the first wife anymore. (I thought that a first wife kept her first right in the house?) No, you say that if you divide this paper in two, the old wife will get the smallest part (she shows me how small it would be) while the new one gets the rest.

Actually the very word for it means "two who are enemies". As a rule, a *havvu* will be in charge and decide more. To have a *havvu* in the house is not very easy, because if a new wife arrives the old one turns into a servant. After all, the new one is the bride in the house, happy and fresh. The old wife has to accept this fact, or she will be sent back to her Father's house with her children. But when they are 5-6 years old they are taken back to their Father's place. However, in Kurdistan they won't give you a divorce even if your husband takes another wife. In our *tajfe* (tribe), there is no way you could have a divorce. Perhaps a new house for the first wife, but apart from that she has to accept it. He keeps his wife without a divorce, and she is not even allowed to socialise with other people without the husband's consent, even in her own Father's house. And she cannot remarry. In other parts of Kurdistan, among the sorani (a kurdish dialect) speaking, they might give you a divorce (cp. All ex. 6: Inconceivable Divorces).

(In our part of the world, in the old days it was the new bride who had to work hard by tending to her mother-in-law.) Yes, it is like that with us too. – There are two different ways of getting a new wife into a house. If the first wife presses for a new one herself, in order that the husband is forced to fetch one, it is like that. Then she will have much to say. In that case, the new wife will be a servant for the older one, she cannot eat without permission from the first wife. She will have the upper hand. But if it is because of a disagreement, you could say '...' (Then it is considered the fault of the first wife?) Yes. You see, for there to be two wives is very common. You just fetch a new one if the man has the need for, or desires a younger wife. It all depends on the man; if he is kind and righteous perhaps he will say to his *havvu* that the first wife is older and has to be respected and assisted. (What ways are there for a wife to get power?) Very few; few wives will have anything else than power over her children and perhaps some daughters-in-law.

(If your uncles and father all had several wives, then you are now breaking this pattern?) I think that it is very wrong of them to have sex freely in order that they do not even know how many children they have. It makes no difference whether they are young or old. When we return one day, my husband may very well take a *havvu*.

(cp. N ex. 11: "My mother's youngest daughter")

In a famous passage of the canonical collections, the Prophet directed some women to give alms "as I have seen that the majority of the dwellers of hellfire were you (women)" he continued: "You curse frequently and are ungrateful to your husbands. I have not seen anyone as deficient in intelligence and religion as you. A cautious sensible man could be led astray by some of you."[22] The Prophet traced this deficiency in women to their unfitness for prayer during menstruation, and their legal value as testimonies in the court being half that of a man.

Among the many controversial issues related to gender, we find that of "cutting women down to a half", as the critics would have it, related to the enactment of islamic penal laws. Following the rules of giving evidence, the lack of male, muslim witnesses, for example when a woman has been assaulted, may bring about either the acquittal of the culprit or a reduced punishment, creating the impression that a crime committed against women is less serious. Also, *diya*, the economic compensation paid to victims of violent crime or their relatives, is correspondingly less for women[23].

According to the underlying dogma of the saudi ulama, women are considered to be *fortunate* to be exempted from such heavy responsibilities[24]. Following this line of reasoning, god has preferred men above women because men are superior in mental ability, good counsel and powers of performance, hence the discretion in matters of divorce and giving evidence have been their prerogative and preserve. Where a husband has the unilateral right to divorce through the institution of *talaq*[25], a wife is entitled to divorce only under very restricted conditions. It should not be forgotten, however, that a woman's affiliation to her husband's kin is secondary to her affiliation to her father's-brothers, who are regarded as her nearest kin and primary protectors. Saudi scholars define the institution of marriage as mutual but unequal self-sacrifice, referring to the fact that in surrendering herself, the wife receives a dowry, whereas the husband receives no such compensation. So, by cancelling the marriage contract, a wife could seem to be prejudicial to her husband, a condition that, according to the authors[26], would declare any contract null and void.

The only reason that can guarantee divorce for women is the impotence of the newly-baked groom, in which case the marriage is never consummated, or his total disappearance. Some law schools entitle a wife to divorce because of her husband's neglect of her sexual needs[27], lack of support, gross maltreatment, or if he suffers from certain serious diseases which make marriage impossible. It was precisely this type of reasoning that provided my client with the grounds for divorce, since it gave her the badly needed, and previously denied, arguments for a divorce: the fact that her husband refused her children, and his abuse of alcohol. Fatherless, she had been married to a man who was twelve years older than her, of no relation to her, divorced and, as it turned out, extremely violent (F ex.1: The Pretraumatisation Period).

The Islamisation of Prison Life

As pointed out above a muslim who repudiates his faith may be considered guilty of a capital offence, in complete conflict with fundamental human rights regarding freedom of religion and conscience. According to the sudanese scholar an-Naim (1990, 23) apostasy may be indirectly inferred by the court from a person's views or actions deemed by it to contravene the basic tenets of islam, regardless of the accused person's conviction to the contrary[28]. A person may thus be liable to the death penalty according to the sharia for expressing islamic views held by the particular authorities to contravene their official view. Apart from the use of torture and the curtailment of civil and political freedoms on the domestic scene, iranian human rights violations include assassinating opponents abroad and executing political prisoners and drug-traffickers in the name of islam thus arousing a fear not unknown to the clients at issue. Capital punishment is, according to Amnesty reports, broadly applied by the iranian regime. Since the introduction of the Anti-Narcotics Ordinance in January 1989 which prescribed a mandatory death sentence for those caught carrying or smuggling drugs, reports from all parts of the country[29] has revealed that anti-drugs operations have been used as a ideological cover-up to justify political arrests, summary executions and other actions amounting to acts of genocide, such as burning entire villages and forced evacuation of dissident tribes in the border areas where there are large sunni minority groups.

Besides the death sentences already referred to in chapter 2 (Psychological Trauma Reconsidered), islamist regimes have been criticised for the severe corporal punishments, and especially the mutilation or dismemberment, that takes place in the name of islam. The so called islamic *hadd*-punishments, relating to fornication, alcohol consumption, theft and highway robbery now interpreted broadly to include terrorism, are considered eternally valid and ordained by god for the transgression of his boundaries[30]. Under normal conditions (but not during *the emergency-like situation* prevalent in revolutionary Iran) a heavy burden of proof is, however, attached to these punishments. This includes the required presence, during the very act of adultery (i.e. the penetrative sexual act) of no less than four trustworthy muslim male witnesses (cp. what is said of the lack of male witnesses above). Judicial abuse is further counteracted by regulations such as the stipulation of eighty lashes for *false accusations of adultery*. Differences of opinion among scholars, as well as between the various muslim sects, together with the stringent conditions for evidence, tend to minimise the utility of these laws under normal circumstances. However, reports of public floggings meted out to, among others, women who have infringed the dress code, continue to be received by Amnesty from Iran (1993).

Illegal sexuality, *zina*, is dealt with in the koranic verse 24:3, according to which extramarital relations are to be punished by a hundred lashes in public[31].

> The fornicatress and the fornicator -
> scourge each one of them a hundred stripes,
> and in the matter of God's religion
> let no tenderness for them seize you
> if you believe in God and the Last Day;
> and let a party of the believers
> witness their chastisement
>
> (Arberry 1964)

In addition, the islamic tradition (sunna), which together with the Koran forms the basis of the sharia, demands that *if they are married,* unfaithful persons should be stoned to death. In Pakistan, for example, the Offence of *Zina* Ordinance of 1979 thus holds that persons are seen to have committed *zina* if they wilfully have sexual intercourse without being validly married to each other. If the person is adult, sane and married, the punishment is stoning to death, otherwise 100 lashes, given in a public place. Perpetrators of prohibited sexual acts such as prostitution, pederasty, homosexuality, fornication or pimping, may also in Iran be punished by execution, public hanging or stoning to death. According to estimates by Amnesty International, more than a thousand women have been stoned to death since the 1979 Iranian revolution, 75 per cent of them during its first years, and this practice still continues[32].

* Fatima ex. 13 (3-5 continued/post-medial)[33]:

SECRETS OF THE PRISON

Fatima recounts that in prison there was a separate building where a cell mate of hers was taken in the early hours to be buried alive for prostitution, and that, another time, she managed to get there by bribing a prison ward to let her go to the toilet on her own. There she saw the carbonised remains of humans and their clothes, and smelled "burned people like in a crematorium", while from the roof there hung other dead bodies. While intermittently denying actually having seen people buried there (previously she had told me that she had seen, with her own eyes, a woman being buried), she eventually broke down in tears and told me that she *had*, after all, been telling the truth when she first said that she had seen it (cp. what is said about dissociation in chapter two: Psychological Trauma Reconsidered). However, her worst memory was of a young boy whose face was all blue:

> They have to dig deep in order to get a person into the ground in a standing position. They took them up again when they were dead. (What do you think he was accused of?) Of selling alcohol... (she is unable to speak and there is a long silence).

> (A world too hard to comprehend?) Who has the right to tell this regime anything. What kind of a regime is that, why do you do things like that (observe the change of perspective by way of emotional 'invasion' here), why are you not human...?

> (Did you get the feeling that those women who did things like that were cruel or brainwashed or stupid? What did you think of

them? How could they do things like that?) But how can you hit women who are pregnant... How can you have the imagination needed to put a woman who is pregnant like that in a hole in the earth (She shows me how they bury them up to their shoulders).

(They buried a woman who was pregnant? I am shocked myself and it is difficult to believe her). Yes (Except for her head?) Yes, precisely. Perhaps you do not believe me, but only listen. (We hear so many things in this house, from all parts of the world, I add somewhat defensively, but that she would die like that? It seems like a silent murder). They have to put her in the earth until she dies. (Buried alive in order that she cannot move?)[34] How can they, how...

(In that way one is slowly tortured to death?) Yes, and afterwards they become all black around the mouth and the eyes. Slowly, slowly they will die. (Did they do this in the prison where you were? I still have difficulties confronting her information.) Yes, there are different cells. (Did they kill them in their cells?) Yes. (How did you get to know about it?) Very secretly I tried to see... (You saw for yourself? I don't seem quite to be able to believe her) Yes, I wasn't able to sleep. And then I heard, very secretly and slowly, a man arriving with a lady. All at once, using electricity... Many, many women had such beautiful faces – their faces were very beautiful. At first the man likes her and has sex with her. (Rapes her before the killing?) Yes, all at once with his kalashnikov, or sometimes using electricity.

(Did you hear people scream?) It was very quiet, no noise, a small scream was heard. I could tell you endless things today, but it isn't enough to explain with my words. (Even if you were perfect in norwegian, words would not be enough to describe such appalling things).

According to traditional practice in some parts of the muslim world such as Iran, convicted adulterers are buried up to their armpits before being stoned to death by a crowd. In January 1994 a woman was condemned to death by stoning in this fashion in Teheran's Evin prison having been found guilty, according to the *Keyhan* newspaper, of killing her husband; in February another woman, alleged to have had an affair with her cousin, was stoned to death in the same prison, charged with adultery and of planning to murder her husband; in March, according to the Teherani *Resalat* newspaper, a third woman was stoned for co-operating with a prostitution ring in the city of Qom[35].

* Fatima ex. 14 (3-5 & 13 continued/medial):

ACCUSED OF LESBIANISM

There were two women with a huge punishment. They were flogged badly due to rumours about sleeping together (lesbianism), which is not allowed in Iran. They were tied up to each other at all times for everyone to see, even if I know they were innocent. All the prisoners had to watch them getting one hundred stripes in the courtyard. I pleaded to be excepted, it was so difficult for me. But this man came to force me to watch. If you didn't watch, you got the punishment yourself. The other one had heart problems. After a couple of strokes she said "Ooh"; then "Please"; she cried "Wait a moment". Afterwards they were left in isolation without medical attention for two months. I saw their bleeding skin loosen. It was in the winter, but they could not wear clothes. I visited them secretly with some medicine. They themselves warned me not to but I didn't care. It made no difference to me. A little help means so much. We became good friends.

According to the saudi ulama, the punishment for adultery was prescribed, out of necessity, to curb once and for all prevalent sexual licence and to prevent confusion regarding paternity in preislamic times. Furthermore, they stress the demanding conditions of proof required as referred to above.

Fourteen centuries have elapsed since that severe penalty was edicted, and we can strongly affirm that fourteen cases of stoning could hardly be numbered in all that time. In this way, punishment by stoning has remained what it always has been, *cruel in principle, but extremely rare in practice* (On Moslem Doctrine and Human Rights in Islam 1972, 29, my italics).

And as if disguising their disparagement of notions of western (im)morality they add:

We suppose that, if such a thing had occurred in the street of the capital of a civilised country, *where complete sexual liberty is allowed,* passers-by would have taken it upon themselves to lynch the performers, even before the case would be laid before a court. Such people would be treated like beasts, and their lives would not deserve any respect (Ibid. 27-28, my italics).

It is important to notice that, although neither the forms of torture nor its prevalence has changed significantly as a result of the revolution, the conditions of prison life were, as the case was with the rest of society, islamised, for example by way of strict gender segregation and the introduction of female torturers.

* Fatima ex. 15 (3-5/9/13-14 continued/medial):

'ONLY WOMEN'

Only women, all of them women. Men were not allowed to enter. There were women who had taken a course in order to learn to hit and had become very tough. Men are not allowed to beat women according to the Koran. If you ask why they beat women, they will deny doing it. This is true since not the men but women beat up women. So strong, so strong they were, these women. Perhaps you will not believe me, but using a wet belt they hit so hard that afterwards the skin was all black for a couple of months. You cannot stand up, only lie in bed. I asked them why they did such things. "Are you married, do you have children?" They answered: "What can I do? I have to do these things". Most had children, unmarried women were not allowed to work there.

Here she makes an exception to the sexual abuse of female inmates by intruding male guards as referred to above, which abuse, however, took place under cover of dark nights, or more commonly, like torture, outside the cells. Most importantly, the transgressions themselves were openly motivated by religious reasoning, often meted out by the ulama (the learned scholars) themselves with explicit reference to the Koran.

* Fatima ex. 16 (12-15 continued/medial):

IN THE NAME OF THE ALMIGHTY

(What about obligatory prayer in prison?) Yes. (Five times?) No, three times. (So you had to pray like a shi'ite?) Yes, those who are sunni put their hands like this (she shows). (Did they pray like that in prison?) No, no. They dared not even say they were sunni, at all. (Were you ever asked?) Yes, they ask you. (Then you are compelled to lie? Or if not, what happened?) They give severe punishments, because if there are both sunni and shi'ite adherents around they start quarrelling about Ali and Hussain and what not.

(Did they refer to the Koran?) Yes, they always did; always. After forty days, they brought the Koran to me, stating that according to its verdict, they had to do what they did; that what they did was in accordance with koranic injunctions. I asked them to show me the law, and they did, but I could not understand it as it was written in arabic. They read it in arabic, and, without any explanation. It is not possible to translate, this book is so important! I didn't understand a thing, but if they imprison me they have to use it. When I was allowed to see the female chief, she took *wuzu* (ritual ablution) and opened the Koran using a pin. It is too sacred to touch.

Afterwards, I saw a *khazi* (religious judge) who knew the Koran by heart and wore a black turban. No one can oppose his decisions. I said that I didn't understand my case. Then he said "Don't talk, kindly sit down. It says here in the Koran that you will have a severe punishment, but if you pay some money I can lessen it". I asked for the amount. "It isn't that expensive, just 100 000 *toman*". "Regrettably I don't have the money. If I end up here, it doesn't matter if it is for life. I have lost my brother, my husband, I have lost everything. Just go ahead, sentence me". "You really do talk a lot" he said. "Okay, I'll send you back to prison". He only sits there to collect money.

The function of canonical texts like the koran (mis)used here, is to constitute a common norm distinguishing between good and bad. Such canonical demarcations are found in many religions which give certain selected texts a qualitatively different status from others. Thus, a canon serves the inward conformity of the group (and a corresponding exclusion of others) by offering criteria for distinguishing orthodoxy from heresy.

Many rights given by the sharia thus follow a classification based on faith, but also gender. The theoretical idea of ascribing rights to human beings by virtue of their independent being does not exist here[36]. Instead rights are bestowed as a function of a person's relationship to god. From a human rights perspective then, this actually makes muslim males the only full citizens of an islamic state; while the position of females to a much larger extent depend on their indirect relationships to god by way of their husbands. According to Hjärpe (1980, 52), it is meaningless to criticise islamic punishments from the point of view of human rights or even out of general humanitarian principles, such references being completely irrelevant to the basic orthodox islamic ideology. I would like him to be wrong.

I do agree that the Koran is a closed body of texts, which cannot be expanded by additional texts of the same status, such as human rights declarations. But, as Thomassen (1992) suggests, canonical texts, despite consisting of a finite number of elements, also have an almost infinite number of possible interpretations and applications. Whenever a text is made the subject of exposition, the process entails both a narrowing and an enlargement of its shade of potential connotations. This means that it is nonsensical to insist on the written text alone, since it makes no sense apart from its adherents and the authority they confer on it. Just as it is important to understand the precise wording of a normative text, it is equally important to focus on those persons who, at a particular time and place in history, set these particular standards and laid down the rules for when to use the cane.

In conclusion, any criticism of the existence of koranic injunctions is readily seen as blasphemous. Criticising the correct application of the injunctions can be more effective, especially if it is done from an islamic point of view. However, the fact remains that: whether or not islam has full control of the judicial system the way it has in Iran and Saudi Arabia, is making considerable progress in certain areas such as the case is in Pakistan and the Sudan, or is on a renewed offensive like in Algeria and Somalia, it will always be difficult for muslim governments to counteract the fundamentalist resurgence for fear of being branded anti-islamic by their own citizens.

9.
THE CUMULATIVE EFFECTS OF TRAUMA

A distinction is generally made between *natural* and *man-made* disasters. To study psychological trauma is to come face to face with human vulnerability in the natural world as well as to confront the capacity for evil in human nature[1]. It is to face man-made destructiveness of such intensity that the prevailing collective traditions, which usually serve to create basic trust in the community, cannot adequately respond to such appalling detrimental experiences (cp. chapter 7: The Collective Dimensions of Trauma). As a result, these forms of suffering tend to be suppressed socioculturally as well as psychologically. Moreover, if the traumatic events are natural disasters – *acts of god* – those who bear witness sympathise readily with the victim. When they are of human design, however, those who bear witness are caught up in the conflict between the victim and perpetrator. The supernatural justification of the infringements themselves and the accompanying lack of shame on the part of the iranian offenders, however, further complicate the picture for those victims who regard themselves as believers in the same religion.

A parallel can, in this respect, be drawn with the opposition from human rights organisations against *impunidad*: when motivated by new-found peace the perpetrators are excepted from criminal prosecution. The human rights organisations fear that the victims are deprived of the possibility of rebuilding their shattered identity by crediting the immoral acts to a sick system of society[2]. This conviction is based on a belief in the therapeutic benefit of 'the method of witnessing' (see p. 20), the aim of which is to transform a private violation into an issue of public concern. Man-made trauma should always be seen in the context of the relationship that exists between the individual and his or her society. From this perspective, the phenomenon of millenarism described in the previous chapters (seven and eight), serves as a historical imprint, which transmits the impact of past catastrophies long before the involvement of modern psychiatry in this area. As a result of the latter involvement, we have come to learn about stress reactions in individual disaster victims. But at the same time, it seems to me, that we have almost lost sight of the collective dimensions of organised social violence which are pushed to an extreme when a whole community, much more 'a way of life' or 'culture', is endangered.

Forced migration represents *a complex and cumulative trauma* which is characterised right from the beginning by a state of emergency, exception and stigmatisation, followed by a range of unforeseen *additional* problems while in exile. But the traumatic experiences resulting from 'past torture' and 'present exile' experienced by these clients do not interact in any simple additive, or confrontational way; rather in an interference pattern. For example, the fragmentation of mental functioning which accompanies PTSD (chapter two: Psychological Trauma Reconsidered) not only deepens, but also complicates the confusion caused by the subsequent cross-cultural exile as envisaged above. Likewise, the loss of impulse control inherent in the psychiatric diagnosis may spill over, worsening the bitterness of ostracism and even racist harassment as experienced in exile by these clients; or the painful memories of *pasdaran* (paramilitary forces) intruding in their private lives in Iran may complicate the ensuing relationships with helping professionals in the exile (i.e. *authority incidents*) even further.

Racist harassment was regrettably evident in all the clients' lives in exile including, for example, quite unpleasant incidents during the Gulf war when they themselves came to be seen as representing the muslim enemy by the ignorant man in the street. Thus Nasreen and her children were subject to a series of assaults ranging from verbal abuse and pestering telephone calls to physical acts of aggression, and their apartment was targeted by unknown assailants. At another time, Aisha's son was hospitalised for two weeks following a gang assault which she perceived as clearly racially motivated. Such encroachments are especially tragic because in addition to the suffering involved in the very act itself, they imply that exiled refugee-victims are somehow called to account for the deeds of their very oppressors.

In a large number of cases the simple extent of the initial traumatic impact may be decisive in determining the outcome. However, where malignant influences exceed a certain limit, such factors seem to decrease in significance as envisaged by the concept of cumulative trauma put forward by Khan (1963). According to him, and supported by Lipton's (1994, 9) concept of stacking, a series of stressful and disruptive experiences (whether at home and/or in exile) may serve to trigger subsequent trauma. Predisposition to PTSD in response to trauma are influenced by the similarity of the current trauma to a past trauma and the number and severity of stressors, the more factors stacked the greater the co-morbidity. When a trauma is staged within an already existing one, the subsequent event may eventually become constantly overwhelming[3]. Unintegrated traumatic memories then demand ever more energy to retain ego functions until real life may, in the worst case scenario, become a fringe phenomena taking place around the nucleus of the trauma; Mollica (1988) uses the expression "to be trapped in the trauma story".

* ALL EX. 7: THE ACCUMULATION OF TRAUMA[4]

THE KURDISH LEGACY:	THE PAIN OF EXILE
inherited trauma	PTSD/depression/somatic pain
pre-flight oppression	racist harassment & 'authority incidents'
death/suffering of relatives	continued 'bad news' from home
destroyed home	frequent change of residence
living in hiding	marginalisation/isolation
warfare/terror	continued fear of agents of the iranian regime (unsolved murder of female acquaintance; Aisha, Nasreen)
imprisonment	husband's arrest (Aisha, Nasreen)
refugee camp	hospitalisations
torture and rape	suicide (Aisha, Fatima)
keeping 'shameful' incidents in exile secret from their own	marital/intergenerational discord/ child custody (Aisha, Nasreen)

The degree of success achieved in coping with past traumatic experience will thus influence a person's vulnerability to later events of this kind. Moreover, PTSD patients who have suffered repeated trauma may, according to Lipton (1994, 76-77) come to court danger while taking unusual risks. Trauma may be followed by resort to pathogenic development and symptom formation, or it may result in recovery. According to Weisæth (1992), psychiatrists with a clinical experience gained in a civilian context tend to be too pessimistic in their prognosis for trauma victims. He suggests that their lack of experience with previously mentally healthy persons and scant knowledge of preventive measures explain this state of affairs. Others, like Herman (1992, 20-23) draw the opposite conclusion: that, due to undervaluing the cruelty of war and their interest in returning clients to the battle field, psychiatrists with experience from the army are unduly optimistic in their evaluations. As long as their subjects continue to function on a basic level, they are assumed to have recovered, irrespective of their subsequent destinies or any follow-up treatment. Despite this overt disagreement, both sides agree on the necessity of increasing the focus on the non-pathological factors involved.

From the standpoint of cultural psychology, the issue could at least be raised as to the extent to which certain, less intensive, traumatic experiences, such as the loss of a child or some types of abuse, which were earlier regarded as more or less expected life crises, have not, in our time and part of the world, become rare cases of traumatic sickness.[5] If left without protection the very biological limitations present in the human infant represent an inevitable source of trauma in relationship to the overwhelming external conditions even under the best circumstances. It is likewise important to acknowledge that PTSD is not caused by mental illness traceable to unresolved conflicts in early life, but to extraordinary environmental stress, which, according to some estimates, affects as much as 30 per cent of the population at some time during their lifetime.[6]

Successful recovery from PTSD may also enhance the individual's ability for further mastery of traumatic events in the way of a constructive immune reaction. But as already Anna Freud (1967, 77) pointed out, when a town is rebuilt better than it was before the earthquake, it is not the earthquake, but the people, who should get the credit. With regard to the ego's attempt to deal with the effects of trauma, it could, perhaps, be said that nothing succeeds like success, but nothing might likewise fail like failure. In conclusion it can be claimed that, despite its frequent association with violations of personal integrity and basic human rights, the issue of the intrinsically pathogenic nature of trauma remains an open one.

The colonial hypothesis within the social sciences holds that there is a causal sequence at work: culture contact – social change – millenarian movement and/or mental disturbance. If tradition changes in a way which renders people abruptly and radically deprived of the direction and support offered by its norms, distress will follow regarding who they are and what will happen to them. Cross-cultural migrants frequently depart with the intent of finding security and, perhaps of gaining a better living, but certainly not in order to become buried in respectless ways on foreign soil (A ex 11: From Ghost to Second *Shahid*). While return is indefinitely postponed, few of the older generation of third world migrants will succeed, and due to growing racism, their very personal security may still be at stake. The lives of many a migrant will end in psychosocial problems, drug abuse, somatic illness and/or a disability pension, when they find themselves ending up on the 'wrong' side of the globe from the point of view of their own ideals. But others, especially among the younger one's not included in this study, will make it, while changing their very misfortunes into challenging opportunities for growth and creativity. And, moreover, their perceived success will also depend on their primary reference group: while the first generation will feel materially better off than those who stayed behind, the next ones will, to a larger extent, compare themselves to their ethnic norwegian compatriots.

Despite the fact that problems often follow from cross-cultural migration, these categories must not be unequivocally confused, since the empirical measures of collective and individual self-esteem are, according to Liebkind (1992, 5), only moderately correlated. There seem to be mounting evidence that the development of mental problems in migrant groups is not so much due to the psychological qualities inherent in the migrant themselves, but, rather, to the interaction between them and the host communities. Stress is most intense for those migrants whose original values differ radically from the new, where there are no available familiar groups to join or support them, and where the receiving country actively encourages rapid assimilation[7]. If my analysis is correct, this seems to be the case to a much greater extent than has hitherto been assumed, especially where organised social violence has preceded exile. Whatever the cause, assuming the refugee client of a forced cross-cultural migration recovers from her traumatic past, the problems of acculturation still have to be addressed.

PART TWO:

THERAPY IN A
CROSS-CULTURAL SETTING

PATTERNS OF EXCHANGE IN
CROSS-CULTURAL TRAUMA THERAPY

On the Issue of Object Relations
in Integrating Traumatic Content

I will now, again, turn to the clinical evidence from a somewhat different angle, and focus on interpersonal coping strategies. One could then ask "Did the clients 'make it' during the period we worked together? What about those whose world is so mutilated by organised social violence that there seems to be no safe place left to flee to? Can they find a way out of the chaos and recover basic safety in the face of the further problems they experience when they must face yet more problems in cross-cultural exile?"

If *integration* of the traumatic content haunting the clients – linked as it is to the internal and external worlds – can be used as an indicator of successful therapy[1], some additional factors must be considered before returning to this issue. First, it must be recognised that the therapeutic outcome as reflected in the narrative content and the accompanying emotional responses, is a collaborative composition between three persons: narrator-patient, the interpreter and the investigator-therapist. And, moreover, that the interrelationships of these three involved persons are tied up with the success of therapy through transference reactions. All of them become active constructors of reality in the process; the narrator-patient selecting and reconstructing his or her past, while reflecting about the present and projecting onto the future; the interpreter and investigator-therapist contributing to this process by way of their reaction to the issues at hand.

'Meaning' is open to negotiation. It is context-dependent in the sense that the alternative is not independence of context, but meaninglessness/nonsense. Highly explicit accounts encompass a piece of the environmental (i.e. psycho-socio-cultural, even bio-physical) *whole* as these become projected onto or invested in, that is, shared with significant others. 'Meanings' are the products of such interrelationships, a bit of foreign land taken home or claimed by feelings, as Smith (1987, 30) would have it. The catalyst that converts a mere location into an inhabited place, here a home in the new country, is the result of deep experience, an experience that allows the empty space to shed itself of its 'frozen' quality as depicted, for example, by N ex. 1 as a house that is strange like a sculpture.

* All ex. 8:

'SUCH COLD INDIFFERENCE'

To all the clients (excepting Fatima, who puts the emphasis on racism), the new 'hosts' appear indifferent and 'cold', somehow cut off from their roots in a confused search for superficial individual gain. This was a view that came to include those kinsmen who opted for 'the Norwegian way', such as Aisha's daughter (A ex. 7: Children Drowning as in an Enormous Ocean), Nasreen's 'modern' kin not included in the examples here or 'Kurds who slip on it' more generally as Aisha would describe such deviating countrymen in A ex. 22. However, in time this impression will become less extreme, a process which, I assume, is helped along by including not only the integration of past traumas but also the correcting interpersonal experience of among others the therapist functioning as some kind of 'mother-of-the-new-culture' as referred to on p. 204.

For Nasreen, this was not articulated until a return visit to iraqi Kurdistan (1993), when she unexpectedly became confused as to where she really belonged. Initially relieved and happy to retrieve the warmth of kurdish company, and proud of showing it to her children (who according to her "were very impressed by the hospitality of being invited to stay in the home of a taxi driver just like that"), she unexpectedly felt "the sting of being just a little bit Norwegian, after all". This was a feeling which, according to her, furthermore, became particularly evident upon listening to broadcasts that urged the local people not to be offended by or act upon the improper dress of refugee children visiting from Scandinavia (there was at the time a co-ordinated group of visitors from that area), while explaining their 'shameful' dressing away by their changed fair complexion which, the argument went, was supposed to be the result of their south-north migration, and had made them dependent on light clothing in order to let the sun's rays through.

It is a therapy-specific privilege to gain access to the intimacies of people's lives in a way which is not without reservation given to the anthropological fieldworker. This implies, however, increased ethical risks, particularly regarding clients whose pain has been inflicted by the deliberate actions of others[2]. As pointed out above, organised social violence may involve the creation of perverse relationships stripped of any moral standards, while a forced cross-cultural exile may complicate the situation further.

Ethics are rooted in the inter-subjectivity of the familial, including the primary objects, and by extension cultural context, a claim that naturally holds true regardless of on which side of the subject-object relationship one is positioned. In this sense, the politics and poetics of the representation of *the other*, whether this happens in a clinical or extra-clinical context, can never rise above, but remains in various ways bound to the surrounding context and the tension between powerful systems of meaning. As an experimental and ethical pursuit, this is, according to Clifford (1986, 10-23), part and parcel of the simultaneous invention of *the others* while at the same time attempting to represent their views. Within the scientific community, there is a growing awareness of the fact that researchers can no longer speak with automatic authority for those who are defined as unable to speak for themselves.

World views do not hold still for their portraits to be painted, and attempts to make them do so necessarily involve a selective focus. In addition to this, there is inevitably the imposition of some form of power relationship between the researcher and his research objects. In order to gain correct information, both fieldworker and therapist must systematically empathise with the experiences and ways of thinking of people who may be very different to themselves. Neither will gain from too much closeness with their informants, but will have to alternate between the inside *emic* and outside *etic* perspective. Just as psychologists can learn from the cultural sensitivity of the anthropologist, the anthropologist would benefit from the psychologist's therapeutic insight into the reciprocal impact between the professional and the client as *objects of expectations* or *attribution* in each other's eyes.

Within the field of anthropology, the postmodernist influence has made itself felt to the extent that the predominant method of the former has come under revision.[3] In the context of the fieldworker's 'craft', one now asks for 'the one who speaks', 'for whom', 'when' and 'where'. The observer himself has become elevated to centre stage, while a more complicated view of *the other* is simultaneously emerging. This *other* is now perceived as some sort of stage on which a performance is repeated to be seen; i.e. from the standpoint of a privileged participant, as Clifford (1986, 12) would have it. The researcher's personal experience, or voice – especially experience of participation and empathy which were earlier hidden away in field notes – is now becoming recognised as being central to the research process itself. Investigators have increasingly begun to write about their field encounters from a self-reflective point of view, including previously irrelevant facts such as their own confusion, strong emotions, nonprofessional transactions and failures as regards informants.

In turn sophisticated or naive, confessional or analytic, such author's accounts provide a platform from which to raise a wide range of interdisciplinary issues concerning the subject-object balance. While participating in the lives of their informants, anthropologists in the field necessarily become part of their 'field' to a greater extent than is required within the confines of psychotherapy. This is since the very frameworks of psychotherapy is meant to exclude or process such influences by the creation of an alternative fictitious stage, that is, through projection (pp. 185 & 196). A major consequence of this crisis of anthropological enquiry has, therefore, been a dislocation of the ground from which the experts can securely represent others. Many voices are clamouring to express their own renditions of tradition in an overall effort to rewrite history from the standpoint of the oppressed. Dialogism and polyphony have increasingly become recognised within the scientific community to the corresponding exclusion of monophonic authority.

Where anthropologists once viewed clearly defined *others* in a way reminiscent of psychiatric nosologies, they must now face these *others* also in relation to themselves. As yet they must do so without the relevant tools for interpreting this encounter – tools which were, however, incorporated long ago into the psychodynamic perspective as a primary working tool. It should by now be clear to both sides that any version of another is somehow related to the construction of a self, but how? One answer to such an interdisciplinary challenge might be found in object relations theory that gives us a glimpse behind the scene. This notion represents a shift in theoretical perspective which, again, is paralleled by a similar shift of emphasis within the psychoanalytical movement: that is from within the confines of viewing *the others* as somehow closed or pent-up intrapsychic entities towards an interactionist perspective. In classical analysis, all explanation of the patient's behaviour was derived from the psychological make up of his or her drives. Theoreticians like Hartmann later enlarged upon this view by focusing on the interdependence of the ego with, and emphatic failures in, the surrounding social milieu. In Fairbairn's (1952, 154) words, the emphasis thus moved towards a libido which is not primarily pleasure-seeking but which has as its basic aim 'the good object'. This was followed by a parallel shift in theoretical focus from the *content of intrapsychic conflicts* towards including the type of *defence mechanisms used in interpersonal interaction*. The change of focus itself was enhanced by an increased interest in pregenital developmental pathology, the treatment of which confronts therapists with deviations from the classical transference reactions and therapeutic technique[4].

What happens in psychodynamically oriented therapy is that, by means of separating the exterior real world from the confines of the therapeutic involvement, unintegrated fragments of the past become re-enacted on the level of object relations as a reflection of an internal 'map for orientation' of the patient. The patient will then try to confirm this scenery emotionally as well as behaviourally in the form of a transference reaction. According to clinical experience, the victims of social violence come to 'know' their past traumas by way of intruding fragments of unintegrated memory[5] or by reliving trauma in transference reactions. Either form of memory entails the grafting of bits and pieces of past traumas onto current situations which are coloured by them and may complicate the problems of exile. There are, of course, degrees of meshing the past with present, but the extent of fragmentation reflected in the ensuing transference reaction, is *one* measure of the parallel distortion of present experience.

Intimacy and Mistrust as Treatment Parameters in a Cross-cultural Setting

Having basic trust in others constitutes a theoretical premise, which is of primary importance in western psychological understanding.[6] The constitution of inter-subjective space is thought to provide the ego with a basic sense of belonging or trust. From birth on every human being experiences the existence of another absolutely necessary (m)other offering primary concern; his or hers first emotional 'container'. This is followed later in life by a variety of more or less conscious ways of encoding this biologically rooted fact cross-culturally[7]. For example, Hundeide (pers.com.; 1989) draws attention to the emphasis placed on verbal rather than physical contact in breeding patterns in modern westernised society compared with those in traditional agricultural contexts.

Regardless of cross-cultural differences, this experience of being 'held' by others and in time becoming able to 'hold' and protect the helplessness or vulnerability of others, is, from a psychodynamic point of view, considered the basis of ethical development. It implies the assumption of responsibility for maintaining an object's 'continuing being' until he or she may, independently, assume and give meaning to human interdependency; i.e. a process which is referred to as a basic universal identificatory project[8]. From this idea of a child carrying a primary object relation there follows, by extension, another according to which the subject always expects *others-as-environment* to fulfil its needs like a protective parent[9]. This is a link that establishes continuous dependence and sensitivity in relation to the acceptance or rejection of an external other (cp. the notion of sociocentric self). There is, according to this psychodynamic relational view, an absolute human need for projection or anchorage in *any* psychosocial environment, notwithstanding however inadequate, for example, violent, that may be.

The relationship of the self to its context is thus marked by 'depositing' in privileged others; others who are considered capable of contributing meaning. No one can ever become completely self-contained but must remain dependent on specific external others and the larger sociocultural field. The point is that basic trust, by its very nature, presupposes something given, something which constitutes the essence of the moral claims people make on each other. It works like a silent but absolute claim for living up to the expectation contained therein. It is only when we have reason to believe otherwise that this common affective bond is challenged or may break down through outside circumstances[10].

Analysis of trauma in the light of feelings of belonging necessarily implies analysis of how social interaction is established as well as detecting the indicators of its disturbance. By breaking this basic trust between humans, trauma disrupts close bonds, precipitates mutual blame or mistrust and creates barriers to intimacy.[11] Every subject has a certain amount of choice regarding in which way to belong, but it is impossible not to do so at all. However, in situations of organised social violence, one is frequently deprived of this possibility of choice (cp. All ex. 3: Impossible Choices). The following regression to ambiguity corresponds to the fear of breakdown or dread of resourceless dependence as depicted in chapter two: Psychological Trauma Reconsidered.

According to Varvin (1998, 65) trauma puts the subject in a position in which he will re-experience not only the helplessness he felt as a child but also the strength and caring received. Hence, according to the clinical rationale, recovery from a traumatic experience is dependent on gaining access to the same level of internalised object relationship at which the damage manifested itself; ideally to provide victims with a new beginning. However, this is complicated by the fact that the psychologically detrimental mechanisms involved in trauma have a distinctly cultural flavour. This is because there are certain passive expectations of the primary nursing object within the register of one's culture which affect the development of the personality, including its bad and good objects.

Writing on Iran Beeman (1976; 1986) introduces two types of communicative systems, one aimed at unequivocal direct communication in everyday dealings, and a second with the opposite aim of multiple interpretation and indirect communication. To western observers directed by their culture and training to think in unambiguous one dimensional terms while arriving at single sets of interpretative criteria, the multiple criteria involved in the latter form of communication may leave an impression of uncertainty and even mistrust in social relations. These fluctuations are, however, predictable results of the variable conditions present. On different occasions, one may be told many different versions of the same story to demonstrate flexibility in dealing with situational demands. Moreover, an emphasis on esoteric ideas of multiple hidden meanings is a feature of the shi'ite principle of *taqia* (dissimulation). *Taqiya* refers to the lawful safe-guarding or protecting of oneself, family or property by way of concealing one's allegiance to the shi'ite religious minority in dangerous situations[12].

Only an outsider would, according to this type of logic, press for a single truth where insiders know there are many more than one, reasoning from the need *to protect external appearances*. Again, we run into a difficult psychocultural issue that might influence diagnostic efforts to evaluate the trauma story purely from the point of view of its fragmentation depicted in chapter two (Psychological Trauma Reconsidered) since there may be other, culturally sanctioned reasons for presenting an incomplete story. This difficulty is due to the fact that the basis for assessing the information contained in a refugee's testimony is highly variable, depending as it does, besides on traumatic avoidance, splitting mechanisms and/or mental repression as depicted by PTSD, moreover, on the relationship between those conversing and their respective views regarding the aims of the particular – here cross-cultural – conversation.

In the specific iranian context, this uncertainty in interacting is reciprocated by the exercising of *zerængi* (cleverness); a communicative operation thwarting any direct interpretation of intent or deliberately leading others astray, while being able oneself to interpret the actions of others successfully[13]. A person exercising *zerængi* may try to create a tendency on the part of others to interpret communication in a particular way, for example by ingratiating himself to another in order to increase the possibility of a request being received favourably or "save face *in a reasonable sort of way*", as my interpreter would explain, adding, moreover, "by reacting at the proper time and in a proper manner. It is very difficult to explain, very Iranian".

The Silence-of-Shame versus the Catharsis-of-*Talking-Therapy*

It would, therefore, be a mistake to interpret *zerængi* as being restricted to situations of pure self-interest. It is not only a matter of furthering self-interest but can arise from altruistic motives, such as the prevalent desire to *protect others* from embarrassment and pain by breaking bad news in stages[14].

* Layla ex. 3 (medial):

LAYLA'S SECRETS

Tragic news must be told slowly, little by little – that is the best way rather than having it thrown in your face as here seems to be the case. In eleven months, I have not even visited my brother. Sometimes I phone him and he visits us. He asks me why he is to come if I only sit there staring. I cannot expose him to the knowledge that I am deeply unhappy. Because he would become sad. I simply say that I'm sad because of the family at home. I do not want him to know that I'm ill or have problems. I answer him that everything is okay with me – just perfect. He must not know because, if he did know it would disturb his own life. He will have sympathy with me and become sad himself too.

(Is it in order to protect him?) People who are more vulnerable have to be protected. For example, our son who had obtained a scholar-ship have to move because I am always so irritable and angry. I can-not stand anything. (Is it your little brother?) Yes, *this is why I have emotional responsibility for him.* I do not wish to expose him to more because of me. If we had been in Iran we would never have got these problems, but if we had, there was the possibility of turning to the elders in the family and talking, somehow emptying ourselves. But now there is no possibility because they are not here. If they phone and ask how things are we will lie to them, tell them that everything is splendid. For example, when somebody set fires to our house it came out somehow. Even the family at home got to know about it – I won-der whether it was an enemy of ours who told them... So the phone rang and they were crying in the other end asking to be informed, but we said only that the tragedy had struck another with the same name, that it had been all a mistake. Perhaps they have realised that we have lied to them but we cannot expose them to such things when they are so far away.

This strategy whereby detrimental actions or bad news are revealed in stages, and as a consequence of which one comes to expect them to be broken to oneself in the same way, has its shortcomings in exile. When lacking complete contextual information there is a tendency among refugees and their relatives to follow the expected stages of message presentation to their worst outcome. A creeping fear frequently befalls clients who, out of lack of personal face to face contact, cannot trust information coming from home. This was deeply imbedded in the reasoning of all the clients in their strive to maintaining the thera-peutic relationship, and also depicted in their frequent PTSD-linked nightmares about the fate of their relatives.

ONE YEAR AFTER HER MOTHER'S DEATH

(And your mother's death?) I had a sort of preparation – I only wished to be able to talk to and be together with her once more before she was to die. I don't know, no one has told me, no one phoned. But death came and her life ended, there is nothing to do about that. Everybody dies and life ends for different reasons; one dies of illness, another of burdens and sad things. But when *adjal* (destiny) arrives, life has come to an end for that person. Everyone has to accept that.

There are many colours of sorrow, though. I never saw my Mother again before her death, I have lost my son, he was so young. Mother gave me a great deal of hope in the world, and now it's gone, God has to give me endurance (I get the feeling that she now comforts herself in the way I would have customary been expected to respond to her agony, but find myself probing into the question of who disclosed the bad news to her, cp. A ex. 16: A Sociocentric Transference? How did you get to know?) I don't know how long ago it was that we were at a *Fatiheh* ceremony. A brother of an acquaintance had a stroke and there were many families present. "I myself have a period of mourning," he said, "My brother was about 40 years old. I lost him a month ago. And you have lost your Mother a year ago". It was so sinister. Once in a while I forget that she is dead, but then I say to myself "Yes – No, it is like that – She really is dead".

(Would you have liked me to tell you? After consulting her husband's therapist and other staff we had decided not to, despite her husband's request that the therapists should disclose the bad news, cp. A ex. 16: A Sociocentric Transference?) I do not know, my mind is so confused. I cannot mourn my Mother as I should do. It wouldn't be good for the children, they are not strong. It lasted a couple of weeks. An Iranian lady returning from a visit home brought a letter with the news of my Mother's death and a cassette. It was for Aisha. She (her mother) asked for me, all her children except for Aisha were there. On the tape she (her mother) says "She (Aisha) must not mourn because she is a foreigner in an alien country". She had to forgive me (for being absent) because, actually she has the right to be treated as a Mother, I am in debt to her (cp. A ex. 11 on her son's debt to herself as a mother in a similar situation in which the approaching death is to separate them). "Aisha must not use black clothes or mourn or mourn, not cry because she is on foreign soil. For the sake of her children, she must not remain alone and cry there" she said. The last days she lived she had said some words for me...

Until her last days she didn't lose her speech, kept her reason, and said "Now you have to take care of each other, but you must take care of Aisha and her children". My brother's wife, who had lost her husband many years ago, wrote a letter with the help of her son comforting me "You must not think that you have lost your Mother. I will take her place, this is what you should feel", she writes in her letter[15].

(She was full of wisdom, your Mother?) Yes, very wise. Despite all the troubles she had, she was a wise woman, she had such an open mind. She never attended any school or read anything, but she knew as much as many professors did. She knew so many things. Both men and women approached her asking for advice, even if they were older than she was. Because I'm so very fond of my Mother, I thought that after her death, life would be very difficult for me to continue. When somebody joked about this, for example, when I got home (i.e. in Iran) and she was not there, not in her place, then I would ask my sister-in-law "Where is my Mother?" and she would say "Don't you know, she became ill some hours ago. We drove her away, she is dead". That is how they would fool around with me. Then I tore out my hair and cried because I thought that after her death I would not be able to go on living anymore. This will drive me mad.

(There follows on the tape) It is her (mother's) wish that "She (Aisha) mustn't cry, because that wouldn't help the dead person. If she comes here and visits the graveyard Aisha can see for herself that other loved ones lie there. God gives endurance and strength to them..." (Who told you?) My brother's wife told my husband on the telephone, but he only said that Aisha is ill, now that she has lost her son (didn't tell me). I dreamt about Mother, and told my husband (cp. N ex. 9: About the Importance of Dreams). He said "My Mother is also dead, yours is old. Perhaps she will die". I will definitely go to Iran, I said. "But how can you do that?" he asked.

(Were you angry when they didn't tell you?) Yes, because after a week their sorrow is old, but for me it is new. "Why didn't you tell me?" I asked him. "When Mother died and they phoned to say that, you (i.e. Aisha) were ill, my heart beat for thinking of you" (he answered). I don't know, perhaps he was afraid of what could happen to me, for this is what they do, they hide it from someone who has lost a loved one, they are afraid that something will happen to that person. But until now, it hasn't happened for anyone (observe that her own father died from such a shock, A ex. 19: What It is All About). The person who hides it is afraid that it may hurt.

There were two brothers who lost their parents. One knows but he says "Little brother must not know because he will mourn so much". We say it is best that you tell him. (Would it have been better if I had told you or not?) On the one hand it is good... When Mother died, they should have phoned from Iran. She was ill. I met the Iranian lady at the airport and she said "I have seen your Mother. She has a room to herself, and your sister-in-law takes care of her". That was how it was before she died. I asked "Has she (Mother) talked about me?" She said "Very much. She talked about Aisha". Because she (Mother) had lost her sight, she had said that she could smell me from that lady who was visiting her all the way from Norway. "If I only could see Mother once more," I said, and the lady got tears in her eyes. "Insh'allah..." she said.

(Were you suspicious in any way?) No, I couldn't imagine that Mother was dead. I wouldn't have accepted her death anyway. Because this lady told me that "The wife of one of your brothers has died". I thought about the children who are alone, without anyone to take care of them. I cried so much, didn't think about the rest, because they with such certainty said that she was not dead... On the one hand, however grown up as you are, when you lose your Mother, you need your Mother. There was a time when I wished no one could call me Mother. I cried so heavily for Mother, I missed her so awfully, and wished to be small again and to long for my Mother. You see, one becomes so small in that sense. On the one hand, everything was going very well, I knew I had been a good daughter for Mother. Actually it was I who should have asked forgiveness, but I never had any need to do that. I had a very good conscience. I can relax completely, because of that. I cannot say that even once I would not have listened to her. I have been obedient all along my life, done as they (her parents) told me to, even if that would have meant throwing myself on the fire, I would have done it. Mother puts it like this "I am completely satisfied with you. If God is as content with you as I am you will have a good life". I do have a good conscience, but I'm still sad.

(It was at a *Fatiheh*?) Two or three days had passed since the death in that family. (What is a *Fatiheh* about?) You sit down together, they try to give hope and say comforting words to those who have lost a near one, the 'owner' of the dead. They start like this "God must give you endurance." We sat there for about half an hour, and then that man says to me "Aisha we have to accept that such things can happen to us in a foreign country. It happened to me, my brother was young and died". Then something happened to my heart, it told me that something had happened to Mother. And when he said, "God is with your Mother" I broke down in tears. When my daughter came she asked "Why is mother crying so much now?" and they told her, and then she put her arm around me and we cried together. We stayed there for an hour. Everyone accompanied us home and stayed with us for two weeks.

(Do they choose someone special to disclose such news?) I don't know, but if a person is far away, it may happen that a child realises that something has happened without really understanding, and wants to break the news quickly. Then they'll stop the child because not just anybody can break the news. These things are very sinister (cp. ch. 10, footnote 17). It should be one of your nearest kin, one of your own, a person of experience. The head of the family or an older person should tell it, should start rebuilding the case somehow, sneak it in slowly, say it in such a way that no mental harm is done for the other (cp. what is said about *zerængi* above). Death is like that for everyone...

(Was it a good thing that they waited before telling you then?) Yes, but I had realised it anyhow. Perhaps it was something that just popped out of someone's mouth. After all, everybody in Norway knew that my Mother was dead. Only I didn't. It is said that those who are the 'owners' of the dead person are blind. They see things, but cannot see the point... (What was it like to hear about it?) It was as if I had got a shock, I didn't know what to do, I wasn't able to cry as I would have at home. It happened among strangers. (What should I have done, I did not know how to do it myself, it was a difficult situation when your husband came to tell me. I thought that if... I clearly have problems with this point, and the client is now comforting me). No, because as I told you, those who told you had said "You must not tell her". Everybody I know knew it. When they talked about their Mothers whom they had spoken to, I said "In eleven years I have spoken with my Mother only once (subsequent to which occasion she brought food to the session cp. All-ex. 11: Artefacts of Exchange), but now she is old and I don't want to worry her. But in actual fact only two months after I had talked to her, she died..."

(I explain to her that we are not allowed to keep such secrets from our clients, and ask her whether I did something wrong by keeping it secret.) No, I wouldn't have liked to hear it from anyone outside. One of your nearest kin should say "*Our* Mother is dead". But every time they thought of saying it, my husband told them not to "because she is sad". Each time I dreamt about my Mother during the last year I would wake up. I could dream that I had my arms around her and we cried or laughed together and talked. When I told my husband he didn't want to talk about it, always said "You just dream and dream". (Was it his responsibility to tell you?) Someone close, my older sister, brother, one who belongs to the family, who carries the same sorrow and pain could have told me how it happened, what happened. But of course it is the will of God...

(Could we have told you? I repeat) I would not have wished to be told anywhere else than at home. It isn't the responsibility of anyone special. No, I don't know. They themselves had had so many worries and thought that "She is filled with sorrow, has been ill, lost a child". They thought like that, but I myself would have wished to hear it from the mouth of my brother or sister. It would have been much easier if I could have been at home in my own place. Here, I was among strangers, couldn't cry as I wished to, and behave as I wished to. But if we had been at home, perhaps there would have been a way out. (How would you have preferred it to be?) They could have phoned or come here. Because, when I left home, I had arranged for the children to be happy. I said "You can eat something good and play, watch a film. I am going on a visit but will be back."

(My son) asked "Where?" and I replied "To someone who is dead that we have to visit" at that he said, "Why do you only visit when someone dies. Why never for a party". But I arranged it so that they should be happy when I was away. But it turned out differently, and (my daughter) had to return home beforehand in secret and switch off the TV. When I arrived at home the kids were very sad, they sat separately in silence, looking at me as if to say, "What happens now?" If they had phoned me at home to give me the news it would all have been much better. I could just have cried. I didn't know what to say or do in the house of a stranger. (Something turned out wrong anyway?) Yes, because it would have been better if I could have cried.

(Perhaps your experience could be of benefit to someone else?) There is a lady who lost her Father and brother in a car accident. Her husband knew. When we mourned my son, he asked "If it is all right for you, could you not tell her the bad news?". I said "It isn't good news, after all she has a Mother who could phone her and comfort her, give her some good words, give her strength." I said to tell her that "Some people get sick, some end up in prison and are tortured and die". I could not mix up her sorrow with that of my own. This thing was left lying until last year when she visited Iraq. She had a suspicion that something had happened to her brother, but she never had suspected anything about the death of her Father. When she asked her Mother "Where is Father?", she said that he was gone to Iran but would be back in some days. This lady tells me that she relaxed for a couple of days at home, before all her siblings gathered around her and told her "Your Father died seven months ago". She said that she thought she would go mad from the news, thought she would never make it. But because there were so many kin around her, many who could hold their arms around her, in a couple of days, she told me, it was all over. Because she had a network (the word used by the interpreter) around her and was in her own house when she heard of it.

(How do you yourself feel right now?) I have pain in my chest. (Were you able to be like a child for a while?) Yes I was, but I was still sad. The children took care of the housework, but because of them – this was after the death of (my husband's) Mother and he was very sad too, and after my son died – I didn't want to show them how sad I was, because of the children. Only a couple of days later I said they could turn on the TV. They said "No, because you are sad, because your Mother died", but I said "It doesn't help you whether you are happy or sad, Mother won't come back again".

(cp. A ex. 11: From Ghost to Second *Shahid*, and her previous more complicated mourning)

Hans Sande (1993) has described the double bind nature of death messages during the palestinian *intifadae*. Such bad news is broken in stages and never by one person alone, as it is not considered to be a private matter. The full truth might not be known until the funeral gathering which confronts the bereaved with ambivalent feelings: of sorrow and abandonment on the one hand, combined with expectations of a willingness to sacrifice by the dead person as advocated in the intoxicating rituals in which martyrdom is glorified. A popular iranian screenplay (*Gav*) of the 1970s, based on a novel by Gholam Hossein Saedi, tells the complex story about a man who has been driven mad because of a missing cow, and after well-intentioned neighbours had protected him from the truth about its death[16].

Internalised explanatory models distinguish the individual as a closed 'ego-strong' system with highly private feelings, in contrast to externalising *open* systems which define the personality more in relationship to surrounding forces. In the latter case, socially sensitive people are formed, people who tend to be highly conscious of their obligations towards the community and, when necessary, are expected to defend its honour even by means of violence. It follows from this sociocentric nature of the personality structure that collective interaction and elaborate precautions also mark behaviour connected with illness; i.e. in order to minimise the vulnerability of the weaker party. Polite manners are given high priority as a necessary result of the individual's assumed vulnerability to her surroundings as further presented below. Ideally, one is expected to adapt towards others to the extent of forgery, exhibit hospitality and respectful distance. Thus, according to Nasreen, a host will be prevented from disclosing bad news to guests, even relatives, while the latter are expected to bear responsibility of reducing the malignant consequences by way of their cautious management of the issue.[17]

* Nasreen ex. 8 (medial):

WHEN YOU ARE PREVENTED FROM DISCLOSING YOUR PAIN

Nasreen was prevented from telling the daughter of her eldest sister[18], visiting from abroad, of the racist harassment which had recently befallen her close family.

> You just have to smile in order that the guests will not become sad. (How is that?) It's difficult to explain, but people can become very sad just because of me. Giving them bad news is simply out of the question – it could give them heart trouble. Only the good things must be said. This concerns the host; a guest is free to disclose bad things. (Did your guest tell you anything sad?) Yes. (What was that?). My aunt and other close relatives are dead. I cried so much. All this illness and warring. My eldest brother has got heart trouble and is out of work. If I tried to contact them, those who tap telephones may intervene saying that they should bring their escaped daughter back.[19] I'm afraid that I might cause problems for them. Our house was levelled to the ground during the war and many kin died. All the memories come back; there is no hope of seeing the family again.

(Cp. N ex. 2: "Like parting with my sister")

This code of silence as regards certain particularly difficult or shameful and, what is more, *contagious* personal problems, comes to affect confidentiality between the superior (usually older) and inferior (usually younger) person, and also between insiders and outsiders as further elaborated below; especially where infringements on the weaker gender or small children are an issue. Added to the unspeakable facets of trauma, this is relatively problematic psychocultural ground from the point of view of a belief in the cathartic effects of talking it all through, in what the legendary patient Anna O. labelled a 'talking cure' or 'chimney sweeping'[20]. From the time Anna O. taught Joseph Breuer the importance of listening to stories of illness as a method of healing, the active work in therapy has rested more with the patient. In the psychodynamic movement, this kind of development has subsequently progressed beyond that which is currently practised in anthropology[21]; i.e. up to the point where there is an intermittent shifting between considering the transference reactions which emerge in the patient and countertransference reactions of the therapist.

In sum, we are faced with a cross-cultural dilemma, unsettling for those who believe in direct dealings as a sign, if not proof, of friendship and trust. This may explain why it has often taken such a long time for a working alliance to develop with this group of clients. Knudsen (1990, 132; also 1993 & 1997) views this undercommunication of personal problems among refugees as a type of coping mechanism. According to him, they find silence to be a far better strategy than talking when they are in an exile situation which is beyond their own control[22]. Irrespective of the possible limits of verbal therapies, the patient confronting the neutral therapist's role may however, in a cross-cultural context, reinforce such a confusing state of affairs.

THE AESTHETICS OF CROSS-CULTURAL
THERAPEUTIC INTERACTION

Challenging the Neutrality of the Therapist's role

In order to gain a better understanding of the dialectical interaction of inner and outer life worlds surrounding cross-cultural therapies, I will now compare certain cultural concepts prevalent in the iranian context with some of the emerging (western-style) therapeutic working alliances and, by extension, the transference reactions of these therapies. Killingmo's (1984) exposition of the principles of dynamic psychotherapy will be used as a benchmark for clarifying the process involved. In a paper on the relationship between theory and technique in psychodynamic therapy, he draws some important demarcation lines, while at the same time criticising the widespread eclecticism in therapeutic interventions "for confusing the principles of validation". This is because, in his view, such a situation invites dubious practice without the necessary measures of control embedded in an articulated theory.

Although the structure and content of therapy may vary, enabling the patient to re-connect with the good objects of the past is considered to be the most important feature of psychodynamic therapy with those who have survived torture or other forms of organised social violence[1]. Because perverted forms of interpersonal relationships have explicitly caused their symptoms, recovery suggests some form of correcting affiliation. In this sense, according to psychotherapeutic thinking, there has to be a similarity between the pathology formation and the curative process. What is more, real life is not thought to possess, in itself, the power to erase such horrendous imprints of the past, which insidiously spill over into and contaminate the present. The undoing of such malignant experiences within the confines of psychodynamic therapy therefore presupposes the role of a neutral therapist who refuses to be exposed in order to remain 'a blank screen' for the reconstruction of the misrepresentations of the past. The patient will come to regard the therapist as some significant figure in their past, and transfer onto the therapist feelings and reactions, which undoubtedly applied to that particular prototype.

I will not touch upon the many definitions of and debate on the concept of transference itself here, but will proceed to treat it mainly from the point of view of the triad of 'the client', 'the interpreter' and 'the therapist'; i.e. the way in which the cross-cultural therapeutic situation occurs. While constructs, which vary across cultures define the potential range of the interactive options available to the individual, any actual blend of choice among them takes place within a given interpersonal setting. The psychotherapist, the interpreter and the patient have to deal, not only with the mutual impact of ordinary, although cross-culturally variable contexts, but with their further transformation through the establishment of a therapeutically separate space. This is because the requirements of the therapeutic setting, as in any dramatic, ritual or other behavioural setting which is 'set apart' and involves a certain amount of make-belief, differs from those of ordinary performance. The very fictitious elements contained in such settings, that is, spatially 'set apart', are made possible by the artificial limits imposed on participants in order to protect them from acting out on their immediate behavioural consequences. It is precisely because of the renouncing nature of the therapeutic contract that the intensification of effect becomes possible, corresponding to what we may experience on stage as we ourselves sit safely among the audience.

Like that of the greek tragedies, the psychoanalytical catharsis, according to Gammelgaard's comparative exposition (1993, 15), occurs when action is suspended in order that affective and cognitive processes may unfold freely within an imaginative, supernatural or here therapeutic space bounded by certain separate arrangements. It is in this 'transferential' borderland between fiction and reality that affects are let loose. However, in order to bring about catharsis proper, Gammelgaard asserts that the events are dependent on a further narrative reconstruction, which will institute a further distance analogous to the artistic experience. I will return to this issue in the next chapter On the Narrative Approach and Meaning-Formation, but will continue here with a further description of the religio-cultural elements involved in the process.

The nature of interaction within the home context of these clients requires consummate skills of adherence to a code of conduct which is based on a double set of conceptual parameters following from status differences (i.e. superior-inferior) and the level of intimacy (i.e. insider-outsider). There are said to be few societies that take the obligations of status as seriously as iranian society does[2]. The farsi language itself which was used in these therapy sessions contains a number of stylistic devices to help individuals to communicate to each other such aspects of relationships. In societies such as those in Kurdistan or Iran, which are run according to hierarchical religious, ethnic or even tribal considerations, there can be no talk of equal opportunity in the western sense. For example, the requirements to follow the strict rules about wearing the veil and avoidance between the genders are a constant reminder of one's status in relation to others. The customary forms of address and courtesy behaviour, which follow very complex patterns, fill a similar function. Thus children, from about the age of six, are expected to address their elders, including elder siblings with suffixes of politeness such as -*khanum* (dear), regardless of their real feelings[3].

It is important to acknowledge the extent to which these formalities carry symbolic functions creating invisible boundaries around particular phenomena and persons credited with much respect. In a cross-cultural therapy context, because the therapeutic message is filtered through an interpreter, the therapist will, however, frequently miss such nuances. It took a long time before I became attuned to the fact that despite addressing the clients by their first names, the interpreter kept using addendums of respect in order to save me from losing face according to socioculturally correct practice.

* Interpreter ex. 1:

"ANYTHING ELSE WOULD BE UNTHINKABLE"

At one point, the interpreter referred to a colleague who was nicknamed 'the Iron Man' because of his insulting literal translations of western-oriented professionals' address to clients, who subsequently refused his help. In the same way, my own interpreter's greetings defy translation, as they include a minimum of added utterances and courtesy behaviour like obligatory kissing considered necessary by her for the sake of keeping your proper distance from clients. For fear of being drawn into an inevitable premature extra-therapeutic communication of this sort, she generally avoids even passing the waiting room. And, like the clients, seems very conscious of who is to enter through a door first, who is to follow whom to the therapist room, to address first the other and so on – all aspects that are easily overlooked by an culturally unaware helper.

While a reference to god is always involved in greetings or the expression of a wish, an experienced interpreter might again avoid literal translation. Had I not recognised the frequent use of *Insh'Allah* and similar expressions by the clients myself, I might not have grasped the importance of the supernatural in their lives, as such expressions were simply and 'correctly' translated by "Let us assume...". In the words of Dziegel (1981, 21) it is essential to keep in mind the extent to which any kurd, whether an illiterate peasant, a small town craftsman or an educated civil servant, has been nurtured by muslim tradition. This is, according to him, true even of those kurds, who may give an impression of religious indifference, readily imitating the modern western life style.

Considering the dynamics of iranian social exchange separately from such mere formalities, social interactions between superior and inferior tend to revolve around the provision of favours, material goods, tribute and service, or else stimulating others to do so by issuing orders or making petitions. The obligations incumbent on the superior demand that they should ideally live up to their status by granting favours to their inferiors, who in turn ensure their support and respect. This brings me back to my starting point: ethnic minority *problem patients* constantly requesting written statements and other concrete favours in various extra-therapeutic issues, from their confused (western-oriented) therapists, as characterised by the concept of *parsitis* (on p. 26).

* Shirin ex. 3 (initial):

"COULD YOU PLEASE MAKE THEM BRING MY FAMILY HERE OR OTHERWISE I WON'T COME HERE ANYMORE"

A typical example of this would be the extremely affect-laden outbursts including seeming difficulty in breathing and constant threats to terminate therapy by Shirin, following her requests for my practical help in getting her extended family to the country, despite repeatedly being told of the impossibility of this request (cp. S ex. 4: "Had my husband witnessed the insulting behaviour of that patient he would never have let me continue to interpret for her" below).

According to classical psychoanalytical understanding, the origin of such persistent and excessive claims which clients keep making on their surroundings is a mere fixation on unsatisfied and often unconscious past needs. However, I believe that there is significant cross-cultural misinterpretation regarding why ethnic minority clients keep trying to draw their therapists into conformity with their own patterns of interaction. Two essentially opposed transference relationships appear in the therapies at issue here which are, again, echoed by a certain countertransference pattern referred to below. On the one hand, clients who are used to the traditional healing practices of the popular religious sector[4] may transfer a premature trust in the miraculous powers of the superior healer onto the therapist. Such was the case with Aisha:

* Aisha ex. 15 (medial):

HOSPITALISED FOR HEART TROUBLE

(What is that stone you have around your neck?) It is to protect against the evil eye, envy, you could say. If someone is jealous, they might have the evil eye, which may be damaging. If, for example, someone says "How many children you have!, how beautiful they are!, or how rich you are!", but forgets to add "May God protect you", one has to ask why they forgot that. It is a special stone, which has to be blue, deep blue. If a child is exceptionally beautiful, or if there is much misery in the family, it is good to have one. When I became ill, I used it because of my children. I bought one for my daughter, but she would rather have gold (like other girls in Norway). "What kind of an eye – how could an eye hurt you?" she asks. She simply cannot understand. I myself got one from my own Mother, which is much bigger.

(Does your family have a Sheikh?) Yes, he is somehow both Sheikh, and a kind of a leader too, and doctor. It is just like with you, that is why I believe in you. Somehow you are my Sheikh, because I'm so happy to come here. It helps to be able to come here and talk, it is very important for me. The Sheikh's grandchild from Sweden came to visit me in the hospital (this says something about the status of her family). He said that if someone is ill and the distance is long, it is an obligation to shorten that distance. Travelling 'on foot' he can bring healing. He brought things, which had become holy from a particular place in Iran, and his Mother had read from the Koran many times over for my benefit. At home, his grandfather sent messengers to visit the sick with blessings. If a lady was ill, he sent a female visitor. But if it didn't help, he came in person. You always have to try and help.

On the other hand, perverted aspects of their traumatic luggage, as depicted in the PTSD symptomatology, may, again strengthened by the socioculturally determined features of mistrust referred to above, become imposed onto the therapist and interpreter as a highly intrusive and negative transference.

* Cp. ex. 1 (Fatima/Layla):

DURING A PERCEIVED ATMOSPHERE OF INTERROGATION

In the initial sessions with Fatima and Layla two separate interpreters, independently of each other, shared my sinister feeling of being caught right in the middle of a fierce interrogation-like atmosphere while being attributed the role of adamant "Islamic sisters".

AND WHAT LAY BEHIND (L ex. 1 continued/pre-medial)

(In Fatima's case I refer to the lengthy treatment of her illness in previous chapters)

It later turned out that Layla had not told the truth about her flight being a mistake ("that actually her family had not been politically active"). She had behaved as if I was some kind of interrogator she could not trust. The change came after she disclosed her nightmares about interrogations and executions that had been tormenting her and which had started after a terrifying escape to a neighbouring country. During the intervening period of one and a half years, she had not dared to tell anyone about the political involvement of her kin. Now she brought a newspaper cutting as 'evidence' of her husband demonstrating against the regime, explaining that she had managed to keep everything at arms length until the last few weeks when it had all begun to surface again.

She is very upset and confused in the session (to the extent that she lost her way when leaving), and her behaviour is characterised by a desperate need to talk (she keeps phoning me between the sessions); she tells me that she constantly talks to herself about painful

197

memories. She is concerned about whether or not she is able to keep secrets, and I wonder whether she may have broken down in an interrogation, without, however, asking her explicitly at the time. As it turns out, three years ago she had indeed been interrogated by a "Mullah" while two Islamic sisters were present (cp. the re-actualisation above). Unfortunately, later she kept re-experiencing everything in her dreams and woke up crying. A week after this interrogation she got "a lump in her throat". This symptom now reappears among her many somatic complaints, coupled with a nauseating feeling of strangulation, and fear of food going down the wrong way. I leave this preliminary occurring information aside while, for the moment, I try to slow down her mounting anxiety and 'premature' narrative.

Later she discloses the episode concerning the fate of some young kin following the killing of a revolutionary guard as described in L ex. 1: Public Demonstrations.

(cp. F ex. 7: On Mental Intrusions)

I also perceive in these clients' behaviour an attempt to provoke the helpers to act as an extension of the joint family in accordance with their expected collective model of interaction, resulting in what could perhaps be labelled sociocentric transference. This applies especially where several family members are in treatment, as is often the case with this group of clients. Dahl (1989, 28) likewise refers to the concept of 'floating transference' in describing a middle eastern patient's tendency to experience his family as a unity that could be represented by one person, his therapist.

*Aisha ex. 16:

A SOCIOCENTRIC TRANSFERENCE?

Aisha initially repeatedly requested that *we* take responsibility (she always referred collectively to the therapists involved in the family during such requests), first for her children (only later becoming aware of the problems involved), then of her husband, whose life she thought was in danger as a result of her children's shameful behaviour (cp. A ex. 10: The Case of Aisha's Daughter Continued). Her husband, on his part, pleaded with several of the therapeutic staff (including me) to take responsibility for breaking the bad news of the death of Aisha's mother to her (cp. A ex. 14: One Year Past her

Mother's Death); only recently, did Aisha express a wish for getting her daughter back in order to solve the problems by herself (cp. A ex. 21: About Exceptions).

The same holds true – and that over an extended period of time – for all the members of this family in their contact with the authorities, i.e. that the staff at the Psychosocial Centre were perceived as some kind of extension or replacement of their (lacking) primary group (often referred to as a collective unit). This is also reflected in the fact that ending these treatment contacts is such a difficult/time consuming matter (cp. below where the clients seem to regard us "as members of the family, more than doctors", All ex. 12; About the Benefits of Therapy).

As early as 1958, Spiegel wrote a paper on transference relations as developed between psychoanalytically trained therapists and irish-american patients. As carriers of the professional values and goals of the american middle class, his team of therapists expected their patients to be able 'to look forward to change' and 'to keep appointment times', unless this type of behaviour was registered as psychological resistance. He found that conflicts, however, soon centred on the future-oriented individualistic values of the therapists as opposed to the veneration of the past and loyalty to the extended family incorporated into the world view of the ethnic minority patients at issue.[5] I quote his further elaboration on their therapeutic stance:

We valued our 'benevolent neutrality' in the domain of morals and hoped to release our patients from their tyrannical super-ego pressures, whether conscious or unconscious. We expected our patients to talk about their thoughts, attitudes, and feelings but, in accordance with our technical job training, were reluctant to talk much about ourselves. And we hoped that, whatever the degree of divergence from our values and goals at the beginning, as therapy progressed and the relationship deepened, our patients would identify with and accept our goals and values. If this did not happen, then we would clearly have to discontinue therapy, or – and this is what actually happened – change our own value orientation as applied to therapy.

Since our patients did not arrive on time consistently, did not value change, could not reveal their feelings if we concealed ours, kept expecting us to tell them to solve their problems, were unable to aim for autonomy and independence from the family, and finally and most importantly, could only make the smallest changes in their strict moral sensibilities, we clearly had to modify our goals and procedures, or else abandon our research and accept failure (Spiegel 1959, 450-51).

The meaning I give my own participation as a therapist-researcher in such a confusing cross-cultural exchange, particularly when sharing with highly traumatised clients their painful experiences, is of necessity strange and abject to me.[6] It may bring about mutual expectations of such an extreme nature that they prove very difficult to handle, thus unduly strengthening transference reactions and the accompanying stress this causes all parties. The pressure to satisfy such expectations is perhaps particularly demanding for an interpreter, who is enculturated into responding to the force of such socioculturally valid claims, as I will discuss below. The typical pattern of countertransference response in helpers includes initial fascination and overinvestment, followed by extra therapeutic activity as 'an advocate for the client', later yielding to feelings of bewilderment, anger and fatigue, if not secondary traumatisation. If unsupervised, this may be followed by emotional withdrawal of empathetic involvement and a sceptical detective-like stance where the helper doubts and tests the credibility of the trauma story (cp. F ex. 13: Secrets of the Prison).

According to Amati (1992, 12), the ethical risk for the therapist working with trauma victims is that the helper colludes unwittingly with the torturing system, accepting as obvious what is unacceptable, adapting to everything. This is why all our concerns regarding the interpretation of the client's experiences are necessary. But again, the dangers involved are coloured by the double influence of trauma and culture. At the outset, it was my intention to venture beyond therapeutic sessions in order to generate complementary source material from a combination of field and team work. Eventually I found this to be more problematic due to a conviction that, while working with untraditional clients when so much else is in a flux, it became *more* and not less important to stay within a well established therapeutic setting. Already the use of an interpreter raises so many problems in it that the situation might easily become difficult to control.

The fact that I myself have at times made telephone calls on the clients' behalf as a result of their own repeated failures with the authorities, I regard as related more to a general shortage of such essential practical assistance as interpreting for this time consuming group of clients. I have, however, been careful to ensure that it should only be an infrequent *link* in an effort to open doors by initiating a *cross-cultural* (never a kurdish) contact, always with the client herself present. Dahl (1989, 27) speaks of an initial more directing or *didactic technique*, later yielding to a more neutral position, which accords with my own experience of such requests declining over time.

The classical problem remains: if the therapist takes part in team work outside of the sessions or assistance venturing across professional and cultural boundaries, undoubtedly in line with the general interdisciplinary requirements of this field, however, in a specific cross-cultural case under scrutiny, the risk of emotional leakage, misunderstanding or manipulation, and even contamination in the eyes of the client is impelling. For therapists themselves to offer concrete help for problems to do with the social welfare or the legal system may, in addition to the quackery involved in their lack of training in the field, also leave the underlying long term problems untouched.

By refusing to provide help outside the scope of therapy (referring such problems to the proper authorities), the whole issue of the cross-cultural disadvantage which affects the client – and which will continue to affect her situation after the therapy has ended – is made explicit; while, at the same time, the client's integrity and increased resourcefulness subsequent to having 'got the (cross-cultural) map right', is to a greater extent acknowledged. The curative element, as aptly stated by Killingmo (1983, 139), lies not in persuading the patient, but in the fact that the therapist has managed to communicate a correct understanding of the origin and function of the particular problem, and, as I would add, *across cultures*.

The greater the cultural distance between the therapist and patient, the easier it is to lose sight of such basic principles of therapeutic interaction. I am specifically referring to certain conditions surrounding the therapeutic contract itself that seem thrown into relief while working in a cross-cultural context. Referring to world wide comparative studies of therapeutic effect, Elsass[7] asserts that *the context* of healing rituals is more important for the outcome than any particular *theoretical orientation (i.e. content)* in itself. In this sense, it is less important which therapeutic concepts are used for describing the content of the client's distress, as whether there *exists a mutual agreement with the client about the frameworks* of the therapeutic setting itself which enables the therapeutic alliance to unfold. This theory-neutral stance also accords with the preliminary findings from an extensive survey of therapeutic effect presently conducted by the Centre for Clinical Psychology at the University of Oslo[8].

Assuming that the systematic exploitation of the emotional relationship existing between therapist and patient (i.e. the *quality* of the therapeutic interaction[9]) is considered to be the essential curative medium, this has implications for what kinds of deviations from the classical technique are possible in a cross-cultural setting. According to Killingmo (1983, 143), selective focusing on certain therapeutic themes is possible, but attitudinal or technical changes which are at odds with the principle of autonomy are more difficult[10]. While using a focused life story approach based on the knowledge of traumatic exposure, I tend to agree with him on the first point, provided that the dangers involved in having a too narrow perspective are duly recognised (cp. "to be trapped in the trauma story"). His other points are, however, linked to the wider issue of being able to distinguish acculturative stress deriving from the more general effects of socioculture and working class membership (cp. the marginalisation of third world migrants in our society). Goldstein, in the *Psychotherapy of the Poor*, summarises the available findings on the influence of social class on the therapeutic outcome as follows:

> The implications of a patient's social class for his psychotherapeutic treatment destiny are numerous, pervasive and enduring. If the patient is lower class, all such implications are decidedly and uniformly negative. In comparison with patients at higher social levels, the lower class patient or patient-candidate seeking psychotherapeutic assistance in an outpatient setting is significantly more likely to: (1) be found unacceptable for treatment; (2) spend considerable time on the clinic's waiting list; (3) drop out (or be dropped out) after initial screening; (4) receive a socially less desirable formal diagnosis; (5) be assigned to the least experienced staff members; (6) hold prognostic and role expectations incongruent with those held by his therapist; (8) terminate or be terminated earlier; and (9) improve significantly less from his own and his therapist's perspective (1973, 93).

According to Goldstein all attempts to avoid such negative outcome through modifications of psychoanalytically based therapeutic techniques are doomed to fail. Reducing social distance by means of the therapist adopting a more active or directive method of treatment, employing concrete language, crises generated by the therapist and other interventions that have been proposed, simply don't work. His proposal is the opposite of Killingmo's: one should actively teach working class people middle class characteristics such as self-disclosure, empathy, articulation of feeling in a self-observing fashion, identification with others, and so on. According to his rationale, no collaborative efforts are, however, required by the therapist in order to identify with or learn more about working class perceptions and values, since the background of the patient is assumed to be responsible for their emotional difficulties. The author accordingly considers middle class values and behaviour the royal road to mental health, while neglecting the degree to which ethnic minority patients get caught up in conflicting value systems as they undergo social mobility and change.

By regarding these middle class values, previously assumed to be a mere obstacle in cross-cultural therapy, as motivating the therapists towards therapeutic success – by overcoming them – Spiegel (1971, 460) declares: "Guided by our deepening understanding of the legitimacy, on both sides, of the value differences, we made changes". Like other authors[11], Spiegel reports on the value of making such changes as: giving brief initial instructions to the patient regarding what to expect in treatment, choosing treatment goals in accordance with the patient's cultural standards or maintaining a flexible technique:

> We made home visits and increased our visibility for other members of the group, disclosed certain aspects of our personal lives when, for example, questioned about the existence and well-being of children and family, became adopted by their network, changes that seemed to help the process along (1971, 451).

Much later and quite unaware of his paper, I had come to similar conclusions. However, I cannot fully agree with him because of his opposition to an approach, which leaves any value choice, decision making or social action, ultimately to the patient. Killingmo (1984, 142) counts introducing time limits, restricting therapeutic aims, preprogramming sessions or giving advice or 'home work' among the more difficult changes therapists are prone to make. Forced to adapt our several years long therapeutic relationships to the uncertain time perspective inherent in the funding of this study (for the clients treatment was free), I myself may at times have violated the principle of non-interference. However, apart from offering information on essential aspects of the therapeutic contract itself; on the uncertainty of the time perspective involved; on the PTSD symptomatology (a most important constituent of these therapies); and my pointing out differences in normative styles pertaining to the change of sociocultural abode to bewildered clients, I have seen little reason to change the basic technique. Nevertheless, I still perceived a craving on the part of the clients to know more about my points of reference than would be indicated by transference reactions in a culturally homogenous setting in which all parties share a greater part of the intersubjective field. From my experience with these clients, I agree with Dahl (pers. com. 1995) asserting that the therapist turns out to be a sort of *mother-of-the-new-culture*.

Despite the value conflicts and countertransference errors involved, a culturally sensitive and professional therapist should, in my view, be able to handle these problems without fundamental changes in procedure. In my therapeutic experience with the clients at issue, they did, in fact arrive on time despite travelling long distances; they did value change when it implied a release of their suffering, and were most genuinely able to reveal their feelings[12]; eventually stopped expecting me to tell them how to solve their problems; and made small changes in their strict moral sensibilities. Most importantly, however, all but one (Fatima), never showed any fundamental preference for aiming at independence from their extended family contexts. Nor did I deliberately give instructions about how to live or, as far as I can see, consciously gratify infantile needs based on suggestion and surrender as a method.

My strategy was based on a conviction that the (transferential) need for an omnipotent healer will (A ex. 15: Hospitalised for Heart Trouble), in combination with the therapist's own narcissism and possible hidden wish for grandeur (cp. countertransference reactions), easily become part of an unconscious alliance, regardless of the cross-cultural context. If the therapist gives in, he or she will be operating with a limited mandate, but if, on the other hand, every aspect of communication is drawn into the transference situation, this may also be a sign of the therapist overestimating the special meaning he or she has for the client.

However, there are other reasons for avoiding such a position also from the point of view of the sociocultural patterns of interaction involved in the interpersonal expectations of these migrant-clients. If a therapist can accept an offered position of superiority, it may become incumbent upon him, according to the traditional expectations of the clients', to grant them certain favours. Being thus bound to those in an inferior position (i.e. here the clients), it is easy to get trapped – in the sense that having bestowed favours once, one might expect more requests to follow. This pattern of conduct may spiral out of proportion in the relationships between ethnic minority *problem patients* and their perplexed helpers, ignorant of the socioculturally determined mutual expectations involved in this kind of other-raising versus self-lowering behaviour.

* Interpreter ex. 2:

OTHER-RAISING VS. SELF-LOWERING

The mechanisms involved were brought to my attention during a home visit to a client (not otherwise included here), who welcomed me with a respectful greeting involving, apart from excessively cordial verbal remarks, lengthy repeated pressing of my lower legs with both hands, finally touching my feet with her fingertips while seated on the floor in front of me. Someone greeted in this way is expected to voice a series of stereotypical blessings upon the junior, the intensity and degree of the response varying with the degree of seniority and other more or less personal factors, of which I was wholly ignorant at the time. The encounter left me quite uncomfortable, with an impression of a ritualised and not very genuine communication, except for the longing she expressed for her extended family; a wish which was also involved in this client's requests for my assistance in getting her joint family to this country (cp. S ex 3).

Defining oneself as inferior in face to face situations offers a tactical advantage in the form of greater maneuvrability, as shown by the case of Fatima below. Although relationships between close perceptual equals likewise involve exchange behaviour, this is of a different and absolute kind, as encoded in the practice of *partibazi* (translated as an 'act of friendship' by my interpreter); that is, presenting the interests of intimate friends/kin to persons in a position of granting privileges, such as employment, licenses, exemptions from certain regulations and the like. In Iran, such obligations of intimate equals are embodied in the institution of *dowreh* that is composed by an *all*-male or *all*-female circle of intimates which meet regurlarly.[13]

People who believe themselves to be subject to the demands of exchange obtaining between intimate equals, are usually those who have life experiences in common, who are directly related to each other, of the same age, and have known each other for a significant amount of time; though sometimes they may have been thrown into similar circumstances for a shorter period. Thus, refugees who have spent difficult and long periods in the same refugee camp may develop binding relationships of a type they would be quite unlikely to form at home. In a sense, the family is a natural *dowreh*, since its members must be able to further each other's interests and to provide for the survival of the unit as a whole.

The ethical values implied in the ultimate fulfilment of both types of exchange are a willingness to enter into extensive self-sacrifice in meeting the needs of the other. When this is a genuine concern, the relationship between intimate equals and non-equals alike is stable and may embody great affection. This is true of the superior who must care for dependants however difficult that may be, of the inferior who follows a leader in all circumstances, and of the comrade who gives all for the sake of an intimate companion. The archetypal model is, in the muslim context at issue here, found in the spiritual bond between the master of a sufi order and his apprentice. It is in fact difficult for western outsiders to quite understand how the emotional commitment to a cousin, brother or close friend in such a setting may reach levels that, in their westerners' view, may have erotic connotations. Equally difficult to understand for westerners is the deplorable situation of a father whose influence or *parti* is not enough to provide adequately for his own family nor protect its members from shame; i.e. following from a lowering of his relative male status and the increased influence of a diversity of outside (often, in his view, young low status female) professional helpers involved in the exile situation. Even where children are perceived to be at fault, the situation is regarded as very embarrassing from the point of view of the inadequacy of the parent to provide and protect.

Courtesy and Withdrawal Behaviour
in the *Triad of interpretation*

Because psychodynamic theory building generally has not proceeded beyond a dyadic constellation in its present explication, the role of the interpreter has so far gained scant attention in comparison with the sufferings and predicament of the clients and the helpers. Therefore, the latter should also ask themselves in what ways the sociocultural patterns prevalent in the home country make themselves noticeable in the triadic constellation while using an interpreter: Where are the interpreter and therapist placed in the picture? 'Who has a way with whom', and 'who plays whom off against the others', at which particular points in time?

In my own experience from these therapies, the interpreter and I have been allied in every conceivable combination. We were drawn into transference relationships, which imply triadic problems of expulsion, and the formation of various alliances. In the present chapter I will focus on the difficulties inherent in the interpreter's role rather than on that of the therapist due to the difficulties involved in such a self-analysis. The situation of the interpreter is especially difficult because s/he is frequently caught up between opposing forces (due to both the traumatic and/or sociocultural 'luggage' involved in these therapies) without, however, possessing the required qualifications inherent in clinical training or often even supervision, nor the experience of him/herself having gone through therapy as part and parcel of that training.

Because of problems in confronting personally highly charged material, clients might sense a certain reluctance and decline from revealing sensitive material because their counterparts (i.e. therapist, interpreter or other 'listener') might not be able to endure these revelations. And, furthermore, this reluctance may again be coloured by cultural notions considering both their content and the form of interaction (N ex. 8: Prevented from Disclosing your Pain). This problem may be further increased by the frequent closeness between client and interpreter in terms of cultural attributes. However, it might also work the other way around, because of the fact that the clients themselves may assume their problems to be contagious, and are, therefore, afraid to disclose them as pointed out on p. 191. From the point of view of the well-educated and well-adapted interpreter used in this study, who had no refugee background herself[14], the most sensitive issues turned out to touch on relational problems regarding the behaviour of compatriots in exile, problems that were again associated with the principles of honour engaging the tradition-oriented clients at issue. In two cases, clients actually said that only when they are able to proceed without translation (i.e. ideally freed from the scrutiny of their compatriots and any possible cultural stigma attached to their 'shameful' problems), would they tell the rest of their story. This was despite the fact that this interpreter was the only one accepted by the said clients for sharing in their trauma-laden secrets, most notably because of her scant contacts with the exiled iranian milieu. One of them, it turned out, even followed her warning and thus came to give me a hint as to what kind of material was involved (cp. F ex. 17; 2 & 13 conducted without the interpreter).

On the other hand, both the client and therapist are totally dependent on the interpreter, who, as time passes, if left poorly supervised may threaten to withdraw from further co-operation and thereby increase her relative position of power. From the start, the relationship of dependence on the interpreter that is inevitably involved in this kind of cross-cultural therapy which requires interpreting, constitutes an opportunity for positive – though premature – transference reactions. Assuming that supervision is adequate, this initial dependence can, if supported by positive ethnocultural identification between client and interpreter, be used to keep the therapy going. The reason for this is the fact that it counteracts the initial mistrust frequently accorded a therapist-outsider and representative of the majority in such a cross-cultural setting.

But again, *in the long run* this positive primary identification with the interpreter, initially perceived in all the cases at hand, may hamper the treatment process in as much as it alone cannot compensate for a proper therapeutic alliance. Moreover, if it poses difficulties for a white middle class therapist to identify with ethnic minority clients and vice versa, such problems can likewise be perceived in the interpreter, to the extent that his or her subculture may also differ from that of the client. When this occurs, three or more cultures are operative in the encounter: in this case, finnish, swedish, norwegian, persian and kurdish.

It was particularly difficult for the interpreter (without a therapeutic education) to handle the subsequently emerging negative transference reactions that were to replace the initially good one, in her experience pertaining only to kurdish women among her iranian clientele. Any well-adapted interpreter-migrant may come to be perceived as a 'traitor', guilty of having changed sides in their more recently arrived – and here somewhat desperate – clients' view, merely by having come to terms with the majority society. Or, as strongly emphasised by the prominent anthropologist Fredrik Barth[15], in the eyes of the kurdish participants of this study a *persian* interpreter may in fact represent in this case an upper class urban dweller, one of the oppressors. On the other hand, in the eyes of a persian interpreter, the clients may be perceived as being trebly stigmatised: as kurds, as sunnites and as illiterate females. Just as the case may be with any other unanalysed/unsupervised 'helpers', their clients may come to represent exotic but needy inferiors for whom it is easy to feel pity, as long as the relationship remains unambiguous and if the client shows them the respect they expect and deem proper.

* All ex. 9:

ABOUT NEGATIVE TRANSFERENCE

Negative transference emerging over time has hampered the interpreter's relationship to LAYLA in particular, perhaps due to this client's upward mobile social aspirations, which had caused confusion on several points as to her social positioning, not least her – relative – age in relation to the interpreter's (i.e. the fact that the client was younger). According to the interpreter "She got on her high horse even though she's only a kurd. She behaves as if she were older than me, but I don't think she really is, but at the same time she always addressed me as 'You' (The polite pronoun)".

It has gone more smoothly with AISHA, perhaps due to her comparatively old age; by conducting herself naturally as a superior while treating both of us with a certain condescension ("'addressing us with 'you' while expecting to proceed through the door first, etc.'");

With FATIMA too it went quite well at the beginning, perhaps due to her unequivocal subordination in relationship to us (again according to the interpreter "'An innate respect resulting from our professional status; she would never ever say 'you' but 'You', and never entered a room before me as she is clearly the younger '") before a sudden change in her behaviour emerged as described below.

NASREEN, on her part, never seems to have challenged anyone's status. "She might proceed first or last in a relaxed way, use you/You forms all mixed up, and is not particularly courteous but behaves more as a girlfriend of equal standing" (that is, intimate, cp. her relationship to her own mother in N. ex. 12: "The youngest daughter of my mother"). With hindsight, the interpreter, however, remembers having initially had to work hard in order to gain her trust ("despite her husband recommending me as an interpreter"). But it is always the interpreter who has to take the initiative.

A common theme in the negative aspects of the transference reactions described here seems to be the extent to which the interpreter and I (the therapist) have been considered to be in either superior or inferior positions in relation to the clients. One might therefore ask: What kind of interrelationships exists between the twofold axis (presented on p. 194) and the therapeutic space as these migrant-clients experience it? The most obvious denominators in the scope of possible intimacy are kinship and gender, but what about the *relevant others*? Both therapist and interpreter are necessary in cross-cultural therapy, and both are outsiders to varying degrees from the point of view of their clients. To what extent have we been considered superior/inferior or even equal insiders/outsiders in our relationship with the clients during the course of these therapies?

* All ex. 10:

'INSIDE-OUTSIDE' POSITIONING

AISHA

The interpreter claims that Aisha regards us – along with herself – as being somehow insiders, albeit inferior. This was expressed through acts such as sharing with us the loss of her deceased son (which she due to the extraordinary circumstances surrounding his death could not wholly share with her kin), allowing herself to cry in our presence, and sharing food with us (All ex. 11: Artefacts of Exchange). Despite this intimacy and the confidence she showed us, we were not expected to break the bad news of her mother's death because we were in actual fact outsiders (my remark; cp. A. ex. 14: One Year After her Mother's Death). Our – to us beneficial – position as somewhat inferior may be due to her unambiguously superior self-image owing to her respectable age and high-status origin (cp. childhood setting A ex. 17: The Guest House);

FATIMA

On the other hand, with Fatima who always follows the rules of courtesy including elaborate greetings to the interpreter (cp. the withdrawal in F ex. 17: "I will never go back to interpreting for her or I lose all my credibility"), we were, according to the interpreter, superior outsiders. I cannot, however, quite agree with her opinion on this point because of the very sensitive material she has, after all brought to my notice despite great anxiety on her part. She also shared her cigarettes, proverbs and even songs with us during sessions.

NASREEN and LAYLA

For Nasreen, we have obviously been insiders for most of the time, according to the interpreter, "somehow like intimate, equal friends". Layla, however, regards us clearly as outsiders and frequently uses us to take care of her more practical arrangements (cp. initial phase of therapy on p.201*) despite the involvement she seems to have had in the process, as became evident in retrospect from her reaction to the inevitable ending of her therapy (All ex.12: About the Benefits of Therapy).

In sum, it seems to be in the more *equal but non-intimate* relationships (like that of Fatima/ Layla) that confusion is prevalent, while in non-equal (Aisha) or intimate equal (Nasreen) interpersonal situations there is less offence or confusion. Among intimates and non-intimates alike politeness and respect for a superior is of paramount importance to these clients' relationships. However, in non-intimate relationships ritual courtesy or *ta'arof* behaviour, which was explained to me as "a kind of modesty from considerations of courtesy" by the interpreter, who added "and not for any other reasons", seems to parallel that of *partibazi* among intimates. This is a social pattern that includes offering food, gifts or compliments and other forms of courtesy behaviour to another person who is seen as either superior or (rarely) inferior. In his classical work on the meaning of such gift exchanging patterns, Marcel Mauss (1996) relied on comparative material from many different parts of the non-literate world.

I will try to develop this issue by further extending its focus from a consideration of the clients' requests for concrete favours and the exhibited courtesy behaviour, to looking at what artefacts they have brought to whom and what the clients themselves say about these objects[16]. They are as follows:

ARTEFACTS OF EXCHANGE

PRESENTS such as flowers (a bigger/smaller bouquet for the therapist/
interpreter) from all clients: cards (from Nasreen/Fatima) and sweets
before holiday breaks (like "Finnish chocolate to the Finnish therapist" from Layla and "sweets for your kids" from Aisha). The most
problematic one, a compoundable cake platter the client (Shirin) had
got from her mother[17], was obviously related to her request for my
help in organising family reunion by influencing the authorities.

I believe these presents are primarily connected to the socially
ambiguous initial phase of client's requests and status-negotiations.
They ceased in all cases when therapy proceeded towards a more
traditional neutral stance.

FOOD such as a traditional dish in celebration of her mother's phone
call (cp. when dead ones visit in Aisha ex. 12: About the Secondary
shahids), obviously more related to a genuine relief regarding her
worries about neglecting intergenerational obligations (Aisha ex. 8:
She who would have Cared for her Old Mother) than to our presence.
On another occasion Shirin presented me with some bread that she
had baked herself; I interpret this to be her way of thanking me for
what she after all had perceived as my having done her a favour in the
above-mentioned matter of the request concerning family reunion.

PICTURES OF CLOSE KIN such as photographs of relatives taken
at home so that I was able to see for myself – concretely – whom
these people missed so much (all but Fatima who owned none/had
lost them during her flight). Layla once brought me a photo of her
most highly respected father with what she in a very moving session
interpreted as godly light illuminating his image, and another photo
depicting her bravely resisting husband "as proof" of his commitment
to the oppositional cause (cp. also what is said about the "shameful
photos" taken at the grave of Aisha's son on, A ex. 5).

SONGS / STORIES of sorrow and hope relating to Fatima's survival in
prison, sung spontaneously during a therapy session (she had lost all
personal items during the flight); others talked with great affection
about the songs their mothers sang to them which brought back memories of their childhood without, however, singing "shamefully 'out of
context'" during therapy sessions. All the clients narrated anecdotes
in order to underscore some important point of their messages (cp.
the metaphorical language used by them).

POLITICAL PAMPHLETS ETC. by Fatima; she and Layla were the only ones whose political motives spontaneously had come under scrutiny during therapy.

A BOOK OF PROVERBS / DIARY / LETTER in farsi to the interpreter (as part of the events surrounding her negative transference depicted in F. ex 17: "I will never go back interpreting for her or I will lose all my credibility"). For years Fatima also kept arriving to the session carrying books in farsi; I interpreted these books as some kind of transitional object connected in her mind to her father who used to read aloud to her when she was a child. She also brought a letter of farewell before an longer separation due to my stay abroad (F ex. 19: 'Dear Nora'); a diary depicting 'their family story', written in norwegian by Nasreen's much-loved son in co-operation with his caretakers, subsequent to the Child Welfare Authorities returning him home (cp. N ex. 5: The Boy who should not have Survived).

VIDEO / FILM such as the one referred to initially on p. 14 by Nasreen (cp. bereavement from a happy childhood when considering her adult traumatic life), and a feature film, about the problems of exile, produced by a refugee who was later murdered by the regime's agents while in exile in a european country (by Fatima).

KIDNEY STONES by Nasreen after a medical check-up for sexual violation which had left no visible scars, perhaps in order to give me at least some concrete evidence of her suffering (she had kept them from an earlier operation).

By emphasising and preserving culturally defined roles, such acts of courtesy, carried out at every turn of everyday life, mark differences in social status; that is, every time friends meet in the street, when several persons proceed through the same door, or engage in the same activity such as eating, drinking or, talking. Such patterns are naturally also reflected in therapeutic interaction. According to Beeman (1986, 57-58) the idea is to defer to your superiors, confer on inferiors, accept after protest or press the favour or tribute involved on an equal, and thereby 'win' community approbation for maintaining social order. One form of negative ritual courtesy is actually a sort of manipulation, which serves to paralyse the recipient (cp. the host/ guest relationship and 'other-raising' behaviour discussed on pp. 190 & 205ff).

In order to implement such strategies of exchange, skilled operators go to great pains to discover which social links actually exist between themselves and people in power. Could this facet of psychocultural communication (i.e. testing the relationships) also explain something of the complex interrelationships involved in the 'problem family' pattern in exile; a pattern which, again, interferes with and further complicates the traumatic one preceding it?

The value placed on formality and the fine-tuning of exchange behaviour in these migrant-clients' pattern of communication contrasts strongly with the informality and 'automation' with which westerners today largely engage in non-verbal communication. There are rewards for the adept and setbacks for the clumsy within any system of exchange. People everywhere vary in their ability to understand the interpersonal contexts in which they find themselves. Moreover, all societies have procedures for bringing incongruous phenomena into line. For example, in Iran one who mixes with everyone is colloquially labelled a *dervish*, likening him to the holy mendicants who operate outside the normal confines of the social system.

Inappropriate acts such as regularly exhibiting responsiveness to children's requests while raving at elders (cp. the normative styles on p. 69) signal that one cannot perceive social situations correctly or is otherwise unknowledgeable about the proper behavioural repertoire.[18] Similarly, people who do not stand, bow or use the proper forms of courtesy, are considered not only rude or impolite (Int. ex. 1: "Anything else would be unthinkable"), but also 'without honour' or lacking in the generally expected respect for their family and elders, as if they were 'without a mother and father'; cp. that the stigma of being orphaned is considered almost equivalent to that of being unprotected and thus a vulnerable person, such as a streetwalker (All ex. 2: The 'bad' woman). It is interesting to note how in the sociocentric structure of these clients' world 'a rude person' refers to someone who lacks any basic social unit like a family and protective parents/kin within which he has been trained. It could almost be likened to declaring someone non-human by virtue of being non-social.

Departures from the normal are duly noticed and, because of their unexpected nature, carry special significance. Emotional expression, such as violating or intensifying socially anticipated behaviour or even total withdrawal, thus becomes negatively encoded as *conduct that falls outside the anticipated normal scheme*. Mixing the cards is a message which carries strong affective overtones (Layla and the interpreter in All ex. 9: About Negative Transference). Ritual courtesy, such as that used by the interpreter in respect of the clients at issue, would thus be quite inappropriate among intimate equals and here serves to endorse a professional neutrality. Using 'outside' speech forms to criticise someone one is not entitled to criticise, is thus more effective than plain remonstration and will trigger an angry response, as will a lax physical attitude accompanied by an incongruent hierarchical language use as a sign of protest.

If displeasure and anger are difficult to deal with in public, they can be managed by an opposite gradual increase in polite language or a growing cold reserve, similar to flattery from someone from whom one is not likely to receive it, and so forth. On the other hand, breaking down in tears is a particularly powerful action from someone in a position of inferiority (frequently a woman). Such behaviour makes it virtually mandatory for the superior person to respond in kind with the appropriate favour (cp. Shirin's fits of violent crying accompanying her request in S ex. 3: "Could you make them bring my family here or otherwise I won't come here anymore"). Other forcible means, used against 'difficult' husbands, are to withhold sexual contact, refuse to do the housework, pretend to be sick, or leave for your parental home in order to pout; a strategy resorted to by Aisha already in connection with her referral to therapy (All ex. 1: Time and Manner of Referral).

Total withdrawal from social interaction carries an extremely powerful emotional message. *Ghar va asti* – to withdraw in anger or the total denial of interaction with an intimate with whom one is displeased in order to test the relationship – carries an unambiguous message, irrespective of gender, age, etc. This is since ideally it puts pressure on the whole social network in which both are involved and forces the parties to reconcile their differences, the actual conflict being more or less lost in the process. According to Beeman (1988, 169), it can, in effect, be regarded as a way of removing an issue of conflict altogether from the scene in a situation where both would otherwise lose face.

My first unexpected encounter with this type of complication concerned a client not otherwise included here but while I was working with the same interpreter.

215

* Interpreter ex. 3:

"I WILL NEVER GO BACK TO INTERPRETING FOR THAT PATIENT AGAIN"

During the visit mentioned above (Interpreter ex. 2: Other-raising vs. Self-lowering), while attending to my comfort as a guest (on a home visit to the client's house), the client managed to offend the interpreter in ways so subtle that I (as an outsider) had no idea of what was going on at the time. Later, she pointed out to me that while fruit had been placed on my plate, accompanied by the required exhortations to eat (accorded a non-intimate outsider), only later did the hostess place a banana-peel so that it came to touch her (the interpreter's) plate as if 'by accident'', after which the interpreter fled to the toilet in order to be able to keep up appearances. After this episode, however, she refused to ever attend to this client again. Later, pondering this visit, the interpreter related to me other experiences of a similar kind which had forced her to withdraw from all contact beyond that which was strictly necessary.

In the interpreter's own words:

> If you expect something from someone else who lets you down, for example from your compatriots or a close girlfriend, and if you are really good friends, who should have known better, it is even worse... Then you go away and 'sulk', I can't find a better word for it. One behaves as if the offender doesn't exist for better or worse. One simply doesn't want to have anything to do with that person. One puts the relationship in 'cold storage', as it were, without destroying the other person, since this type of behaviour doesn't imply revenge.

By preventing aggressive expression, this kind of withdrawal or extreme avoidance behaviour enables a group to remain on equable terms despite internal misgivings, especially with those to whom one is somehow unequivocally linked, such as kin or compatriots in exile. I will end this section by pointing out the process involved in the two cases in which such mechanisms of withdrawal became particularly evident in the course of treatment.

* Shirin ex. 4 (1-2 continued/pre-medial):

> "HAD MY HUSBAND WITNESSED THE INSULTING
> BEHAVIOUR OF THAT PATIENT'S HUSBAND HE WOULD NEVER
> HAVE LET ME CONTINUE TO INTERPRET FOR HER"

In fact, this contact nearly ended prematurely after, among other things, an argument involving the client's ex-husband (who was unwilling to accept that she ventured outside the house alone and/or attended treatment sessions, which she in fact did in secret) and a sorani (a kurdi dialect) interpreter who was used in this particular case.

* Fatima ex. 17 (post-medial):

> "I WILL NEVER GO BACK TO INTERPRETING FOR HER
> OR I'LL LOSE ALL MY CREDIBILITY"

After an extended period of extreme courtesy behaviour on the part of the client, as described by the interpreter who made the above comment in interpreter ex. 3: "I will never go back to interpret for that client again", as especially characteristic of this client (All ex. 9: About Negative Transference), a change paralleled the emergence of a negative transference reaction. This happened in the case of a client who had consistently refused to use any other interpreter and who, therefore, had been allowed to use this specific interpreter to accompany her outside the confines of the therapy in one of the very rare instances requiring somatic intervention and where the degree of honour at stake was so high that an exception had to be made. From that time on the client's reputation was perceived as resting with the loyalty of the interpreter as the interpreter herself pointed out to me.

The episode was brought on in my view when the interpreter unexpectedly took offence when the client corrected and indirectly criticised her translation, as a consequence of which the interpreter then totally withdrew. I was left to proceed without her assistance with the client who at that point fortunately spoke some norwegian. Out of curiosity, and because there were no alternatives, I went along with this arrangement in the hope of being able to discover what kind of material was involved. As it turned out, the client proceeded in the expected direction, dwelling on issues of lost honour. Eventually she brought in a close friend to interpret her "real story", as she put it at the time.

217

The story, presented in F ex. 2: "Promise me never to speak of my mother as being dead", highlighted the fate of unprotected children, in particular vulnerable girls. It further opened up a wholly disassociated part of her self involving the death of – among others – her mother. Only after a period of patiently listening to these new aspects of her story while at the same time making my views about the use of a friend (herself traumatised and affected by the story) as an interpreter very clear to her, did I manage to proceed alone. Following my parallel consultation with the 'withdrawn' interpreter concerning the therapeutic necessity of remaining on post in clinical work were negative transference to emerge, the interpreter managed to return to her work at interpreting for this client. But this only occurred after my mentioning the client's request for her return to interpret, quite unaware as I was at the time of having perhaps thus played the role of a mediator.

After this episode, the client now began to heap compliments on the interpreter, she even gave her a book to read and similar gifts, increasing the embarrassment of the interpreter even further, while I, on my part, had to ensure my 'neutral' presence in the alliance as I had during the early phase of this therapy. Only after a period of mutual mistrust and the accompanying unfolding of her further story, did the storm settle to the honour of both.

The mutual respect for precedence naturally applies irrespective of gender. The whole area of same-sex etiquette, like that between the gender, ranges in its expression from stereotyped gestures of deference and courtesy behaviour to the maintenance of social distance, or the more extreme measures involved in complete avoidance. It includes such devices as described above in forms of address and reference, modes of greeting and leave-taking, precedence in sitting and eating arrangements or other gestures displaying the relative status and/or kinship positioning of the interacting persons. For example, it is very rare for a younger woman to sit freely conversing in front of an older one, especially if they come from different kinship groups. This might explain why Aisha is the one who feels most free to narrate in the presence of the interpreter and myself, both of whom she perceives as clearly younger than herself (cp. All ex. 9, 10). But, again, one cannot dismiss the possibility of the 'double effect' of culture and trauma in dealing with avoidance behaviour among this category of clients. This is because, after a time, persons suffering from PTSD learn to promptly avoid specific triggers that cause distress; triggers that may also be involved in the therapeutic dynamics of the kind discussed here.

To sum up Spiegel (1976, 462) concludes his cross-cultural examination with a discussion of the inevitable link between transference phenomena and the traditionally required neutral position of the therapist. Distinguishing the therapeutic alliance from transference aspects, as he does, implies viewing transference as selective attention in a new relationship which, though no simple repetition of the old relationship, includes a number of the same elements. In a cross-cultural setting the therapeutic alliance has to be very carefully constructed as a collaborative venture over an extended period of time in order to avoid unnecessary infringing on the norms of the clients' major group affiliations.

If prestige, for example, is important to the hierarchical values of the primary group at issue, the therapist should perhaps initially be presented as a prestigious – or at least respectable – person to the client's family. This is especially important where gender issues are involved because husbands, as a rule, must give their permission for any therapeutic involvement to take place. By the therapist's attending to such concerns, the client is given breathing space before eventually opting for either side of the perceived – and multileveled – normative value systems concerning gender and hierarchy as presented on p. 69 (for example, autonomy versus dependence on husband), depending upon how he or she sorts out the said conflicts in exile. As for the clients themselves, diverse features of the normative styles involved will, however, contribute to their vulnerability. Rather than being of a unilinear nature, adaptation is a multilinear process, which always involves selecting from a number of different alternatives and normative or explanatory combinations as discussed in the next chapter: On the Narrative Approach and Meaning-Formation. Adaptation can take different form in different contexts, on occasion exhibiting various forms of conformity and at other times resistance.

Provided that the basic bond between therapist, migrant-client and his or her primary group – as well as the interpreter – have been accepted, there will generally be a positive tone in the therapeutic sessions in time allowing for the detection of transference and countertransference responses. However, during an extended initial phase while client and therapist are negotiating the interrelationships involved in the tripartite therapy structure, the sustaining power of the therapeutic alliance,[19] must be given extra attention in order to build up the relationship. Because the working alliance during therapy is so vulnerable to various normative breaches which may result from the traumatic and culturally diverging past of the client (relative to her new environment), there will, in addition, be an increased need for focusing on the maintenance of the relationship.

I will end this section by referring to the mechanisms behind the subsequent resolution of Fatima's case (i.e. the one involving the interpreter's withdrawal as a result of my failure to cater to her proper supervision) in which I myself came to play the role of a mediator without at the time being aware of it.

* Fatima ex. 18 (17 continued/post-medial):

MORE ABOUT WITHDRAWING

(What can you do in order to solve such a conflict? I ask the interpreter, talking about this pattern of withdrawal more generally, outside sessions). You have to turn to a third person, who is respected by both the parties. Someone experienced, preferably an older person who acts as a mediator and witness. This person becomes a sort of co-signer or guarantor that the conflict will never repeat itself even if it frequently does, for example, in marriage quarrels. One cannot approach the offended party by oneself. If someone sent me a letter trying to justify their behaviour, I wouldn't accept such an apology. I would read it, tear it up and simply forget about it. If they had, instead, gone to my boss and publicly admitted their fault, it would have passed, but contact just between the two of us is not enough.

If my friend ever wronged me, she would go to a third friend of ours, who would then approach me bringing my friend's apologies and assuring me that she didn't mean to do it, that she regrets it and so on. If it's a bigger thing, it has to be done properly. If one tries to apologise for one's own behaviour the situation gets even worse: It's as if one repeats the offence by reminding the other of it. It should be rephrased somehow. For example, when a client's husband (referring to int. ex. 3: "I will never go back to interpreting for that client again") repeatedly phoned me at my office – his wife didn't dare to phone herself – explaining that it was all a misunderstanding, that wasn't directed against me personally, but just that they didn't like the idea of having an interpreter at all. I knew that wasn't true, but still accepted this mediated apology (observe that this extra-therapeutic communication had appeared without the knowledge of the therapist).

So the question remains: Where does the therapist fit into this complicated picture? Which elements can be judged therapeutically relevant for the selective application of norms involved in cross-cultural gender mobility among tradition-oriented and traumatised refugee women? It is important to find this out and make it explicit in order to protect the migrant-clients from unnecessary pain.

Transformation of Basic Schemes:
About the Benefits of Therapy

Now, let me return to the question of outcome. Killingmo (1983, 144) criticises psychotherapeutic outcome research, often of a comparative character, for producing uncertain results despite the effort put into it[20]. Innovations in therapeutic theory and technique do not, in his view, stem from this type of research, but from detailed casuistic studies and clinical observation. He points out two main reasons for this state of affairs: First the use of theoretically incongruous criteria for measuring effect, and secondly inadequate demarcations of the concept of psychotherapy itself, which are frequently based on a medical model resembling that of the natural sciences (as further developed in chapter 14: On Methodological Choice and the Study of Sensitive Issues) with a clear beginning and end. An end which is again thought to coalesce with the cessation of symptoms. In addition there is the implicit idea of the therapist applying certain techniques when treating a 'passive' recipient.

The psychodynamic approach of Killingmo clearly deviates from the kind of medically oriented model he criticises; in many respects it resembles a humanistic research model, but for its added emphasis on an applied perspective. Its aim is to resume and proceed with an – in principle – indefinite development that has somehow come to a halt. This development is initiated by a working relationship, which unfolds as highly personal team work without leading to any clearcut end. The therapist's reconstructive emphatic interpretations may ideally bring the client to a point from which s/he can go ahead on her own as an inquiring strategist in life: to put the ego back where it should be, in charge, as Freud would have it. Evaluating the benefits of therapy is, therefore, better done in relation to the unique individual developmental profile in evidence at the outset, and the quality or 'match' of the therapeutic interaction, rather than to any particular diagnosis or category of symptoms such as PTSD. Instead of attempting to answer the unanswerable question of a clear-cut and predictable *outcome* from the point of view of the research design used in the present study, I will instead proceed to reflect on what the participants themselves say about its benefits. That is before summarising, on the basis of the interdisciplinary lesson, some principles of treatment in cross-cultural trauma therapy for further consideration.

From a sociocentric point of view the western-oriented individualistic therapeutic context offered to the tradition-oriented traumatised clients in exile embodies a deviation from 'good form'. In the cases at issue here this deviation has, however, been accepted and, in time, even valued. This has, among other things been evidenced from the fact that they, despite having to travel lengthy distances (at least an hour and a half each way), nevertheless turned up regularly over many years. Like most western clients do, also these refugee clients express experiencing beneficial effects from the therapy they have received (i.e. rather irrespective of its theoretical foundations as pointed out above), which is not to say that it has therefore been successful. For such an evaluation the design of this study is not particularly purposeful.

* All ex. 12:

ABOUT THE BENEFITS OF THERAPY

Without exception including Shirin, despite the premature conclusion of her treatment, the clients were happy to have had the opportunity to reflect on their sensitive problems: a typical remark being "this is the only place where I can do that". Fatima is very adamant in this regard, stating that she "would be dead if it were not for this possibility" and she has since maintained therapeutic contact with another therapist. Layla says that because she considers me (the therapist) an irreplaceable member of her family, she would rather keep her problems to herself than change therapist which, however, she willingly does when, after a touching final session she is forced to confront my forthcoming absence; like Aisha and Nasreen, she too has some experience with other therapists. In her last session she returns to the issue of reunion with her family, after having circled around the subject in tears before broaching it. She then presents me with a gift of flowers, reminding both of us of the fact that our sessions have in her case regrettably ended prematurely.

On her part Nasreen, though marked by the gravity of the situation and deeply thankful, bids farewell without further ado, on the whole confident of being able to make it on her own.

What follows is a quotation from the session in which Aisha got to know about the approaching imminent conclusion to her therapy in about half a years time:

> (I'm not quite sure how to raise the issue, because you have made me aware of your customary practice of presenting a problem little by little, while at the same time it is important for you to know in time). Yes? (And you are right in the middle of this difficult time with your daughter (cp. A ex, 10: The Case of Aisha's Daughter Continued). Shall I do it the way it is done in Norway, just say it straight out the way it is?) Yes, you can, because what ever is to be said, good or bad, must, after all, be said. (It concerns my work situation, which is going to change...)

I emphasise the fact that ideally she herself can choose when to end therapy, but point out that reality often puts restrictions on us, and propose various alternatives of how she can either conclude or continue with another therapist. Taking refuge in her religious belief she says:

> I do realise that this is life. The world is like that, family and friends move on, only God remains, without changing. But people do change and move on and disappear. It's the natural order of things. That's just how it is, it is the way of Destiny. – Yes, I did become very sad because I haven't thought of you as a doctor but as one of my closest kin to whom I could talk right from my heart. And that has been a very good thing. I have complete trust in you. But, as I said, people have to part with each other. This is what happens sooner or later. (I have told you that I'll write about your experience, try and get people to understand many wise things you have pointed out to me in order that perhaps someone who arrives later will be spared the experience of some of the unnecessary pain involved in exile). Insh Allah ('God willing').

If the migrant-client is receptive to treatment, in terms of her ability to articulate feelings, and develops an observing ego function and other standard prerequisites for getting well, there should, in my view, be no reason why the difficulties imposed by sociocultural divergence could not be overcome in cross-cultural trauma therapy. There are, however, several issues that have to be discussed when assessing the suitability for and benefit from therapy of multitraumatised clients in cross-cultural exile.

I. THE BENEFIT OF A LONG-TERM PERSPECTIVE
AND FIRM, CONSISTENT BOUNDARIES

Since the traumatic condition of the clients results from an earlier assault on the integrity of their ego, successful treatment in these cases seems above all to be dependent on firm and consistent therapeutic boundaries; as a buffer against the many additional problems of their exile situation that is intruding in the process (cp. chapter one: The Interdisciplinary Challenge, on the pattern of migrants *problem families*). For this reason it is especially important to evaluate the stability of the surrounding external situation of a refugee client being referred for treatment, before embarking on more insight-oriented therapy. Still, in the experience of the Psychosocial Centre for Refugees, many clients have managed to establish a working alliance with their therapists without this external security in their day-to-day lives. In fact, it seems that for some therapy was the only way they could establish any security at all[21]. On the other hand, it is quite common for a client beginning treatment initially to spend quite a long time – while he or she keeps 'coming and going' – before getting settled into or used to the idea of therapy, in short, for basic trust to develop between client and therapist, and also interpreter. The fact that severely traumatised people may suffer, in addition to the insecurity of their exile, from pronounced problems of ego functioning, often makes a long term therapeutic perspective beneficial.

I quote from a letter, accompanied by a dried rose, sent to me by Fatima before our last session prior to an inevitable six month break from therapy, because it highlights a slowly re-emerging and hard won basic trust, which in her case had been particularly slow in coming. And which trust in the case of these traumatised refugee-clients often seems to necessitate, not only an extended initial period of therapy while negotiating mutual roles, but, moreover, a similarly extended concluding phase in which to make sure there is enough time to work through unrealistic dependencies awakened in the process.

* Fatima ex. 20 (pre-concluding):

"DEAR NORA"

I do not know how to begin this letter, but I do know that much now that the word goodbye is very difficult. Like the proverb says, "Becoming attached to someone is an easy matter, but ending the relationship, is like dying slowly". This is the reason why I cannot attend the last session. I do hope that you will not take offence at my discourtesy, because to me you are like a kind mother, a loving sister and a great doctor. With this in mind, I will, from now on, try to convince myself that you are still here. In the hope of seeing you as soon as possible, and good luck!

In conclusion cross-cultural therapy seems – perhaps more than anything else – to necessitate a longer time-perspective than the case is in ordinary therapies, because of diverse factors such as the extended initial as well as concluding phases of therapy and the fact of the extra time already needed for mutual language translation: a fact that makes sessions shorter than an hour unlikely to succeed; mine were as a rule one and a half hours long.[22]

2. THE EXTRAORDINARY CHALLENGE OF THERAPEUTIC ROLES

In cross-cultural trauma therapy, the role of the therapist and interpreter are easily obscured and certainly very demanding due to many complex factors inherent in both interpersonal violence (*the torture trauma*) and cultural interpretation (*the cross-cultural or exile trauma*) as presented under the heading *Between the Devil and Deep Blue Sea* in chapter three. Although the aim of analytic understanding and creating intersubjective meaning from the material brought by the client remains the same, its implementation is more difficult because both sociocultural and extreme psychosocial factors impinge on the situation. Moreover, the dynamics are changed by the presence of at least three individual persons of diverse sociocultural backgrounds (client, therapist, and interpreter). By sharing the process with another involved professional (the interpreter), the therapist may come to lose his or her role as the one who carries primary therapeutic responsibility, a fact that leads to various boundary-related problems concerning formal procedures, time limits, and so on (as presented above).[23] All these changes require from all parties both an ability to patiently wait for the therapeutic alliance to develop and to endure the mechanisms of splitting involved in the triadic constellation that may unfold during the further process of therapy.

3. THE IMPORTANCE OF THE SILENCE, NARRATIVE REFLECTION AND DREAM-LIFE THAT SURROUND TRAUMA

Because the clients are marked by buried trauma and shattered security, meaning/morale, time-orientation, basic trust and future hopes; these must somehow be restored if the hidden is to be uncovered, abreaction is not to turn into retraumatisation. On the other hand, the silence surrounding the patient's trauma must somehow be confronted[24]. Displeasing experiences of strong affect due to feelings of shame and/or guilt, ambivalence and confusion must be endured. Much must be grieved for and the religio-culturally determined and contradictory values addressed in order for the clients to face the reality of their changed situation.

I challenge therapeutically more experienced colleagues to consider such difficult issues further. In this last section, however, I merely want to point out the added significance oral narration has for these largely illiterate migrant-clients. If there is any common ground between western-oriented therapy and their traditional world, it is found in the importance they put on sharing in narration (cp. metaphorical communication in F ex. 3: The Power of Harsh Words; N ex. 3: A Sexually Abused Woman's Secret; A ex. 6/7/ 9/11) and, moreover, at least in the case of these kurdish women, their confidence in dream interpretation.

* Nasreen ex. 9 (medial):

ABOUT THE IMPORTANCE OF DREAMS

Two days after they (the police) had come to fetch my husband, I had this dream, that it was his wedding. (Why a wedding?) I don't know, but when I was in Iran I would tell my Mother or Father, and they would come up with an explanation. Dreaming about money or a wedding is not a good sign. Sometimes you dream about something two or three days in advance. It's happened to me many times.

(What about the bad dreams you had after arriving in Norway?) If Mother had been here it would have been easier, because she could interpret dreams. I don't know why people dream at all. (How did your mother explain that?) I don't know because she never told me why (cp. A ex. 3: About the Meaning of Life). (But those gloomy dreams?) Yes, dreams are sinister. (Do you believe that they contain a sort of message?) Yes, I think so. But I haven't thought about what it is that makes them so important. We always tell each other our dreams on the following day, but the other person might make a joke of it and say "You must have had too much food". But I would reply "No, I didn't".

(Is there any difference between dreams?) Yes, but I just wanted to ask, do you never dream? (Of course, we do.) Perhaps for you who live here, they're not that important, but they are for us, whose family remains there. If we dream about something we say "Aha, perhaps something s happened there". (That is what I am trying to find out, what *you* think about it) Yes, for us it's very important.

(Were you reassured when you told them?) Yes, because that's how it is, the others say "It isn't anything to worry about, that's for sure. You shouldn't think too much about it". (Is it a comfort?) Yes, of course, because when you are able to tell the others, they can find out if anything has happened, if that's the reason for my having this dream, or if something is going to happen; then I just wait to see what happens. Yes, you wait for three-four days and see how things develop.

(Your parents must have had much experience with dreams then?) Yes, because they were old-fashioned, so they knew a lot. Dreams are very valuable for me, and very important. *Only God knows how important this really is to me.* For me, every dream is important. The night I had this particular dream I got out of bed to make tea. My daughter fetched a cup of tea, and I said "You know what, I had this dream that it was father's wedding". She just laughed. But then I said "Only God knows, you see I'm very sad and concerned by this. Why his wedding?" And then two days later the police came to get him.[25]

(next she relates what actually happened) I've already told you. (About the sinister experience?) Yes, because on the day I met him (her husband) he was to bring me something, but he was late. When I finished tidying up and was on my way out, I met him. And he said that he would help me out while I was ill. I replied "You just go up and sit down there while I'm out"'. And he did, but when I returned he was gone. He had disappeared for us.[26] I told my daughter how worried I was. "He'll come back, that's for sure" she said. It was late and he hadn't showed up. Then the police came, they had a letter giving them permission to search the house. (My daughter) asked "Where is my Father?" And they said that they had him. (Did they arrest him in your house?) Yes, while I was out...

(Why do good dreams turn into something sad?) For me it is always that way. "A wedding, for example, – what kind of an event is that?" Then I thought "Now I had a dream about a wedding. May God help us". (Why is a wedding so bad?) Everyone says so, it's not good. It really isn't, that's what they say. (But you do associate a wedding with something good?) Yes, because then, you know, the opposite comes true. (Is it reversed in the world of dreams?) Yes, then it turns out the opposite way. For me it is always the opposite. My Mother thought that way too. That's just how it is. (So you prefer not to have good dreams?) No, this is what I think to myself. (If you dream something sad about your family, would it be reversed then?). You know, *sometimes, concerning the family and that kind of thing, it isn't clear to me what it's like*, if it's something good or bad, so I don't bother because it won't be cleared up anyway. (In that case you'll forget about them?) Yes, because you know, it's more than ten years since I came out [since her flight]. And I don't really know whether they're dead or alive. So for me, I forget this thing and think that there's no use in...

(But at times, when you do remember, do you get anxious?) Yes. (If you dream that your brother has heart trouble, would you be afraid then or think that it is the reverse that counts?) Yes No, in that case I would be very frightened, because I would think that then he really does have heart trouble. If his heart stopped, then everything would come to an end. If that happened, I would think about it day and night. (So it isn't merely an issue of reversal, but it may come true?) Yes, it sure can...That's the way it is, sometimes it's the same way as in the dream. (How can you know which way it is?) No, I don't know, one has to figure it out for oneself, sort out how it is. (Then you need the help of the elders?) Yes. (Your Mother had heard many dreams, hadn't she?) Yes, that's true.

(Is it difficult for you to talk about these things?) Yes, of course it is. (Only sad, or are there any good memories too?) That's exactly why I get sad, but now and then some good memories might also turn up. (Are you sad now?) Of course, because then it always turns out to be just the way it started – all over again.

(Cp. A ex. 14: One Year Past her Mother's Death)

Again, as reflected in this quotation, one runs into difficulties inherent in the double effect of or even conflict as between sociocultural understanding and psychological theory about trauma. In this case the difficulty seem to arise from the fact that the collective tradition of dream interpretation – to which this client is accustomed from childhood on – doesn't fit the nightmares that according to our psychological understanding are considered a direct result of her post traumatic stress disorder. A fact which, again, could explain why/how the ensuing psychocultural confusion might generate feedback and further complicate the PTSD related symptoms of disorganisation.

4. THE CULTURAL SENSIVITY REQUIRED FOR BRIDGING THE PAST WITH THE FUTURE

Because the condition of these clients is marked by helplessness in the face of overwhelming external events (organised social violence) that involve their past as well as their future life quality as migrants in exile, the focus of therapy should not merely be on the client's psycho-history, but also on the equivalent history of her sociocultural status. Therapists who work cross-culturally should be aware of what it is like to be involved in different sociocultural traditions following a forced migration, and what it is like to get confused without, however, recognising the origin of the confusion as Nasreen clearly does in the above example: About the Importance of Dreams. He or she should be able to understand deviant versus conforming behaviour not just for what regards middle class western standards, but many other ethnic and social class standards as well. In this way they will not unnecessary confuse the client even more, but be basically supportive of him or her. It is, for example, in my view, important initially to consider the family as a whole supportive unit, to keep it together where possible, to strengthen the parental roles from the outset which are shattered by both traumatic experience and cross-cultural migration and to be aware of any developing unwanted imbalances in gender patterns by way of being attentive to the sociocentric structure of relationships prevalent at home. In this way the traumatised clients are given a certain breathing space before having to confront the further problems of exile (cp. the concept of time out on p. 278 below).

ON THE NARRATIVE APPROACH
AND MEANING-FORMATION

Refugee Narratives and 'Time'

Following on from the preceeding analysis of the emerging cross-cultural therapeutic space from an interactionist perspective, I will now proceed to consider *the identificatory migratory process* as it is reflected in the clients' narratives. The stories told to me by the participants in this study vary a great deal, for example regarding issues such as time, context and persons involved. When the clients narrate, the culture of their origin and primary reference group speaks through their mouths, so to speak. Moreover, for a psychologically competent listener, the story can to a certain extent also reveal the traumas of the narrator's lives, such as those depicted in this study. I would however go even further and claim that the story itself changes as a result of the narrative encounter, the main reason being that there are several ways of listening to it. For example, therapists who are used to listening to the suffering of their patients, are attuned to the fact that the emerging illness narrative will shape the events *in retrospect*, so as to distance – or actually integrate – an otherwise frightening reality (chapter two: Psychological Trauma Reconsidered).

Outside of the therapeutic setting, retrospective narrating is frequent in the ageing population, in situations marked by catastrophe, or where such a situation was only narrowly avoided. In such cases, it is evident how the story holds a moral purpose, while stressing certain core themes as a sort of summation of one's life trials. It functions like the recitation of a myth, reaffirming the values under siege while at the same time pointing the finger of condemnation towards the perceived injustice (cp. the witness story). The *raison d'être* of the process is not primarily fidelity to the (historical) facts, but rather validity in the bestowing of subjective meaning. In general, for the person telling the story of her life, the first function is not to describe the past as it was, but to confer a certain subjective meaning to it. This creative rearranging plays an instrumental role in allowing the subject – by way of mediation – to incorporate her past into the script of her present life as well as her hopes for the future. From an analytical point of view the *forms* of life stories may therefore be just as important as the events which they describe. Indeed several authors have stressed the relationship between the cognitive ordering of time as a coping mechanism and the mental health problems of migrants.

It seems that during periods of acute stress, the relative emphasis people place upon past, present and future events are affected. As long as the traumatic experiences of the past continues to live on inside the survivor encapsulated as 'a foreign body', time seems to stand still in this area of her personality. According to Varvin and Hauff (1998, 119), the main purpose of therapy for severely traumatised patients who tend to be incapable of accepting the possibility of a future for themselves, is to get their internal clock started again so that the trauma can be integrated as a part of the past. It seems to me that the clients somehow perceive their future to be foreshortened, thus also lacking energy to plan for it. According to Beiser's study (1987, 437-38), thai refugees arriving in Canada focused their problems on the present situation to the relative exclusion of both the past and future, as a coping strategy, I would add.

Indeed, it seems that the re-emergence of the traumatic past into the subject's consciousness carries with it a risk for developing severe depression (cp. the risk of retraumatisation), especially if the person slips into nostalgia (cp. Aisha & Nasreen below). Knudsen (1990, 126; also 1988), however, challenges these conclusions on the basis of his own anthropological data, collected from vietnamese refugee camp dwellers, which, quite to the contrary, confirm a strong future-orientation. According to him, getting these asylum seekers to talk about the present was problematic, which he interprets and I would agree, as a mechanism of survival considering the fact that the camp was a real hell in which they were presently involved, and about which they could do very little.

The cognitive ordering of time in narration thus varies contextually according to the psychocultural level of stress as well as with the strategic presentation of its content, or the information sought in interaction. According to my experience from these clients' treatments, the main point seems to be that, at diverse points in time, the subjects, depending on their mental status *and* phase in migration (level of integration), select or repress elements from different points in time and settings. Events, which then tend to be presented and serve as strong contrasts between past retrospection and perceptions of the present or future. The ensuing illness story may thus be more or less past-/present- or future-oriented according to a variety of interdisciplinary factors and situational demands.

As Knudsen (1997; 1983) points out, refugee narratives contain information that changes with regard to the context and with regard to identity management strategies over time, vis-à-vis various sets of significant others. It is not a mere life story but, simultaneously, a more or less conscious strategy for self-presentation. In addition to the content and interpersonal exchange being indicative of the psycho-socio-cultural variables surrounding it, such stories can be related to, or chosen from among, a number of available *forms of relating*. There are many types of solutions that can create meaning in the course of a person's life; for example, whether one views misfortune as being due to the maliciousness of others or as a result of one's own neglect (cp. the concept of locus of control[1]), or finds a goal in some superior value system which postpones relief until some later date or place; for example in the idea of paradise after death. Or perhaps one might, for various reasons, simply have been called by a bad destiny (A ex. 3: About the Meaning of Life & N ex. 6: A Memorate of *Adjal*).

Eriksen (1990) proposes a typology for illustrating a number of such available life stories which create meaning in autobiographical material (See illustration below). According to her, the A:D structure combination, i.e. re-evoked memories of a happy past or childhood and a difficult, disharmonious present situation, is the most compli-cated. Here, informants have to address the conflict ridden problem of explaining why everything went wrong, despite the fact that it started off so well, a situation which is typical of the adult refugee who is free of primary traumatisation (like Aisha/Nasreen). By extension of the same strictly formal logic, that would make the opposite B:C structure (like that of Fatima) the least complicated one.

If subjects fail to reach inner consistency in processing the contra-dictory evidence of their narration (in respect of the past, present and future) disintegration is likely to follow. As long as this lack of coher-ence continues they will be liable to various symptoms of stress and subsequent solution seeking behaviour, such as may become chroni-cally contained in the PTSD symptomatology and exile stress following in its wake. Despite the fact that this is the point at which the role of the therapist is actualised in the lives of forced refugees, the narrative

AUTOBIO-GRAPHY LIFESPAN	positive evaluation in presentation	negative evaluation in presentation
PREVIOUS EXPERIENCES	A	B
PRESENT EXPERIENCES	C	D

approach remains an aspect of mental health care studies that has so far been rather neglected. Awareness of a more complete process, including a full appreciation of the role of the client's narrative *as such* (when analysed as a text), would contribute to our understanding of traumatisation as it is unfolded in the lives of refugees-on-the-move, especially while cast in the difficult role of patients-on-foreign-soil.

Differences in narrative style show up both in the content (the themes presented) and the way of telling the stories (the forms of mediation or coping strategies). Across ethnocultural and religious boundaries, men, for example, tend to present themselves as initiators in the stories they relate, while females seem more attuned towards *relationships* and will more easily include and credit significant others in their life stories. Such differences of gender are seen in the very language used: men use "I" more often than women, particularly the tradition-oriented women of this study who prefer collective expressions. A husband who tells *his* story with a concern for chronological accuracy may, according to Bertaux-Wiame (1990, 257), however, constantly have to turn to his wife for help, who will again subdue his self-willed image in a web of surrounding circumstances and persons influencing the reconstruction.

Such issues of style are not merely a conscious choice, but reflect forms of real life, in this case the condition of women in kurdish society as producers of what their society define as their proper products: children, not merely biologically but socioculturally produced. Life stories entail different relations to life and hence to the act of telling about it. The psychologically relevant aspects of a patient's life come to the surface in the clinical material not only through biographical

233

data, but also through a number of other channels. These facts are, moreover, transferable to *the how, why and when* a particular help is chosen. Furthermore, meaningful illness stories entail a specific adaptational response to the 'Why' of the development of their lives, classifying its favourable and unfavourable elements according to some coherent explanatory principle, frequently with their roots in childhood experiences; these could be said to constitute a sort of archaeological structure for the psychotherapist.

The Architecture of Kurdish Social Interaction and the Clients' Childhood Settings

I will argue that human memory selects, rearranges and endows certain events or categories with a symbolic meaning, to the point of turning them into personal myths. For example, place as *Home-place* appears to be pre-eminently an emotionally charged, almost sacred, category of nostalgia, a word derived from the greek *nostos*, to return home. Moreover, place as Home-place lies at the heart of psychodynamic ideation, filled with reveries of childhood memories: moments of special significance, private or shared, considered incomprehensible to outsiders lacking intimate knowledge. In this sense home is not simply the place where one is born or happens to live, but a place for memories to be housed. As such it is unique; there is no place like home.

On the basis of these largely smithian (1987) assumptions, I will take the three core patient's [2] childhood settings, or Home-places, as a starting point for depicting their basically sociocentric selves – that is, in juxtaposition to the average kurdish woman's prescribed role – and their ensuing coping strategies in exile. In her book *Children of the Jinn. In Search of the Kurds and their Country* (1980), Kahn relates how, through bitter fieldwork experience, she had to learn not to expect to meet people individually; rather kurdish women under normal circumstances at home always appear in a group setting (A ex. 5: The Shameful Photographs). The picture on the cover of this publication was chosen in appreciation of the various ways the participating women of this study have in fact – due to the extraordinary circumstances of their lives – been left alone with their children in the absence of kin/husbands; and of their individual ways of participation in the process of therapy while they have been driven into a foreign exile; i.e. in sharp contrast to the sociocentricity of their expected role.

Kahn would meet the women either at reception-like arrangements in their homes, where the eldest woman presided and asked more questions than she evasively answered, or outside of it, under the supervision of men, because it was unthinkable for a woman of that area to go out alone. Her experience echoes the problems western-oriented therapists encounter when trying to reach a working alliance with this category of exiled clients as described in the previous chapters. But there are of course also subcultural variation in their gender patterns, such as those resulting from Aisha's background in a feudal family of *agha* landlords, Nasreen's background in the urbanising upper-middle social strata, and Fatima's background in the lower class sector of rural emigré families to the poor districts of the towns (All ex. 2: The Kurdish Legacy).

Persian feudalism is based on the hereditary prestige of owning a village as Aisha's kin did, or a piece of land as was the case with Nasreen's family, while Fatima's family was too poor to own anything but their tragically collapsing house (F ex. 2:"Promise me never to speak of my mother as being dead"). The joint family including its servants is a structure firmly rooted in this kind of persian feudalism, with the *pater familias* as the main focus of loyalty and manager of common affairs. As the head of the family, though absent for much of the time given that he stays in some other locale with his additional wives and their children, he is treated as the absolute source of law and order. Together with his kin, the kurdish *agha* (landlord or *pater familias*) has formed a privileged aristocratic group in a traditional enclave remaining largely isolated from urban life styles despite living in the capital for parts of the year, like Aisha's extended family did.

The common land owning unit is the village (the landlord owns the village), and its chief responsibility the maintenance of its guesthouse. Kurds are well known for their hospitality; On the whole they believe in offering only the best to their guests, often the best part of the house, the best food and their best social presentation is reserved for guests. In Aisha's case two large rooms of her family's lodgings delineated the separate worlds of women respectively men and visitors. In the latter male room, a 'throne seat' was reserved for the landlord himself, while a small door gave access to the female quarters.

Through this small door food was passed back and forth, and those persons entitled to enter it, especially small boys up until the age of about six, also passed freely from one room to another.

* Aisha ex. 17 (medial):

THE GUEST HOUSE

Imagine there is a house, and then there is a wall there in the house (she shows me while gesturing on a piece of paper), and a small door in the wall. The men could have access to the women's side of the wall which separated the genders. They could come in to fetch food or chat to their children or wives. Women were not permitted to move as they pleased, but the small boys had a separate room apart from the girls, where they could sleep – just the same way it was organised for the men. When they grew up and wanted to stay up late, they didn't return to sleep there but stayed with the men.

Until about the age of 13 we (the girls) were allowed to go out and play, but after that age we had to stay at home. If there was a wedding or some other party we had to ask nicely to go out. Otherwise, everything came to an end... (i.e. there would be trouble). We were not permitted even to leave the house. You know, when I myself grew older and became a mother, I asked Mother "Why did Father lay down such strict rules, that males and females had to be separated, stayed together during nights only, and that boys and girls could not see each other?" She said that it has been like that right from the beginning, that there had been a generation before (my) Father's which was like that too. She could not say for how long it would last, but that that was how it should be, she said.

In this home context, the men largely lived apart from the women; slept in separate rooms, kept apart during social gatherings, and had separate foray outside of the house or in a separate space attached to it, where they socialised, smoked, ate and even slept. They were not allowed to enter the female side except for doing business considered necessary such as fetching food, talking a little to their wives, or, very discretely spending time during the night with them. At the latest about the age of twelve, boys were definitely removed outside the confines of the world of the women, which was not considered suitable for men to dally in, and praised for having 'learned shame'. The years between six to twelve were considered a period of learning, but from that age on also the boys were expected to show respect towards the women by spending little time among them.

In Papanek's (1973) well known studies on purdah, the home world of women is likened to a symbolic shelter reflecting the asymmetrical relationship existing between the gender categories within the traditional muslim context. However, women from the smaller kurdish provincial towns, to which Nasreen's family of employees[3] belonged, experienced less segregational pressure than Aisha did, obliged as they often were to share in the men's efforts to earn a living. Some of Nasreen's female kin did precisely this, working in nursing and in education, as well as earning money as dressmakers.

From the point of view of examining what iranian interaction (including gender) patterns are relevant to cross-cultural therapies, the contrast between the external or outward (*zaher*) and the internal or inward (*baten*), which corresponds to the insider-outsider axis touched on in the previous chapter twelve (The Aesthetics of Cross-cultural Therapeutic Interaction), is a most useful dichotomy. This contrast governs a variety of spatial aspects from collective life to personal orientation, including a twofold concept of the self comprising *a public and a private core self*[4]. The private self is thought to house one's true feelings, protected by the public one from external disruption and trauma.

* Nasreen ex. 10 (9 continued/medial):

THE LIVING-ROOM OF DREAMS

Nasreen, who had sought me out for what turned out to be persistent nightmares about her family back home, felt her biggest loss to be the common family evening gatherings. Every single night, until her mother died and the revolution dispersed the family, they all gathered in a living-room decorated with cushions and rugs to eat, talk and interpret each others dreams (see N ex. 9: About the Importance of Dreams). Her father (when visiting from the household of his other wife) would sit at the far end with the others, everyone in their proper place according to their age and gender, which also accorded them the right to speak or attention.

One must know how carefully to operate such a distinction between the internal and external spheres in order to stay out of trouble (cp.

the shameful problems of exile). The internal *baten* is the seat of the strongest feelings such as romantic passion or *gheiret*, a term connoting a sense of indignation or the violent angry outburst at a personal affront which is difficult to control (cp. the *authority incidents*). Despite the unsettling character of the emotions contained herein, their expression on appropriate occasions is not merely socially sanctioned but *demanded* (cp. the obligatory nature of ritual emotion). The sharing of private experience, such as listening to music, drinking tea, smoking or reading poetry, belong in this area and are usually carried out in intimate situations only (All ex. 10: "Inside-Outside" positioning, and the difficulties in establishing a therapeutic alliance earlier referred to).

In contrast to this, in the external *zaher* area one's true feelings are concealed and a public face put on, marked by controlled polite expression and hospitality. Although a necessary concomitant to life, and a buffer for the delicate 'inside' areas, the *zaher* area is, however, not highly valued in moral terms, but considered the realm of personal manipulation[5], corruption and worldly influence. My point here is that a clients' interaction even in exile may be highly contextualised depending on factors like these, a most important concern still being the explicit recognition of hierarchical distinctions based on such principles as age, gender, genealogical seniority and degree or kind of incorporation into the group[6].

Now looking at parental relationships (cp. chapter five on the violation of intergenerational obligations), it could be said that: Like the father of Nasreen, Aisha's father had remained a distant, though beloved, person whom she could only meet on his explicit request or subsequent to the mediation of her elder brother, and that furthermore in rather formal circumstances, the transcending of which boundaries created immediate anxiety[7].

* Aisha ex. 18 (medial):

ON THE LAP OF THE PATRIARCH FATHER
FOR A LITTLE TO LONG

In retrospect Aisha remembers herself as having been the favourite daughter of her father, who, after all, had some privileges as compared to the other women of the household (cp. A ex. 4: Purdah of the Heart); but she also remembers the ensuing fear from having possibly transcended the limits of what is considered proper behaviour by her people when she used to sit on his lap although she was already past the first signs of puberty.

The father-daughter-relationship is based on the same principles of gender subjugation as that which exists between husband and wife, in addition to the further age hierarchy involved. The relationship between a brother and his sister is more intimate, and is therefore frequently used as a pretext to allow a young man, labelled 'brother' for the purpose, to socialise with a girl, on condition that he is to protect her and to refrain from sexual advances (cp. *as-if strategies* discussed below). Of the available female roles, such as reflected in the folk tales of the area, that of a mother, especially a post-menopausal one, is the least ambiguous and most positively loaded one, associated with the widest possible freedom of action.

* Nasreen ex. 11 (medial):

'MY MOTHER'S YOUNGEST DAUGHTER'

When she was a mere toddler Nasreen's father took another wife, stating the need for labour attending to his many animals as the reason. According to her, no one wanted her father to take a new wife but her mother was not the type to start a quarrel (cp. N ex. 4: 'If it had not been because of us'). However, like her siblings, she herself refused to play along and often quarrelled with her half-siblings, a disunion which has remained until this day. It was at the time more than five years since she has heard anything about "that part of the family", and she didn't even know where they now lived (observe that this is a deviation from the norm).

Like her mother and herself, Nasreen's father was illiterate apart from having learnt the Koran. Because he refused to educate his daughters from his first marriage, at an early age she decided that her own children were not to suffer from illiteracy. At home a scribe was used only on particularly important occasions, never otherwise.[8] Everything was based on spoken interaction.

However, it turns out that Nasreen (like Layla) took part in the decision as to whom she would marry. Although according to tradition she was engaged to her mother's-sister's- son, her father nevertheless didn't force his daughters to marry into the family. She herself was consulted, and did not like this particular boy. She says that she turned

239

down many proposals before marrying her brother's friend without too many costs involved. He paid the bride price to her father, who used a part of it to help them set up a separate household next door.

She was thus an active participant in her own marriage and is content with her choice even though it ended in divorce as a result of his violent (PTSD-linked) behaviour subsequent to the torture to which he had been subjected (He continues to stay with them for periods of time). She wants her children to be able to choose their spouses by themselves, but when her daughter was prevented from marriage by norwegian age rules despite having reached the kurdish marriageable age of sixteen, she found this difficult to deal with. Despite the fact that she would have preferred her daughter to marry her sister's son, the latter came to marry a non-kin kurdish refugee without opposition by her mother or the kind of problems Aisha had to experience in relationship to her children (cp. A ex. 4: Purdah of the Heart).

> My husband is angry, he shouts and sometimes hits us. (Are you afraid of him?) When he is angry he has to do *something*. I'm afraid of being hurt. (Is it difficult for him to control himself?) He has no self-control at all. He became that way when we arrived here. (Was it a mutual decision to split up?) We talked it over, and I said that "It would be much better if we went our different ways because something could happen". At first, when we were newly wed, our married life was very good (she still seems genuinely fond of her husband).

> (What was the best part of that life?) He never asked where I was going when I went out, I was permitted to visit my Mother whenever I wanted to. This made me very happy. (He gave you rather a lot of freedom?) Yes. (Had you been afraid that it would be otherwise?) Yes. I thought that I would not be able to see my Mother so often. But it didn't turn out that way! (She is obviously content while telling me this). I was so terribly fond of my Mother, I liked to spend a lot of time with her. You see, my Father had two wives so I have several half-sisters younger than me. But I'm my Mother's youngest daughter (Does it mean something special?) I don't know, it isn't special in that (traditional) way, but nevertheless I was very fond of Mother, and Mother was very fond of me. That was just how it was: I was terribly fond of my Mother, and Mother was terribly fond of me.

> (What did you do when you were together?) We sat together, talked together, perhaps laughed together, cooked together.

Because my Mother wasn't old at all (You were good friends?) Yes, just like good friends (cp. All ex. 9 & 10). I do have to say, that I have so many happy memories about Mother.

(What about her grave?) You know, it is such a big cemetery, but they have put up a fence around the spot which is only for our family. I pray to God that there will be a day when it will be possible to visit it. That is what one most wants. (What would you do if you had the possibility?) You sit down and just start crying (she cries when telling this). I'm so very fond of Mother; Father too, but I'm particularly fond of my Mother. You sit beside the grave. (Would you take something with you?) Yes, we take flowers and some candles to light beside the grave. And you decorate the grave. But I can't go there...[9]

(Is there any difference at what time of the day you go?) No, we go at midday. They say it is good to visit the dead, who are there on Thursdays. (Do you think that you would start crying before reaching the grave?) That's for sure, if you have very many burdens inside of you, how could you not? (Would you have gone there alone?) If I could have gone there now, I would have gone alone (cp. Aisha ex. 14: One Year After her Mother's Death, according to whose custom this was not allowed). Stayed for four-five hours. (Would you have you done something else or merely cried and cried?) You could pray, or recite some Koranic verses, and you cry and talk to them (Some particular verse?) Yes, you read a verse called The Conclusion (actually it is called the Opening) *Fatiheh* from the Koran. (Why is that?) That I don't know. (How does it go?) I can't remember. Yes, you cry and sit down and just talk. (In that case you would have told her all you needed?) (She cries.) Yes, just told everything then...

(Where do you think she is now, would she be able to hear you if you were there?) That I have to say I don't know. (Do you believe in a life after death?) I don't know, the others claim that there is one, but I don't know. I keep wondering "How can you live when you are dead?"

The difference between the outward and internal self creates a parallel structure in the social and even physical environment toward which its energies are directed, as reflected in the gender based spatial arrangements permeating the traditional muslim life world. In its architectural form the internal part of the house is represented by the *anderun*,

241

the heart of social peace, the space within the household, which is the most private, secluded and female. It is also the seat of family intimacy – the living-room where dreams are interpreted – where one – especially the women – may find safety from the outside world and can give free reign to expression of one's feelings and thoughts. Its opposite is the *birun*, the public reception area of the household where strangers are entertained without endangering the private female sphere of the family (A ex. 17: The Guest House above).

Almost every piece of behaviour reinforces and reaffirms this distinction. In inside as opposed to outside situations, people are expected to carry themselves differently. While outside, movement is restricted, the body stiff, and eye contact or verbal interaction is avoided across the genders. The processes of other-raising versus self-lowering involved in courtesy behaviour between perceived unequals clearly belong in outside situations where emotions are restricted, far removed from the expectations associated with a therapeutic atmosphere (cp. Int. ex. 2: Other-raising vs. Self-lowering). On the other hand, in inside situations, people are more expressive. The intimate male visitor may proceed unannounced to the inner quarters of the household, be offered a pyjamas, and, while he is offered refreshments, they will most likely not be pressed on him as they would be in outside situations. He is free to come and go without being extensively greeted or exhorted to eat more than he wishes to[10].

Within the inner confines of the house, siblings including half-brothers and –sisters, and cousins of the joint family, who are considered to be the closest intimate equals (like siblings), may sprawl on the floor and adopt a generally relaxed attitude. But the moment an older relative enters, they immediately pull themselves into a respectful sitting position (cp. what is said about Aisha being uncomfortable with her daughter's behaviour when in the presence of their father in A ex. 4: Purdah of the Heart). To do otherwise would violate normal expectations as presented above.

The case of Fatima in many ways offers an exception from the rule, anchored as it is in the plight of people 'without a public voice' in the poor districts of large towns. Both her parents were forced to take almost any job; the father running a small teashop while the mother worked as a cleaner on low wages. Also, the fact that her father was shi'ite while her mother was sunni created problems from early on. Furthermore, the fact that she became an orphan left her very lonely and in the end wholly cast off from familial networks in a world she rightly perceived of as being full of dangers for such an unprotected female.

* Fatima ex. 20 (2 continued/post-medial):

THE HOME DESTROYED

Differently from the other clients, she initially came to my therapy sessions alone, displaying, furthermore, a remarkable independent character and a will of her own, quite different from the others. The home, she knew, had been a badly constructed house for which her parents had worked hard before it collapsed, burying them all, an event which was to give her life its out of the ordinary quality under the auspices of her married elder sister who maltreated her, until she fled and joined a run-away teenage brother in the city. His later disappearance, however, left her completely alone and, again, unprotected; this time quite literally naked in the street, robbed by strangers on the outskirts of a large metropolis in which the proper place of respectable females where officially out of sight.

Fatima describes the relationship between her parents as being very good ("They were very fond of each other"; cp. F ex. 2: "Promise me never to speak of my mother as being dead") and their family life as being isolated from other kin. Her own relationship to her remaining siblings was bad. Following her father's advice and encouragement, she managed to acquire an education and describes herself as "at the outset, an organised person with top-level grades and aspirations" (which was also my impression, that she was on the whole a highly motivated, dedicated and conscientious person). This was not achieved, however, without opposition from her relatives, mainly for economic reasons (at this point she has yet to tell me about her fate as an orphan). Later, she was to work with tasks which were generally looked down upon by the iranian establishment, such as nursing or taking up music and dancing.

It follows from the narrow confines of the prevalent female image as also reflected in the folk tales of the area, that even when right at the centre of attention during marriage negotiations, the ordinary kurdish woman still remains a minor character on a stage publicly dominated by men (F ex 10: 'Nothing but a Widow'). She does not appear independently until she is left alone for some reason, for example in

243

old age, or if she is considered somehow deviant or morally corrupt (cp. the exceptions treated in the next chapter: Symbolic Shelter in a Changing World). In the folk tales, what we might see as colourful female characters are thus as a rule represented by 'bad' or evil personalities whose acts are somehow considered extraordinary and out of place. Only such deviant or otherwise exceptional women have the power to influence the larger scheme of things, in which case their abnormal behaviour is given close attention by their surroundings. While most 'good' wives are less interesting and occupy a passive withdrawn position, there are examples of more colourful treacherous wives. Like old wives, they constitute a favourite and much less unambiguous female character in the folk tales of this area, as well as in its jokes and conversations[11].

According to Jonathan Smith (1987, 25-29), it has been the persistent claim of humanistic geographers that *place as Home-place* is best understood as a locus of subjective meaning. Place, many claim, is the beginning of our existence, just as much as a parent is. Like memory, however, it remains a complex and deceptive arena which appears to be primarily a matter of the past, yet in actual fact equally part of the present. Moreover, it is as much an external affair as it is an internal one: the axis of orientation, or how we place ourselves in relationship to our experience. In this sense, we are both placed and bring place into being, since it is neither wholly a creation of the inherent personality structure, nor a question of what forms or leaves an imprint on personality. Undifferentiated space, lacking any significance other than strangeness, becomes 'place' only when we get to know it better and are able to endow it with subjective meaning, so aptly described by Nasreen in N ex. 1: A Topsy Turvy World. It is perhaps ironic that home is frequently perceived as most meaningful from the perspective of distance.

Models for Adaptational Choice:
From Cause towards Meaning Resolution.

Long term refugees in cross-cultural exile struggle to establish continuity in their life course. This struggle confronts them daily with problems on many levels not just stemming from their traumatic past, but with the normative contrasts between the new and old sociocultural setting as well. To them, not only is their past always present,

osity about alternative ways of thinking – which resulted from her being an orphan of mixed religious affiliation in the 'wrong' cultural setting. She was to move from the extremely unstable conditions and maltreatment of her childhood and youth, towards the brave struggle of a young woman for her husband's love at home, and again abroad, while militating against the image of 'a fallen woman' attributed to her by the surroundings.

— *Separation anxiety and intermittent desperation* (a suicide attempt; hospitalisations).

— *Intruding thoughts* and fear of re-experiencing torture ('injured basic trust').

This intelligent client's few existing relationships were highly emotionally charged, somewhat ambivalent and certainly complicated, at the same time while she herself appeared to be a curious mixture of a dependent and stubborn person, who managed to become somewhat 'special' also in the eyes of the interpreter and myself as her therapist.

(cp. All ex. 2: The 'Bad' Woman)

In effect, trauma gives rise to a conflict with which the ego deals, with varying degrees of success and in varying ways. The overall balance between progressive and regressive developmental forces will, eventually, determine the psychological outcome. At one end of the scale is assimilation and eventual mastery (Nasreen?), at the other various degrees of failure of resolution, with persistent symptom formation and prolonged depression (Aisha?). Character traits occupy an intermediate position, representing various degrees/types of fixations on the trauma, which are ego-syntonic and periodically do not manifest the negative effects associated with symptoms (Fatima?).

From these – separately – emerging casuistic client profiles I will now turn to the research issues (set forth in italics below) summoned in the concluding chapter Defining my Concern on Sensitive Issues, while, simultaneously, summing up the central tenets of the inter-casuistic analysis:

As initially pointed out (All ex.1: Time and Manner of Referral) Aisha arrived in therapy with her husband, followed by her eldest son as a chaperon, before she eventually was allowed to visit me on her own, and despite initial resistance also to use public transport even if she by doing so felt naked and unprotected (cp. what is said about gender mobility in the next chapter: Symbolic Shelter in a Changing World).

On the other hand *Nasreen*, despite coming on her own, had been encouraged by her husband, who had received therapy himself and knew the staff, to attend my sessions.

Fatima, who was referred by her solicitor during a period of conflict with the authorities, atypically came alone as she had no close person in the country at the time. In addition to suffering from PTSD as the others did, she had briefly been hospitalised for making a suicide attempt while desperately awaiting the reunion with her beloved husband.

– How did the clients themselves construe the trauma?

THE FIRST SINGLE-CASE ANALYSIS (Aisha)

From the outset, it was evident that the motivating factor behind Aisha's – and her husband's – request for therapy was not her past traumatic experiences, despite the fact that these experiences constituted an enormous burden for her and were continuously re-actualised and worked through as part of the therapy. Aisha and her family's prime motivation for therapy was based, rather, on *material needs and demands* directed at Norwegian Welfare Authorities (this seems to be a result of what they experienced – quite correctly so – as their loss of status in exile), in their own words: "in order for her to be able to function as a housewife again" (level 1).

After a long time in therapy, a reorientation in the direction of ruminations about her *neglected obligations, bereavement* and *despair* in relation to her dead son and kin back home, accompanied by a severe depression, became evident (level 2).

Before Aisha ended the sessions in persistent reflections about *her role as a responsible mother* in relationship, on the one hand, to her own (now deceased) mother as a role model and, on the other, the changing gender role of her daughters in exile (level 3). This theme had, however, been implicit in the very first session (cp. the breach in functioning as a housewife).

Though this client will experience first a relief of her PTSD symptoms, they are soon replaced by an extended period of depression only slightly improving towards the end of our time together. Only towards the end of our sessions does she again manage to take an active role in the relationship with her children, while at the same time struggling to keep her disintegrating family together *under alien cultural pressure*.

THE SECOND SINGLE-CASE ANALYSIS (Nasreen)

In Nasreen's case, the initial wish for relief soon changes into *grief and longing* for her kin back home and *intergenerational problems* emerge (level 1).

Subsequent to this, her own *personal trauma story* emerges, followed by a deep and long-lasting depression which replaces the PTSD symptoms (level 2).

The situation is further complicated by her exile problems, especially the *loss of custody* of her son, (before his return home by the Child Welfare Authorities) which happened to coincide with the return home of an older brother (he had earlier moved away from home receiving support from the social security services) and the successful marriage of her daughter. Taken together, these factors make *recovery* and a successful conclusion to therapy in her case possible (level 3).

A prerequisite on the part of the Child Welfare authorities for returning the custody of her son, however, seems to have been her own divorce from a husband suffering from outburst of anger due to PTSD and the absence of her eldest son (whose return was therefore kept secret).

THE THIRD SINGLE-CASE ANALYSIS (Fatima)

Fatima began therapy in the hope that demands would be made towards the authorities in Norway, in her specific case concerning the *reunion* with her husband. It was not long, however, before her own traumatic experiences from the past emerged expressed *through very strong/trauma-laden reactualisations* (level 1).

Her therapy deals precisely with mastering these (remembered experiences and intruding reactualisations) as expected by western-educated

251

therapists, even if she (like the others) waits for years to disclose *sexual violation* (level 2).

In time, however, her earlier *deviant gender role*, which was already evident to me from the outset judging from the fact that she arrived alone to sessions, and not accompanied by her husband or any other family member or 'protector'; and from the independent action she had taken against the authorities, eventually crystallises as the main theme of therapy and her coping (level 3).

Depending on external circumstances (unemployment and her partly self-imposed social *isolation* for fear of disclosing her past), Fatima fluctuates between marked improvements and recurring relapses (though they become less malignant in time) in the form of reactualised anxiety. Such relapses and the accompanying anxiety render her very *dependent* on the mainly supportive treatment contact (cp. F ex. 19: 'Dear Nora').

In sum, the above analysis can be said, first of all, to confirm theoretical expectations about problems relating to the prevailing kurdish gender role. Fatima's deviance can be given predictable reasons. From childhood on, she appears to have been at odds with the sociocultural norms of her surroundings, a fact which will become all the more evident as she experiences greater, if ambivalent, acceptance in relationship to the norwegian culture and gender roles. Let me now relate these findings to research issue 3, as presented in the concluding chapter fourteen, about coping, and focus on how, after many years of treatment, it all turned out.

– How does the narrative structure reflect the clients' ability to cope?

Based on clinical presuppositions the extent (i.e. amount, persistency and subjective significance) of traumatisation, as well as the survivors' predisposition in terms of earlier deviance or psychological problems, should have decisive impact on the therapeutic outcome. Such evaluations gave my supervisor misgivings about the benefits of offering Fatima a more ambitious therapeutic treatment at the time. Moreover, from the point of view of uniculturally determined expectations concerning a proper kurdish woman's life course and expected happiness in life, her position as an unprotected and traumatised orphan was, likewise, weak; that is, were it not for the new possibilities opened up by her exile. But then, as it turned out, the turn the therapeutic process in her case took (her coping rather well in exile) was somewhat unexpected, irrespective of which perspective is made a basis of the evaluation. According to clinical evaluation she was obviously pre-traumatised and according to cultural analysis highly prestigmatised.

While Aisha and Nasreen moved from PTSD symptoms to marital problems, prolonged depression and the need to rely on disability pension, and both their families were threatened by disintegration; Fatima unexpectedly (but in tune with the motif of her life depicted above: the survival of the underdog) moved from a near mental breakdown, a suicide attempt followed by hospitalisation and being defined as a rather serious case, to further education and even work, while her married life is marked by harmony. Subsequent periods of unemployment and unavoidable separations from her husband, however, seem to immediately trigger a reaction and her dependence on the treatment continues.

It is thus obvious that both explanatory hypothesises ('culture' and 'trauma') need revision in relationship to the emerging interdisciplinary picture while they come to interact in various ways. In spite of the relatively happy childhood of Nasreen and to a lesser extent Aisha[12], the psychologically deprived (orphaned) Fatima after all seems to have managed somewhat better in the exile situation. Could it be that the culturally determined relatively greater acceptance of her gender role in the host society carries more weight than the influence of the socially condemning norms of her previous setting, and that, moreover, to the degree that it will overshadow the psychologically malign factors of her past? My reflective guess would be both yes and no. Moreover, a structural review of her story yield an uncomplicated (C:B) narrative structure. Counter-arguments would be that the picture is complicated by the suicide of Aisha's son and the murder of a female friend under extremely obscure circumstances in exile. Fatima has not experienced similar trauma in this country, but was imprisoned in solitary confinement and cruelly tortured in Iran before her flight, while Aisha, though witnessing extreme violence during her years of imprisonment, was herself targeted to a lesser degree. Nasreen occupies a middle position in this sense, having been imprisoned and sexually molested before the flight, and, then, intermittently having lost custody of her son while in exile.

An open question also remains as to what degree Fatima's case reflects a much more frequent situation among the poorer sectors of large urbanising centres in the Third world, a strata of society not usually represented among the lower-middle class/upward mobile immigrants to the West. In other words, her deviance was in fact given a certain amount of support already at home by her own deprived parents, especially her father; and her problems has to be seen in relation to the co-ordinated social ambitions of her poor family and herself. This is also supported by the expressed positive attitude of her father, against the common practice of the neighbourhood, regarding the education of his daughters and his thereby overt breach of gender rules (F ex. 11: Taking part in Muharram Celebrations as a Little Girl).

In conclusion, while Aisha and Nasreen have ended up in the wrong place, in a strange and frightening foreign culture, Fatima was according to her own testimony "born to the wrong culture" and thus to a larger extent prepared for the challenges offered by the host country. Through migration she had, quite simply, in some ways achieved a higher quality of life, despite her starting point being so weak. Perhaps she had also learned to cope with problems, attuned to them as she had been from bitter childhood experience (cp. DESNOS on p. 42). Therefore: Should the importance of the unexpected devastation of a happy life on the verge of adulthood, as in Aisha's case, be more strongly emphasised? In Aisha's view, it all started the day her brother was tortured to death and her father died from shock, and, according to her, her luck hasn't turned since (A ex. 19: What It is All About). A similar pattern was also found in Nasreen's case, which shared a somewhat same type of traditional background (though not as pronounced), that is, immediately prior to a sudden and prolonged depression. With the help of a most happy/trustful and relatively more flexible past (as compared to Aisha's past), she re-emerged from her depression as the psychologically most fortunate of this group of clients.

In conclusion, I would like to present a lengthy quotation from one of Aisha's post-medial sessions following upon her release from a somatic hospital as an example of a successful therapeutic session involving what therapists would call an emotional breakthrough, that is, a step towards acquiring increased intersubjective meaning.

* Aisha ex. 19 (3/15 continued/medial):

WHAT IT IS ALL ABOUT

(Were you afraid?) No, I'm not afraid of the illness itself but I wish that they could find out *what it is all about*. I have great pain and they cannot find out what causes it, that is what I'm sad about. Actually, I'm not afraid of the pain itself. However, on that evening when I had gone to bed there was nothing especially worrying, I was okay. And suddenly I get this pain. But actually, the worry I have inside me is always there. That's just the way it is; when I get ill I sweat a lot. It's like some kind of sting or heavy weight on my heart, and it becomes difficult to breathe.

But what I do want to ask you is why Norwegian doctors don't manage to find out if someone is ill, what the reason is? I don't believe that I would have that kind of pain if all was well. They say that "Perhaps it's this or perhaps that", but have never said a hundred percent for sure. I did have this pain in my head but they said "Perhaps it is a migraine, perhaps not". (May I ask you whether it is common for a doctor in your home country to have much authority?) Yes, it is, because doctors have such a big influence. If they say something, you don't doubt it because a doctor couldn't lie. You see, sometimes that's just how it is; if you have a pain and they find the reason, that's much better for the sick person who doesn't know what's wrong with her. If the doctor could only examine me and find the reason, because if I complain of pain here, they answer perhaps it is this, or perhaps that... They ask lots of questions, sitting there behind a computer. Go on then! Just look at the machine, but my pain isn't there. It's in my body. So if they could find out the reason and give me medicine, that's the best for someone who's ill, someone who understands and prescribe medicine. It isn't nice to walk about with half the body aching and then be told "No, there's nothing wrong with you after all".

An older lady from India that I got to know had just returned from the hospital – she had been in Norway for many years – but all they did was to give her a pill now and again. In the end she travelled home to India and they said that if she wasn't operated on she would die. Because they couldn't operate on her in India, it was to be done here, but here they couldn't even find the reason for her illness. That's how it is with me too when I have this pain in my legs, in my head or in my chest. They say that it's nothing, but worry. Perhaps that's a better way, but personally I think that it's best if you find the reason for why you are sick – or else you are not sick, really.

(So you are a little afraid that perhaps it could be something dangerous in your case too?) Yes, that's true, because they say that it's nothing to worry about, but I can feel my own pain (Hmm). And when I climb the stairs my heart beats so fast, it kind of stings and then it burns. (Have you thought at all about what the reason for this could be?) No, no I haven't, only that when there is pain I feel sad and so I think that "Perhaps my heart will stop". (But there's nothing particular which you think about except that your heart may stop?) Yes, it could very well happen because I worry too much, since I'm in a situation that is putting a great deal of pressure on me, I have to carry these burdens. Perhaps, I don't know myself. But at times there is much pressure and many burdens inside me and then I notice it...

(Your Father, his heart stopped, didn't it?) Yes, it was a heart attack. (Do you think that this has made you more vulnerable?) No, I'm not sure, but I think that it was just because of all the burdens he was carrying, because he didn't have any heart trouble. But because my brother was killed, and he heard that, he suddenly got a heart attack. (I do remember that. Did you experience it yourself?) Yes. (Did you see him die?) Yes, that's exactly how it was (she has never told me this before): when he died, or had been ill for two weeks since the stroke and his arms and legs had become slack like that. During those two weeks he wasn't dead, but he couldn't speak anymore. But on the day when he died he was much more alert and asked all the children to gather around him. He reached for my hand and I took his finger in mine like this. He was reading the Koran when he died.

(Do you remember your age at the time?) I was 12 or 13. (So you were quite young.) Yes, but I remember everything very well. (Do you remember the first stroke?) You know, I couldn't understand why he had become like that, but I saw that his mouth had become lopsided, and he couldn't talk. They had fetched the corpse of my brother. And he said to me "Can you take my hand?" as he was about to go out. He was a big, strong man and I gave him my arm for support. Only the wife of one of my brothers and I were present. And when he got that stroke he fell over and hit his head. (So you were actually present when it happened too?) Yes, I believe that he had become like that when he heard the news of my brother's death. But I knew nothing of what was going on, what it was with his heart, strokes and all that. But I was there with him. Afterwards my Mother and some others came to put him to bed.

(Where were you taking him when you were supporting him?) You know, it was like this: he *had to* go out. For the last weeks he had stayed in bed, and because I always stayed at home I tried to give him company. Everybody else just cried. And everything became chaotic and helter-skelter, confusing. He kept telling me "Take my hand, I'll want to go and see what's wrong with (his son/my brother), what he does, why there are so many people assembled here at our place." So I was there simply to... and he kept giving me his hand all the time, like this. And I was supposed to help him get up but couldn't do it. (Did he know at this point what had happened to your brother?) Not really, you know it seemed like he had forgotten all about it. Because only after they told him he became like that. And afterwards he kept talking to himself like this: "Now he's coming" and "Where is he then?" and things like that. (Do you know who told him?) No I don't. I can't remember, I only heard that everyone had gone from the house to the mosque howling and crying and behaving like that. My brother's wife kept hitting herself on the head and tearing her hair and crying, so my Father called for me. I didn't realise *what it was all about*, I didn't know what had happened to my brother. I thought that I had done something wrong and was about to get a beating.

But when I came there he said "They say that they've killed M., I'm going to see for myself *what it is all about*". I was supposed to help him out. But I never managed to help him. (He said that to you then?) Yes. (And you tried to help him when he fell?) Yes. (It must have been a frightening experience for you). Yes, when my Father became like that, I didn't know what had happened to my brother. I never thought anyone could kill or execute my brother because he was so strong, so then I stayed with my Father all the time instead of being out with the others mourning. Two of my other brothers also disappeared for two weeks; they fetched the corpse. Father kept drawing my arm towards his all the time and in a way said that I should stay with him.

I spent much time by his side, those last weeks before he died he didn't call for the others. It was only Aisha who fetched his shoes, who was allowed to take him out and all that, so I wiped away my tears, and pretended there was nothing unusual about that. When he asked, it was as if his tongue was paralysed and he couldn't speak properly. Somehow he drew me nearer to him and reassured me, "When I'm well again I'll buy you this and that" and so on. Then he would ask "Where is Mother?" and I would answer "I don't know if they're only outside in the garden or with the sheep" and things like that. I can't remember everything, only how very sinister it all was. It was a horrible experience. (Was it sinister when you saw him fall ill and thought that he might die?) Yes, *from that particular day until today my life has been very sad.*

257

(Were you happy to be able to stay with him though?) No, I don't think it made any difference because I knew I was going to lose my Father... (You said that they brought your brother's corpse home?) It was during the Shah's regime, and the soldiers came. On that same day they washed and buried him, but four days later they dug him up again and took the corpse with them. (The corpse of your brother?) Yes, that's right, they had taken the corpse with them because they had killed him by blowing out his brains. I don't know what they had filled it in with (his head), meat or what, because the blood kept running. They took it with them, and took both my brothers too. They never returned the corpse at all. This was the last time I saw him, and there was three times sorrow in this way, that is including my Father's forthcoming death.

(When misfortune hit, it hit very hard all at once) *Yes, from that particular day onwards it all started* (She sighs and cries, and uses her hanker-chief.) *From that day on our fate has never changed.* My Mother cried all the time; there were many small children in our house, and we had no Father. (So it took many years before you married, you kept mourning for years). Five years. No, you know my Father had said "That girl will marry my brother's son". I was given away, but after this I didn't want any wedding, nor did I feel like wearing red clothes or anything. I wanted to stay with my parents, I wanted to stay with my brother. But when my Mother lost my brother and then her husband, I became very fond of my Mother. In a way she became like a child again, very vulnerable, losing her husband and son at the same time (cp. A ex. 14: One Year after her Mother's Death). So I wanted to stay with her, to help and support her. (Did you ever imagine that such things could happen, or was it a complete shock for you?) I never imagined it.

If this quotation is representative of the core point of Aisha's trauma story, compared to which the other above mentioned breaches of honour are secondary consequences, then in Fatima's case it could be considered to be her mother's death and subsequently becoming orphaned (F ex. 2: "Promise me never to speak of my mother as being dead"). It is more difficult to point to any overall core theme in Nasreen's case, although it must clearly include the confusing image of coexisting polar opposites in an 'upside-down' world (N ex. 1: A Topsy-Turvy World); the subsequent loss of custody of her son (N ex. 5: The Boy who Should not have Survived), as well as, the happy memories of her childhood (N ex. 11: "My Mother's youngest daughter").

A personal belief system represents a more or less functional 'internal' map in relation to the outside world, on the basis of which subjects interact with others around them. Extreme social violence disturbs this inner map rather drastically, a process which is, no doubt, reinforced by a subsequent forced exile in a culturally remote area as experienced by these migrant women. By shattering the confidence in and ability to cope with internal/external circumstances, traumatic experiences, especially when strengthened by a forced cross-cultural migration, call into question our deep-seated values and shatter our expectations in the very construction of reality. However, while a map can be modified without too many costs, a belief system is a more complicated matter, at the same time linked both to the outside and to the inner world, defining what is real or unreal.

According to Gammelgaard (1993, 234), therapeutic reconstruction constitutes a creative, if painful, search in the process of which some things may become articulated for the very first time. It is in the process of thinking over and over again about one's helplessness in the face of external events, that the traumatic past is mentally caught up with and made sense of, on condition that there is some earlier basic trust to rely on, I would add. In this way, 'talking therapy' may offer a possibility for replacing the mere intrusive repetition of trauma by interpersonal/historical mediation. The aim of the treatment is to replace the affect-provoking intrusive memories with less reiterative affect-elaborating images rendered possible only from a certain distance to the immensely tragic events, and, in this way going beyond the mere lifting of what has been labelled psychological repression. Memorising, in the form of simple repetition, merely serves mental resistance and retraumatisation.

The psychodynamic aim of these therapies have been in combining emotion with articulation so that traumatic events become more bearable by way of letting them unfold as a coherent personally meaningful narrative. It is, I believe, in this kind of memory space – between the self that was and will always remain in the past and the exiled self which is now remembering – that a traumatic past may be, if not conquered, at least made bearable. This cathartic effect does not derive from the mere purification of affects accompanying the memories, but from letting them gradually unfold as part of a dialectical process in which the client appropriates her life history in the same kind of continuity of meaning that a meaningful illness narrative represents.

259

By analogy to the collective ritual use of myths, illness stories can, under favourable therapeutic conditions, offer ultimate form and meaning to suffering. Threatening and chaotic life experiences are worked through in order to attain what Erik H. Erikson (1968) notwithstanding religious or other affiliation once called "integrity as an end product of life", but during this process, the meaning aspects of the experiences will change as it seems spontaneously, even for those who continue to believe in them.

POSTSCRIPT

13.

SYMBOLIC SHELTER IN A CHANGING WORLD

Gender Mobility in a Cross-cultural Setting and the *As-if* Strategies

Ideally, all interaction, whether cross-cultural or not, presupposes that the parties know how, and in what ways, to find a place in and to fulfil their duty within the system. No one, however, is ever completely merged with existing codes, but will inevitably find themselves in some kind of a more or less reiterative or renewing relationship to these codes. At the same time they could not be anything specific without a relationship to these codes, as illustrated here, for example, by contrasting the role of Aisha as enclosed by her traditional gender role ('The Frog in a Well' in All ex. 2) with that of Fatima as 'the fallen woman' rebelling against the prevalent gender code of her culture of origin. In real-life situations, not to mention cross-cultural ones where it is not possible for everyone to know their exact position vis-à-vis others, nor to comply with it, a good deal of energy is spent trying to establish mutual positioning, as pointed out when considering the initial phase of these therapies conducted across cultural dividing lines, as well as what I have called withdrawal behaviour in preceding chapters.

Norms display a double face; On the one hand, they have grown out of and been adapted to the conditions of a particular domain over time. On the other hand, they are always somewhat anachronistic and ill fitting at particular points in time, posing problems with which individuals and institutions alike somehow have to cope. My primary focus has been on the emotional strain produced when third world migrants suddenly are forced to accommodate to alien norms and in circumstances in which massive trauma is involved. Psychologically their situation is found to be extremely difficult and vulnerable, since they are chronically faced with intricate circumstances in which it is necessary to grasp future possibilities without, however, unduly violating their past.

The interplay of contradictory impulses and their resolution through an ongoing process of reformulation becomes the essential challenge of the migrant-clients' life (cp. the concept of *system-oscillation* put forward above). In such a setting it seems to me that the object or audience of correct conduct is not so much the complete outsider or stranger (here, the majority population), nor the close insider, as it is certain persons intermediate to these. Such would be for example members of one's wider kinship circle, the neighbours of the residential district, or even other muslim compatriots to whom one's family may be known. Avoidance and courtesy behaviour are connected to social group approval of persons whose opinions about one's respectability matter[1].

According to Vatuk (1982, 68), beyond domicile in places where one is a total stranger or anonymous, the strict behaviour patterns prevalent at home become less necessary: that is, when one travels so to say out of station to where there are few chances of meeting relatives and friends. It is evident from this why the interpreter used in this study, in her capacity as an outsider in the local refugee milieu, was in fact the only one accepted by the clients for sharing their secrets. And also why the two clients who were most uneasy in their present role as patients (Layla and Fatima) refused to share the waiting room with compatriots who might have recognised them (cp. the stigma frequently attached to psychological problems).

Forced migrants have to struggle with a conflicting desire to return to the reassuring predictability of the past and the conflicting impulse to abandon it and submerge themselves in the present circumstances of their exiled life. The social disruptions following from a cross-cultural exile require renewed consideration of certain basic assumptions, the most significant of which in this case are linked to ruptures of the delicate balance between gender and age-group distinctions within the joint family. Ruptures which may result in intergenerational breaches (as presented in chapter five) *backwards* (the secrets kept from their own) as well as *forwards* (the loss of children by way of 'shameful' events), often risking the dissolution of the whole family (the frequent separations).

As a result, professional helpers may encounter refugee families in which the men have lost the powers formerly accorded to them rather abruptly, at the same time as they confront new and ever so demanding alien external conditions. And, who therefore, to the utter despair of their wives (who may request for separation), either rule authoritatively at home or alternatively, seem to pass more and more of their time outside the house in 'men only' gatherings (a further development of a pattern prevalent also at home; A ex 17: The Guest House). Sometimes they might even disappear abroad without notice, away from the 'shameful' problems accumulating in exile, again an accentuation of the extraordinary war-like situation already prevailing in their country of origin (cp. the absence of men in All-ex. 5).

* Aisha ex. 20 (13 continued/post-medial):

HUSBAND AND COUSIN

It was like this: after a while my husband calmed down. After two or three years in the country he would frequently say to me: "You have been a good wife to me; you have understood and supported me" and the like. But nowadays, when I talk to him about such matters, that is between married couples and their quarrelling, I add that "as well as being spouses we are male and female cousins (cp. the endogamic marriage practice in N ex 12: "My mother's youngest daughter" and A ex 19: What It is All About). If I had another cousin anywhere else in this world who I had reason to believe needed my help, then I would have offered it to him".

I tell him that "I'm exactly the same wife who helped you before. I will help you again". But he only shouts and says that "Such old stories are just rubbish. I don't want to have anything to do with it. I'm fed up with all the norwegian paper-work (the bureaucracy of the norwegian authorities) and I want to be by myself somewhere in peace and quiet, I don't want to have to think about you". That's what he says (in utter despair).

Submitting to the will of elders and/or men somehow has to be adapted to the requirements of personal responsibility inherent in the norms of the majority culture. While great pride is still taken in a positive group identity, exiled women are frequently forced to take primary responsibility for running the family while at the same time trying to make their humiliated husbands look good in public. The children are often well aware of the strains this is imposing on the family (A ex 2: "When they trampled upon our honour"). This choice of running the family more or less like a man implies taking an active role vis-à-vis the social and welfare authorities to an extent by far surpassing their traditional gender role. Was it not for the redefinition of this public area of interaction (i.e. social and health care) as a female one of domestic relevance; and for the fact that their husbands frequently avoid the same authorities because the majority of the employees are young (in their eyes 'low status') females equipped with a confusingly great deal of power over the domestic spheres of their clients, these women would not be in a position to fulfil this new role.

Where the practices of gender segregation and avoidance behaviour are undergoing change, as the case is here, this is usually done without the approval of older, more conservative, members of the family. Just as the reality of a divorce or other 'shameful' problems in exile are withheld from the latter relatives (cp. the excuses needed in order to attain this). This brings a fear of disclosure that somehow has to be acknowledged in the therapeutic process with these migrant-clients. One important way to circumvent the critical problems inherent in 'shame' used by the clients themselves seems to be by way of what I have called *as-if strategies*. This is seen, for example, when Nasreen reports talking to her own people as if her sexual trauma had happened to some other third person thus making it after all possible for her to communicate the matter; or when Aisha in order to be on the safe side talks to me as if her daughter's 'shame' was only imagined; or Shirin as if following an unavoidable divorce she could somehow have become male because of the subsequent need to run the household like a man.

* Shirin ex. 5 (1-2/4 continued/medial):

THE WOMAN WHO TURNED OUT A MAN

Sometimes gender roles are maintained with such resolution that they are almost impossible to alter within their context. As a consequence of the eventually inevitable publicity around her divorce, Shirin came to define herself in terms of the male-option (i.e. posing as a male) thus avoiding the stigma of 'a bad woman', a choice supported also by her divorced husband, who had initially resisted her even moving outside of the house.

(cp. S ex . 4: "Had my Husband witnessed the insulting behaviour of that patient's husband he would never had let me continue to interpret for her")

One can also perceive such an as-if pattern in the above mentioned habit of designating any young/virile man who associates with an unmarried woman, her 'brother' or the fate of Muslim female mystics who – if successful – likewise become addressed as males by their followers.[2]

My point is that the stricter the system, the more flexibility is also required for somehow circumventing it, for example by undergoing the hymen (re)operations available for the elite in many Muslim countries, requests for which can be expected to rise also among migrants in Europe. The restriction and control of people and their roles to a common small scale arena like the village life of the traditional 'system' or 'normative style' (as presented on page 69) allows for little tolerance of overt deviance, while it, among other things, renders the changing of gender roles nearly impossible from within the system itself (cp. the sanctions involved as presented in chapter four: Violation of Gender). Moreover, it poses similar difficulties in identifying any one particular person responsible for excerpting repression where social control is so collectively anchoraged as the case is here (cp. the notion of sociocentricity).

* Aisha ex. 21 (4-7/10 continued/pre-concluding):

ABOUT EXCEPTIONS

(What if she is ashamed of herself?) If I only knew; but I do think that she has done something that she is ashamed of. Or she is very proud and stubborn, and wants to inflict pain on us. It has to be one of these two alternatives. She has managed to talk at the Social Security Office and to her doctor, but they won't tell us. (Perhaps it is because they are not allowed to from reasons of confidentiality. If we believed that the very worst has happened, what possibilities would then remain?) What do you mean? What could be worse than that, for a girl or woman? It is like this: the girl or woman does something, like has sex with a boy then, – I don't want to think that, but it is the worst that can happen to her, that she has been in contact with some boy, *no matter if she wanted it or not herself* (cp. *the innocent without status*, for example rape victims on page 76ff). But she was young then, so she has run into trouble. That's the very worst that could happen to her, in my opinion.

(Will it be found out when she is married?) Yes (Is it required that you prove your virginity?) Yes, if she marries a Kurd it has to be like that. If she thinks that she has moved into the Norwegian society and culture, that Norwegians accept it, that you should be free and have a good time and all that, before in time finding a partner of the same mind who shares the same views. It won't pass. They would never let her survive this thing. You know, next year the Child Welfare Authorities won't be able to say anything, they cannot protect her. After all she is no Salman Rushdie who has bodyguards and people who use lots of money to take care of him and hide him. *Norway is a small country, everybody knows you.* If she imagines that she can do what she likes without interference from anyone, it won't work. They would never let her survive (cp. externalised control, page 112-113).

That is the truth, they will take her life. I see no alternative, if it goes too far. If too much time hasn't already been lost, if she turns to me, I could do something for her. But if things go on like this we'll lose her. But if they (the professionals) reason with her, and make her come back before too much time passes... Establish contact between us so that she'll tell us what has happened to her, who has done this thing to her; perhaps the person who did it is fond of her. Perhaps they could marry and we could arrange it that way – if he is Norwegian or whatever, it doesn't matter.

(So you see the same kind of solution which was in practice here in older days, that they marry each other?) You know, I reckon that once she has married that person, afterwards she'll be able to marry a Kurd too, because you can find that way (i.e. the right way to act) because if she has been married once, don't you think? But if she thinks that she can have fun for years and then marry without being a virgin, it won't work. *Even if they (the relatives) don't hurt her, her husband might because she isn't what she is supposed to be.* They may lose respect, punish, shave her head and smear yoghurt on it or cut off her nose (cp. A ex. 6: Donkey Ride into Death). There are a hundred different laws from the old days and they are still in use.

But I won't presume that she has done it. (We have no reason to assume so, but if the worst were to happen, it is best to be prepared.). No, it is true that it is only an assumption, but I do think that when she keeps on running away from us so persistently, it has to be something she has done and is ashamed of, something that she is so terribly ashamed of that she doesn't dare to face up to it.

All she can do is to run away from and dissociate herself from us. It'll only be for a while and afterwards she'll be all on her own in this world, no-one will support her, no one will help her. As I said, she isn't anyone famous but just a naive refugee girl, there is no-one to put body-guards at her disposal or anything like that. They just let her loose and she can do what she likes.

(You said that she could marry again with a Kurd?) In that case it would be nothing to speak of, even a donkey would realise that if it is someone who has been married, then it has to be a woman and not a mere girl in that sense (i.e. a virgin). In that case, she wouldn't be a problem. Because if you take someone who has been married, then she has been together with a man before. But if she imagines that she could slip into marriage while posing as a virgin, I tell you, that it's just a dream, wishful thinking. It wouldn't pass.

(Is blood still required as evidence?) Perhaps not like in old days, that the bride had to be in that room until she had lost her virginity and all the ladies would examine the sheet (cp. F ex. 10: 'Nothing but a Widow'). In any case, you have to get some kind of proof or at least her husband will, if he isn't all lost, realise that she isn't a virgin. I have no idea what would really happen, but this is what I think might happen, it isn't certain, but if it really turns out to be like that, I would be very worried for her. I don't know how it will end, and I have told her many times before "that we don't need to talk as mother and daughter (cp. as-if strategy & A ex. 20: Husband and Cousin) but you can talk as if we were friends". I told her plainly that "If someone were to start touching your trousers or things like that, you have to think clearly, to use your head. But if something does happen, you must tell me, you must not hide it. Of your Father and sisters and girl friends, your Mother is the nearest to you, and I can help you".

(I explain that this was the practice of respectable old families if a mistake happened in Norway too, that they were married, and that in muslim countries rich people may have an operation). In Iran I haven't heard of such operations, but I do know that at the time a girl is to move to her husband's house she is required to visit a doctor. It is the kind of doctor who does that kind of examination, and as a rule some member of the husband's family is present in order to make sure that everything is in order[3]. In Iran among Farsi-speakers, Kurds or Turks, it's happens (i.e. that the bride is not a virgin) – perhaps once every 100,000 times. But this is the first time I hear about operations.

(Perhaps it would be wise to try to approach your husband about the issue; the different possibilities you have if it would turn out to be that bad, because of course I assume that he wouldn't want to take her life?). I DARE NOT. No – I dare not mention anything. If only he himself would notice that she has been near to, that is has had sex, with someone... That is, if this person who has done this thing to her will have her as his wife, it's okay. But if he gets to know about her having done this thing, and if she has been away for months and has been hiding from us, then her life will be in danger or she might be injured so she'll end up in hospital or something like that. And he can't take any steps, because the shame is so great. But I couldn't tell him that "Now listen to me, perhaps our daughter has done it, and now we have to operate on her." No, I say this because of what she has done outside marriage; you have to get rid of it, that shame.

No, no, concerning that I cannot say *anything*, because if it did happen it is – I was about to say – illegal, this thing. It is like this, when the men who hold the power get together, and girls do not have any power, she has to turn to me and say "Mother, it has happened to me, help me." Then my husband will have to travel away somewhere, he must not know about it. When he says this thing (i.e. threatens her), he just has to do it. I tell him "Think positively, think that she hasn't done anything wrong, you must stop thinking that she has done anything wrong". She has to come to me so that I can help her when he is absent.

Whatever the means of upholding respect and the ideals of male-female, age or other normative distinctions, they are always context-bound, and, as such, vulnerable to change when the context changes, for example, through the mechanisms involved in cross-cultural migration. All societies apply their norms selectively, for example, according to a woman's marital or social status, age and position in the life cycle, or depending on other somehow exceptional circumstances, such as travel or pilgrimage[4]. For example, many modernising muslims explain (away) their relaxed following of required religious rules by reference to the fact that they see their exile as an extended form of travel which allows for greater flexibility.

No society can uphold its ideals *in toto*, nor can it seclude *all* women from *all* men under *all* circumstances. In the widespread geographic area that harbours gender segregation as something most people desire, it is, in practice, most particularly associated with people who are not poor (cp. the higher status and strict segregational practice of Aisha's kin as compared to the lower status and greater flexibility in gender issues of Fatima's family; Nasreen being positioned somewhere in between these extremes). Moreover, all societies define some categories of men, such as 'brothers', and types of social situations as 'safe' from the point of view of a woman's sexual vulnerability or 'shame'.

The extent to which a woman is in actual fact secluded has varied and still varies a great deal[5]. In other words, the rigid system of purdah is, after all, to some extent flexible and has been subject to constant modification, despite the fact that the basic principle of female modesty has remained relatively unaffected, to this day surviving western influence. The traditional black cloak or *burqa* is itself a fairly recent liberating invention, the introduction of which gave urban women a degree of mobility within the public arena which was previously unknown. According to Hansen (1961, p. 65), only twenty years ago wearing the *burqa* was considered a statement of emancipation in many parts of the muslim world. The increasing tendency to abandon it when among total strangers is thus a further development along this path[6].

From the point of view of the social psychology involved in this type of migration, it is important to note that the internal part of the house, *anderun* (see p. 242) as a protective space or symbolic shelter, can be extended to other sorts of localities and modes of relationships (for example the transpositioning of childhood settings in the previous section: The Architecture of Kurdish Social Interaction and Adaptational Choice). Its *portable* facets are evident, apart from the use of a mobile *burqa*, for example in the practice of bringing rugs, cooking utensils and other provisions from the female sphere at home (thus transposing its protective symbolism) outdoors on a picnic, or in the importance attached to finding hospitality in the homes of kin while travelling. In marriage arrangements, the assurance that members of the involved families will indeed become admittees to each other's *anderun*, where they can find a pyjamas, take a nap, or eat in the company of their extended kin, is a vital consideration[7]. Even distant kin are routinely expected to visit one another[8], and there is strong pressure to socialise with them (again only the 'deviant' Fatima complained about this obligation).

Notwithstanding other differences in affiliation, such as those to do with the muslim and hindu faith, it could be of interest here to compare the present situation of the exiled women of this study with the colonial discourse regarding female seclusion in nineteenth century North India in order to highlight some important facets of gender mobility.[9] This is because the impulse towards social reform in the north indian bengali society at the time was based on an indigenous (emic) response to the presence of the colonial western regime and its standard of civilisation. Subsequently, a new bengali middle class began to emerge, a stratum of society which directed a great deal of attention towards its own women and their important role in child rearing practices as 'the shapers of the coming generations'. In the bengali community, during this period of rapid change under alien pressure, it was considered necessary to educate women in order to inculcate modern values. At the same time, however, a female ideal was constructed representative of the very best of both sides.

Bortwick (1982, 134) depict the ensuing process of selection by which western ideals were adapted to house the indigenous society and were eventually slotted into the ideology of the reformers of that time. Since the dominance of western colonial ideals in the exterior world was very real – then as it is now – an adaptation to the new and more lax disciplinary techniques towards women were required in order to master the changing socioeconomic existence (alongside colonials in a form of compromise). Simultaneously, however, it became vital to maintain control of the women as representatives of the privately sheltered familial realm, perceived as important symbols of ethnic purity and continuity as they were, a realm thought to contain the true inner self depicted above, and by extension, the collective identity of the whole nation. In this way, the colonialist underdog could be superior after all, since his women were not like their boundary-protecting stereotype of 'shameless' western women. This is a type of images that can be found also among contemporary tradition-oriented migrants to the West, in which the inner *spiritual* realm and its respectable women are portrayed as the strong side of the indigenous albeit materially inferior culture, which has to be preserved and protected against overwhelming western modernising influences at all costs.

Women were thus in a key position in the process of adaptation at the time of the western colonial power, as they are, again, now in the contemporary world. While in the material exterior sphere male imitation of western norms become more and more inevitable (at least among those of working-age), by contrast, indigenous values still reign supreme in the idealised female domestic world. Though a certain adaptation to western ideals is called for in respect of external attributes, this fact do not seem to influence the traditional virtues of womanhood. On the contrary, home-life acquire a new and strengthened role as a place where indigenous qualities find expression and are to be preserved. Like the women of the emerging bengali middle class, the migrant-clients at issue here, acquire a particularly important role in the transmission of their own cultural heritage under changing circumstances.

The symbolic significance of the female seclusion pattern renders it almost impossible to transcend its limits without ado. The seclusion of women is a function of a family's value in an economic sense, but it also becomes indicative of their social worth or 'honour' in order that the higher the status-aspirations, especially among the lower middle classes, the more important the chastity of women becomes[10]. The solution sought by the bengali reformers to the problems inherent in the uneven cultural contact situation of the times was to give womanhood as a concept a new content as the guarantor of important national and ethnic values. Through use of the image of the *bhadramahila*, the female parallel to the *bhadralok* 'respectable gentleman', it now became possible for women to move outside of the confines of their traditional sphere without thereby endangering their feminine virtues[11]. While women appeared as more autonomous subjects in a new arena their roles as mothers and wives were simultaneously given a new emphasis and importance[12]. They could attain greater mobility only on condition that they displayed even more modesty.

However, the relative shift from the physically rigid boundaries of externalised notions of 'shame' towards the more flexible internalised mechanisms of self-control and individual 'guilt' implied in this process of social mobility, ultimately made freedom of movement possible without the anarchy predicted by supporters of the old system (such as Aisha), provided that this freedom given to women was compensated for by an assurance of their continuing 'purity' within the confines of the family.

* Aisha ex. 22 (1-2/4/6/13 continued/medial):

KURDS WHO SLIP UP

Following upon the arrival of a few kinsmen "who knew the (cultural) rules", Aisha pointed out to me that the kurds are here "only on a visit", and should not lose their proper, customary behaviour (cp. the so called 'myth of return' harboured by migrants). She told me the following story:

> The girls (i.e. the visitors) immediately withdrew to the kitchen to serve me. They know what is expected from them. It is embarrassing to socialise with 'the other Kurds' whose way of treating guests or whose behaviour differs from ours. I don't know if they learnt it here, but I don't find it to be proper behaviour, for example that their men help in the kitchen. It isn't proper, it has to do with showing respect. You have to know your place. No, I find it very difficult to accept. My husband would never enter the kitchen. I could never put up with that.
>
> They say that it is detrimental to the refugees that they won't adapt, but I disagree. They don't think, they don't understand what kind of customs they have, and it frightens the Kurdish men. The children learn one thing, Mothers and Fathers something else, and this leaves them very confused about how they should behave. It shouldn't happen so quickly that one is frightened and feels pressed to adapt, or that they threaten the families with the police, if not the authorities threaten to take the children away...

The differences among the kurds here referred to by Aisha connotes kurds who practice father's-brother's-son (for example Aisha's kin) as against mother's-sister's-son (for example Nasreen's kin) marriages[13]; as this practice relates to other further dissimilarities, such as besides linguistic ones (badini versus sorani), for example, the strictness of seclusion practice, the possible flexibility in choosing a spouse (especially for daughters), divorce practices and managing the accumulating intergenerational problems in exile, which seem to follow in the wake of a forced cross-cultural migration; compared to Aisha, Nasreen has, after all, done rather well in this sense.

We might well be tempted to ask what exactly it was, in our case study from Bengal that most effectively counteracted the feared process of westernisation; a fear that is so evident among the clients at issue here? According to Bortwick (1982, 130) it was decisive that purdah, at least as much as isolation, represents a world view with a certain innate flexibility (cp. the metaphorical walls of 'the purdah of heart' in A ex. 4). Women in purdah are, after all, brought up to adapt to the new circumstances following from their inevitable marriage and subsequent life in the 'alien' home of their parents-in-law and to be attentive to the decisions of their new relatives/superiors[14]. What the british colonialists in retrospect seemed to have overlooked at the time, and what we are busy overlooking again today, is a deeper understanding of the role the notion of *freedom from the self*[15] – in conjunction with what I have, in this publication, denoted as the *sociocentrisity* of these clients – by way of subordination and dependence, played as a cornerstone in the construction of the joint family group[16]. And the key position women had in it.

The women of both eras have had to carry responsibility for protecting their familial 'honour' while nourishing and bringing up their children, just as such qualities as true modesty or patriotism have been filled with an almost sacred authority right up to the present time. But in the present situation, the clients at issue here (representatives of tradition-oriented third world migrants to the West), seem to face somewhat poorer odds than their bengali forerunners, perhaps due to the increased influence of the 'foreign' authorities in their very homes (cp. what is said about *clientification* as a reactualised trauma in chapter six).

* Aisha ex. 23 (10 continued/pre-concluding):

"THEIR CULTURE AND MINE"

Theirs is a modern culture, but we are not 'modern'. We cannot manage, and the girls suffer. I have told them that they must not think that they have reached another world, and believe that they can slip into that new world. They have to remain what they are. I've told my daughters many times that girls have to be virgins when they marry, and if not they lose respect. It is said that one has to walk with one's head bowed down through life (she means that they loose respect by this) and that is not an easy destiny (cp. F ex 10: Nothing but a Widow).

When I quarrel with my husband, what can he say to me since I am able to keep my head high and say "You cannot divorce me as long as I myself am not 'stained'" (i.e. with any kind of loss of respect). It is very important to be able to say that one has 'a clean face'. But if something were to happen to me, the very smallest thing which I had done, he be able to say "You have been a bad girl, you lost your virginity in your father's house"; this would be the worst thing that can happen to a girl, losing her virginity while she is still living with her parents.

275

Their life has changed, but actually their new lifestyle harms everyone, at least those of us who are refugees. I don't go around complaining about *why* their culture is like that, *why* they accept this. I only
complain that I'm a refugee in this place. Because I think that their
culture, well, it suits *them* and they know how to behave and see it
as acceptable...

But I do think it would have been much better if instead of bringing the refugees to *their* country, they had drowned the whole lot of
them[17],so that it wouldn't have turned out like this .

In sum, the importance of detecting the psychosocial implications and
stress factors involved in the confrontation between western (health)
ideologies and the traditional thinking of these clients is a necessary
supplement to understanding their traumatisation and the ensuing
PTSD symptomatology. Just as it is similarly important to grasp how
individual psychological changes are conditioned by socioeconomic
changes on the macro level. In the end female seclusion practices will
last as long as they are beneficial to the group. Their abolition among
the middle- and upper-status oswals in the former state of Mewar
(indian Udaipur) likewise show how women can give up the practice
of seclusion without the loss of self-esteem so painfully experienced by
my clients, provided that the decision was a more collective one enjoy-
ing wide support. According to an in-depth study of 25 families in this
region by Mehta (1976; 1982), the transition in this particular case
was, in fact, smooth, notwithstanding the major changes in life style.

Despite the fact that roles in the muslim traditional setting are rigid
in terms of status and gender markings, individual mobility through
and around them may, under certain conditions simultaneously affecting the group as a whole, be quite rapid. According to Beeman (1986,
51), more than anything else, the fact that *an individual's status is
relative to his or her social context including other people* (the very
sociocentricity of the clients) is what gives iranian social life its particular flavour. The fact that perceptions of status thus vary depending
on the specific communal setting being attended to, seems to render
these clients prisoners of their communication system, but its masters
too. Untraumatic change, however, is dependent on at least a minimum of collective acceptance.

In sum, there are two major foci of concern with reference to these
largely tradition-oriented migrant-clients' interpersonal communica-

tion which lead them to organise their experience (new and old; good as well as tragic) on a sliding scale with idealised absolute goals at both poles: that is the contrasts of superior/inferior and of outsider/insider. Few can fully fulfil such expectations, but as cultural ideals they inspire and direct positively valued behaviour in their proper setting.

Divided History – Divided Mind:
In Search of Collective and Individual Memory

From the point of view of the individual in society, culture as a system of public, collective meanings is largely taken for granted. However, when confronted with cultural diversity through cross-cultural experience, it becomes evident how it is foremost an issue of *cultivated* surroundings; something that is simultaneously rooted in and nurtured by individual as well as collective experience. Culture confronts us as individuals when entering the world, as previously given patterns formed by others, which summon us, harshly or gently, and more or less ambiguously depending on our position in the landscape, on time and other factors, such as here migration and extraordinary traumatic experience. In the words of Geertz (1973, 57[18]) we find it already current in the community when we are born, and it will remain, with additions, subtractions and alterations that we may or may not have had a hand in, in circulation after our death. While alive we make use of and live by a more personal construction of collective culture, as exemplified in this study through the diverse options taken by its kurdish female subjects in a western exile.

A most important theme, which follows from the refugee-specific situation, therefore concerns the meaning of various types of normative boundaries which are crossed; boundaries which are perceived by those involved against a backdrop of culturally defined ideals. In other words, considering the meaning of a 'good' life in an anticipated/familiar social context one could ask as I have done:

– What kind of 'meaning' will the innumerable transgressions and ruptures encountered by refugees have?
– How are elementary forms of human rights violations conceptualised?

277

– What about fellow members of one's group who deviate from the norms, such as divorced women or westernised children, prematurely dead or 'mad' relatives and violated people in general?

The way such problems are handled is dependent on both collective and individual meanings, which again may be liable to further aggravate the refugee dilemma of abandonment, deprivation and lack of belonging. The frequent tragic fates of many third world migrants, and especially traumatised refugees, in our welfare societies, could be understood as a sort of inverted pilgrimage. A process, that is marked by a gradual removal from the starting point in a 'holy place' or 'mythical past' (i.e. place as Home-place) by way of more or less violent ruptures towards an unknown and frightening future on foreign soil. The life of a refugee is, therefore, readily defined in the negative, on the basis of perceived breaches in time, place and behaviour. It is frequently about sorrow, anger and 'guilt' or 'shame' on the individual level, and about powerlessness, defeat and punishment/persecution on the collective one; and, that is, followed by a risk of additional discrimination and even racism in their country of exile.

In order to understand the accompanying psychosocial effects, it would be useful to compare the position of the cross-cultural, and especially forced migrant, with an opposite, that of the adventurous holidaymaker in our time and part of the world. This is since a range of features contrast the positive element of holidaymaking with the negative sides of *refugeism* described here, despite their common origin in a departure from familiar surroundings. Both phenomena may, in Victor Turner's (1969) terminology, be characterised as *liminal* in the sense that they are situated outside everyday occurrence. Such *time out* is marked by conflicting wishes for freedom and security, loneliness and shoulder-to-shoulder contact, or adventure – but – without danger.

A central feature of the holiday trip when viewed as an escape route from the pressures of modern western life, is an intermittent freeing of the holidaymaker from the rules prevailing at home. As a surplus phenomenon it offers a possibility to experiment without the risk attached to a change of roles within the home context. But that which gives increased possibilities for a lucky few means reduced freedom for other, more unfortunate ones. Real-life experiences of escape can be described as a form of *serious tourism*: that is, when the 'parenthetical' situation threatens to become permanent, this often constitutes a problem in itself. For westerners on holiday who would find themselves on an exotic beach ready to enjoy the freedom of a foreign context, when the possibility of safe return was indefinitely postponed, the stay would immediately feel more like a hostage-type bondage or compulsive captivity than actual freedom.

Because the psychological travel time is much longer than an intercontinental flight would indicate, the 'captive tourist' will come to suffer a range of mental upheavals paralleling the refugee experience. She or he may, for example, be seized by a fear of the unknown (cp. the sculpture-like quality of Nasreen's home in exile in N ex 1) – and an accompanying desperate longing for return to the recognisability and monotonous routines of the home context; for all that the holiday dream was supposed to provide a release from. Adventure holidays are, after all, highly organised risk-taking, a sort of willed culture shock that may be compared to the creative timing out process in which every artist is more or less deliberately involved.[19]

Like an asylum seeker facing an uncertain future, the *forced tourist* is banished to living in the constant insecurity of the present (cp. what is said about time-perception in chapter 12: On the Narrative Approach and Meaning-Formation). Again, the democratic and jovial breakdown of social roles which marks holiday time as a 'time out', has its parallel in the forced loss of status and disempowerment or role confusion from which marginalised third world migrants in our society frequently suffer (A ex 2: "When they trampled upon our honour" & A ex 9: "We came as guests but are treated as beggars"). The stay is more likely to be coloured by an involuntary break in networks, turning out to be a journey into isolation instead of a different kind of community. Like the forced migrant, the captive or cowardly tourist will be overcome by all the new experiences, deprived of the reduction of risk offered by a guided package tour (N ex 1: A Topsy-Turvy World; A ex 3: About the Meaning of Life). The opportunity to relax in secure but dissimilar surroundings is replaced by an exhausting and confusing refugee experience.

In sum, change which is planned and consistent with one's purpose in life is more readily experienced as improvement and to a greater extent incorporated into a broader range of 'meaning'. But when it is forced and moreover inconsistent with one's aims and values in life, it is often experienced as a loss.[20] Where environmental change in some cases brings a pleasantly coloured experience of increased quality of life, it is in other cases marked by distaste, suffering or loss. This is especially the case where the psychological incompatibility or distance between the home context and the forcedly encountered and unfamiliar host context is perceived as great, even more so where there is a parallel loss of power (A e 23: "Their culture and mine"). Leaving familiar surroundings may, depending on the degree of choice – and change – involved[21], bring diametrically opposed results: the blissful freedom of the holidaymaker or the mentally upsetting escape of traumatised refugees in cross-cultural exile (*the exile or 'culture' trauma*). But, the distress and disability that may again follow from the preceding tragic events affecting the refugees (*the 'torture' trauma*), similarly imply an involuntary shift between social positions and accompanying life worlds that complicates the matter further. In particular, chronically ill or traumatised refugees can, regardless of their migration, be considered captives in a little known borderland where they are engaged in a desperate search for moral justification, which could bring meaning to confused aspects of their experience. In the meantime, their lives will be marked by the sick person's continual uncertainty about the possibility of return to 'the normal'; even more where various factors depending on migration and trauma act jointly on the situation of the clients under scrutiny here.

While the refugee experience is characterised by the constant disturbance of psycho-socio-culturally rooted normative boundaries which mark the position and tasks of man in life, much of therapy is about giving space or *refuge* to the accompanying feelings of shame and loss. Trauma survivors may come to lose their basic trust in their own ability to deal with events in their lives in a meaningful way (cp. 'the ultimate victory of the good'), as their children may lose trust in the ability of their parents to deal with and protect them against evil (cp. intergenerational ruptures). The disturbed relationships between outer and inner reality brought about by organised social violence (interpreted along cultural lines) further add to the vulnerability and mental agony of the exile experience: an exile which presumes a greater psychic mobility of the individual, especially from a tradition-oriented context.

The changes following from cross-cultural migration seem to force the subjects to redeem their existence individually where it was earlier given or lost only as a member of the kinship group, tribe or religious denomination (cp. chapter three: The Torture-versus-Exile Trauma). Quite unexpectedly, they confront a need to ponder existential issues, about what man must do in order to be allowed to live (cp. to "those who should not have survived" in N ex. 5 or *the innocent without status*). I have therefore had a double aim in the course of my investigation/therapeutic work: first that the clients should become able to affirm and integrate the breaches of confidence encountered during socially organised violence *and* their psychocultural dislocation in exile. And second, to describe and analyse at length the mental processes involved in the process so as to contribute to the interdisciplinary efforts that I regard as crucial in the field of comparative religiocultural research generally and, more particularly, in psychology at the present time.

Thematically, the emerging clinical material of this study centres on abstract loss and normative transgressions, which result from the shift of belief systems (*the 'cultural' trauma*) and/or traumatisation (*the 'torture' trauma*). This shift, moreover, highlights the relationship between frustrated professionals and minority *problem patients* who increasingly demand their attention. Third world refugees in exile share many universally common psychosocial problems concerning language skills, culture shock and marginalisation: some are diagnosed as suffering from PTSD, they have been exposed to repression, followed by acute uncertainty due to separation from their families and, often, by an undecided legal status. Many more than those who openly acknowledge such acts, turn out to have been tortured and sexually violated. Furthermore, some of them are harassed by their own even in exile, as well as by the host people.

So why do we need knowledge about the 'cultural' issues involved in forced migration? Paradoxically, through the acquisition of such knowledge we learn more, not only about those affected, but about the structure and organisation of our own mentality and community life as well. That is when we have something to compare with, especially something that is so close to home and everybody has an opinion about here in this country – i.e. immigrants. The unknown turns out to be a mirror through which we become aware of the shades of our own 'invisible culture', i.e. that part which we all too frequently take for granted. For example, it shows us how in the West an increasing belief in man *as an independent subject* guides our ways of relating to new and unknown features of the cross-cultural encounter. And these situations also tell us something generally important about multicultural development and majority-minority constellations, which we as therapists are party to, for example, not only by way of our migrant-clients' concern for 'shame', but, moreover, by way of our own increasingly important role as vendors for socioculturally expected 'proper' behaviour in our own culture.

I would like to conclude that cultural understanding is in no way a 'device' to get out of the problem of trauma, which remains as tragic as ever no matter how we conceptualise it. Without a certain knowledge of its impact, however, there is no way for mental health workers and researchers, who wish to engage in the humane venture of easing its burden on the subjects and fight its causes, to participate in and thus understand the clients' experience. Perhaps one could regard and treat the condition of these refugee-clients in therapy as a sort of psychological 'rest' or regression, however emotionally upsetting/demanding it simultaneously is. A period of *time out* that aim at putting them in a position to cope – not only with their past traumas – but, moreover, with the more or less desperate search for new frames, a search that is a direct result of the additional burden placed on refugees through cross-cultural migration.

It seems to me that the clients' trauma story is not only a story of past tragedies, but when followed by a forced cross-cultural exile it is equally about their own response to a changing and radically different environment. Through this process the focus of the clients' trauma story shifts from being symptomatic of a history of psychosocial assault to becoming a story about psychocultural reinterpretation. Should refugees be better prepared for this task, in addition to coping with their past traumas, and if so, how can we as professionals best help them prepare?

14.
ON METHODOLOGICAL CHOICE AND
THE STUDY OF SENSITIVE ISSUES

Defining my Concern on Sensitive Research

As for its subject material, the present work is bound by what a few cases of kurdish women refugees with trauma-related and/or adaptational problems brought into an extended number of therapeutic sessions. In many ways the clients represent hitherto invisible migrants, who have seldom been the focus of research despite a considerable exposure to the scrutiny of the public health system. While the perspective of studies in migrant mental health has up to now been poorly integrated into studies in the field of cultural research, the postulations of this work have developed out of themes raised by my earlier work on the ideological encounter between muslim migrants and the norwegian society[1].

Any research design carries at least a minimum of such more or less implicit theoretical formulations which serve as a blueprint for the study. If the aim of the study is to develop interdisciplinary insight, the focus of the research issues should either be similar to those previously studied or deviate in some clearly defined ways. I myself ventured into this project with a question of common concern to scholars working in the field: *How does the refugee-trauma influence a life course?* With one exception the informants of this study showed clear signs of post traumatic stress at the outset of treatment.

At this point I introduced 'the cultural factor', until now largely neglected, from the point of view of the treatment ideology; which put me in the position to pose a more specific question: *How do the kurdish migrant-clients themselves construe their trauma?* This emic perspective brought a set of new problems linked to the interrelationships between the effects of organised social violence and adaptational problems viewed as a psychological handicap, as envisaged in chapter two (Psychological Trauma Reconsidered) and three (The *Torture* vs. *Exile Trauma*) of this publication. Culturally distant exile is inevitably about life worlds in more or less violent confrontation, and coping with this type of exile is therefore dependent upon mastering radically altered psycho-socio-cultural conditions.

This interdisciplinary affiliation between traumatisation and culture-of-emergency-like situations turned out to be productive also when considering the fact that cultural analysis traditionally leans so heavily on functional generalisations, with less sense of conflict and chaos than the case is within the field of psychology. In his Elizabeth Coulson lectures quoted by Voutira & Harrell-Bond (1993), John Davis suggested an integration of the comfortable 'anthropology of maintenance' with 'the anthropology of suffering', claiming that;

> To bridge the gap between the two requires the recognition that the causes of human suffering are essential features of all societies, rather than being unique to any particular case, or pathological per se.

I have therefore stressed the psychological resources inherent in the actual transmission of, here oral, tradition carried out by the clients on a very personal level and in a cross-cultural setting, and asked further: *How does the narrative structure (of a client's account of her own trauma) reflect both psychocultural trauma and coping?* If cultural research were to benefit from viewing man made violence and emergency-like circumstances as potential features of *any* cultural context, then the strategies for psychocultural survival utilised by refugees could likewise be viewed with a semblance of normality, regardless of the overt nature of the pathology involved. Because of the axiomatic link between crisis and pathology in the field of psychology, little is in fact known about how previously healthy individuals cope with malignant situations. Which is not to assume that a client is always free of pretraumatisation.

For the same reason, the functionalistic comprehension of 'the cultural whole' as a stable organisation would in my opinion benefit from incorporating psychological knowledge about the impact of crises, and vice versa. In order to highlight such interdisciplinary questions without affront to the therapeutic requirements of this study, a multiple case study design was chosen[2]. This method has been chosen precisely because it is well-suited for posing explorative issues in contemporary real-life contexts in which the relevant behaviour cannot be manipulated (as the case is in an experimental setting); in other words where the investigator has little control over a large number of potentially relevant variables.

In addition to its interdisciplinary nature, the present work is embedded within complex therapeutic treatment processes which are marked by psycho-socio-cultural change and confrontation. Under such conditions a qualitative case study approach offers a detailed close-up observation that may preserve the complicated and subjectively meaningful aspects of the material[3]. Also, participant observation and in-depth interviewing become important methods in the field of minority, and particularly refugee studies which frequently deal with sensitive or controversial issues. The reason for this is that these issues rely on sustained and intensive interaction between the researcher and his or her subjects in the cause of which any additional/ adverse problems that may affect the subjects (especially what is revealed in the interviewing situation) are more easily detected. In this way the clients can, hopefully, also be better protected. Sometimes the mere knowledge that someone is attentive to your plight is helpful, the idea Amnesty International rests on.

While this kind of research frequently touches upon power relationships – even criminal stigmatisation[4] – on human atrocity and immense suffering, it becomes especially demanding for the researcher too. Hence the reference to *secondary traumatisation* or even social stigmatisation from the refugee specific setting; unwelcome effects that are perhaps seen more clearly within the context of the refugee assistance scheme which is so to speak expected to remedy the situation.[5] In addition to ordinary research skills, refugee research requires cultural sensitivity and political sophistication from its practitioners. The very ways of posing questions may sharpen sensitive ethical dilemmas and affect the involved parties who are at risk both from the internal psychological impact of the traumatic material itself, and externally from its (mis)interpretation by various interest groups in the society at large.

Besides its interdisciplinary character the subject theme of minority and especially refugee studies, time and again turns out to be of a sensitive kind. By sensitive I mean studies which bear a potential risk of unwelcome social consequences or psychic costs for the participants or some social category that they may represent. For a closer scrutiny of the concept see Renzetti & Lee (1993, 3-13), who, among other things, distinguish between a broader definition denoting all some-how controversial studies which may have social implications for the subjects involved (i.e. almost any applied social research), and, more specifically, research which is, moreover, likely to become threatening for the parties involved, such as those dealing with socially discrediting or deviant behaviour.[6]

It is perhaps enough here to remind the reader of the uneasy relationship between the study of islam and the debate on orientalism or human rights issues on the one hand[7], as well as the growing xenophobia directed at third world migrants in many western countries on the other.[8] In addition to topics which touch on deviance and social control, Lee and Renzetti (1993, 6) add a few more of relevance here, that are likely to be perceived as sensitive. They are where research intrudes into the private sphere or some deeply personal experience, impinges on the vested interests of those in power or deals with things sacred to those who do not wish them profaned.

But what particular issues are considered sensitive naturally varies cross-culturally; and what is initially believed to be a sensitive issue thus might not be such after all. For example the registration of personal belief in the scandinavian context has not been considered necessary, or even *comme il fault* with reference to its sensitive nature as it is believed – besides to be a highly personal experience and private issue – to touch upon racist controversies. But in many countries from where the migrants come it is quite to the contrary considered the first and foremost identifying – that is public – and normally quite unproblematic issue for its firm believers. Research which at the outset may appear quite harmless can, likewise, later turn out to be potentially risky for its more or less unprepared practitioners[9]. Against the background of the overall political tensions concerning minority issues such studies may be dragged into the research external area of press sensational writing or misused for political purposes.

It is not the topic in itself so much as its relationship to the social surroundings in which the research is carried out, that is of importance here. And that brings me to the role of the researcher. In addition to those implications which apply to the primary vulnerability of the research subjects who, as a rule, have not initiated the process themselves (for example, third world migrants who might suffer stigmatisation from focusing on the problematic aspects of their exile situation), sensitive research may be burdensome to the researcher as well.

Despite the fact that the power within the subject-object relationship of the research setting itself largely belong with the researcher, this is – of course – not the case in respect of the surrounding research external community setting. In such a setting a researcher into deviant groups who rely on emic involvement and/or a human rights commitment might become viewed as more or less contaminated by the research topic him or herself.

Because ethics and politics become intertwined in refugee research, especially when it is performed in a multicultural community context, it frequently evokes responses from those who learn about it. Refugee studies certainly raise a range of problems relating to ethics as well as politics, in addition to problems relating to the refugee specific psychosocial setting. Moreover, in an increasingly bureaucratised world, the researcher in refugee issues is frequently dependent on formal permission by the *gatekeepers* by which I mean those who monitor the researcher's access to the empirical material, such as, for example, authorities set to review the use of sensitive or personal data, or some other corporate bodies involved in the issues or subjects of one's choice – including the credentials or formal status that may be required for entering the field, such as in my case, for example, as a clinical psychologist in addition to my interest and parallel education in cultural analysis.[10] Lee & Renzetti (1989, 9-10) add to this picture the issue of legal restrictions that increasingly may affect not only health workers, but researchers as well. Researchers in the field have to consider what particular kind of person they themselves represent; their public image, so to speak, or the attributional links between themselves and those whom they depend on for carrying out their scientific work.

By extension, research on sensitive issues thus raise a whole range of problematic issues of methodological relevance. It affect almost any stage in the research process rendering problematic the collecting, holding and/or dissemination of research data. And the problems that may arise from it in hindsight take many forms, such as political, ethical or legal, as well as those that, depending on the surrounding context, affect the personal lives and security of its participants. All considerations that are worth serious academic pondering, not the least from the point of view of the choice of research method and design.

Polarities of Methodological approach:
An Issue of Varying *Inputs* as well as *Outputs*

The typological arrangements in figures 1-2 below contrasts what could perhaps be labelled a Natural Science-oriented (NSC) – and by extension medical – versus a Humanistic (HUM) Model – in which I include the social sciences as well.

SOME POLARITIES IN THE METHODOLOGICAL APPROACH

wiew of social reality *as external to actor*	*wiew of reality* *as socially constructed*
quantitive/hard data (restricted)	qualitative/soft data (flexible)
sample generalisation (measurement/replication)	content contextualisation (*'verstehen'*/interpretation)
research assistance	researcher as participant medium
social survey/ experimental design	unstructured interviews/ participant observation/ case study design

It is representative of a division which often – though not quite consistently – is equated with quantitative *hard* versus qualitative *soft* data approaches.[11] Here I have registered certain main differences between the two approaches which are of relevance to my argumentation. They include – besides the disparities in viewing reality as indicated on top of the scheme – a restricted focus which demands a high level of precision or 'operationalisation' and offers few – if not only one single – opportunity for measurement and data collection, versus one which – quite to the contrary – requires greater flexibility of performance.

The HUM approach gives many more *opportunities for revision and contact*, not only between the researcher and his or her research subjects but, more importantly, also as between the theoretical – here interdisciplinary – analysis and collecting the empirical material; modes of operation that in the NSC model are viewed – and thus methodologically protected – as highly separate operational units, which by way of their very separateness ensure or strengthen the validity of the analysis at issue. In this type of argumentation the researcher is supposed, first to formulate explicit propositions about the topic to be investigated and design the research *in advance* specifically to answer these questions and – note – nothing else, all else being considered irrelevant surplus or somehow *disturbing* data.

For this reason researchers are also cautioned not to change the focus of their inquiry during the research process in order to minimise errors that could interfere with the replicability of the research design and with reaching a statistically relevant measurement. Again, the HUM researcher may, contrary to the NSC methodological practice, encourage paying attention to the unique features of the *surplus* material that emerges, or, even more radically, s/he may start off with one proposition (for example, an economic one) and reach conclusions that relate to seemingly entirely different aspects by way of unexpected connections (for example, ending up in shamanistic rituals). As complementary or even competing views the said scientific approaches depend on a different kind of input; to the extent that the very *disturbing* factors (in terms of reliability) of the one approach, factors, which are as a consequence ruled out as errors, may in fact be considered to be ideal material on which to base further investigation by the other; that is, a material that has emerged while taking *a closer look* at the subject's overall situation, and in the case of interviewing going beyond the selfsame research questions into considering their wider – here interdisciplinary – context (i.e. contextualisation).

Thus the controversies in methodological approaches are reflected in the employment of methods used for gathering data, for example in their level of standardisation for predefined and controlled stimuli versus flexibility in including a shifting focus that is tailored to deal with *exceptional or otherwise unaccessible material*[12]. In the NSC type of design the researcher is counselled to study the levels of correlations between types of treatments and their effects through examining a large number of passively recipient cases (hypothesis testing). But by choosing such a design s/he simultaneously comes to avoid the detailed study of those *agents which bring about these effects*, causes which are better attended to within HUM designs, in which the issues are to a larger extent considered from the subjects' point of view (emically, cp. Weber's term *verstehen*); while the researcher is free to concentrate on whatever numbers are favourable from the point of view of the theoretical interests, if it be one single case.

While the natural science approach is modelled on the requirements of highly structured experimentation with the ideal of bringing *the world out there into a controlled (closed) laboratory* in mind, the latter model – derived from within the field of the humanities – venture the opposite way *out there into the field*, being among other things, built *around participant observation in natura* (under field conditions) with an accompanying flexibility of thought and action characteristic of unstructured methods.[13] And that is the very aspect that, with certain modifications makes the latter type of approach better suited for attending to problems of the kind discussed in this publication, because it is about an intensified attentiveness in relationship to the surroundings (cp. for example, the notion of *socially organised* violence used in this publication).

A representative sample of the population at large (i.e. generalisation) is a matter of particular further concern to the NSC model. For this reason the type of measurement that are chosen should encompass a large, but minutely exact, battery of input. A number of seemingly rather prosaic factors, such as the very wording of a question, or even if it has been used before (i.e. is standardised) – for example, cross-culturally *in a wide variety of testing situation while remaining the same* – may seem more important than pondering its conceptual relevance to those being asked to respond as long as they *do* respond.[14] This is, of course, in order to minimise errors which hamper the replicability of the research design and reach a statistically relevant outcome. And, again, in contrast to the unique *processual* features of much HUM research which is difficult to replicate at will. That is also why in the latter case, instead of instrumental precision, one goes for educating the *researcher as a participant medium*.

However, such differences in scientific outlook doesn't merely concern the issue of the scientific procedure itself or even its design, but, moreover, they turn on how the end product is construed when taken as a *genre;* for example, when published as articles of few words and figures or extensive monographs punctuated by quotations and detailed description. While the choice of method thus implies a different degree of control over the input, as a consequence it produces differing though not incompatible results. It is not only an issue of different input but of ending up in a different style of presentation, as well. For example, the self-conscious endorsement by qualitative researchers of literary devices is not seldom outright rejected by quantitative quarters. On the other hand, already the employment of certain scientific concepts (like causal or independent variables and reliability) may bring negative expectations regarding the nature of the presentation among qualitatively oriented scholarly readers.

Thus, the issue of research design is to a certain extent also about the criteria on which we base our evaluations, because the way of posing the problems as well as presenting the findings are so different. The NSC methodology is based on the assumption that the only reliable source of knowledge is one which facilitates the prediction of future events. And yet human action is often indeterminate – or made determinate only in the course of social negotiation (that is socially constructed) – and therefore, according to adherents of HUM designs, remains open to various interpretations depending on contextual variation such as here a range of cross-cultural or multidisciplinary factors.[15]

In order to get away from the subjectivity and error of what is perceived – frequently rightly so – as a naive qualitative enquiry by scholars of opposite persuasions, a whole apparatus is set up to ensure a neutral distance between the researcher and his or her subjects. However, while it does counter some problems, it raises others which follow from killing off relevant information in the name of reliability, if not acquiring or amassing inadequate knowledge. The strategic retreat to 'surface certainty' tends to sweep away the imaginative underpinnings of an analysis, resulting in a product which, to its critics, may seem shallow and absolute in a very restricted sense only. And the results of which are not infrequently turned over in a cross-cultural or historical context.

On the face of it the differences between a qualitative and quantitative approach would seem to be a technical one, but while they remain merely different ways of gathering data for some scholars, these concepts have increasingly come to denote divergent assumptions about the very nature of research within the social sciences[16].

Some Problems of the Medical Model
in Studying Sensitive Issues

To sum up the preceding discussion, it could be said that the nature of the methodology or route a researcher decides to take to the empirical material will govern the type of input required. The emphasis here is either on controlling the research variables and their exact form (the very wording of a questionnaire remaining the same notwithstanding the context) as a measurement of what is considered to be approachable *out there* irrespective of the investigator's relationship to it (while minimising the subject-object interaction) or – quite to the contrary – on emphasising the reviewing of the context and quality, that is, the level of rapport in the relationship between the researcher and his or her subjects, while utilising a larger flexibility of both focus and content. Writing on method Knudsen (1983, viii) uses the term 'unstructured conversations' to describe this phenomena:

> We attempted to let the refugees guide the conversations themselves, as it is their own thoughts on the situation in the camp, and on the past and future, which are of primary importance. For this reason we have not collected systematic data...

The problems encountered in the NSC model are thus both of a structural and pragmatic kind. For one thing, the very conceptual starting point may be at odds with the particular reality under study, while, at the same time, its cross-cultural revision might be difficult in as much as this type of design tend to treat irregularities as irrelevant 'errors' to be discarded. For example, the use of self-assessment scales, such as the Harward Trauma Questionnaire widely used in psychiatric research, in a cross-cultural setting may pose problems already when considering the translation of its measurable concepts into some smaller language of a non-literate context. But, what is more, *in wrong hands* the very way of implementing such a survey, may, in the eyes of the immense trauma focused on in this and similar instruments, and the accompanying emotionality involved and presumably aroused by the intervention itself, appear as an – if not unethical, at least often – a premature questioning or testing of helpless and hapless refugees. This is why it is so important that such research is done by clinically experienced persons, to the exclusion of less well-versed research assistants.

Whenever we are to ask research questions which are not straight-forward and simple to answer (i.e. restricted in the above sense) but charged with subjective meaning for the objects of our research, or that are somehow considered as sensitive in nature, such a question in itself may produce different answers at different points in time, because it initiates a process of reflection and after-thought. And, that is, without these different answers thereby necessarily being wrong or invalidated, to use a more scientific term, as they would be in a design built on the natural science model. For example, the straightforward asking of a tradition-oriented refugee client whether s/he has been raped will almost certainly bring instant denial and accompanying lengthy attempts at keeping its occurrence a secret of the sort touched upon in this study.

The way of posing research questions is a frequently encountered problem in clinical research generally, and especially when it is, more-over, cross-cultural in nature, because the research tools commonly used have traditionally relied so heavily on diagnostic procedures and testing batteries developed in line with the NSC model against the backdrop of a unicultural western context. A feature which, again, becomes especially highlighted when using face to face interview methods. As the counter-argument runs, such a model fails to take account of its appropriateness in studying people and is accused of not acknowledging the fact that – as opposed to natural phenomena – this type of research may in fact *come to affect the subjects in deci-sive ways*. Somewhat paradoxically, the softer the research technique becomes, with an increasing closeness to the subject, the harder it therefore, according to Yin (1994, 26), is to carry out. Unlike statisti-cal analyses, there are few precise formulae to guide the investigator. Marked as soft approaches are by closeness to and flexibility vis-à-vis the field, even *after* data collection has started, much more is depend-ent on the researcher-implementator's own style of rigorous thinking and suitability for this type of research.

The qualitative approach is unstructured in the sense that, although it has a clear purpose and plan, little control is in evidence in order to encourage people to open up and express themselves in their own terms and, preferably, in their own time. As such it is more dependent upon the investigator's basic knowledge of the research issues involved than it is on minute details of the design itself, which is why it requires his or her presence as a participating medium or an *educated observer*. Collecting loosely structured data where one tries ones best *not* to restrict the subject from the outset while making use of rather loose theoretical propositions, is not merely about collecting already existing facts. Researchers are not regarded as a mere recording instruments and, observe, neither are interpreters, but variables to be included in the analysis.[17]

Moreover, because the data collection procedures are dependent on a continuous dialogue with theoretical issues there is little room for research assistants. The end result is an expanded *contextualised* protocol ideally abounding in conceptual richness and personal relevance, revelatory of both the researcher and research subjects and chronicling both the process and content of the process. It is, however, not my intention to dwell on the differences between diverse scientific models as such in this connection, except for merely regretting the fact that such issues of conflicting scientific procedures have brought a tendency to marginalise 'soft approaches' within the social sciences, and a parallel – and, at times, defensive – criticism of 'hard data approaches' within the field of cultural studies. But problems frequently also arise from half-hearted attempts to combine such different approaches without acknowledging their independent character; attempts which as a consequence may confuse more than solve the problems involved.

That brings me to the next issue connected to the difference in scientific outlook of interest in this connection. An issue, which has, so far, been less considered, but, nevertheless is, in my view, of increasing importance particularly in areas of cultural, and especially refugee studies. As an extension of the above mentioned flexibility demand, it is about the subject-object relationship, while reminding us that such differences also relate to diverse conceptualisations of *the role of the researcher* in relationship to his or her research subject (*Figure 2*). It is the inclusion of contextual factors in the soft method research design, which makes it necessary to take a closer look at the effect of the researcher as well.

As part and parcel of the postmodern impulses the role of the researcher has come under closer scrutiny. Frequently critical voices are heard demanding that the author behind the product be accountable, inquiring about *whose* history or cultural interpretation, rather than, as the case is in the hard data procedure, about how representative the research sample is. By *de*-anonymising the person behind a particular product one wishes to reach a greater reliability and also extend what perspectives that are mediated as 'Truths' within the public sphere, not seldom to the benefit of a post-colonial, feminist or micro historical presentation.[18]

SOME POLARITIES IN THE SUBJECT–OBJECT INTERACTION

restricted focus/content (surface/etic)	flexible/associative content (in-depth/emic)
preformulated/-coded structured questionnaire subject respondent	open-ended/informal 'conversation with a purpose' subject informant/interactionist
(measurement/replication)	('*verstehen*'/interpretation)
short term/neutral interaction	long term/trusting interaction
assymmetrical control/distance	closeness/mutuality/ dependence

Research projects of a kind that may have unforeseen, not seldom political implications, presuppose the acknowledgement of the vulnerability, not only of its subjects, but also of the researcher. The said developments have, for example, given rise to intense debates about the right of the research subjects to gain insight into research results, and the responsibility of the researcher to see to it, or the power of the powerless – quite often minority groups – to influence what kind of research is done on them; or about the further issue of whether, in the word of the anthropologist Hylland Eriksen[19] a professionally good researcher could not simultaneously be unmoral as a person, to take just a few examples which have been debated lately.

Scholars in many fields have been quite naive when it comes to such problematic aspects of the role of the researcher; in my experience they have as a rule been personalised and retold as gossip. What is important here is the fact that this has happened without the information being substantiated or taken seriously as a problem of research. Such backbiting should be brought to light as a problem of method, and the students better prepared to handle the mass media, political and other authority figures who may take active part in deciding on their research findings. I don't mean to say that real conflicts of interest are thereby necessarily done away with; my claim is of course more modest, like minimising the personal pain and problems of public relations that may result from *unprepared* practitioners in the field.

The problems that may arise in connection with sensitive research are not so much about personal shortcomings or defeat, but, more often than not, about unintentional politicisation of research problems and findings, and, above all, about an unfortunate personification of a more general problem. Such a state of affairs may bring self-censorship which, again, might render our research and its results innocuous. A development that poses greater responsibility not merely on how we choose to focus our studies – the ratio between critical as well as understanding perspectives – but also on how we are to prepare for the possible research external utilisation of it.

Summing up the Interdisciplinary Challenge: On Context-dependent Data and Professional Ethics

In the efforts to systematise problematic aspects that may arise from sensitive research there is much to gain from interdisciplinary co-operation. One thing that I myself have learned while carrying a double role as clinician-psychologist and cultural researcher/field worker, is that, while anthropology has a long experience from fieldwork concerning the subject-object interdependence, it has, nevertheless, shown less systematic efforts at understanding it theoretically. Psychology, on the other hand, has a lot to recommend itself when it comes to instruments for analysing such interdependencies in the form of theories about what are called attributional links and transference reactions or, more generally, object relations, while it still lacks in cultural sensitivity. In addition, clinicians largely work through subject-object relations: in psychodynamic approaches that is their primary instrument. Moreover, they have the benefit of the *closed therapeutic* or *free exploratory space*, which permits in nature experimentation of a kind that offers the flexibility of a qualitative design while it still simultaneously represents a more controllable research situation than what is possible in fieldwork, in which the researcher – however unwillingly – is to a much larger extent drawn into the confines of his or her field as envisaged by among other things the so called *arrival stories* (i.e. of researchers into new and alien field circumstances).

During the project under scrutiny here, based as it has been on year-long therapeutic contacts, I have learned a lot about cross-cultural relations, especially, about relationships between different gender, age or in/out groups, from the way the clients related to me. Among others things, I have learned from their occasional withdrawal behaviour (chapter 11: The Aesthetics of Cross-cultural Therapeutic Interaction), or their viewing the mental health professionals as some kind of extended kin, as well as from their misunderstood expectations about getting help with practical issues (chapter 10: Patterns of Exchange in Cross-cultural Trauma Therapy). Among the more sensitive factors I – the therapist-researcher – had to confront in this connection, was the refugee research specific danger of retraumatisation by way of the reactualisation of the traumatic situation during the treatment process, which may, not only affect the clients/research subjects but the interpreter and therapist/ researcher as well.

The methodological starting point for this study was in an interdisciplinary challenge coming from the field of cultural studies, and perceived within the mental health care sector, as to where the encounter between helper and client should take place, and how it may affect their relationship (chapter one; The Interdisciplinary Challenge). The classical problem is worth reiterating here: If the therapist takes part in team work across professional dividing lines undoubtedly in line with the general interdisciplinary requirements of this field, where there is a particular case, say of child custody, under scrutiny, a risk of emotional leakage, manipulation/misunderstanding and even contamination in the eyes of the client may become impelling. For therapists to offer concrete help for problems pertaining to the social welfare or legal sectors may, in addition to the quackery involved from their lack of training, also leave the underlying long term problems untouched.

The area of refugee assistance/research thus seem to require both cultural sensitivity and a certain political sophistication, not only from its minority subjects, but from its professional practitioners as well. Many important interests may be involved, which makes it necessary for a researcher cum therapist to consider his or her intervention from the point of view of maximum validity and minimum offensiveness on the part of its vulnerable subjects as envisaged by the concept of *compassionate scholarship* (that is, in analogy with that of the emphatic therapist).[20] A professional does wisely to reckon with the possibility of sanctions from infringements by those in power or by way of somehow incriminating or sensitive material becoming known: for example the harassment of exiled persons by their homelands' regimes, or, in the case of asylum seekers, that the empirical data may somehow throw suspicion on their motives.

A main difference between the methodological approaches here referred to – and illustrated by reference to minority studies – is in *the closeness of the researcher to his field*. One could perhaps state that while the researcher draws nearer to his field in *soft* approaches, the theories remain further away from the empirical data in that one creates greater vistas, while the opposite is true for those that work with hard data designs, that there is a tendency to exclude meta level theorising as speculative due to the strict demands for operationalisation, in the same way as the effect of the researcher is to a greater extend excluded from the picture. Though in both cases choices made must naturally be made explicit as must the researcher relate to a qualified discussion between experts who has some kind of relationship to the kind of empirical material or theoretical thinking that is at issue in the particular project.

There is professional agreement about the fact that the relationship between empirical facts and theory is problematic, mediated as it is through the work of the researcher and aided by some kind of measurement. Both sides in what has been called a science war[21] accuse each other of renouncing the truth: While one side claims that the other merely produces fiction and speculations in the head of the researcher; they are themselves accused for loosing themselves in numerical brick bracketing. A criticism that reminds us about the fact that also statistical validation is dependent on conceptual refinement, is about a certain percentage of *something*. Numbers without context remain meaningless. That is, before what solutions are sought to the said mutually agreed upon problem, assume different forms. While the *soft* approach among other things seeks to include the effect of the researcher in the analysis, the *hard* one, quite to the contrary, wants to exclude it. This is because, unlike a conventional structured intervention which seeks to hold constant the researcher's impact – as it does of all inputs – its counterpart recognises the interactivity or mutual dependence and psychological positioning of the researcher and his or her research subjects, as well as, the wider context it involves.

Moreover, in a qualitative approach theories are not considered bare logical apparatuses for prediction, which is why they must not be judged on their predictive power alone, but on the plausibility of the image of the world they help to create: i.e. here the theories function to *anticipate* reality. The ultimate aim of a case study is therefore not to assess the prevalence or frequency of a particular clear-cut phenomena in the context-independent manner of a positivistic confirmation. Rather, the aim of such a study is in the utilisation of extended networks of theoretical implications that, while never complete in themselves, are nonetheless crucial to its scientific evaluation. In this way the present study has been about questions, but not necessarily about their answers.

Again, for those of us who have limited ourselves to collecting our empirical material in interpersonal – not least therapeutic – situations it is moreover important to remember that while the choice of *soft* methods frequently arise from difficulties in accessibility on the one hand, it may, on the other, bring a range of unwinding problems which result from the increased involvement by the researcher in his or her field of enquiry (cp. the problems in ending the therapeutic contacts indicated in chapter 11: The Aesthetics of Cross-Cultural Therapeutic Interaction). This fact reminds us that the subject-object relationship here referred to is not a question of a private but of a professional closeness/distance. Sensitive research issues may impinge on any social research, however, not seldom, without the awareness of the involved parties, but it is most evident in research contexts that tend to sharpen ethical dilemmas such as those of minority and refugee studies.

Many contemporary research problems, among which are those pertaining to migration and forced exile, depend on an interdisciplinary or, at least, a cross-culturally valid approach. The very problems that are raised takes the researcher into a multitude of subjects, and here it is in the words of Meyer[22] "the very questions that tell, not the 'domicile' of the answers". However, interdisciplinary work is never easy because the nature of social life colours academic life in order that, by extension, also scientific disciplines come to carry features of it for better or worse. Researchers who challenge traditional scientific boundaries may unwittingly trigger problems of identity and even 'warfare' – instead of advancing interdisciplinary co-operation – in defining the objects of study or legitimating competing accounts of reality. In the name of science we are in for a certain amount of unhealthy division of what scientific reality is in fact all about. Despite the fact that research activity is frequently described in geographical metaphors, using terminology like 'a field of knowledge' or 'ground-breaking facts', nevertheless our research problems increasingly defy the limits of traditional subjects. What is thus kept apart in reality goes together.

NOTES

INTRODUCTION

1. A notable nordic exception is found in the works of Henny Harald Hansen (1958; 1961), based on her stays in Kurdistan. See also Wikan (1978; 1996), who has written on middle eastern women; while Agger (1994) and Dahl (1998) focus on refugee women from a more restricted psychotherapeutic and medical perspective.

CHAPTER I

1. For example Alver & Selberg 1992; Ingstad & White 1995.
2. Agger & al. 1990; Aron 1992.
3. For example Hofer & Niedermüller 1988; Bertaux 1981; Watson & Watson-Franke 1985.
4. In Norway Akman 1995; Eriksen 1994; Fuglerud 1996; Kamalkhani 1988, Longva 1997 besides Ahlberg 1990.
5. In Norway for example Dahl 1993; Lavik & al 1996; Varvin & Hauff 1998.
6. Rosenbaum 1988; Peterson & al 1993.
7. Rutter 1987.
8. Gullestad (1984) was the first anthropologists to study ordinary common people in Norway.
9. Berger 1969; Berger & Luckmann 1971; also Geertz 1973.
10. Cp. my introduction of the concept system-oscillation in chapter 3: The Torture versus Exile Trauma.
11. Figley 1995.
12. Berry 1992; Levine; Schweder & Levine 1984; Schweder 1991; Stigler & al 1990.
13. In Norway Nobakht 1993.
14. Illiteracy, of course, must not be confused with social status.
15. Observe that those two clients who initially complained about nerves had both been in contact with therapeutic treatment before I met them.
16. Grünfeld 1991.

17. Ibid.

18. The examples of this study will from now on be dated according to the following categories: initial (the period of negotiating a working relationship); medial (including the more intensive intermittent); and concluding phases of the therapy.

19. See Goffman 1961.

20. Here I exclude the role of the professional helpers in influencing the course of events, important as it may be in the escalation of such unfortunate interpersonal 'incidents'.

CHAPTER 2

1. Among the kurds one still finds groups who confess to zoroastrian doctrines. Zoroastrianism (founded c. 1200 BC) was the original dualistic faith and state religion of Persia; at the time a most powerful religion with great influence on the developments of the later middle eastern world religions (i.e. Judaism, Christianity and Islam; for example Boyce 1984). However, the introduction of islam into the area brought an end to its dominance and persistent and harsh oppression followed. Thus Aisha still relates stories about the fate of her ancestors who were drowned en masse by their muslim enemies.

2. Lindblom-Jacobsen 1988; Allodi 1982; Stover & Nightingale 1985.

3. According to Lipton (1994, 78) drastic changes in lifestyle, behaviour and personality may indeed result from PTSD to the extent that formerly well adapted persons may even loose their job and home, and become addicts living on the street.

4. For the physical and medical effects of severe and long-lasting trauma see Yehuda & McFarlane 1979.

5. Cp. also the emotionally highly charged, repetitive-compulsive, almost 'epileptic'-like fits of Shirin in ex. 3, which were, almost certainly, according to traditionally accepted/expected behaviour rather than any peculiarity of her own, and, despite her lack of post traumatic stress symptoms.

6. The latter may, of course, influence the acting-out behaviour of traumatised and desperate refugees as perceived by their counterparts during the 'incidents' occurring in response to authority referred to in the previous chapter.

7. For example Lipton 1994.

8. Kardiner 1941; Horowitz 1986.

9. Ahlberg 1981; Ludwig 1966; Maslow 1964; Schafer 1958.

10. Tasman & Goldfinger 1991.

11. Ahlberg 1981, 66.

12. In Fatima's case, this includes both her kin, that of a fellow participant in shi'ite Muharram celebrations who flogged himself to death while she was carried on the shoulders of her father in the same procession, and the suicide of a woman unhappily in love with the wrong man, all while she was still a small child.

13. Loewenstein 1991.

14. For example Lipton 1994, vi.

15. If I were forced to diagnose the clients who form the subject of this book, they would, except for the control case of Shirin's adjustment disorder, likewise fit this picture.

16. Ahlberg 1976.

17. Spiegel 1991, 41; Hopper 1991; Varvin 1999.

18. For example Bustos 1990.

19. For example Danieli 1980 & 1984; Major 1996.

20. Laub 1993, 301.

21. Varvin & Hauff 1998.

22. Observe also the pre-Khomeini roots of other clients' tragedy.

23. Cp. their vulnerability as presented in the next chapter: The Torture vs. Exile Trauma.

24. I myself cannot help imagining Fatima herself as a kind of 'Lioness' or Survivor, here defending her vulnerable status or symbolically 'bad' breath.

25. Cp. the fact that AD's body was covered with, and she herself fed on, her own excrements.

26. Observe that 40 is a period of time frequently resorted to in connection with ritual purification.

27. At War with Humanity 1982.

28. Human Rights in Iran Newsletter 9 1993.

29. Cp. the cross-cultural debate on human rights violations on pp. 148 ff. below.

30. Cp. violations of intergenerational obligations in chapter five.

31. For an exposition on her theories see Weininger 1984.

32. For example Bowlby 1953; 1969; Balint 1968; Fairbairn 1943; 1952 and Mahler & al 1975.

33. Cp. cumulative effects of trauma in chapter nine.

34. *Mut'a* or *sigheh* (the farsi term used by the client) is a temporary but fully valid marriage practice among shi'ites which can be contracted

for 99 years during which time the wife cannot be divorced. However, after the period stipulated in the contract it is automatically dissolved. It is forbidden among sunnites and – when conducted for a short period only – generally looked down upon by its critics as a form of legalised prostitution.

35. Furst 1967, 16.
36. Cp. the therapeutic concern for 'getting the clock started again' on p. 231.
37. Cp. also Fatima's episodes of mental breakdown and Nasreen's flashbacks in N ex. 1/2/9.
38. Cp. N ex. 9: About the Importance of Dreams.
39. See chapter ten: Patterns of Exchange in Cross-cultural Trauma Therapy.
40. Laub 1993, 299.
41. See for example Varvin & Hauff 1998.
42. Lindy 1988.

CHAPTER 3

1. A somewhat pejorative term used for a learned theologian in Iran. Momen (1985, 245) agrees with Aisha in that, on the whole, iranian women are regarded as not worth any substantial education, too emotional to be trusted with any important decision and, if unveiled, liable to lead men astray.
2. Hinnels 1997; Ahlberg 1990.
3. cp. Douglas 1995.
4. Lau 1986, 234-5.
5. For example Østerberg 1999; Heelas 1996; 1998.
6. That is, not considering a growing fear of its environmentally harmful consequences.
7. Cp. the debate on orientalism; Said 1978.
8. Hjärpe 1980; Vogt 1993; Assad 1994.
9. Cp. pp. 147 ff. on human rights.
10. On the issue of religion in Kurdistan see Kreyenbroek 1966.
11. Cp. similar developments within the Pakistan Movement as treated by the author (1990).
12. Høybraaten 1992; Gellner 1992; Heelas & al 1996.
13 For example Berg Eriksen 1991; Kurten 1990.

CHAPTER 4

1. Cp. the islamisation of prison life in chapter eight: The Millenarian Heritage of the Modern Age.
2. For example The Human Rights Watch Global Report on Women's Human Rights 1995.
3. For example Agger 1990.
4. For example Douglas 1966; Goody 1990; Sabbah 1988; Wikan 1996.
5. At War With Humanity 1982, 104.
6. Jeffrey 1979, 21.
7. See Papanek 1973; Papanek & Minault 1982; Minault 1992 and Sharma 1978.
8. Cp. also the premigrational absence of fighting or imprisoned men.
9. Cp. chapter 13: Symbolic Shelter in a Changing World.
10. Cp. the difficulties involved in mother tongue language teaching to children without environmental language support.
11. The national epic of the kurds, Meem u Zeen, by Ahmed Khani, is largely built on the same pattern as that of Romeo and Juliet (Bois 1985, 127; also Shakeley 1993).
12. See also Goody 1990.

CHAPTER 5

1. Cp. chapter 11: The Aesthetics of Cross-cultural Therapeutic Interaction.
2. Vatuk 1982, 60.
3. Observe the more traditional Aisha's strict adherence to the norm as compared to the more modern Nasreen.
4. Dervishpour's unpublished sociological data from 1994.
5. I thank psychologist Hassan Namwar for providing me with a information on the increasing problem of divorce among iranians in Norway.
6. Interestingly, the statistics also show that while arab women never marry swedes, iranian women increasingly do, and that such marriages seldom end in divorce in the way marriages between iranian men and swedish women frequently do.
7. Maududi 1980.

CHAPTER 6

1. Cp. what is said about 'authority incidents' in chapter one: The Interdisciplinary Challenge.

2. Since many refugee men arrive precisely at a time in their lives when taking an additional wife would be considered if they were at home (that is, in areas where polygamy is still practised) it might be wise to take this possibility into account when dealing with their marital problems.

3. Cp. what is said about 'the sociocentric transference' on pp. 198ff.

4. For example, Reichelt & Sveaass 1994.

5. Note that this aspect is again a reflection, although perhaps by comparison an extremely limited one, of a parallel oppressive involvement in private affairs by the iranian regime, as depicted in the section on human rights violations below in chapter seven: The Collective Dimensions of Trauma.

6. Hagen & Qureshi 1994.

7. Østerberg 1990.

8. For example Knudsen 1990.

9. Cp. also Kurten 1990.

10. See also, for example Holloway & Fullerton 1994.

11. Cp. for example, *Aisha*'s daughter, who has now begun to 'think like a Norwegian' in A ex. 10.

12. See Hundeide 1988 & 1989; also Erikson 1968 & 1978.

13. It is a widely acknowledged fact that many indigenous interpreters do try to avoid mediating facts which they know/assume to be of such a 'shameful' nature that under ordinary circumstances they would never become articulated (See also the interpreter examples in Part II).

14. Cp. the notion of shame above & A ex. 22: Kurds who Slip-up.

15. Miller 1984, 156-185.

16. Observe the two norm breaches here lumped together as almost equal by the client; having an extramarital baby and setting up a separate household. The son's behaviour at the time also caused a fear in the client, of the father-in-law/girl's father carrying out violent reprisals against her son.

17. Cp. the theories of Mary Douglas on purity and danger, 1966.

18. Cp. the frequent disappearance of the clients' husbands as an alternative to violence and other *avoidance or withdrawal behaviour* as depicted in chapter 11: the Aesthetics of Cross-cultural Therapeutic Interaction.

CHAPTER 7

1. See, for example, Honko 1979 for an overview.

2. For example Kligman 1988.

3. I thank psychologist Hassan Namwar, who worked with war-injured soldiers on the iranian front prior to his own escape, for initially having focused my attention to such occurrences.

4. Imam as quoted in Kashani 1988, 41.

5. *Kerbela* used here as a metaphor of the inclination towards mourning and martyrdom in Shia Islam, is the name of a most important locality south west of today's Baghdad, where Ali, the brother-in-law of prophet Muhammed and progenitor of Shia Islam, lost his son, Muhammed's grandchild Hussein, in internal disputes; events that are re-enacted yearly in the so called *ta'zieh* passion plays. On the history and doctrines of the Twelver Shia which dominates in Iran, see for example Momen 1985.

6. This was a prominent symptom haunting this client for a long time, and especially pronounced during the session in which she 'finally' disclosed the 'public demonstrations' of the regime that had involved her own kin; see L ex. 1.

7. The general muslim term for 'religious festival'.

8. A spiritual person or member of the learned theologians or ulama (cp. The pejorative term used for the same category of persons in Iran is *akhund*, as in A ex. 3: About the Meaning of Life).

9. Cp. the discussion in chapter 8: The Millenarian Heritage of the Modern Age.

10. On iranian religious gatherings see Momen 1985, 238-.

11. Cp. what is said about altered states of consciousness on p. 42.

12. Bowker 1970; Holm & Bowker 1994.

13. For example Burridge 1971; Lanternari 1963; Worsley 1968.

14. For example Oberoy 1987.

15. Cp. Muhammed's *Hijra,* emigration or actually flight from Mekka to Medina in 622 where the first islamic society was founded.

16. For example Fischer 1980; Keddie 1983.

17. Alho 1976, 62-3.

18. Corinthians 1:20-22.

19. Islam has never actually abolished slavery, although Muhammed encouraged the emancipation of slaves. But muslim history has nevertheless seen slaves who did attain great opportunities of wealth and power, and the children a slave girl has by her muslim master are

regarded as legitimate, as is his marriage to her. Even caliphs are said to have had slaves as mothers (Levy 1965, 85-9).

20. Boff & Boff 1986, 10; Stålsett 1997.

21. Despite my focus on refugees from fundamentalist governments like that in Iran, it should not be forgotten that there are yet others who are forced to leave or are severely persecuted precisely *because* of their islamist convictions; this happens in countries like Algeria, for example.

22. The latest of which has been going on in the former Yugoslavia as *ethnic cleansing*.

23. Mamiya 1988, 210-11.

24. For the interested reader examples of such movements can be found, for example, in the classical work of Cohn (1962) or Burridge (1976) and literature on the so called suicide cults of modern times.

25. See also Harrell-Bond 1986; 1992.

26. For example, Liebkind 1993, 4.

27. Weaks 1978; Kreyenbrook 1992; Kinnane 1994.

28. Ghassemlou 1980; Schneider 1991.

29. On muslim law schools see Levy 1965; Anderson 1959; Coulson 1978.

30. There has also been yezidi among our clients. See Schneider 1986; Næss 1986.

31. For example, Kreyenbrook 1998.

32. According to the dogma of shi'ite Islam, Muhammed was followed by an entourage of twelve infallible imams, the first of whom was his cousin and son-in-law Ali, and the last of whom is still alive 'outside this world'. Like Christ, this Mahdi, as he is called, is expected to return in order to establish true theocracy on earth.

33. There has been no association with the non-religious P.K.K. (Kurdish Workers Party) founded in 1978 in Turkey by Abdullah Ocalan among my clients.

34. *Genocide in Iraq* 1993; *Unquiet Graves* 1992.

35. Presentation given at the Third European Conference on Traumatic Stress, Bergen (Norway) June 1993.

36. Cp. what is said about ritual violations above.

37. For example Bettelheim 1943; Krystal 1968.

CHAPTER 8

1. Cp. the internalisation of good and bad objects in object relations theory as presented in Part Two.
2. In a thesis that I cosupervise, architect Hans Skotte (University of Trondheim) ponders the relationships of various internally displaced third world refugee groups to their psycho-physical environments with regard to reconstructive aid models.
3. Blaschke 1991; Schneider 1991.
4. S ex. 3: "Could you please make them bring my family here or otherwise I won't come here anymore".
5. Though the wealthy are as likely as the poor to live in ghettos, they can afford to keep such stress factors at bay.
6. Ahlberg 1988.
7. See also Fischer 1980; Gule 1988; Vogt 1993.
8. For example Lindholm 1990; 1992.
9. Religious Rights in Pakistan 1991, 13-29.
10. A practice that I have regrettably also encountered in the narratives of kurdish/iranian clients (for example, in A ex. 19: What It is All About).
11. For example Caplan 1987.
12. This matter is dealt with at length in Ahlberg 1990.
13. an-Naim 1987, 13.
14. Human Rights in Iran Newsletter 15 July 1993.
15. Human Rights in Iran Newsletter 1993, 5.
17. See Stang Dahl (1992, 104-112) for a treatment of this new veil in the egyptian context.
18. Anderson 1968; Mernissi 1987; Layish 1995.
19. See the Koran Interpreted according to Arberry 1964, verses 24:31, 33:33, 33:53 and 33:59.
20. On Moslem Doctrine and Human Rights in Islam 1972, 163.
21. According to Stang Dahl (1992, 158-60), many egyptian wives are not even made aware of the existence of other wives.
22. Sahih al-Bukhari translated to english by Khan (1976, vol. I, 182-4).
23. An-Naim 1990, 39; Ahlberg 1990, 189.
24. On Moslem Doctrine and Human Rights in Islam 1972, 175.
25. All the sunni schools of law accept divorce by talaq-ul-bida, i.e. through a one-sided three-fold declaration by the husband without the need to

give any reasons or any legal proceedings (Ahlberg 1990, 187; Layish 1975).

26. On Moslem Doctrine and Human Rights in Islam 1972 1972, 176.

27. A rule relating to the practice of polygamy requires the husband to visit his wives regularly, preferably every fourth night (Stang Dahl 1992, 148).

28. Cp. what is said about the ahmadies on p. 149.

29. Human Rights in Iran Newsletter 9, 1993.

30. For example Anderson 1959.

31. In addition to this, an adulterer/ress may only marry another adulterer/ress, or an idolater/ress.

32. Also Sahebjam 1993.

33. This session was conducted without an interpreter (cp. F ex. 17: "I will never go back to interpreting for her or I lose all my credibility").

34. At this point, I was still not aware of the stoning and burying of women alive as a recurrent punishment in Iran.

35. Human Rights in Iran Newsletter 15 & 16 & 17, 1994.

36. An-Naim 1990, 22.

CHAPTER 9

1. Staub 1989.

2. Lavik 1990, 174-5.

3. Furst 1967, 95: Krystal 1968.

4. Included in this chart are the accumulated trauma of the three main participants of this study as further envisaged in chapter nine: On the Narrative Approach and Meaning-Formation.

5. See for example Hodne (1980, 17; cp. p. 128) for changes in the number of dead bodies that people at different times in history have had to confront, depending on varying social expectation in their surroundings. Cp. also the concepts of *adjal* (destiny) and *jihad* (holy war) as culturally alternative explanations of misfortune, which leaves the afflicted person relatively more free of guilt.

6. Personal communication with Weisæth at a research seminar held at the Psychosocial Centre for Refugees 1993.

7. Dahlgaard 1991.

CHAPTER 10

1. Varvin 1998; 1999.
2. Allody & Cowgill 1982; Comas-Diaz & Griffith 1988; Cohn 1991.
3. On postmodernism and psychology see Kvale 1994.
4. Freud found them unanalysable because, in his view, their narcissistic lack of object-orientation did not form any basis for transference reactions. See, for example, Kohut 1971 & 1977; Kernberg 1980.
5. Cp. what is said about the broken narratives in chapter two: Psychological Trauma Reconsidered.
6. Mahler 1968; Mahler & al 1979; Winnicott 1953; 1958; 1971.
7. For example Roland 1998; Kakar 1981.
8. Amati1990, 3-4.
9. Hägglund 1976.
10. Kurten 1990; Voutira & Harrell-Bond 1993.
11. Compare this to what has been said earlier about the divorce rates on p. 92ff.
12. For example Momen 1985, xxii.
13. Beeman 1986, 27-30.
14. Kashani 1988, 44; Beeman 1976, 39.
15. Cp. N ex. 2: "Like parting with my sister" and footnotes 18 & 19 below, on other examples of this kind of role-shifting behaviour pertaining to sociocentric values.
16. Beeman 1986, 31.
17. The interpreter subsequent to her withdrawal from Fatima's therapy as depicted below (F ex. 17: "I will never go back to interpreting for her or I lose all my credibility") gave the following explanation: (What happens if you just throw bad news in somebody's face?) You just wouldn't do a thing like that. For example, when my mother died my sister could not break the news on phone but had to travel all the way here. For days I had to reassure her – I had my misgivings – before she dared to tell me. And even that was only after her young son had told me that grandmother was so ill that she would almost certainly never recover.
18. This sister, subsequent to the death of her mother from cancer (after the latter had returned from pilgrimage) a few years prior to Nasreen's flight, was now perceived, as the a successor 'Mother' to whom her affection was transferred.
19. Following her own father's death, Nasreen likewise considers her eldest brother to be her 'Father'.

20. See Dahl (1989) for a furter discussion of the matter.
21. This is despite the anthropologist's parallel theoretical concern with the subject-object balance depicted here.
22. In a resreach project on the psychosocial and cultural adaptation of unaccompanied minor refugees under my auspices such issues of secrecy has turned out to be of utmost importance (Hjelde 1998).

CHAPTER 11

1. Varvin 1999, 385.
2. Beeman 1986, 12.
3. Cp. with the age for learning 'shame' in A ex. 17: The Guest House.
4. It should be observed that alternative therapeutic pursuits might proceed independently of the current one, and without the awareness of the psychotherapist.
5. I.e. in line with the dichotomy of normative styles presented on p. 69.
6. Cp. my own insisting behavior in A ex. 14: One Year Past her Mother's Death.
7. Pers.com. 1991; see also 1992.
8. The study was presented by Monsen at a seminar in Oslo recently arranged in honour of professor Anni von der Lippe (*Where is clinical research in psychology heading at present?*).
9. Skovholt & Rønnestad 1992.
10. See also Gullestad (1992) on the concept of autonomy in psychoanalytic theory building.
11. Jacobs et al 1972; Hoen-Saric et al 1964.
12. Although, while confronting their immense tragedies, we were quite frank about our own reaction to the gross human rights violations involved.
13. Beeman 1981, 44-49.
14. If unanalysed, such a background may hamper the therapeutic process by reactualising the interpreter's own traumatic past.
15. Pers.com. 1990; also 1954.
16. In a follow-up study funded by Trondheim University and The Norwegian Research Council I will look into this issue and the more general meaning of emotionally charged artefacts in the refugee surrounding.
17. Without having the possibility of taking much along.

18. I myself have repeatedly been the source of amusement for both interpreter and client because of such clumsiness.

19. I.e. which is so fundamental for containing the internalised bad objects involved in refugee trauma.

20. A view largely shared by Rønnestad (pers.com.; Skovholt & Rønnestad 1992) on the basis of extensive interviews of practising psychotherapists.

21. Varvin & Hauff 1998.

22. In fact the slow turnover of patients (as reflected in the PSCR Annual rapports) is today perceived as a persistent problem of our clinical work at the Psychososcial Centre for Refugees that should merit further attention in relation to the difficulties involved in the concluding phase of cross-cultural therapies.

23. Moreover, the existing professional guidelines for interpreters are not convertible to the requirements of the therapeutic context without qualification.

24. Cp. The *Unspeakability* of Trauma and Broken Narratives in chapter two: Psychological Trauma Reconsidered.

25. Nasreen's husband was accused of participation in a passport falsification affair, but soon released due to lack of evidence.

26. Observe that during the flight of her family Aisha's husband had likewise disappeared, forcibly removed by the iraqi police (cp. N ex. 2: "Like parting with my sister"; F ex. 7: On Mental Intrusions).

CHAPTER 12

1. Lefcourt 1981-84.

2. That is, the ones who have been longest in therapy in order for a focused life story to emerge.

3. Though members of her family were employed outside home, they were also dependent on some agriculture for a living.

4. Beeman 1988, 12-14.

5. Cp. zerængi and ta'arof as discussed in the previous chapter: The Aesthetics of Cross-cultural Therapeutic Interaction.

6. Cp. Int ex. 2 & 3; F ex. 18: More about Withdrawing.

7. Again, Fatima's situation differed somewhat in that she had a rather close – even untraditional (See F ex. 11: Taking part in Muharram Celebrations as a Little Girl) relationship to her father, whom she

simultaneously feared very much for his, in her view, fair but extremely harsh punishments.

8. At one time during our contact there occurred an incident when a social worker visiting the family left her scarf behind and subsequently shocked the client by sending her a written note instead of fetching it personally; thus making it "such a big (i.e. written) issue" that she felt as if she were being accused of having stolen it.

9. Cp. the fact that for Aisha the norwegian graveyard where her son was buried because of his tragic death, was in her mind after all transformed into "a small piece of Kurdistan in Norway" (A ex. 11: From Ghost to Second *Shahid*).

10. Cp. the greetings by the interpreter in Int.ex.1: "Anything else would be unthinkable" and food offered in Int. ex 3: "I will never go back to interpreting for that patient again".

11. Jafarnejad, no date.

12. Excepting, that is, the 'inherited trauma' involved in the mere fact of being a kurd, which had hit Aisha's family especially hard as a result of its high social position, thereby giving rise to what could perhaps be assumed to be a shared 'inherited depression' in the female line (for example A ex. 19: What It is All About).

CHAPTER 13

1. Cp. what is said about withdrawal behaviour in chapter 11: The Aesthetics of Cross-cultural Therapeutic Interaction.

2. Schimmel 1982; Gilhus 1997.

3. See The Human Rights Watch Global Report on Women's Rights (1995, 418-443) reporting on such forced virginity exams from Turkey.

4. Cp. the fact that while on hajj (the pilgrimage to Mecca) gender and other social distinctions are expected to be intermittently discarded according to islamic doctrines.

5. Beck & Keddie 1979.

6. One also has to remember that Aisha, Nasreen and Shirin wore the traditional kurdish female dress until the day of their departure, when they suddenly, for the first time in their lives, had to get accustomed to quite different clothing in addition to all the other changes involved in their migration.

7. Beeman 1986, 73.

8. Guest houses such as that of Aisha's home were traditionally set up to be able to allow kinsfolk to visit.

9. Mehta 1976; Bortwick 1982.

10. For example, Jeffrey 1973, 25.

11. Bortwick 1982, 109.

12. Cp. the redefinition of female activity in respect of the norwegian health and social welfare authorities as of domestic concern referred to above.

13. See Barth 1954.

14. Problems in this regard is a frequently cited reason for conducting marriage within the kinship group, in order to make it easier for a young bride to adapt to the new circumstances (cp. A ex 13: *Havvu* & A ex 22: Kurds who Slip-up).

15. This phrase is, moreover, built into many religious expositions that – independently of the particular (here muslim or hindu) creed – aim at supporting such collectivist norms (cp. the distinctive normative styles on p. 69).

16. Cp. Roland 1988; Kakar 1981 & Goody 1990.

17. It could be mentioned here that at this point Aisha had just told me about the old days in Iran when people from her tribe were drowned en masse because they were non-muslim zaratushtrean.

18. Also Berger & Luckman 1971.

19. For example Ehrenzweig 1971.

20. The opposite features described here are similar to those referred to on page 42 in relation to altered states of consciousness, that is, when manifested either as highly traumatic PTSD or creative so called peak experiences.

21. In addition to predisposing personality characteristics.

CHAPTER 14

1. Ahlberg 1990.

2. In order to arrive at overall conclusions in this type of design both the results of the individual cases and the multiple- or cross-case analyses can and should be the focus of the study. An ideal outcome thus illustrates both the principle of literal replication (similar outcome) from case to case, and theoretical replication across cases: a contrary outcome, but for comprehensible reasons (Yin 53-59).

3. Holter & Kalleberg 1982; Kvale 1996.

4. Cp. the highly vulnerable situation of those applying for political asylum in relationship to their more – or less – honest 'advocates' and hosts.

5. Enrique Bustos (1990) has written an enlightening article on the 'splitting mechanisms' operating at the organisational level of the professional helping system concerned with refugees in scandinavia. A phenomenon that may reflect the PTSD-related mistrust found among its clients.

6. As a group refugees are often lumped together with AIDS- or rape victims, drug users and the kind, in the same way that the living areas to which they tend to be allocated in the West, like those of voluntary migrants, often cluster around the red light districts of our deprived inner city areas.

7. For example Lindholm 1992; an-Naim 1990; Ahlberg 1994.

8. Shahid & van Koningsveld 1991; Metcalf 1996. At present, national asylum policies within the European Common Market and associated countries like Norway, are in the process of being co-ordinated in order that what has by the critics been denoted as the *fortress Europe* (to keep third world foreigners out) will be erected around it. And those few asylum seekers who do manage to cross the borders, moreover, have to endure negative stereotypes among their western hosts. Hostile attitudes that are nurtured by the north-south enemy constellation of the post-communist era, and, however unfairly, tend to equate them with their very oppressors. This is especially the case for adherents of the muslim faith.

9. For example, a PhD-project in medical anthropology (under my guidance; Hjelde 1998) on the psychosocial adaptation of unaccompanied minor refugees, has raised some initially quite unexpected issues connected to the more or less 'terrible secrets' that the subjects themselves may harbour concerning their 'real' identities; such secrets as having provided false age, name or familial relationships to the immigrant authorities. A leakage of which kind of sensitive information, in the last instance, might threaten their very juridical status and thus protection in exile. Another potentially sensitive study by psychology students of mine (Sinnes & Nielsen 1997) focus on the attitudes of preachers, belonging in the religious revivalist laestadian movement of northern Scandinavia and Finland, towards mental health professionals and their treatment. This movement which is characterised by a strong regional profile, is frequently viewed as a sort of ethnisised version of Christianity intended for the sami and the originally finnish immigrant or kveni minority.

10. In an article Interviewing *Survivors of Marital Rape*, Bergen (1993), examines how a vast majority of those institutions approached refused him access to the empirical material, from reasons ranging from a plain refusal to acknowledge the occurrence of rape among their clients (cp. repression of traumatic material by the victims as well as by their surroundings described in chapter two: Psychological Trauma Reconsidered) or protecting them from overexposure to researchers, to the likelihood of their resisting such a critical scrutiny as a research process may be when done by conducted by outsiders.

11. Bryman 1992; Holter & Kalleberg 1996;Yin 1984; Silverman 1989; Haavind 1992.

12. It is questionable whether access to the material that has emerged in the present work would have been possible by using a NSC frame.

13. Bernard 1988.

14. Therefore, very strong reasons must be given for altering any basics of, say, a test on post traumatic stress when used cross-culturally; an example is measuring 'survivor's guilt' despite the fact that this item has been tailored to a christian world view. A recurring problem in this type of approach when it is used in a cross- or multicultural setting is also to get enough respondents, especially, where communication is done in writing and there is no trade-off (like 'treatment for data') involved?

15. Kjørup 1996: Gilje & Grimen 1993; Kjelstadli 1992.

16. For example Glaser & Strauss 1967; Engelstad & al 1996; Giddens 1993; Cernea 1991.

17. For a discussion of the processes involved see Bjerre Nielsen 1995.

18. For example Kvale 1992; Milner 1994; Knudsen 1997.

19. In a feature article entitled *Good researchers – bad persons* in Dagbladet 12.3.1997.

20. Alver 1997.

21. For example, the debate following upon Sokal's deliberately nonsensical article published in 1966.

22. In a feature article 'Tinned knowledge' in *Dagbladet* 5. March 2000.

APPENDIX:

List of Clients' Narratives Found in the Text

Aisha:

Nasreen:

Fatima:

Cp. ex.:

Interpreter:

INDEX

322

BIBLIOGRAPHY

ACHTE, K & AL (eds.) Traumatic Stress – Psychology and Psychopathology. Proceedings of the Symposium on the Psychopathology of Traumatic Stress. Jyväskylä: Gummerus Psychiatrica Fennica 1992.

AGGER, I & BUUS JENSEN, S. Testimony as Ritual and Evidence in Psychotherapy for Political Refugees. *Journal of Traumatic Stress* 1990, 1, 115-130.

— The Blue Room: Trauma and Testimony Among Refugee Women. London: Zed Books 1994.

— Psychotherapeutic Understanding of Women Exposed to Sexual Violation in Political Detention. *Nordic Sexology* 1994, 12, 1-12.

AHLBERG, N. Some Psycho-physiological Perspectives on Ecstasy. *Religious Ecstasy*. Stockholm: Almqvist & Wiksell 1981, 63-73.

— Pakistanske muslimer i Norge: Religiøs variasjon og konflikt. *Chaos. Dansk-norsk tidskrift for religionshistoriske studier* 1988, 10, 12-23.

— New Challenges – Old Strategies. Themes of Variation and Conflict among Pakistani Muslims in Norway. Helsinki: Transactions of the Finnish Anthropological Society 1990, 25.

— Muslimska invandrarkvinnor i migrationsperspektiv. *Islam i forskningens ljus*. Holm N (ed.). Åbo: Religionsvetenskapliga skrifter 1990, 21, 183-214.

— På flukt fra virkeligheten med eller uten retur. Noen kulturpsykologiske synspunkter på muslimske flyktninger. Oslo: *Kirke og kultur* 1991, 4, 309-315.

— The Impact of Forced Migration on Muslim Rituals: An area of Cultural Psychology? *The Problem of Ritual*. Ahlbäck T (ed.). Stockholm: Almquist & Wicksell, 1993, 2-14.

— Religion, Oppression and the Issue of Human Rights. *Human Rights Violations and Mental Health* Lavik & al. (eds.) Oslo: Scandinavian University Press 1994, 143-178.

— Eksemplets makt. Noen ideer til forståelsen av muslimske migranters dilemma. *Hva er kasuistikk?: Om moralsk læring og refleksjon i tilknytning til forbilder og eksempler*. Wetlesen J (red.). University of Oslo: Skriftserie for HF's etikkseminar 1998, 3, 187-206.

— Methodological Choice and the Study of Sensitive Issues. *Approaching Religion*. Ahlbäck, T (ed.) Stockholm: Almquist & Wiksell 1999, 9-31.

AKMAN, HACI. Landflyktighet. En etnologisk undersøkelse av vietnamesiske flyktninger i eksil. University of Bergen (1995): thesis (287 p).

ALHO, O. The Religion of the Slaves. Helsinki: Folklore Fellows Communications 1976, 217.

ALLODI, F & COWGILL, G. Ethical and Psychiatric Aspects of Torture: A Canadian Study. *Canadian Journal of Psychology* 1982, 27: 98-102.

— Psychiatric Sequelæ of Torture and Implications for Torture. *World Medical Journal* 1982, 29 (5), 71-75.

ALVER, B & SELBERG, T. Det er mer mellom himmel og jord. Folks forståelse av virkeligheten ut ifra forestillinger om sykdom og behandling. Bergen: Vett og Viten 1992.

— & ØYEN, Ø. Forskningsetikk i forskerhverdag. Vurderinger og praksis. Oslo: Tano Aschehoug 1997.

AMATI, S. Ambiguity as the Route to Shame. *International Journal of Psychoanalysis* 1992, 73, 329-341.

AMNESTY INTERNATIONAL. Written Statement to the 49th Session of the United Nations Commission on Human Rights. February 1993.

ANDERSON, J.N.D. Islamic Law in the Modern World. Westport, Conn: Greenwood Press 1959.

— Family Law in Asia and Africa. London: Allen & Unwin 1968.

AN-NAIM, ABDULLAHI AHMED. Human Rights in the Muslim World: Sociopolitical Conditions and Scriptural Imperatives. A preliminary inquiry. *Harvard Human Rights Journal* 1990, 3, 13-52.

— Religious Minorities under Islamic Law and the Limits of Cultural Relativism. *Human Rights Quarterly* 1992, 9, 1-18.

ARBERRY, A.J. The Koran Interpreted. Oxford & New York: Oxford University Press 1964.

ARON, A. Testimonio. A Bridge between Psychotherapy and Sociotherapy. In: Cole E & Rothblum E D. *Shattered Societies, Shattered Lives. Refugee Women and theirMentalHealth*. New York: The Haworth Press 1992, 67-89.

ASSAD, T. Genealogies of Religion. London: John Hopkins University Press 1994.

At War with Humanity. A Report on the Human Rights Records of Khomeini's Regime. A Publication of The People's Mujahedin Organization of Iran (PMOI), May 1982.

BAILLY, L & AGRALI, S & AMBIAVAGAR, S. Evaluation des Sequelles des Psychotraumatismes dans la Populationm du Kurdistan d'Irak. Paris: L'Association Pour Les victimes de la Repression en Exil (AVRE) 1992.

BALINT, M. The Basic Fault. London: Tavistock Publications 1968.

BARKUN, M. Disaster and the Millennium. New Haven and London: Yale University Press 1974.

BARTH, F (ed.). Principles of Social Organisation in Southern Kurdistan. Oslo: Universitetets Etnografiske Museum Bulletin 1953, 7.

— Father's Brother's Daughter Marriage in Kurdistan. *South-Western Journal of Anthropology* 1954, 10, 164-71.

— Ethnic Groups and Boundaries, Oslo: Universitetsforlaget 1969.

BATUK, S. Purdah Revisited. A Comparison of Hindu and Muslim Interpretations of the Cultural Meaning of Purdah in South Asia. *Separate Worlds. Studies of Purdah in South Asia.* Papanek & Minault (eds.). Delhi: Chanakya Publications 1982, 55-78.

BECK, L & KEDDIE, N. Women in the Muslim World. Cambridge, Massachusetts and London: Harvard University Press 1979.

BEISER, M. Changing Time Perspective and Mental Health among South-East Asian Refugees. *Culture, Medicine and Psychiatry* 1987, 28(5), 437-464.

BEEMAN, W.O. Status, Style and Strategy in Iranian Interaction. *Anthropological Linguistics* 1976, 18, 305-22.

— Language, Status and Power in Iran. Bloomington: Indiana University Press 1986.

BENEDICT, R. Patterns of Culture. Harmonsworth: Penguin Books 1946.

BENNET, G. Traditions of Belief. Women, Folklore and the Supernational Today. Harmonsworth: Penguin Books 1987.

BERGEN, R KENNEDY. Interviewing Survivors of Marital Rape: Doing Feminist Research on Sensitive Topics.

RENZETTI, C & RAYMOND, M (eds.) 1993, 197- 211.

BERGER, P L. The Sacred Canopy. Elements of a Sociological Theory of Religion. New York: Anchor Books 1969.

— & LUCKMANN, T. The Social Construction of Reality. Harmonsworth: Penguin 1971.

BERNARD H. Research Methods in Cultural Anthropology. London: SAGE 1988.

BERRY, J & Co. Cross-cultural Psychology: Research and Applications. Cambridge: Cambridge University Press 1992.

BERTAUX, D (ed.). Biography and Society. The Life Historical Approach in the Social Sciences. Beverly Hills: SAGE Publications 1991.

BETTELHEIM, B. Individual and Mass Behaviour in Extreme Situations. *Journal of Abnormal Social Psychology* 1943, 38, 417-52.

BJERRE-NIELSEN, H. Seductive Texts with Serious Intentions. *Educational Researcher* 1995, 1, 4-12.

BLASCHKE, J. Kurdische Gesellschaften in Deutchland und West-Europa. Ein Überblick über Soziale und Kulturelle Situation. Schneider R (ed.) 1991, 2.1.-1-15.

BOFF, L & BOFF, C. Liberation Theology. From Confrontation to Dialogue. San Fransisco: Harper & Row 1986.

BOIS, T. Kurdische Volksdichtung. Spiegel der Kurdische Seele. Bonn: Kurdische Institut 1985.

BORTWICK, M. The Bhadramahila and Changing Conjugal Relations in Bengal 1850-1900. *Women in India and Nepal.* Allen, M & Mukherjee, S (eds.). Canberra: Australian National University Monographs on South Asia 1982, 8, 105-134.

BOSERUP, E. Women's Role in Economic Development. London: Allen & Unwin 1970.

BOWKER, J. Suffering in Religions of the World. Cambridge: Cambridge University Press 1970.

BOWLBY, J. Some Pathological Processes set in train by Early Mother-Child Separation. *Journal of Mental Science* 1953, 99, 265-72.

— Attachment and Loss. Vol. I: *Attachment.* New York: Basic Books 1969.

BOYCE, M. Zoroastrians. Their Religious Beliefs and Practices. London: Routledge & Kegan 1984.

BRACKEN, P.J. & GILLER, J.E. & SUMMERFIELD, D. Psychological Responses to War and Atrocity: The Limitations of Current Concepts. *Social Science and Medicine* 1995, 40, 1073-1082.

VAN BRUINESSEN, M.M. Agha, Scheich und Staat. Politik und Gesellschaft Kurdistans. Berliner Institut für Vergleichende Sozialforschung: Edition Parabolis 1989.

BRYMAN, A. Quantity and Quality in Social Research. London: Routledge 1992.

BURKERT, W. Structure and History in Greek Mythology and Ritual. Berkeley: University of California Press 1979.

BURRIDGE, K. New Heaven, New Earth. A Study of Millenarian Activities: Oxford: Basil Blackwell 1971.

BUSTOS, E. Dealing with the Unbearable: Reactions of Therapists and Therapeutic Institutions to Survivors of Torture. *Psychology and Torture.* Suedfeld, P (ed.). New York: Hemisphere 1990, 143-63.

— Psychodynamic Approaches in the Treatment of Torture Survivors. *Torture and its Consequences – Current Treatment Approaches.*

Basoglu M (ed.). Cambridge: Cambridge University Press 1992, 86-102

CAPLAN, L. Popular Conceptions of Fundamentalism. *Studies in Religious Fundamentalism.* Caplan, L (ed.). London: Macmillan 1987, 1-24.

CATANI, M. Social-Life History as Ritualised Oral Exchange. *Biography and Society. The Life Historical Approach in the Social Sciences.* Bertaux, D (ed) 1981, 211-224.

CERNEA, M. Putting People First: Sociological Variables in Rural development. Oxford: Oxford University Press 1991.

CLIFFORD, J. & MARCUS, G.E. Writing Culture. The Poetics and Politics of Ethnography. Berkeley, Los Angeles & London: University of California Press 1986.

COHN, J. Proceedings of the International Symposium on Torture and the Medical Profession. XIX Tromsø-Seminar on Medicine. *Journal of Medical Ethics* 1991, 17 (supplement).

COHN, N. The Pursuit of the Millennium. London: Mercury Books 1962.

COMAS-DIAZ, L. & GRIFFITH, E.H. Clinical Guidelines in Cross-cultural Mental Health. New York: John Wiley & Sons 1988.

COSTA E SILVA, J.A. & LEMGRUBER, V.B. Posttraumatic Stress Disorder and Violence in Inner Cities, 29-34. *Traumatic Stress – Psychology and Psychopathology.* Achte (ed) 1992, 29-34.

COULSON, N.J. A History of Islamic Law. Edinburgh: Edinburgh University Press 1978.

CRAPANZANO, V. TUHAMI. Portrait of a Moroccan. Berkeley, Los Angeles & London: University of California Press 1980.

DAHL, C.I. Some Problems of Cross-cultural Psychotherapy with Refugees Seeking Treatment. *The American Journal of Psychoanalysis* 1989, 1, 19-32.

DAHL, S. Rape: A Hazard to Health. Oslo: Scandinavian University Press 1993.

— & MUTAPCIC, A. & SCHEI, B. Trauma, Events and Predictive Factors for Post Traumatic Symptoms in Displaced Bosnian Women in a War Zone. *Journal of Traumatic Stress* 1998, 1, 137-45.

DAHLGAARD, O S. Flytting og psykisk helse. *Sykdom, sjel og samfunn. Festskrift til Nils Johan Lavik.* Notaker, H & Pedersen, W (eds.). Oslo: Pax forlag 1991, 26-41.

DANIELI, Y. Countertransference in the Treatment and Study of Nazi Holocaust Survivors and their Children. *Victimology: An International Journal* 1980, 5, 355-367.

— Psychotherapists Participating in the Conspiracy of silence about Holocaust. *Psychoanalytic Psychology* 1984, 1, 23-42.

DEGHANI, A. Torture and Resistance in Iran. Memoirs of a Woman Guerrilla. The Iran Committee (no date, no place).

Diagnostic and Statistical Manual of Mental Disorders. Fourth Edition. Washington DC: American Psychiatric Association 1994.

DOUGLAS, M. Purity and Danger: An Analyses of Concepts of Pollution. London: Routledge & Kegan 1966.

— Thought Styles. London: SAGES 1995.

DURKHEIM, E. Elementary Forms of Religious Life. New York: Free Press 1965.

DZIEGIEL, L. Rural Community of Contemporary Iraqi Kurdistan facing Modernization. Krakow: Agricultural Academy in Krakow, *Studia i materialy* 1981, 7.

EHRENZWEIG, A. The Hidden Order of Art. Berkeley, Los Angeles & London: University of California Press 1971.

EITINGER, L. Concentration Camp Survivors in Norway and Israel. Oslo: Universitetsforlaget 1964.

— Rehabilitation of Concentration Camp Survivors following Concentration Camp Trauma. *Psychotherapy and Psychosomatics* 1969, 17, 42-9.

ELSASS, P. Strategies of Survival: The Psychology of Cultural Resilience in Ethnic Minorities. New York University Press 1992.

ENGELSTAD, F. & GRENNES C.E. & KALLEBERG, R. & MALNES, R. Samfunn og vitenskap. Samfunnsfagenes oppgaver, arbeidsmåter og rolle. Oslo: Ad Notam 1996.

ERIKSEN, A. 'Livets goder og livets mørke' – erfaring og tolking i autobiografisk materiale. *Nordnytt* 1990 41, 12-23.

ERIKSON, E.H. Identity, Youth and Crises. New York: Norton & Co 1968.

— (ed.) Adulthood. New York: Norton & Co 1978.

ERIKSEN, T. HYLLAND. Kulturkonflikter i praksis: perspektiver på det flerkulturelle Norge. Oslo; Ad Notam Gyldendal 1994.

ERIKSEN, T. BERG. Freuds retorikk. En kritikk av naturalismens kulturlære. Oslo: Universitetsforlaget 1991.

FAIRBAIRN, W.R.D. The Repression and the Return of Bad Objects. *Psychoanalytic Studies of the Personality*. London: Tavistock Publications 1943.

— Psychoanalytic Studies of the Personality. London: Tavistock Publications 1952.

FIGLEY, C. (ed.). Compassion Fatigue: Coping with Secondary Traumatic Stress in Those who Treat the Traumatised. New York: Brunner/ Mazel 1995.

FERRAROTTI, F. On the Autonomy of the Biographical Method. *Biography and Society. The Life Historical Approach in the Social Sciences.* Bertaux, D (ed)1981, 199-28.

FIGLEY, CH. (ed) Trauma and its Wake. The Study and Treatment of Post-Traumatic Stress Disorder. New York: Brunner/Mazell 1985.

FISCHER, M.J. Iran from Religious Dispute to Revolution. Cambridge, Massachusetts and London: Harvard University Press 1980.

FREUD, S. Standard Edition. London: Hogarth Press 1964.

Fuglerud, Ø. Mellom stat og nasjon. University of Oslo: Department of Anthropology. Dissertation 1996.

FURST, S (ed). Psychic Trauma. New York: Basic Books 1967.

GAGNON, N. On the Analysis of Life Accounts. *Biography and Society. The Life Historical Approach in the Social Sciences.* Bertaux, D (ed.) 1981, 47-60.

GAMMELGAARD, J. Katharsis. Sjælens renselse i psykoanalyse og tragedie. Copenhagen: Hans Reitzels forlag 1993.

GEERTZ, A. Ethnohermeneutics in a Post-modern World. *Approaching Religion.* Ahlbäck, T (ed.) Stockholm: Almquist & Wiksell 1999, 73-86.

GEERTZ, C. The Interpretation of Cultures. New York: Basic Books 1973.

GELLNER, E. Postmodernism, Reason and Religion. London and New York: Routledge 1992.

Genocide in Iraq. The Anfal Campaign Against the Kurds. New York: A Middle East Watch Report 1993.

GHASSEMLOU, A.R. Kurdistan in Iran. *People Without a Country. The Kurds and Kurdistan.* Chaliand, G (ed.). London: Zed Press 1980, 107-134.

GIDDENS, A. New Rules of Sociological Method: A Positive Critique of Interpretative Sociologies. Cambridge: Polity Press 1993.

GILHUS, I. Laughing Gods, weeping Virgins: Laughter in the History of Religion. London: Routledge 1997.

GILJE, N. & GRIMEN, H. Samfunnsvitenskapenes forutsetninger. Innføring i samfunnsvitenskapenes vitenskapsfilosofi. Oslo: Universitetsforlaget 1993.

GLASER, B. & STRAUSS, A. The Discovery of Grounded Theory: Strategies for Qualitative Research. Chicago: Aldine 1967.

GOFFMAN, E. Asylums. New York: Doubleday 1961.

GOLDSTEIN, A.P. Structured Learning Therapy: Towards a Psychotherapy for the Poor. New York: Academic Books 1973.

GOOD, M-J DELVECCIO & GOOD, BYRON J. Ritual, the State, and the Transformation of Emotional Discourse in Iranian Society. *Culture, Medicine and Psychiatry* 1988, 12, 43-63.

GOODY, J. The Oriental, the Ancient and the Primitive. Systems of Marriage and the Family in the Pre-industrial Societies of Eurasia. Cambridge and New York: Cambridge University Press 1990.

GRÜNFELD, B. Uførepensjonering og langtidssykdom i Oslo – en bydel-sundersøkelse. Oslo: *Tidskrift for Den Norske Legeforening* 1991, 9, 1088-1092.

GULE, L. Menneskerettighetene i Islam. Bergen: Chr Michelsens Institute. Programme of Human Rights Studies Working Papers 1988, 15.s

GULLESTAD, MARIANNE. Kitchen-table Society: A Case Study of the Family Life and Friendship of Young Working Class Mothers in Urban Norway. Oslo: Universitetsforlaget 1984.

GULLESTAD, SIRI. Å si fra. Autonomibegrepet i psykoanalysen. Oslo: Universitetsforlaget 1992.

HAGEN, G. & QURESHI, N. Barnevernets møte med etniske minoriteter. Oslo: Norges Kommunal og sosialhøgskole, Nota Bene 1994, 1.

HANSEN, HENNY HARALD. The Kurdish Woman's Life: Field Research in a Muslim Society, Iraq. Copenhagen: Nasjonalmuseets skrifter 1961, VII.

— Allahs døtre: blandt muhammedanske kvinder, Kurdistan. Copenhagen: Munksgaard 1958.

HARRELL-BOND, B. Imposing Aid. Emergency Assistance to Refugees. Oxford: Oxford University Press 1986.

— & VOUTIRA, E. Anthropology and the Study of Refugees. Draft 1992 (11p).

HARTMANN, H. Egopsychology and the Problem of Adaptation. New York: International Universities Press 1958.

HAUFF, E., LAVIK, N.J, DAHL, C.I, SVEAASS, N. Psykososiale problemer blant flyktninger i Norge. Oslo: *Tidskrift for Den norske legeforening* 1989, 17-18, 1867-74.

— Stresses of War, Organised Violence and Exile: A Prospective Community Cohort Study of the Mental Health of Vietnamese Refugees in Norway. University of Oslo: Department of Behavioural Medicine & Psychosocial Centre for Refugees, dissertation 1998.

HAUGSGJERD, S.G. Grunnlaget for en ny psykiatri. Oslo: Pax forlag 1986.

HEELAS, P & LASH, S & MORRIS, P. Detraditionalization: Critical Reflections on Authority and Identity. Oxford: Blackwell 1996.

— (ed.) Religion, Modernity and Postmodernity. Oxford: Blackwell 1998.

HELMAN, C. Culture, Health and Society. Boston: Wright 1992.

HERMAN, J. Trauma and Recovery. New York: Basic Books 1992.

HINNELS, J.R. The Study of Diaspora Religion. *A New Handbook of Living Religions.* Hinnels, J.R. (ed.). Oxford: Blackwell Publishers 1997.

HIRSHMAN, A.O. Exit, Voice and Loyalty: Responses to Decline in Firms, Organisations and States. Cambridge, Massachusetts and London: Harvard University Press 1972.

HJELDE, KARIN. Secrets, Silence and Sadness. Resettlement and Care of Young Unaccompanied Refugees. *International Journal of adolescent medicine and Health* 1998, 10, 11-18.

HJÄRPE, J. Islam som politisk ideologi. Oslo: Gyldendal 1980.

HODNE, B. Å leve med Døden. Folkelige fortellinger om døden og de døde. Oslo: Aschehoug 1980.

— & KJELSTADLI, K & ROSANDER, G. Muntlige kilder. Om bruk av intervjuer i etnologi, folkeminnevitenskap og historie. Oslo: Universitetsforlaget 1981.

HOEN-SARIC, R., FRANK, J.D. & al. Systematic Preparation of Patients for Psychotherapy 1. Effects of Therapy Behaviour and Outcome. *Journal of Psychiatric Research* 1968, 2, 267-281.

HOFER T. & NIEDERMULLER, P. (eds). Life History as Cultural Construction/Performance. Proceedings of the III:rd American-Hungarian Folklore Conference. Budapest: The Ethnographic Institute of the Hungarian Academy of Science 1988.

HOLLOWAY, H.C. & FULLERTON, C. The Psychology of Terror and its Aftermath. *Individual and Community Response to Trauma and Disaster: The Structure of Human Chaos.* Ursano & al (eds.). Cambridge: Cambridge University Press 1994, 31-45.

HOLM, J. & BOWKER, J. Human Nature and Destiny. London: Pinter Publishers 1994.

HOLTER, H. & KALLEBERG, R. (eds.). Kvalitative metoder i samfunnsforskning. Oslo: Universitetsforlaget 1982.

HONKO, L. Theories Concerning the Ritual Process. *Science of Religion Studies in Methodology.* Honko, L (ed.). The Hague: Mouton Publishers, Religion and Reason 1979, 13.

337

HOPPER, E. Encapsulation as a Defence against the Fear of Annihilation. *International Journal of Psycho-Analysis* 1991, 72, 607-624.

HOROWITZ, M. Stress Response Syndromes. Northvale, NJ: Jason Aronson 1986.

HOWELL, SIGNE & MELHUS, MARIT (eds.). Fjern og nær. Sosialantropologiske perspektiver på verdens samfunn og kulturer. Oslo: Ad Notam Gyldendal 1994.

Human Rights in Iran Newsletter (by The Organisation for Human Rights and Fundamental Freedoms for Iran), 1993, 9.

The Human Rights Watch Global Report on Women's Human Rights. New York: Human Rights Watch 1995.

Human Rights Watch World Report 1990. New York: Iran Human Rights Developments 1991, 437-453.

HUNDEIDE, K. Barns livsverden: en fortolkende tilnærming i studiet av barn. Oslo: Cappelen 1989.

HAAVIND, H. Analyse av kvinners historier: Bearbeiding and makt og splittelse Ms 1992 (34 p.)

HÄGGLUND, T. Dying, a Psychoanalytic Study with Special Reference to Creativity and Defensive Organisation. Helsinki: HYKS monografia sarja 1976, 61 (diss.).

HØYBRAATEN, H. Christian Monoteism, Ethical Autonomy and Secular Society. Paper given at a Seminar on Islam and Human Rights in Oslo 1992.

INGSTAD, B. Kulturelle faktorer i pasient/helbreder forholdet. *Tidskrift for samfunnsforskning* 1985, 547-561.

— & WHYTE, SUSAN REYNOLDS (eds.). Disability and Culture. Berkeley: University of California Press 1995.

Iran. Human Rights Developments. In Human Rights Watch World Report 1990. New York 1991, 437-446.

Iran. Photographs and Documents on the Continuing Grave Violations of Human Rights. A Report on 64 Forms of Torture Practices by the Khomeini Regime. Published by the International Relations of the People's Mojahedin Organization of Iran (31 pp.) (no date).

Iran. Violations of Human Rights. Documents sent by Amnesty International to the Government of the Islamic republic of Iran. Amnesty International Publications 1987.

JACOBS, D., CHARLES. E., JACOBS, T., WEINSTEIN, H., MANN, D. Preparation for Treatment of the Disadvantaged Patient: Effects on Disposition and Outcome. *American Journal of Ortho-psychiatry* 1972, 4, 666-673.

JACOBSEN, D. Purdah and the Hindu family in Central India. *Separate Worlds. Studies of Purdah in South Asia.* Papanek H & Minault (eds.) Delhi: Chanakya Publications 1982, 82-109.

JAFARNEJAD, M. Kvinne-eventyr og historier fra Iran. Published at own expence in Trondheim, no date.

JEFFREY, P. Frogs in a Well: Indian Women in Purdah. London: Zed Press 1979.

KAHN, MARGARET. Children of the Jinn. In Search of Kurds and their Country. New York: Seaview Books 1980.

KAKAR, S. The Inner World. A Psycho-analytic Study of Childhood and Society in India. Oxford: Oxford University Press 1978.

— Shamans, Mystics and Doctors. Boston: Beacon press 1982.

KAMALKHANI, Z. Iranian Immigrants and Refugees in Norway. University of Bergen. Studies in Social Anthropology 1988, 43, MA thesis (214 pp.)

KARDINER, A. Traumatic Neurosis of War. New York: Hoeber 1941.

Kashani, H.M. Grief and Psychological Adjustment to Forced Migration: A Study of Recent Iranian Migrants to the USA. Berkeley: The California School of Professional Psychology, dissertation 1988.

KEDDIE, N R. (ed.) Religion and Politics in Iran: Shi'ism from Quietism to Revolution. New Haven and London: Yale University Press 1983.

KERNBERG, O. Internal World and External Reality. New York: J. Aronsen 1980.

KHAN, MASUD. The Concept of Cumulative Trauma. *The Psychoanalytic Study of the Child* 1963, 18: 286-306.

KILLINGMO, B. Hva er dynamisk psykoterapi? *Nordisk Psykologi* 1984, 3, 129-146.

KINNANE, D. The Kurds and Kurdistan. Oxford: Oxford University Press 1964.

KJELSTADLI, KNUT. Fortida er ikke hva den en gang var. En innføring i historiefaget. Oslo: Universitetsforlaget 1992.

KJØRUP, S. Menneskevidenskaberne. Problemer og tradisjoner i humanioras videnskabsteori. Roskilde Universitetsforlag 1996.

KLEIN, M. Mourning and its Relation to Manic-depressive States. *Contributions to Psychoanalysis* 1921-1945. London: Hogarth Press 1940.

KLEINMAN, A. Patients and Healers in the Context of Culture: An Exploration of the Borderland between Anthropology, Medicine and Psychiatry. Berkeley: University of California Press 1980.

339

— Rethinking Psychiatry. New York: The Free Press 1988.

— The Illness Narratives: Suffering, Healing and the Human Condition. New York: Basic Books 1988.

— Writing at the Margin. Discourse between Anthropology and Medicine. Berkeley: University of California Press 1995.

KLIGAN, G. The Wedding of the Dead. Ritual, Poetics and Popular Culture in Transylvania. Berkeley, Los Angeles & London: University of California Press 1988.

KNUDSEN, J.CHR. Boat People in Transit: Vietnamese in Refugee Camps in the Philippines, Hong Kong and Japan. Bergen: Department of Social Anthropology, dissertation 1993.

— Cognitive models in life histories. *Anthropological Quarterly* 1990, 63, 3, 122-33.

— Eksilets representasjoner og forskernes fortolkninger. *Norsk antropologisk tidskrift* 1997, 1, 5-11.

KOHUT, H. The Analysis of the Self. A Systematic Approach to the Psychoanalytic Treatment of Narcissistic Personality Disorder. New York: International Universities Press 1971.

— The Restoration of Self. New York: International Universities Press 1977.

KREYENBROOK, P.G & SPERL, S. The Kurds. A Contemporary Overview. London: Routledge 1992.

— & ALLISON, CH (eds.). Kurdish Culture and Identity. London: Zed Books 1966.

KRIS, E. Psychoanalytic Explorations in Art. New York: International Universities Press 1952.

KRYSTAL, H. Massive Psychic Trauma. New York: International Universities Press 1968.

KURTEN, T. 'Basic propositions' och förståelse av livsåskådningar. *Teologinen Aikakausikirja* 1990, 96, 142-152.

KVALE, S. Interviews: An Introduction to Qualitative Research Interviewing. London: SAGE 1996.

— (ed.). Psychology and Postmodernism. London: SAGE 1994.

LANTERNARI, V. The Religion of the Oppressed: A Study of Modern Messianic Cults. New York: Knopf 1963.

LAU, A. Family Therapy Across Cultures. *Transcultural Psychiatry.* Cox, J.L. (ed.). London: Croom Helm 1986, 234-45.

LAUB, D & AUERHAHN, N. Knowing and not Knowing Massive Psychiatric Trauma: Forms of Traumatic Memory. *International Journal of Psycho-Analysis* 1993, 74, 287-303.

LAVIK, N.J. Psykiatriske synspunkter på "livsritualer"- med særlig henblikk på ungdomsårene. Oslo: *Kirke og kultur* 1977, 1, 2-16.

— Organised Violence and Mental Health – Historical and Psychological Perspectives on the 20th Century. *Pain and Survival. Human Rights Violations and Mental Health.* Lavik & al (eds.). Oslo: Scandinavian University Press 1994, 85-116.

— & CHRISTIE, H & SOLBERG, Ø & VARVIN, S. A refugee Protest Action in a Host Country: Possibilities and Limitations of an Intervention by a Mental Health Unit. *Journal of Refugee Studies* 1996, 9, 73-88.

— & HAUFF, E & SKRONDAL, A & SOLBERG, Ø. Mental Disorder among Refugees and the Impact of Persecution and Exile: Some Findings from an Out-Patient Population. *British Journal of Psychiatry* 1996, 169, 726-732.

LAYISH, AHARON. Women and Islamic Law in a non-Muslim State. A Study based on Decisions of the *Shari'a* Courts in Israel. New York: John Wiley & Sons 1975.

LEFCOURT, H.M. Research with the Locus of Control Construct. New York: Academic Press 1981-84.

LEFEBVRE, H. The Production of Space. Oxford: Basil Blackwell 1991.

LEHMANN, A. Att berätta om sitt eget liv. Kulturmöten og kulturell förändring. Malmö 1985, 199-206.

LEVY, R. The Social Structure of Islam. New York & London: Cambridge University Press 1965.

LIEBKIND, K. Ethnic Identity – Challenging the Boundaries of Social Psychology. *Social Psychology of Identity and the Self Concept.* Breakwell, G (ed.) Surrey University Press 1992.

LINDBLOM JACOBSEN, M. Att arbeta med tolk i psykoterapi på psykoanalytisk grund. Erfarenheter från RKC. *Psykisk hälsa* 1988, 1, 57-64.

— Några tankar efter ett års klinisk erfarenhet med torterade flyktningar. *Psykisk hälsa* 1988, 1, 102-8.

LINDHOLM, T. The Cross-Cultural Legitimacy of Human Rights Prospects for Research. Oslo 1990: Norwegian Institute of Human Rights Publication no 3, 35.

— Article 1. *The Universal Declaration of Human Rights: A commentary.* Eide, A & al (eds.). Oslo: Scandinavian University Press 1992, 31-56.

LINDY, J. Vietam: A Casebook. New York: Brunner/Mazel 1988.

LOEWENSTEIN, R.J. Psychogenic Amnesia and Psychogenic Fugue: A Comprehensive Review. *Review of Psychiatry.* Tasman A & Goldfinger S (eds.), 1991, 10, 65-99

LONGVA, ANH NGA. Walls Built on Sand: Immigration, Exclusion and Society in Kuwait. Boulder, Colo: West View Press 1997.

LUDWIG, A. Altered States of Consciousness. *Archives of General Psychiatry* 1966, 15, 225-233.

MAHLER, M., Pine F. & Bergman A. The Psychological Birth of the Human Infant. New York: Basic Books 1975.

— On Human Symbiosis and the Vicissitudes of Individuation. Infantile Psychosis. New York: International Universities Press 1968.

MAJOR, E. War Stress in Transgenerational Perspective: Norwegian Concentration Camp Survivors and Two Other Groups and their Children: A Comparative Investigation. Oslo: The Armed Force Joint Medical Service dissertation 1996.

MAMIYA, L. The Black Muslims as a New Religious Movement. *Conflict and Co-operation between Contemporary Religious Groups.* International Symposium Proceedings by Chuo Academic Research Institute. Tokyo 1988, 177-200.

MANI LATA. Production of an Official Discourse on *Sati* in Early Nineteenth Century Bengal. Economic and Political Weekly. *Review of Women Studies*, 1986 April 1986, 34-5.

MANSELLA, A & FREEDMAN, M.S & GERNITY, E.T & SCARFIELD, R.M (eds.) Ethnocultural Aspects of PTSD: Issues – Research and Clinical Application. Washington D C: American Psychological Association 1996.

MASLOW, A. Religions, Values and Peak-Experiences. New York: Viking 1964.

MAUDUDI, ABUL A'LA. Human Rights in Islam. London: The Islamic Foundation 1980 (39 p.).

MAUSS, MARCEL. The Gift. Forms and Functions of Exchange in Archaic Societies. London: Routledge & Kegan 1969.

MAYER, A.E. Islam and Human Rights. Different Issues, Different Contexts, Lessons from Comparisons. Paper given at a Seminar on Islam and Human Rights in Oslo 1992 (37p).

McGOLDRICK, M & PEARCE, J.K & GIORDANO, J (eds.) Ethnicity and Family Therapy. New York: The Guillford Press 1982.

MEAD, M. Male and Female. New York: William Morrow 1949.

MEHRDAD, DERVISHPOUR. Skilsmässan i Iran. En jämförelse mellan decenniet före och decenniet efter revolutionen. University of Stockholm: Department of Sociology 1992.

— En bild av kvinnornas försämrade situation i Iran. *Sociologisk forskning* 1993, 3, 47-62.

MEHTA, RAMA. From Purdah to Modernity. Nanda B R (eds.). *Indian Women from Purdah to Modernity.* New Delhi: Vikas Publishing House 1976, 113-128.

— Purdah Among the Oswals of Mewar. *Separate Worlds. Studies of Purdah in South Asia.* Papanek H & Minault (eds.) Delhi: Chanakya Publications 1982, 31-49

MERNISSI, F. Beyond the Veil. Male-Female Dynamics in Modern Muslim Society. Bloomington: Indiana University Press. 1987.

METCALF, B.D. Making Muslim Space in North America and Europe. Berkeley: University of California Press 1996.

MILLER, J. The Social Construction of the Person: How is it Possible? *Culture Theory: Essays on Mind, Self and Emotion.* Shweder R A & Levine (eds.). Cambridge and New York: Cambridge University Press 1984, 156-185.

MILNER, ANDREW. Contemporary Cultural Theory. Newcastle: Ahteneum Press 1994.

MINAULT (eds). Separate Worlds: Studies in Purdah in South Asia. Delhi: Chanakya Publications 1992, 139-163.

MOLLICA, R.F. Cultural Dimensions in the Evaluation and Treatment of Sexual Trauma. Psychiatric Clinics of North America 1989, 12, 2.

— The Trauma Story: The Psychiatric Care of Refugee Survivors of Violence and Torture. *Post-Trauamtic Therapy and the Victims of Violence.* Ochberg, F.M. (ed.), New York: Brunner/Mazel 1988, 295-314.

MOMEN, MOJAAN. An Introduction to Shi'i Islam. The History and Doctrines of Twelver Shi'ism. New Haven and London: Yale University Press 1985.

NAMWAR, H. Adferdsterapi ved behandling av tvangsforstyrrelser. University of Oslo: Department of Psychology, MA thesis 1992.

— Økende skilsmisseprosent blant iranske flyktninger i Norge 1993, ms. (4 p).

NENOLA-KALLIO, A. Studies in Ingrian Laments. Helsinki: Academia Scientiarum Fennica, FF Communications 1982, 234.

NOBAKHT, MANSOUR. Sosial endring, globalisering, og multikulturalisme. Hvor er psykologien? *Tidskrift for Norsk Psykologforening* 1993, 30, 140-144.

NÆSS, R. Being an Alevi Muslim in South-Western Anatolia and in Norway. The Impact of Migration on a Heterodox Turkish Community. Paper prepared for the Symposium on the New Islamic Presence in Western Europe, Stockholm 1986 (ms. 34 p).

OBEROY, H. From Punjab to Kalidistan: Territoriality and Metacommentary. *Pacific Affairs* 1987, 60 (1), 26-41.

On Moslem Doctrine and Human Rights in Islam. Issued by the Ministry of Justice in Riyad & Dar al Kitab Allubnani in Beirut 1972.

PAPANEK, H. Purdah: Separate Worlds and Symbolic Shelter. *Comparative Studies in Society and History* 1973, 3, 289-325.

— & MINAULT, G. Separate Worlds. Studies of Purdah in South Asia. Delhi: Chanakya Publications 1982.

PENTIKÄINEN, J. Oral Repertoire and World View. An Anthropological Study of Marina Takalo's Life History. Helsinki: Academia Scientiarum Fennica, FF Communications 1978, 219.

PETERSON, CH. & MAIER, S.F. & SELIGMAN, M.E.P. Learned Helplessness: A Theory for the Age of Personal Control. New York: Oxford University Press 1993.

PLISKIN, J. Silent Boundaries. Cultural Constraints on Sickness and Diagnosis of Iranians in Israel. New Haven and London: Yale University Press 1987.

RACK, P. Race, Culture and Mental Disorder. New York: Tavistock 1982.

REICHELT, S & SVEAASS, N. Creating Meaningful Conversations with Families in Exile. *Journal of Refugee Studies* 1994, 7, 39-47.

Religious Rights in Pakistan. *The Review of Religions* 1991, LXXXVI, 13-29.

RENZETTI, C & RAYMOND, M (eds.). Researching Sensitive Topics. London: SAGE 1993.

ROLAND, A. In Search of Self in India and Japan. Towards a Cross-cultural Psychology. Princeton: Princeton University Press 1988.

ROSENBAUM, M. Learned Resourcefulness, Stress and Self-regulation. *Handbook of Life Stress, Cognition and Health.* eds. Fisher S & Reason J. New York: John Wiley & Sons 1988, 483-495.

RUTTER, M. Psychosocial Resilience and Protective Mechanisms. *American Journal of Orthopsychiatry* 1987, 57, 316-331.

SABBAH, FATNA A. Woman in the Muslim Unconscious. New York: The Athene Series. Pergamon Press 1988.

SAHEJBAM, FREIDOUNE. Den stenede kvinnen. Oslo: Pax forlag 1993.

Sahih al-Bukhari, translated to English by Khan. Lahore 1976, I, 182-4.

SAID, E. Orientalism New York: Pantheon Books 1978.

SANDE, H. Palestinian Martyr Widowhood – Emotional Needs in Conflict with Role Expectations. *Social Science and Medicine* 1993, 1, 231-56.

SCHAFER, R. Regression in the service of the ego. The Relevance of a Psychoanalytic Concept for Personality Assessment. *Assessment of Human Motives*. Lindsey, G (ed.). New York: Rinehardt 1958.

SCHIMMEL, A.M. Reflections on Popular Muslim Poetry. *Contributions to Asian Studies* 1982, 17, 17-26.

SCHNEIDER, R. Die kurdischen Yezidi. Ein Volk auf dem Weg in den Untergang. Fur die Gesellschaft für bedrohte Völker. Göttingen: Pogrom-Taschenbücher 1986, 1011.

— Kurdischer Widerstand. Fluchtgrunde, Staatliche Repression und Konfliktlinien Zwischen Kurdischen Organisationen.*Kurden im Exil. Ein Handbuch Kurdischer Kultur, Politik und Wissenschaft.* Band 1. Berliner Institut fürVergleichende Sozialforschung: edition Parabolis 1991, 2.4.-1-18.

SEBEK, M. Anality in the Totalitarian System and the Psychology of Post-totalitarian Society. *Mind and Human Interaction* 1992, 4, 1, 53-59.

SHAHID, W.A.R & VAN KONINGSVELD (eds.) The Integration of Islam and Hinduism in Western Europe. Kampen: Pharos 1991.

SHAKELEY, FERHARD. Kurdish Nationalism in Mem u Zin of Ehmed-i Xani. University of Uppsala, MA thesis 1993, (63 pp.)

SHARMA, U. Women and their Affines: The Veil as a Symbol of Separation. *Man* 1978, 13 (29), 218-233.

SHWEDER, R.A & LEVINE. Culture Theory: Essays on Mind, Self and Emotion. Cambridge and New York: Cambridge University Press 1984.

— Culture and Moral Development. Stigler & al. *Cultural Psychology* 1990, 130-204.

— Thinking Through Culture. Cambridge: Harvard University Press 1991.

SIIKALA, A.L & HOPPAL, M. Studies in Shamanism. Helsinki: Finnish Anthropological Society 1992.

SILTALA, J. Suomalainen ahdistus. Keuruu: Otava 1992.

SKORUPSKI, J. Symbol and Theory. A Philosophical Study of Theories of Religion in Social Anthropology. Cambridge and New York: Cambridge University Press 1976.

SKOVHOLT, T.M & RØNNESTAD H. The Evolving Professional Self: Stages and Themes in Therapist and Counsellor Development. Chichester: Wiley Series in Psychotherapy and Counselling 1992.

SMITH, J. To Take Place. Towards Theory in Ritual. Chicago & London: The University of Chicago Press 1987.

SOKAL, A. Transgressing the Boundaries: Towards a Transformative Hermeneutics of Quantum Gravity. *Social Text* 1996: 46/47, 217-252.

SPIEGEL, J.P. Some Cultural Aspects of Transference and Countertransference. *Science and Psychoanalysis: Individual and Family Dynamics.* Vol II Masserman J (ed.). New York: Grune & Stratton 1959.

— Cultural Aspects of Transference and Countertransference Revisited. *Journal of American Psychoanalysis* 1976, 4, 447-467.

SPIEGEL, D. Forword & Dissociation and Trauma Ch. 12. *Review of Psychiatry* Section II, vol. 10: Dissociative Disorders. Tasman, A. & Goldfinger, S.M. (eds.). Washington DC: American Psychiatric Press 1991, 143-50.

SPIRO, M.E. Burmese Supernationalism: A Study in the Explanation and Reduction of Suffering. Englewood Cliffs, N.J.: Prentice Hall 1967.

STANG DAHL, T. Den muslimske familie. Oslo: Universitetsforlaget 1992.

STAUB, E. The Roots of Evil. The Origins of Genocide and Other Group Violence. Cambridge: Cambridge University Press 1989.

STIGLER, J., SHWEDER R.A. & HERDT, G. (eds.). Cultural Psychology: Essays on Comparative Human Development. Cambridge: Cambridge University Press 1990.

STOVER, E & NIGHTINGALE, E.O. The Breaking of Bodies and Mind. Torture, Psychiatric Abuse and the Health Professions. New York: W.H. Freeman and Co 1985.

STÅLSETT, S. The crucified and the Crucified: A Study in the Liberation Christology of Jon Sobrino. Oslo: Faculty of Theology, dissertation 1997.

SUMMERFIELD, D. Addressing Human Responses to War and Atrocity: The Limitations of the Western Psychiatric Models – and other Challenges in Research and Practice. Medical Foundation for the Care of Victims of Torture in London 1993.

SWARTZ, S. Individualism-Collectivism. *Journal of Cross-cultural Psychology* 1990, 21, 2, 139-157.

TASMAN, A & GOLDFINGER, S.M (eds.). Dissociative Disorders. *Review of Psychiatry* volume 10, Section 2. Washington DC: American Psychiatric Press 1991, 143-276.

THANWI, ASHRAF ALI. Bahisti Zewar. Heavenly Ornaments. Delhi: Dini Book Depot 1979.

THOMASSEN, E. Målestokken og spanskrøret. Kanon som religionsvitenskapelig term. Copenhagen: *Chaos. Dansk-norsk tidskrift for religionshistoriske studier* 1992, 18, 5-18.

THORSEN, E. Det fleksible kjønn. Oslo: Universitetsforlaget /Det blå bibliotek 1993.

TURNER, V. The Ritual Process. London: Routledge 1969.

— Dramas, Fields and Metaphors: Symbolic Action in Human Society. Ithaca, NY and London: Cornell University Press 1974.

— Betwixt and Between: the Liminal Period in Rites Passages. Lessa, W.A. & Vogt, E.Z. (eds) *Reader in Comparative Religion: An Anthropohological Approach.* New York: Harper Collins, 1979, 234-43.

— The Ritual Process: Structure and Anti-structure. Ithaca, NY: Cornell University Press 1991.

Universal Islamic Declaration of Human Rights. London: Islamic Council 1981 (19 p.).

UNQUIET, GRAVES. The Search for the Disappeared in Iraqi Kurdistan. *Middle East Watch*: Physicians for Human Rights 1992.

URSANO, R.J & McCAUGHEY, B.G & FULLERTON, C.S (eds.). Individual and Community Response to Trauma and Disaster: The Structure of Human Chaos. Cambridge: Cambridge University Press 1994

VAN DER KOLK. Psychological Trauma. Washington DC: American Psychiatric Press 1989.

VARVIN, S. Report from The First Standing Conference on Psychoanalytic Research by the International Psychoanalytic Association. London 1991, April 5-6 (ms. 10 p)

— Psychoanalytic Psychotherapy with Traumatised Refugees. Integration, Symbolisation and Mourning. *American Journal of Psychotherapy* 1998, 52, 64-71.

— & HAUFF, E. Psychoanalytically Oriented Psychotherapy with Torture Victims. *Caring for Victims of Torture.* Jaranson I & Popkin J M (eds.). Washington DC: American Psychiatric Press 1998, 117-30.

— & STILES, W.B. Emergence of Severe Traumatic Experience: An Assimilation Analysis of a Psychoanalytic Therapy with a Political Refugee. *Psychotherapy Research* 1999, 9 (3), 381-404.

VATUK, S. Purdah Revisited: A Comparison of Hindu and Muslim Interpretations of the Cultural Meaning of Purdah in South Asia. *Separate worlds: Studies in Purdah in South Asia.* Papanek, H. & Minault (eds.) Delhi: Chanakya Publications 1982, 55-75.

VOGT, K. Islams hus. Oslo: Cappelen 1993.

— Reise i Iran. Oslo: Cappelen 1997.

VOUTIRA, E. & HARRELL-BOND, B. In Search of the Locus of Trust: The Social World of the Refugee Camp. Paper presented at a Workshop on Trust and the Refugee Experience at an International Symposium on Traumatic Stress in Bergen (Norway) 1993 ms. (13 pp).

WATSON, L & WATSON-FRANKE, M-B. Interpreting Life Histories. New Brunswick: Rutgers University Press 1985

WEAKS, R.V. Muslim Peoples. A World Ethnographic Survey. Connecticut: Greenwood Press 1978.

WEBER, MAX. From Max Weber: Essays in Sociology. Edited and translated by H. H. Gerth and C. Wright Mills. New York: Oxford University Press 1946.

WEININGER, O. The Clinical Psychology of Melanie Klein. C Thomas Springfield Illinois 1984.

WEISÆTH, L. Prepare and Repair: Some Principles in Prevention of Psychiatric Consequences of Traumatic Stress. *Traumatic Stress – Psychology and Psychopathology. Proceedings of the Symposium on the Psychopathology of Traumatic Stress.* Achte, K. & al eds. 1992.

WIEBE, D. Appropriating Religion: Understanding Religion as an Object of Science. *Approaching Religion,* Ahlbäck, T (ed.), Vol I, Stockholm: Almquist & Wiksell 1999, 253-272.

WIKAN, U. Behind the Veil in Arabia: Women in Oman. University of Oslo: Ethnographical Museum, dissertation 1978.

— Mot en ny norsk underklasse: innvandrere, kultur og integrasjon. Oslo: Gyldendal 1995.

— Tomorrow, God Willing: Self-made Destinies in Cairo. Chicago: University of Chicago Press 1996.

WILSON, J.P & RAPHAEL, B (eds.). The International Handbook of Traumatic Stress Syndromes. New York: Plenum Press 1993.

WINNICOTT, D.W. Transitional Objects and Transitional Phenomena. *International Journal of Psychoanalysis* 1953, 34: 89-97.

— Collected papers. London: Tavistock Publications 1958.

— Playing with Reality. New York: Basic Books 1971.

WORSLEY, P. The Trumpet Shall Sound: A Study of Cargo Cults in Melanesia. New York: Schocken 1968.

YEHUDA, R & McFARLANE, A.C. Psychobiology of Posttraumatic Stress Disorder. New York: Academy of Science 1997.

Yin, R.K. Case Study Research. Newbury Park: SAGE, Applied Social Science Methods Series 1989, 5.

Østerberg, D. Det sosio-materielle handlingsfelt. *Kulturanalyse*. Frønes, I (ed). Oslo: Gyldendal 1990, 66-79.

— Byer som fortetninger i landskapet. *Plan & Arbeid* 1990, 6, 2-4.

— Det moderne. Et essay om vestens kultur. Gyldendal 1999.

Printed in the United States
113423LV00005B/103-111/A